Substantive Law in Investment Treaty Arbitration

International Arbitration Law Library

VOLUME 21

Editor

Professor Julian D.M. Lew QC has been involved with international arbitration for more than 40 years as counsel, as arbitrator and as an academic. He has held the position of Professor and Head of the School on International Arbitration, Centre for Commercial Law studies, Queen Mary University of London since its creation in 1985. He is now an independent arbitrator at 20 Essex Street, London.

Introduction

Since its first volume published in 1993, this authoritative practitioner-oriented series has published in-depth and analytical works on niche aspects of international arbitration, authored by specialists in the field.

Objective

This authoritative and established series covering in-depth analyses of niche areas appeals to both practitioners and academics.

Frequency

A volume is published whenever an interesting topic presents itself.

The titles published in this series are listed at the end of this volume.

Substantive Law in Investment Treaty Arbitration

The Unsettled Relationship Between International Law and Municipal Law

Second Edition

Monique Sasson

Published by:
Kluwer Law International B.V.
PO Box 316
2400 AH Alphen aan den Rijn
The Netherlands
Website: www.wolterskluwerlr.com

Sold and distributed in North, Central and South America by:
Wolters Kluwer Legal & Regulatory U.S.
7201 McKinney Circle
Frederick, MD 21704
United States of America
Email: customer.service@wolterskluwer.com

Sold and distributed in all other countries by:
Quadrant
Rockwood House
Haywards Heath
West Sussex
RH16 3DH
United Kingdom
Email: international-customerservice@wolterskluwer.com

MIX
FSC® C103993

Printed on acid-free paper.

ISBN 978-90-411-6103-1

e-Book: ISBN 978-90-411-6110-9
web-PDF: ISBN 978-90-411-5575-7

© 2017 Kluwer Law International BV, The Netherlands

All rights reserved. No part of this publication may be reproduced, stored in a retrieval system, or transmitted in any form or by any means, electronic, mechanical, photocopying, recording, or otherwise, without written permission from the publisher.

Permission to use this content must be obtained from the copyright owner. Please apply to: Permissions Department, Wolters Kluwer Legal & Regulatory U.S., 76 Ninth Avenue, 7th Floor, New York, NY 10011-5201, USA. Website: www.wolterskluwerlr.com

Printed in the United Kingdom.

Table of Contents

Preface		xi
List of Abbreviations		xiii

Introduction: The Unsettled Relationship Between International Law and Municipal Law ... 1
I   The International Law Commission and the Role of Municipal Law ... 1
II   *Barcelona Traction* and *Renvoi* to Municipal Law ... 3
III   Investment Treaty Protection and the Continuing Relevance of Municipal Law ... 8
IV   Two Categories of Interaction Between International Law and Municipal Law ... 11
      [A]   International Law Standing Alone ... 11
      [B]   *Renvoi* to Municipal Law ... 11
      [C]   The Contract-Treaty Problem ... 12
V   Role of Municipal Law in the Investment Treaty Context ... 12

CHAPTER 1
Attribution under the Law of State Responsibility ... 15
§1.01   Introduction ... 15
§1.02   ILC Article 4 and the Meaning of 'State Organ' ... 18
      [A]   ILC Article 4 and State Organ ... 19
      [B]   *The Genocide Case*, *De Facto* State Organ and the Role of Municipal Law ... 24
      [C]   Investment Treaty Awards ... 25
           [1]   *Eureko v. Poland* and the Question of Separate Personality ... 25
           [2]   *Bosh International et al. v. Ukraine* and the Attribution of Obligations Stemming from Undertakings ... 28

Table of Contents

		[3]	*Salini Costruttori S.p.A. and Italstrade v. Morocco and Noble Ventures v. Romania*: The Notion of De Facto Organ	30

§1.03 Para-Statal Entities and the Role of Municipal Law 33
    [A] *Maffezini v. Spain:* The Structural and Functional Tests ... 36
    [B] *Encana Corporation v. Ecuador* and 'Governmental Nature' ... 38
§1.04 Investment Treaty Provisions on Attribution: *Lex Specialis* and the Role of Municipal Law 39
    [A] *United Parcel Service of America v. Canada* 39
    [B] *Metalclad Corporation v. United Mexican States* 41
§1.05 Conclusions 42
    [A] State Organs 42
    [B] Para-Statal Entities 43

CHAPTER 2
Article 42 of the ICSID Convention and the Relationship Between International Law and Municipal Law 45
§2.01 Introduction 45
§2.02 The Relevance of the Historical Background of Article 42(1) 48
    [A] The Vienna Convention, Articles 31 and 32, and the Principles of Treaty Interpretation 49
    [B] The Two Antecedent Draft Conventions 51
    [C] ICSID Convention: *Travaux Préparatoires* 52
    [D] ICSID Convention: Article 42 59
§2.03 Jurisprudence from *Klöckner/Amco* to *Wena* 60
    [A] *Klöckner v. Cameroon* 60
    [B] *Amco Asia Corp. v. Indonesia (Amco Asia)* 62
    [C] *Wena Hotels Ltd v. Egypt* 64
§2.04 The Three Schools of Thought in Light of the ICSID *Travaux* 66
    [A] The Complementary/Corrective Interpretation 66
    [B] The Reisman Interpretation: BITs Require Application of International Law 68
    [C] The 'Tribunal Discretion' Interpretation 70
§2.05 Conclusion 72

CHAPTER 3
Investor Nationality under Municipal and International Law 75
§3.01 Introduction 75
§3.02 Investor Nationality and Municipal Law 76
    [A] The Investment Treaty Background 76
    [B] Nationality and Diplomatic Protection 78
    [C] Arbitral Decisions on Investor Nationality 80
        [1] *Fakes v. Turkey* and Effective Nationality of Individuals 81
        [2] *Tokios Tokeles v. Ukraine* and the Question of Tenuous Links to the State of Incorporation 83

	[3]	*Plama Consortium v. Bulgaria,* Corporate 'Control', and Denial of Benefits Clauses	86
	[4]	*Ceskoslovenska Obchodni Banka A.S. v. The Slovak Republic ('CSOB v. Slovakia')* and the Question of State Control of Corporations	92
	[5]	*AFT v. Slovak Republic and Tenaris S.A v. Venezuela*: The Concept of Corporate 'Seat'	93
	[6]	*Soufraki v. United Arab Emirates* and Proof of Nationality	97
§3.03	Conclusion		99

CHAPTER 4
From Property to Investment 101
§4.01 Introduction 101
§4.02 The Role of International Law in Defining Property 104
  [A] European Convention on Human Rights 104
  [B] Inter-American Convention on Human Rights 106
  [C] The 1959 Abs-Shawcross Draft Convention on Foreign Investments 107
  [D] Harvard Draft Convention on International Responsibility of States for Injuries to Aliens 108
  [E] The OECD Draft Convention on the Protection of Foreign Property 109
§4.03 The Role of Municipal Law in Defining Property 111
  [A] The PCIJ and the ICJ 111
  [B] Investment Treaty Tribunals 112
    [1] Intangible Rights 113
      [a] *Pope & Talbot Inc. v. Canada* 113
      [b] *Encana Corporation v. Republic of Ecuador* 114
    [2] Contracts 115
      [a] *In the matter of Revere Copper and Brass Inc. and Overseas Private Investment Corporation* 115
      [b] *Eureko v. Poland* 116
      [c] *Waste Management Inc v. Mexico* 117
      [d] *Emmis International Holding B.V. et al. v. Hungary* 118
    [3] Legitimate Expectations 119
      [a] *Tecnicas Medioambientales Tecmed SA v. Mexico* 120
      [b] *Metalclad Corporation v. Mexico* 120
      [c] *Biloune and Marine Drive Complex v. Ghana Investment Centre* (and the Government of Ghana) 122
      [d] Other Investment Treaty Tribunal Decisions and the ECHR 123
§4.04 Definition of 'Investment' 125
  [A] Early Investment Treaties: Multilateral and Bilateral 126
  [B] The ICSID Convention 128

Table of Contents

§4.05	The Role of Municipal Law in the Definition, Registration Requirements, and Legal Validity of Investments	133
	[A] Definition of an Investment	133
	[1] Mihaly International Corporation v. Sri Lanka	133
	[2] Fedax v. Venezuela	134
	[3] Salini Costruttori S.p.A. and Italstrade v. Morocco ('Salini v. Morocco')	137
	[4] Mitchell v. Congo	138
	[5] Pantechniki SA Contractors & Engineers v. Albania ('Pantechniki') and 'Inherent Meaning' of Investment	140
§4.06	Registration Requirements	141
§4.07	Legal Validity of Investment	143
§4.08	UNCITRAL Investment Arbitration Proceedings	145
§4.09	Conclusion	147

CHAPTER 5
Shareholders' Rights 149

§5.01	Introduction	149
§5.02	Shareholders' Rights Pre-*Barcelona Traction*	153
	[A] Awards Pre-*Barcelona Traction*	154
	[1] *Ruden*	154
	[2] *Delagoa Bay* and East African Railway Company	154
	[3] *El Triunfo*	155
	[4] *Kunhardt & Co.*	156
	[5] *Baesch e Römer v. Venezuela*	156
	[6] The *Alsop* Claim	157
	[7] The *Shufeldt* Claim	157
	[B] Treaties Pre-*Barcelona Traction*	158
	[1] Treaty of Versailles (1919)	158
	[2] The Mexican Claims Conventions	159
	[3] Treaty of Peace with Italy (1947)	160
	[4] The Algiers Declaration	161
§5.03	ICJ Judgments on Shareholders' Rights	163
	[A] *Barcelona Traction, Light and Power Company Limited*	163
	[B] *Elettronica Sicula S.p.A.*	166
	[C] *Diallo*	168
§5.04	The ILC's Articles on Diplomatic Protection	170
§5.05	European Court of Human Rights	172
§5.06	Investment Treaty Disputes	175
	[A] ICSID	176
	[B] NAFTA	177
	[C] Shareholders' Indirect Claims in Investment Treaty Disputes	178
	[1] Loss of Value of Shares	181

		[a]	*CMS Gas Transmission Company v. Argentina (CMS v. Argentina)*	182
		[b]	*Compañia de Aguas del Aconquija SA and Vivendi v. Argentina (Vivendi II)*	184
		[c]	*Azurix Corp. v. Argentina*	186
		[d]	*Enron Corp. and Ponderosa Assets L.P. v. Argentina*	188
		[e]	*Poštová Banka As and Istrokapital SE v. The Hellenic Republic*	190
	[2]	Claims on Behalf of the Company: *GAMI v. Mexico*		192
§5.07	Conclusion			193

CHAPTER 6
Treaty Versus Contract Claims, and Umbrella Clauses: When a Contract Breach May Become a Treaty Breach — 199

§6.01 Introduction — 199
§6.02 History of the Distinction Between Treaty and Contract Claims — 202
    [A] Draft Conventions or Codifications — 202
        [1] Garcìa Amador Reports on State Responsibility — 202
        [2] Harvard Draft Convention on International Responsibility of States for Injuries to Aliens (1961) ('The Harvard Draft') — 203
        [3] Foreign Relations Law of the United States (Restatement 3rd of Foreign Relations Law) — 203
    [B] Awards and Judgments — 205
        [1] *Affaire Martini* — 205
        [2] *Illinois Central Railroad Company (USA) v. United Mexican States* — 206
        [3] *International Fisheries Company (USA) v. United Mexican States* — 207
        [4] The PCIJ and the ICJ — 207
    [C] Principles to Be Drawn from Draft Conventions/Codifications and Awards/Judgments — 210
§6.03 Distinction Between Treaty and Contract Claims in International Investment Disputes — 213
    [A] *Aguas del Aconquija – Vivendi* and the Separation Between Treaty and Contact Claims — 214
    [B] *Noble Ventures v. Romania* and the Violation of the FET Standard — 216
    [C] The Relevance of Contractual versus Governmental Acts — 217
    [D] *Waste Management Inc v. Mexico* — 219
§6.04 The Historical Background of Umbrella Clauses — 220
    [A] Premise: Abs-Shawcross Draft Convention 1959, First Modern BIT, OECD Draft Convention, and 1998 Draft MAI — 222
    [B] Outcome: Umbrella Clauses and Draft Conventions — 224

Table of Contents

§6.05		Four Schools of Thought Concerning Umbrella Clauses	225
	[A]	The 'Negative' Interpretation: *Société Générale du Surveillance SA v. Pakistan*	225
	[B]	The 'Automatic' Interpretation: *Fedax N.V. v. Venezuela; CMS Gas Transmission Company v. Argentina; LG&E Energy Corp., LG&E Capital Corp., and LG&E International Inc. v. Argentina*	227
	[C]	The 'Iure Imperii' Interpretation: *Pan American Energy LLC and Bp Argentina Exploration Company v. Argentina; El Paso Energy International Company v. Argentina*	228
	[D]	The 'Enforcement' Approach: *Société Générale Du Surveillance SA v. Philippines*	229
§6.06		Umbrella Clauses: Attribution and Parties to the Undertaking	233
§6.07		Assessment of the Four Schools of Thought	235
§6.08		Conclusion	239

Conclusion: The Unsettled Relationship Between International and Municipal Law		243
I	The Necessity of *Renvoi* in the Investment Treaty Context	245
II	*Renvoi* in This Book's Six Chapters	248
III	The Need for Treaty Arbitrators to Apply Municipal Law	251

Appendices 253

APPENDIX I
Hermann Abs and Lord Shawcross, *Draft Convention on Investments Abroad* (1959) 255

APPENDIX II
Treaty Between the Federal Republic of Germany and Pakistan for the Promotion and Protection of Investments (1959) 259

APPENDIX III
Harvard Draft Convention on the International Responsibility of States for Injuries to Aliens (1961) 271

APPENDIX IV
Organisation for Economic Co-operation and Development Draft Convention on the Protection of Foreign Property (1967) 277

Preface

The first edition of this book was published about eight years ago. This second edition is justified not so much by the accelerating appearance of investment treaty awards as by the continuing, serious flaws in the application of international law by investment treaty arbitral tribunals. I believe that at least some of the ongoing criticism of investor-State arbitration is attributable to what the public perceives as the troubling flexibility of international law in the decisions of tribunals, to the disadvantage of States. Although the alleged favouritism of the regime towards investors may be overplayed, the public perception implicitly – and accurately – recognizes that when arbitrators assume unfettered discretion to create international law in the absence of a settled 'international' rule, rather than search for the *municipal* law content of international law, tribunal decisions lack a sound legal foundation. That is, as a matter of international law, arbitrators need to be attentive to the circumstances where municipal law supplies the necessary substantive legal rule.

The investor-State arbitration regime is still relatively youthful, and the problem of substantive law is extremely difficult. Moreover, sitting on a treaty tribunal (or pleading before a treaty tribunal) understandably prods the participants into thinking that they are part of a process where municipal law should not have a significant role. While that is understandable, weakness in properly applying the substantive law in the case is not excusable; sound results in individual cases depend on the correct application of the law governing the merits of the dispute. International investment arbitrators need to be experts in the substantive law. That inevitably entails deep knowledge of the historical development of international investment law as well as treaty arbitration case authorities, and an appreciation of the role of municipal law in the application of international law. This second edition is designed to be of direct assistance in all these respects.

I have maintained the overall structure of the first edition, but I have added one chapter, on Article 42 of the International Centre for Settlement of Investment Disputes (ICSID) Convention,[1] and I have updated all parts of the first edition. The updating has

---

1. This Chapter is a revision of a chapter previously published as 'The Applicable Law and the ICSID Convention,' Ch. 10 in *ICSID Convention After 50 Years, Unsettled Issues*, ed. Baltag

Preface

also involved rethinking and revising certain descriptions and arguments in the first edition. I have also sought to rework many passages so that the prose is more digestible.

As noted in the first edition, this book is a revision of the doctoral dissertation that I completed at Cambridge University under the supervision of Professor (now International Court of Justice (ICJ) Judge) James Crawford. I remain indebted to Judge Crawford and to Cambridge, particularly Hughes Hall College, for the opportunity to study in such an intellectually vibrant setting. A number of scholars either provided comments on the first edition or commented on iterations of certain chapters in this second edition, and I am very grateful to them: Franco Ferrari, Loukas Mistelis, Linda Silberman, Michael Reisman, Amal Bouchenaki, Rocio Digon, Andrea Bjorklund, and Zachary Douglas.

On matters relating to nationality and seat under international law, I served as an expert witness in a treaty arbitration, which helped me to refine my views on those topics. Sarah Vasani, Egishe Dzhazoyan, and Thomas Sprange instructed me in the case and demonstrated their own deep knowledge in this area. An appointment in April 2015 as scholar in residence at the Center for Transnational Litigation, New York University School of Law, directed by Professor Franco Ferrari, gave me an opportunity to conduct necessary research at a great institution.

Two professors in Italy continue to have an enormous influence on my career in the law: Andrea Giardina and Maria Beatrice Deli. They have been, and remain, wonderful mentors, as does Dr Julian D M Lew QC. It is privilege to publish in a Kluwer series edited by Dr Lew.

Finally, I wish to acknowledge the encouragement of my husband, Laurence Shore, in producing this second edition. He commented (usually helpfully) on every chapter in this second edition, a true labour of love.

(Kluwer, 2017), 273-300. I thank Dr Baltag for kindly permitting me to use the chapter in this book.

List of Abbreviations

ECHR	European Court of Human Rights
ECJ	European Court of Justice
ECT	Energy Charter Treaty
IACHR	Inter-American Court of Human Rights
ICJ	International Court of Justice
ILC	International Law Commission
MAI	Multilateral Agreement on Investment
NAFTA	North American Free Trade Agreement
OECD	Organisation for Economic Co-operation and Development
PCIJ	Permanent Court of International Justice
UNCITRAL	United Nations Commission on International Trade Law

Introduction: The Unsettled Relationship Between International Law and Municipal Law

> Especially in the fields of injury to aliens and their property and of human rights, the content and application of internal law will often be relevant to the question of international responsibility. In every case it will be seen on analysis that either the provisions of internal law are relevant as facts in applying the applicable international standard, or else that they are actually incorporated in some form, conditionally or unconditionally, into that standard.
>
> – International Law Commission, Section 7 of its Commentary on Article 3 on State Responsibility.

I   THE INTERNATIONAL LAW COMMISSION AND THE ROLE OF MUNICIPAL LAW

Article 3 of the International Law Commission (ILC) Articles on State Responsibility provides that the 'characterization of an act of State as internationally wrongful is governed by international law. Such characterization is not affected by the characterization of the same act as lawful by internal law'.[1]

Investment treaty tribunals are usually careful to characterize a violation of the relevant treaty as a violation of international law. However, the 'anxiety to dismiss any thought that national law can be invoked as a defence to the breach of an international obligation' often causes tribunals to refer to 'some alternative source of international obligation' that 'can be invoked to displace rights and obligations established by treaty'.[2] That anxiety is at odds with the legal reality that the application of national law

---

1. Crawford, *The International Law Commission's Articles on State Responsibility: Introduction, Text and Commentaries* (the 'ILC's Articles on State Responsibility') (Cambridge, 2005), 86.
2. *Venezuela Holding BV, et al. v. Venezuela*, Decision on Annulment, 9 Mar. 2017, para. 187, available in Investment Treaty Arbitration website: https://www.italaw.com/sites/default/files/case-documents/italaw8536.pdf.

is necessary if and when it is incorporated by reference in the international law rule or because it is the part of the dispute's factual matrix.[3]

In some instances, international law must refer to municipal law to derive the precise meaning of a legal concept. In its 2010 judgment on the merits in *Diallo*,[4] the International Court of Justice (ICJ) explained that compliance with international law may depend on compliance with municipal law (with the caveat that the applicable municipal law must itself be compatible with other requirements of international agreements):

> It follows from the terms of the two provisions[5] cited above that the expulsion of an alien lawfully in the territory of a State which is a party to these instruments can only be compatible with the international obligations of that State if it is decided in accordance with 'the law', in other words the domestic law applicable in that respect. *Compliance with international law is to some extent dependent here on compliance with internal law*. However, it is clear that while 'accordance with law' as thus defined is a necessary condition for compliance with the above-mentioned provisions, it is not the sufficient condition. First, the applicable domestic law must itself be compatible with the other requirements of the Covenant and the African Charter; second, an expulsion must not be arbitrary in nature, since protection against arbitrary treatment lies at the heart of the rights guaranteed by the international norms protecting human rights, in particular those set out in the two treaties applicable in this case.[6] *[Emphasis added]*.

In cases like *Diallo*, the ICJ is 'called upon to "apply" municipal law, not as such, but as being incorporated into international law'.[7] The interpretive task of investment tribunals is to consider the proper application of Article 31 of the Vienna Convention on the Law of Treaties (Vienna Convention) to treaty provisions containing a juridical concept. What approach, then, should a tribunal take if the term at issue cannot, as an initial matter, be understood by consulting a general dictionary, but instead would send the tribunal to a legal dictionary? What are the rules for interpreting such terms, particularly where the legal dictionary does not contain an accepted *international law* definition of the term?

When a Bilateral Investment Treaty (BIT) contains a legal concept, the interpretation of the concept may require the application of municipal rules. In these circumstances, the tribunal is still applying international law, but in doing so must refer to

---

3. Crawford, *supra*, 101.
4. Ahmadou Sadio Diallo (*Republic of Guinea v. Democratic Republic of the Congo*), Merits, Judgment (30 Nov. 2010), I.C.J. Reports 2010, 639.
5. *Id.*, 663, para. 64: Art. 13 of the Covenant reads as follows: 'An alien lawfully in the territory of a State party to the present Covenant may be expelled therefrom only in pursuance of a decision reached in accordance with law and shall, except where compelling reasons of national security otherwise require, be allowed to submit the reasons against his expulsion and to have his case reviewed by, and be represented for the purpose before, the competent authority or a person or persons especially designated by the competent authority.' Likewise, Art. 12, para. 4, of the African Charter provides that: 'A non-national legally admitted in a territory of a State party to the present Charter, may only be expelled from it by virtue of a decision taken in accordance with the law.'
6. *Id.*, para. 65.
7. 'Article 38', by A. Pellet, in *The Statute of the International Court of Justice*, eds. Zimmermann, Tomuschat, Oellers-Frahm and Tams, 2d ed. (Oxford, 2012), 731, at 783.

municipal law in order to give meaning to the term, consistent with its context in the BIT and the purpose and object of the BIT. Municipal law is relevant to the extent that international law must refer to it to determine the existence of rights on the international plane. In such cases, a *renvoi* to municipal law, or to municipal legal systems, is a crucial aspect of the application of international law.

The investment treaty regime, however, has tended towards the exclusion of municipal law. The purpose of this book is to demonstrate when and why such exclusion is improper, as a matter of international law. In particular, I consider key matters of substantive law in which a *renvoi* to municipal law is necessary if an investment treaty tribunal is to reach a sound result under international law. In setting out the foundation of this *renvoi*, it is first necessary to discuss *Barcelona Traction* and a few other important cases from the ICJ and its predecessor, the Permanent Court of International Justice (PCIJ), and then to explain the continuing significance of such cases in the investment treaty regime.

II   *BARCELONA TRACTION* AND *RENVOI* TO MUNICIPAL LAW[8]

In his separate opinion in *Barcelona Traction*, Judge Morelli explained the relationship between international and municipal law in the context of diplomatic protection. He emphasized that there is no subordination between the two; rather, 'the very existence of the international obligation depends on a state of affairs created in municipal law'.[9] In *Barcelona Traction*, the ICJ majority, and not only Morelli, determined that it had to refer to municipal law – not merely take cognizance of it – to resolve questions of shareholders' rights versus company rights under international law. Investment treaty tribunals may believe that their *lex specialis* realm relieves them of the need to know these landmark diplomatic protection decisions, but that belief diminishes the legal reasoning of BIT awards.

---

8. The Institute of International Law, Rapporteur M. Andrea Giardina, EIGHTEENTH COMMISSION, 18th Commission PLENIERE, 13 Sep. 2013, *Legal Aspects of Recourse to Arbitration by an Investor Against the Authorities of the Host State under Inter-State Treaties* confirms at Art. 4 that arbitral tribunals, 'when referring to notions defined in municipal law, such as that of nationality or legal personality, shall at the same time respect the relevant rules of international law'. In the Travaux Préparatoires, the Eighteenth Commission commented that: 'With regard to companies and other legal persons, the starting point for any reconstruction of the topic according to customary international law is obviously the decision of the International Court of Justice in the *Barcelona Traction* case of 5 February 1970, according to which diplomatic protection of companies is a right for the State in which the companies have been incorporated and have their registered office, and not for the State of which the majority of shareholders are nationals, provided, however, that connections with the State in which the companies have been set up are real and not fictitious.'
9. '*[N]o subordination of international responsibility, as such, to the provisions of municipal law is involved; the point is rather that the very existence of the international obligation depends on a state of affairs created in municipal law, though this is so not by virtue of municipal law but, on the contrary, by virtue of the international rule itself, which to that end refers to the law of the State. … [T]here is on the one hand a set of rights conferred by the municipal order on the company and, on the other hand, within the same legal order, another, quite distinct set of rights conferred on the members. Each set of rights is entitled to its own, distinct international protection.*' Barcelona Traction, Light and Power Company, Limited, Judgment, *ICJ Reports* (5 Feb. 1970), 3; Separate Opinion of Judge Morelli, 234–235, paras 4 and 5.

The particular issue in *Barcelona Traction* was whether Belgium could seek reparation from Spain for damages suffered by its nationals, shareholders of a Canadian company. The ICJ addressed this question by considering whether the Belgian shareholders had suffered an injury to a *right*, as opposed to an *interest*. The ICJ concluded that Belgium had failed to establish *ius standi*: the violation of the company's rights and the resulting damage to the shareholders did not constitute a violation of shareholders' rights. The analysis of the company's rights versus the shareholders' rights was undertaken in accordance with the 'relevant institutions of municipal law'.[10] In particular, the ICJ stated that it had 'not only to take cognizance of municipal law but also to refer to it. It is to rules generally accepted by municipal legal systems which recognize the limited company whose capital is represented by shares, and not to the municipal law of a particular State, that international law refers'.[11]

The case featured an array of approaches to the relationship between international and municipal law in the application of public international law. At one end of the spectrum, Judge Morelli opined that if international law does not regulate certain concepts, a *renvoi* to municipal law must be conducted. At the other end of the spectrum, Judge Gros opined that only international law should apply; municipal law should be ignored, and economic realities had to be considered. In between – though much closer to Morelli – stood the ICJ majority, with its *renvoi* to municipal legal *systems* rather than municipal law of a particular State. The majority's 'municipal legal system' referred to universal principles drawn from municipal laws. The application of principles differs from the application of international law alone, because the source of these principles is a comparative analysis of municipal laws.

The ICJ majority's approach, then, was that rights had to be defined in accordance with municipal legal systems if there were 'no corresponding institutions of international law to which the Court could resort'.[12] Since in *Barcelona Traction* the shareholders were not vested with any rights under municipal law, and economic damage did not equate to injury to a right on the international plane, Belgium had no right of action.

The ICJ and Morelli approaches could have led to different results, because the ICJ looked to rules generally accepted by the 'municipal legal systems', whereas Morelli focused exclusively on the respondent State's municipal law. Judge Morelli's view was that under international law each State was required to respect foreigners' rights, and in *Barcelona Traction* the extent of shareholders' rights had to be determined in accordance with the Spanish legal system.[13] However, both approaches were fundamentally similar in requiring a *renvoi* from international law to another set of rules for the determination of shareholders' rights.[14]

---

10. *Barcelona Traction*, 37, para. 50.
11. *Ibid.*
12. *Ibid.*
13. *Id.*, Separate Opinion of Judge Morelli, 235, para. 5.
14. The term *renvoi* is used in this book to mean a *renvoi* to the substantive law of a State and not to its conflict of laws rules. *See*, on *renvoi*, Dicey, Morris and Collins, *The Conflict of Laws* (London, 2006), 73.

Judge Gros' Separate Opinion and Judge ad hoc Riphagen's Dissenting Opinion rejected *renvoi*. Judge Gros believed that *renvoi* led to the supremacy of municipal law over international law, by referring the assessment of the existence of a right to municipal law.[15] He considered rules of municipal law to be mere facts in evidence. According to Judge Gros, the *renvoi* method ignored the point that an irregular expropriation was a breach of international law.[16] Alien shareholders, he remarked, should not run the risk of seeing their investment disappear as a result of unlawful acts, even if those acts are formally targeted at a domestic corporation.

Gros focused on economic realities to determine whether reparation may be sought.[17] Riphagen's dissent went even further: he regarded international law and municipal law as completely separate spheres. Under his approach, the treatment of aliens is, he stated, regulated by rules of customary international law.[18]

Gros's economic realities approach echoes the position taken almost a half-century earlier in *Certain German Interests in Polish Upper Silesia*.[19] The PCIJ had ruled in 1926 that 'municipal laws are merely facts which express the will and constitute the activities of States'.[20] The PCIJ would not interpret a municipal law 'as such',[21] but could decide whether its application conformed with a State's international obligation. In *Barcelona Traction* the ICJ majority and Judge Morelli also did not interpret municipal law as 'such'. Rather, they applied international law, and in doing so emphasized the need, in certain circumstances, to refer to municipal law. Municipal laws were not merely facts that expressed the will of States. This approach, *renvoi* to municipal law, or municipal legal systems, was not something invented in *Barcelona Traction*. Despite the PCIJ's ruling in *Certain German Interests*, the *Barcelona Traction* approach had long been an aspect of the application of international law.

The matter of *renvoi* had previously been discussed in the Advisory Opinion on the *Exchange of Greek and Turkish Population*.[22] The PCIJ had to interpret the word 'established' in Article 2 of the Convention of Lausanne of 30 January 1923, concerning the exchange of Greek and Turkish populations,[23] and whether to apply Greek and Turkish law to determine if a population was 'established'. Since the Convention of Lausanne did not define the term, the PCIJ had to assess whether there was an implied reference to Greek and Turkish law. In resolving this issue, the PCIJ distinguished between (a) the national status of a person, which 'can only be based on the law of that State, and whereas, therefore, any convention dealing with this status must implicitly

---

15. *Barcelona Traction*, Separate Opinion of Judge Gros, 272-273, paras 9-11.
16. Id., 273-274, para. 12.
17. Ibid.
18. *Barcelona Traction*, Dissenting Opinion of Judge Riphagen, 335-338, paras 3 and 4 in particular.
19. *Certain German Interests in Polish Upper Silesia* (Merits), Judgment, 25 May 1926, PCIJ Series A, No. 7, 1.
20. Id., 19.
21. Ibid.
22. *Exchange of Greek and Turkish Population*, Advisory Opinion no. 10, 21 Feb. 1925, PCIJ, Series B, No. 10, 6.
23. Id., 7.

refer to the national legislation';[24] and (b) a mere situation of fact, defined by the Convention without any *renvoi* to national legislation.

The PCIJ observed, *inter alia*, that (i) a central purpose of the Convention was to save Constantinople from the loss it would have suffered as a result of the exodus of its Greek inhabitants, who were a key economic part of its population; and (ii) 'established', unlike the term 'domicile', had no connection with any particular system of law.[25] The PCIJ stated: 'Whereas the natural status of a person belonging to a State can only be based on the law of that State, and whereas, therefore, any convention dealing with this status must implicitly refer to the national legislation, there is no reason why the local tie indicated by the word "established" should be determined by the application of some particular law. It may very well be that the Convention contemplated a mere situation of fact, sufficiently defined by the Convention itself without any reference to national legislation.'[26]

The PCIJ therefore concluded that the term 'established' should be construed according to its natural meaning and not by reference to national legislation. In doing so, it dealt with the interpretation of a term that it did *not* consider to be a term of art or an expression of a 'legal nature', which appeared in a 'self-contained' treaty that had as a central object the non-remission of the term to a possibly differing national law treatment. Notably, the Advisory Opinion clearly indicates that when a treaty refers to, but does not interpret, a legal concept for which a recognized international law standard does not exist but which can be based on the law of a State, a *renvoi* to the municipal law *is* called for, as the treaty implicitly refers to the municipal law. Unless the interpretation of the concept under municipal law otherwise conflicts with the intention of the State parties to the relevant treaty, a *renvoi* to municipal law is the proper application of international law.[27] In the *Advisory Opinion*, one discerns a clear Vienna Convention approach (well before that Convention was drafted): the assessment of a term's ordinary meaning, in context, and in light of the treaty's object and purpose. Importantly, one ascertains from this *Advisory Opinion* that determining the 'ordinary meaning' of an expression of a 'legal nature', in context, and in view of the treaty's purpose, may well necessitate a *renvoi* to municipal law.

Subsequently, the PCIJ confirmed that interpreting a term under international law may require a *renvoi* to municipal law. In his Individual Opinion in *Consistency of Certain Danzig Legislative Decrees with the Constitution of the Free City*, Judge Anzilotti explained that the PCIJ was created to 'administer international law',[28] and that, despite being separate systems, international law may refer to municipal law:[29]

> [The] Court, in performing its function as an organ of international law, may have to consider municipal law from two entirely distinct standpoints. In the first place, it may have to examine municipal law from the standpoint of their consistency

---

24. *Id.*, 19.
25. *Id.*, 18–19.
26. *Id.*, 19.
27. *Id.*, 19–20.
28. *Consistency of Certain Danzig Legislative Decrees with the Constitution of the Free City*, Advisory Opinion, 4 Dec. 1935, PCIJ, Series A/B No 65, 41 at 61–62.
29. *Id.*, 63.

with international law. (...) Secondly, *the Court may find it necessary to interpret a municipal law*, quite apart from any question of its consistency or inconsistency with international law, simply *as a law which governs certain facts, the legal import of which the Court is called upon to appraise. [Emphasis added].*

In previous writings, Anzilotti had identified two different categories of *renvoi*: (i) substantive *renvoi*, under which the rule of municipal law becomes a rule of international law, and (ii) formal *renvoi*, where the reference to a rule of municipal law serves only to determine the applicability of the international law rule without the rule's migrating from the international law plane to the municipal law plane or vice-versa.[30] Anzilotti considered formal *renvoi*, by which there is no transformation of rules, to be the category most frequently applied by international courts and tribunals. He gave as specific examples of this category the protection of nationals and the determination of nationality by *renvoi* to municipal law.

The PCIJ's discussions of *renvoi* provide guidance that is applicable to the task of interpreting certain terms in BITs under international law. This guidance is consistent with the general rule of interpretation prescribed decades later in Article 31(1) of the Vienna Convention, which controls the interpretation of all treaties. This is unsurprising, since the Vienna Convention is an expression of customary international law. But the PCIJ's guidance also gives substance – i.e., *renvoi* to municipal law – to the Vienna Convention's three-step interpretive approach when the term at issue is a legal concept directly related to a State's definition of nationality. The *lex specialis* status of BITs is not resistant to this *renvoi* approach, precisely because the approach is consistent with Article 31(1) of the Vienna Convention.

Discussions of *renvoi* to municipal law in the diplomatic protection arena are of particular relevance for investment treaty tribunals, when one considers that while investment treaties lay down international standards of protection, the beneficiaries of this protection are entities or individuals – the investors – in relation to their individual investments. These beneficiaries are subject to municipal law, which governs the underlying investment that such treaties address.

An important issue is whether the *renvoi* should be to rules generally considered applicable in municipal legal systems or to the rules of a specific State. Again, the customary international law of diplomatic protection provides useful guidance. In *Barcelona Traction*, a majority of the ICJ adopted the former approach,[31] whereas Judge Morelli posited the latter, i.e., *renvoi* to the rules of a particular State, as the preferred approach.[32]

---

30. Anzilotti, *Il diritto internazionale nei giudizi interni* (Bologna, 1905), and *Corso di Diritto Internazionale, Introduzione, Teorie Generali*, vol. I (Padova, 1955), 55–63; *see also* Ruda, 'The Opinions of Judge Dionisio Anzilotti at the Permanent Court of International Justice', *EJIL* 3 (1992), 100 at 102–103, and Gaja, 'Positivism and Dualism in Dionisio Anzilotti', *EJIL* 3 (1992), 123 at 134–138.
31. *Barcelona Traction Light and Power Company, Limited*, Judgment (5 Nov. 1970), *ICJ Reports* 1970, 3 at p. 37, para. 50.
32. *Id.*, Separate Opinion of Judge Morelli, pp. 233–235. Both views are *obiter dicta*, as the issue did not have to be decided in *Barcelona Traction*.

The ICJ majority's approach has been criticized – properly, in my view – on the grounds that it does not indicate how the 'rules of municipal legal systems in general' are to be determined.[33] These rules apparently mean common principles of municipal legal systems, but the concept is vague, and suggests that relevant 'customary municipal rules' (or 'transnational municipal rules') exist and can be applied for such a purpose. If international law does not define certain terms, the *renvoi* must overcome the absence of that definition.[34] This book argues that the solution is not to refer to municipal rules in general, which in many circumstances will be too general and abstract to apply in the context of a dispute, to the extent that any commonality can be discerned. The *Barcelona Traction* majority's 'rules in general' approach has not been applied, to my knowledge, by any international court or tribunal. The majority's approach is particularly unsound in relation to *ratione personae* issues. It could lead to tribunals reaching results by asserting a notional 'general municipal rule' where one does not exist.

Judge Morelli's 'specific municipal system' approach, however, has the advantage of legal rigor and greater certainty in interpretation. Moreover, in the context of jurisdiction *ratione personae* under BITs, where a contracting party's municipal law on nationality typically applies to the determination of who is an 'investor', Judge Morelli's method of *renvoi* results in the proper application of Vienna Convention Article 31(1).

III INVESTMENT TREATY PROTECTION AND THE CONTINUING RELEVANCE OF MUNICIPAL LAW

The ICJ's and Judge Morelli's guidance seem, at first glance, less appropriate when the arena is investment treaty protection rather than diplomatic protection. But the *lex specialis* nature of BITs does not render customary international law irrelevant, nor does it prevent municipal law from having an important role in constructing a substantive law framework. As noted above, the beneficiaries of this treaty protection are entities or individuals in relation to their individual investments, which in turn are subject to municipal law. In his Hague Lectures, predating *Barcelona Traction*, Sereni argued that an 'attempt at applying international law to private relations would be tantamount to seeking to apply the matrimonial laws of France or England to relations between cats or dogs'.[35]

However, a rigid separation of municipal law and international law is too categorical to apply to investment treaty disputes, in which the application of international law often requires reference to municipal law. The interplay between international and municipal law has led one scholar to refer to the investment treaty regime as

---

33. Thirlway, *The Law and Procedure of the International Court of Justice, Fifty Years of Jurisprudence* (Oxford, 2013), 102–108.
34. Brownlie's *Principles of Public International Law*, 8th ed, ed. Crawford (Oxford, 2012), 53–54.
35. Sereni, 'International Economic Institutions and the Municipal Law of States', *Recueil des Cours* (1959), I, 133 at 210. *See also* Triepel, 'Les rapports entre le droit interne et le droit international', *Recueil des Cours* (1923), I, 77 at 81.

Introduction: Relationship Between International Law and Municipal Law   III

having a 'hybrid or sui generis character'.[36] Investment treaty disputes demonstrate municipal law's crucial role in defining the content of the subject matter regulated by the applicable international law standard. The key issue in this context is not which law – municipal or international – prevails, since there is normally no direct conflict. Rather, the issue is how these rules of law should interact. But given the approach taken by a number of investment treaty tribunals, there is a predicate question to be addressed: Is there even a genuine role for municipal law or should 'economic realities' prevail in guiding a tribunal's assessment of the non-international aspects of a dispute?

Economic realities cannot substitute for the existence of a right. If municipal law does not deem these realities to constitute a right, can international law nonetheless protect them? The European Union (EU) Commission has rejected this approach, and stated in its Reading Guide[37] on the Transatlantic Trade and Investment Partnership (TTIP) that:

> The draft TTIP text also includes provisions clarifying that the Investment Tribunal will apply exclusively to the provisions of TTIP, in accordance with international law. The Investment Tribunal would only be able to take a domestic law of each Party taken into account as a matter of fact. Where the Tribunal would be required to ascertain the meaning of a provision of a domestic law of a Party it would have to follow the interpretation made by that Party's domestic courts. The draft TTIP text further clarifies that the meaning given to domestic law by the Tribunal would not be binding on domestic courts. This further guarantees that the autonomy of the EU legal order is fully preserved.[38]

Under the EU-Canada Comprehensive Economic and Trade Agreement (CETA), introduced by the EU Commission as a 'clear break from the current ISDS [Investor-State dispute settlement] system' and showing the 'commitment to work together to establish a multilateral investment tribunal', an investment tribunal will only apply the agreement, in accordance with the principles of international law, when adjudicating upon claims submitted by investors. It cannot decide on matters of EU or Member State law. It can only look at EU or Member State law as a matter of fact, for example to make sure that the investor does in fact hold the property rights in question. It will therefore not interpret EU or Member States law in a manner binding on EU courts or EU governments. CETA also plainly states that determining whether a Party's measure is legal under domestic law remains the monopoly of the Party's competent authorities.[39]

Investment treaties protect foreign investors and their investments by setting an independent international law standard such as, fair and equitable treatment and prohibition against expropriation without compensation. But international law often

---

36. Douglas, 'The Hybrid Foundations of Investment Treaty Arbitration', *BYIL* 74 (2003), 151.
37. *See* EU European Commission, Reading Guide that sets out the main elements in the draft text on Investment Protection and Investment Court System in Transatlantic Trade and Investment Partnership, 16 Sep. 2015 available on the Commission website: http://europa.eu/rapid/press-release_MEMO-15-5652_en.htm. *See also* Douglas, 'Property Rights as the Object of an Expropriation', in *Building International Investment Law, The First 50 Years of ICSID*, eds Kinnear et al. (Kluwer, 2016), at 347.
38. Reading Guide, *supra*, 4, 'Next Steps'.
39. News on CETA available from the EU Commission website, 29 Feb. 2016: http://trade.ec.europa.eu/doclib/press/index.cfm?id=1468.

does not regulate the *right* it protects. Therefore, the standard's application should be determined by *renvoi* to municipal law, despite the differences from the diplomatic protection context. The determination of whether a contractual right constitutes an investment first requires an analysis under the relevant municipal law to determine whether the right exists, and any limits to which it may be subject. The second step is to determine whether this right gives rise to investment protection. The enquiry into the relevant municipal law, however, does not determine whether there has been a violation of international law. As the *Vivendi* Ad Hoc Committee observed, 'a State may breach a treaty without breaching a contract and *vice versa*'.[40] Article 3 of the ILC's Articles on State Responsibility, quoted in full above, further explains that the 'characterization of an act of a State as internationally wrongful' is not 'affected by the characterization of the same act as lawful by internal law'.[41]

International law's supremacy in the event of a conflict with municipal law[42] is not the focus of this book. Rather, the central topic is municipal law's role in providing the substance for concepts such as contracts, property rights, and shareholders' rights, which are relevant in the investment treaty context but are not regulated under international law. Applicable law clauses state the problem without resolving it.[43] Even where parties have sought to exclude municipal law and have referred exclusively to international law, the latter does not define or regulate contractual or property rights related to an investment. These are in principle governed by the law of the host State (which is also usually the applicable law of the investment contract).[44] Municipal law has a role represented by the definition of the contents of the property rights in dispute.

The chapters that follow analyse the unavoidable interaction of municipal law and international law in investment treaty arbitration and the consequences stemming from rejecting the application of municipal law when it is relevant. In a number of these arbitrations, the tribunals have struggled with the dichotomy between 'commercial' and 'international' law issues. The underlying problem is that municipal and international law are concerned with the same thing: an investment arising out of a legal relationship that did not exist before municipal law created it. The municipal law of the host State determines whether a right exists and in whom it vests; the investment treaty and public international law establish whether the right is an 'investment' and whether it is protected by an investment treaty. The typology set out below is designed to provide a starting point for understanding the international law/municipal law interaction.

---

40. *Compañiá de Aguas del Aconquija-Vivendi ('Vivendi')*, Decision on Annulment of 3 Jul. 2002, *ILM* 41 (2002), 1135, para. 95.
41. Crawford, *supra*, 86.
42. *See*, in general, Borchard, 'The Relation Between International Law and Municipal Law', *Va. L. Rev. 27* (1940), 137.
43. Douglas, 'The Hybrid Foundations of Investment Treaty Arbitration', 195.
44. *Id.*, 198.

IV TWO CATEGORIES OF INTERACTION BETWEEN INTERNATIONAL LAW AND MUNICIPAL LAW

In investment treaty arbitration, the relationship between international law and municipal law can be characterized as falling into three categories. This book explores the second and third categories, in which there is unavoidable interaction.

[A] International Law Standing Alone

In the first category, international law is the only applicable law; municipal law plays no role. Because international law regulates the entire dispute, no reference to municipal law is called for. This category includes, for example, contracts regulated by international law. In the *Eurotunnel* case,[45] a dispute arose under the Treaty of Canterbury (12 February 1986) and an associated concession agreement concerning the development of the Channel Tunnel. In 2003 the Eurotunnel Group commenced arbitration against the United Kingdom and France pursuant to the concession agreement's arbitration clause, alleging damages caused by the governments' failure to protect the tunnels, the terminal areas, and freight facilities from incursions and related delays.[46] The applicable law was the provisions of the Treaty of Canterbury. The tribunal defined the concession agreement as a 'free-standing agreement governed by international law'.[47]

This book does not analyse this category, in which there is no interaction between international and municipal law. Moreover, this category is not commonly implicated in investment treaty cases.

[B] *Renvoi* to Municipal Law

In the second category, international law defines certain concepts, but a *renvoi* to municipal law is necessary for these concepts to apply in the investment protection context. The definition of State organ, for example, belongs to this category. International law defines the term 'organ', but there still must be a *renvoi* to the definition of the same term under municipal law. The *renvoi*, however, does not complete the analysis. As discussed in Chapter 1, it constitutes the initial step. After the *renvoi* to municipal law, the content of municipal law must be tested against international law. This category also applies for concepts such as 'investment' and 'property', 'investor's nationality', and 'shareholders' rights', where there is no international law definition.

---

45. *The Channel Tunnel Group Limited & France Manche SA v. The Secretary of State for Transport of the Government of the United Kingdom of Great Britain and Northern Ireland and le Ministre de l'équipement, des transports, de l'aménagement du territoire, du tourisme et de la mer du gouvernement de la République Française (Eurotunnel)*, Partial Award dated 30 Jan. 2007, ILR 132 (2008), 1.
46. There were further claims based on civil penalties against the Group and the support given by the UK and France to a company operating ferry services in the cross-Channel transport market.
47. *Eurotunnel*, 44, para. 146.

International investment law generally protects shares and shareholders' rights. Investment treaties do not, however, define 'shareholder' or a 'share', and typically do not require that shareholders must own a majority of the shares or control the company's administration to qualify for treaty protection. Several investment treaty arbitral decisions have defined shareholders' rights as comprising an entitlement to receive compensation for damages suffered by the company due to a violation of an international obligation *vis-à-vis* the company. Such protection has been deemed to cover not only the ownership of the shares, but also a company's assets. Among the questions arising in this context is whether economic reality should be relevant over and above the existence of a legal right.

[C]   The Contract-Treaty Problem

Finally, there is a category that concerns the contract-treaty 'problem' in international investment cases: whether or in what circumstances an alleged breach of contract may constitute a breach of a State's international law obligation entails an analysis of the relationship between international and municipal law. As a matter of customary international law, a State's breach of a contract between an alien and the State does not as such entail State responsibility. The investment treaty arena poses a different set of problems for arbitral tribunals. As noted above, the foundation of an investment is a contractual relationship. The difficult task for investment treaty tribunals is to determine the possible jurisdiction under investment treaties for contractual disputes. Chapter 6 considers this issue, and umbrella clauses. The central question is whether an alleged breach of an umbrella clause transforms a breach of contract claim governed by municipal law into an international law claim. An associated question is whether umbrella clauses apply to contracts entered into by instrumentalities of the State with a separate personality.

V   ROLE OF MUNICIPAL LAW IN THE INVESTMENT TREATY CONTEXT

This book does not simply observe that there is a complex interplay between international and municipal law in investment disputes; rather, its purpose is to develop a systematic approach to the interplay. The task is how to characterize an internationally wrongful act when, as Judge Morelli stated, 'the very existence of the international obligation depends on a state of affairs created in municipal law, though this is so not by virtue of municipal law but, on the contrary, by virtue of the international rule itself, which to that end refers to the law of the State'.

This book analyses six areas in which the application of international law and municipal law – or the municipal 'legal system' – has triggered debate in the investment treaty context: (i) the application of the principle of attribution; (ii) applicable law in the International Centre for Settlement of Investment Disputes (ICSID) regime; (iii) the definition of the concepts of investment and property rights; (iv) the definition of the concept of nationality; (v) shareholders' rights; and (vi) the difference between treaty claims and contract claims, and umbrella clauses. In these areas, the alternatives open to arbitral tribunals range from complete exclusion of municipal law to complete reliance on municipal law. Neither extreme assists the development of international investment law, which requires a more nuanced approach to the role of municipal law than many arbitral tribunals have implemented to date.

CHAPTER 1
Attribution under the Law of State Responsibility

§1.01 INTRODUCTION

Article 2 of the ILC's Articles on State Responsibility[1] identifies the two elements of an internationally wrongful act of a State:

(i) conduct 'attributable to the State under international law';[2] and
(ii) conduct that 'constitutes a breach of an international obligation of the State'.[3]

This Chapter analyses the first element, attribution of conduct to a State, in the context of investment treaty disputes, and focuses on the respective roles of international law and municipal law in such attribution.

Scholars have long debated whether municipal law can contribute to the assessment of State attribution under international law. Article 3 of the ILC's Articles on State Responsibility ('characterization of an act of State as internationally wrongful') stands

---

1. See, generally, *The Law of International Responsibility*, eds. Crawford, Pellet and Olleson (Oxford, 2010); Dupuy, 'Relations Between the International Law of Responsibility and Responsibility in Municipal Law', Ch. 15 in *The Law of International Responsibility*; Crawford, *State Responsibility, The General Part* (Cambridge, 2013); and Crawford, *The International Law Commission's Articles on State Responsibility* ('The ILC's Articles on State Responsibility'). See also *Hamester v. Ghana*, Award, 18 Jun. 2010, available on the Investment Treaty Arbitration website: http://www.italaw.com/documents/Hamesterv.GhanaAward.pdf, para. 172: '[i]t is clear that Article 2 is not an autonomous basis for attribution. Rather, its purpose is to give a general definition of what constitutes an internationally wrongful act of a State. Article 2 does not create a general obligation on the part of States to prevent any act interfering with an investor's rights. The article only articulates the elements of the definition of an internationally wrongful act of a State, which can be an action or an omission. Either has to fulfill two cumulative conditions: it must be attributable to the State and it must violate an international obligation of the State'.
2. Crawford, *The ILC's Articles on State Responsibility*, 81.
3. Ibid.

as the major outcome of this debate. Under Article 3, as previously discussed, the 'characterisation of an act of a State as internationally wrongful is governed by international law', and 'is not affected by the characterisation of the same act as lawful by internal law.[4]

However, in an ILC meeting before the adoption of the Articles on State Responsibility, the Drafting Committee clarified that:

> [A]rticle 3 did not consider internal law to be irrelevant to the question of whether conduct was internationally wrongful; rather it provided that international law governed the question of characterisation, taking into account internal law to the extent that it was relevant. In other words, there could be situations when internal law was relevant to the question of international responsibility and that was reflected in the wording of article 3.[5]

The ILC's position that municipal law may be relevant to the application of international law remained consistent during the discussions preceding to the adoption of the Articles on State Responsibility. The drafters commented that although the 'characterization of an act as unlawful was an autonomous function of international law not contingent on characterization by national law',[6] this 'did not mean that internal law was irrelevant to the characterization of conduct as unlawful; on the contrary it may well be relevant in a variety of ways'.[7] This Chapter's central task is to identify, in the investment treaty context, municipal law's role in the attribution of conduct carried out by either a State organ or a para-statal entity exercising elements of governmental authority.

First, it is necessary to determine whether the Articles on State Responsibility apply in the investment treaty context. It has been argued that a 'distinct regime of international responsibility'[8] applies to the relationship between the host State and the investor, and that Part II and III of the Articles on State Responsibility do not apply in investment treaty arbitration. The Commentary to ILC Article 28[9] is more nuanced. It clarifies that 'while Part One [Articles 1-12] applies to all cases in which an internationally wrongful act may be committed by a State, Part Two has a more limited scope. It does not apply to obligations of reparation to the extent that these arise towards or are invoked by a person or entity other than the State'.[10] The Articles on State Responsibility that are most relevant to this Chapter are Articles 4[11] and 5[12] of Part I,

---

4. *Id.*, 86.
5. ILC's 2681st meeting of 29 May 2001, the summary of which is recorded in the ILC *Yearbook* 2001, vol. I, 91, para. 14.
6. Report of the International Law Commission on the work of its Fiftieth Session, 20 Apr. 1988 to 12 Jun. 1988 and 27 Jul. 1988 to 14 Aug. 1998, A/53/10, ILC *Yearbook* 1998, vol. II (2), 79, para. 346.
7. *Ibid.*
8. *See* Douglas, *The International Law of Investment Claims* (Cambridge, 2009), 96.
9. Article 28, *Legal consequences of an internationally wrongful act*, 'The international responsibility of a State which is entailed by an internationally wrongful act in accordance with the provisions of Part One involves legal consequences as set out in this Part.'
10. Crawford, *The ILC's Articles on State Responsibility*, 193. *See also* Art. 33 on State Responsibility, 209–210.
11. Article 4, *Conduct of organs of a State:*

Chapter 1: Attribution under the Law of State Responsibility   §1.01

which apply to all international obligations 'of the State and not only those owed *to other States*'.[13]

Given the applicability of ILC Articles 4 and 5, the next step is to determine if the investment treaty at issue contains a provision on attributing conduct to the State, and in particular contains provisions on the definitions of 'State organ' and 'governmental activity'.[14] ILC Articles 4 and 5 on State Responsibility have a 'residual character'. That is, under ILC Article 55, Articles 4 and 5 apply only in the absence of a *lex specialis*.[15] Some investment treaties provide a *lex specialis*, and displace customary international rules on attribution.[16] In certain other treaties, such as the Energy Charter Treaty (ECT), a specific treaty provision may nonetheless be deemed to be consistent with customary rules. For example, Article 23(1) of the ECT states that:

> Each Contracting Party is fully responsible under this Treaty for the observance of all provisions of the Treaty, and shall take such reasonable measures as may be available to it to ensure such observance by regional and local government and authorities within its Area.[17]

This ECT provision has been interpreted as restating rather than amending the customary rules on attribution.[18]

In the absence of a specific treaty provision, then, the ILC's Articles on State Responsibility, to the extent that they reflect customary international law,[19] should

---

1. The conduct of any State organ shall be considered an act of that State under international law, whether the organ exercises legislative, executive, judicial or any other functions, whatever position it holds in the organization of the State, and whatever its character as an organ of the central government or of a territorial unit of the State.
2. An organ includes any person or entity which has that status in accordance with the internal law of the State.

12. Article 5: *Conduct of persons or entities exercising elements of governmental authority*, 'The conduct of a person or entity which is not an organ of the State under article 4 but which is empowered by the law of that State to exercise elements of the governmental authority shall be considered an act of the State under international law, provided the person or entity is acting in that capacity in the particular instance.'
13. Crawford, *The ILC's Articles on State Responsibility*, 193, [emphasis in the original].
14. *See*, on State responsibility and attribution in the investment treaty context, Dolzer and Schreuer, *Principles of International Investment Law* (Oxford, 2012), 216–227; and Cohen Smutny, 'State Responsibility and Attribution: When Is a State Responsible for the Acts of State Enterprises? *Emilio Agustín Maffezini v. The Kingdom of Spain*', in *International Investment Law and Arbitration: Leading Cases from the ICSID, NAFTA, Bilateral Treaties and Customary International Law*, ed. T. Weiler (London, 2005), 17.
15. Article 55, *Lex specialis*, 'These articles do not apply where and to the extent that the conditions for the existence of an internationally wrongful act or the content or implementation of the international responsibility of a State are governed by special rules of international law.'
16. *See* below the discussion of *United Parcel Service of America v. Canada*.
17. Dolzer and Schreuer, *Principles of International Investment Law*, 218. *See also* Art. 22 of the Energy Charter Treaty.
18. Dolzer and Schreuer, *supra*, 218.
19. Shaw, *International Law* (Cambridge, 2014), 84–86 and, with regard to investment dispute arbitration, *see* Crawford and Olleson 'The Application of the Rules of State Responsibility', in *International Investment Law*, eds Bungenberg, Griebel, Hobe and Reinisch (Baden, 2015), 411–441, at 419–420.

guide a tribunal's analysis of the attribution issue. The tribunal must then look to customary international law and municipal law's role in the definition of 'State organ' and 'governmental authority'. This stage can be broken down into two major parts.

The first part is whether the municipal law status of a State organ is relevant to the international law standard. In particular, municipal law's role, if any, must be assessed in: (a) the meaning of the term 'State organ'; and (b) the elements required to find that a *de facto* State organ's conduct should be attributed to the State. The second part concerns the definition of an entity exercising governmental activities ('para-statal entities') and how tribunals should apply municipal law to determine the scope of activity carried out by a para-statal entity. In conducting this analysis, there is a need to navigate between two extremes. On the one hand, there is the concern that States may seek to use municipal law to avoid international responsibility by labelling an entity as being outside of the State structure. On the other hand, municipal law cannot simply be ignored; it supplies the content of the State structure, because customary international law does not define State organ or entity. Moreover, the definition of State organ is further complicated by the fact that State structure is often determined by practice and convention rather than formalized in statutes. The difficulties in working through these issues do not absolve tribunals from performing the tasks, expressly and meticulously.

§1.02   ILC ARTICLE 4 AND THE MEANING OF 'STATE ORGAN'

If an investment protection treaty contains provisions concerning attribution to the State of conduct carried out by its organs or para-statal entities, the treaty's wording is essential in determining the role of municipal law in the arbitral tribunal's analysis. This wording: (i) may contain the rules for attribution and a definition of State organ or governmental activity such that no *renvoi* to municipal law is called for; or (ii) may refer to municipal law for the definition of State organ or governmental authority. However, in the latter situation, the *renvoi* would not be dispositive, because there is an overarching international law standard that cannot be displaced.

If an investment treaty does not contain any rule on attribution, customary international law must provide the rule. In this circumstance, similar to situation (ii) above, what does municipal law contribute to the definition of State organ?

Although international law provides a list of categories of 'State organ' for purposes of attributing State responsibility (*see* below), it also refers to municipal law as providing the substance or content of these categories. That is, for the international law category of 'State agency', municipal law provides the actual designation of whether an entity qualifies as a 'State agency'. If municipal law does not consider the entity an organ, international law nonetheless requires that the structure of the State and its relationship with the entity must be considered to determine whether the entity is under the State's *de facto* control. A finding of *de facto* control would justify equating the entity to a *de facto* organ. Much of the attribution debate in the investment treaty context concerns how to categorize entities that are not de jure (pursuant to municipal law) organs of a State.

ILC Article 4 addresses the relationship between international and municipal law by using the term 'includes': a State organ for the purpose of attribution of State responsibility *includes* any organ that has this status under to the relevant municipal law. In other words, any organ under municipal law is an organ under international law, but at the same time any organ that is not categorized as such under municipal law may still be considered a State organ for purposes of attributing State responsibility.

The Article 4 definition was tested before the ICJ in the *Case Concerning the Application of the Convention on the Prevention and Punishment of the Crime of Genocide* (the '*Genocide* case').[20] The ICJ considered whether certain individuals could be considered a *de jure* or *de facto* organ of a State. This decision illustrates, albeit in a context different from investment treaty arbitration, how the principle contained in Article 4 is applied and how the relationship between municipal law and international law should be characterized. Before examining the *Genocide* case, it is important to examine ILC Article 4 more closely.

[A] ILC Article 4 and State Organ

ILC Article 4 states that the 'conduct of any State organ shall be considered an act of that State under international law'. This rule is of 'a customary character',[21] as noted in the Commentary to Article 4. The ICJ confirmed this in the *Genocide* case, where it recognized this rule as being one of 'customary international law'.[22]

The Commentary to Article 4 explains that the 'reference to a State organ covers all individual or collective entities which make up the organization of the State and act on his behalf'.[23] Any State organ can therefore commit an internationally wrongful act. The Commentary further states that no distinction is made between 'legislative, executive or judicial organs'; the reference to 'State organ' must be interpreted 'in the most general sense'.[24] Article 4, however, does not define State 'organ', and does not attempt to list individuals or entities that come within the category. Article 4(2) clarifies the relevance of the State organ's internal status, but again does not attempt to define a State organ from an international law perspective.

Article 2(b)(i) of the ILC's Articles on Jurisdictional Immunities of States and their Property,[25] which was subsequently adopted by the 2004 United Nations Conventions on Jurisdictional Immunities of States and their Properties (not yet in force),

---

20. *Case Concerning the Application of the Convention on the Prevention and Punishment of the Crime of Genocide (Bosnia and Herzegovina v. Serbia and Montenegro)*, Judgment of 26 Feb. 2007, available on the ICJ website at www.icj-cij.org/docket/files/91/13685.pdf.
21. Crawford, *The ILC's Articles on State Responsibility*, 95, citing the ICJ in *Difference Relating to Immunity from Legal Process of a Special Rapporteur of the Commission on Human Rights*, ICJ Reports (1999), 62, at 87, para. 62.
22. *Genocide* case, 138.
23. Crawford, *The ILC's Articles on State Responsibility*, 94.
24. *Id.*, 95.
25. The ILC adopted this Draft at its forty-third session (1991). The Draft was submitted to the General Assembly in order to convene an international conference to examine the Draft and adopt a convention on the subject. In 2000, the General Assembly decided to establish an Ad Hoc Committee on Jurisdictional Immunities of States and their Property. On 2 Dec. 2004 the General

provides a definition of 'State'. According to Article 2(b)(i), 'State' means 'the State and its various organs of government', and Article 2(b), sections (ii), (iii), (iv), and (v) list political subdivisions, agencies, or instrumentalities and representatives of the State. The Commentaries on Article 2(b)(i) explain that the 'State and its various organs of government' include:

> the State itself, acting in its own name and through its various organs of government, however designated, such as the sovereign or head of State, the head of government, the central government, various ministries and departments of government, ministerial or sub-ministerial departments, offices or bureaux, as well as subordinate organs and missions representing the State, including diplomatic missions and consular posts, permanent missions and delegations. The use of the expression 'various organs of government' is intended to include all branches of government and is not limited to the executive branch only.[26]

The Commentaries further remark that:

> Just as the State is represented by its Government, which is identified with it for most practical purposes, the Government is often composed of State organs and departments or ministries that act on its behalf. Such organs of State and departments of government can be and are often constituted as separate legal entities within the internal system of the State. Lacking as they do international legal personality as a sovereign entity they could nevertheless represent the State or act on behalf of the central Government of the State, which they in fact constitute integral parts thereof.[27]

Thus, the definition of 'State' that applies to questions of State immunity comprehends all branches of government, 'not limited to the executive branch only'.[28] This broad definition can also be invoked in relation to State responsibility, in so far as the definition allows for the concept of 'organ' to be treated in the 'most general sense'.[29]

The only difference between the usage of the term 'organs' in the context of State immunity versus that of State responsibility concerns the relevance of the distinction between *acta iure imperii* and *acta iure gestionis*. This distinction is *not* relevant in matters of State responsibility with regard to State organs. The ILC sought the views of governments on whether 'all conduct of an organ of a State is attributable to that State under Article 5 (attribution to the State of the conduct of its organs), irrespective of the

---

Assembly, by its resolution 59/38, adopted the United Nations Convention on Jurisdictional Immunities of States and their Property.

26. Commentaries on Art. 2(b)(i) of the ILC's Articles on Jurisdictional Immunities of States and their Property, 14–15, available on the ILC website: http://legal.un.org/ilc/texts/instruments/english/commentaries/4_1_1991.pdf.
27. *Id. See also* the Resolution adopted by the Institut de Droit International, during the Session in Basel, 2 Sep. 1991, on *Contemporary Problems Concerning the Immunity of States in Relation to Questions of Jurisdiction and Enforcement*: Art. 3 states that '2. The fact that an agency or political subdivision of a foreign State possesses a separate legal personality as a consequence of incorporation or otherwise under the law of the foreign State does not in itself preclude immunity in respect of its activities'. (Text available at: www.idi-iil.org/idiE/resolutionsE/1991_bal_03_en.PDF).
28. *Id.* (Commentaries on Draft Art. 2(b) (i), 15).
29. Crawford, *The ILC's Articles on State Responsibility*, 95.

Chapter 1: Attribution under the Law of State Responsibility §1.02[A]

iure gestionis or *iure imperii* nature of the conduct'.[30] The members of the Sixth Committee who responded to the query affirmed the irrelevance of such a distinction.[31]

As mentioned above, ILC Article 4(2)'s description of the role of municipal law in defining State organ uses the word 'includes' in the non-exhaustive sense: 'an organ *includes* any person or entity which has that status in accordance with the internal law of the State'. Municipal law does not limit how a State organ is identified from an international law perspective,[32] and instead may add to the internationally accepted understanding of what constitutes a State organ. This must be the case; otherwise, a State could improperly limit its liability under international law by using its internal law to define narrowly the persons or entities having the status of a State organ. The Commentary to Article 4 observes that 'a State cannot avoid responsibility for a conduct of a body which does in truth act as one of its organs merely by denying it that status under its own law'.[33] Nonetheless, as discussed below, at least one arbitrator, the dissenter in *Eureko v. Poland*,[34] has read 'includes' in ILC Article 4(2) to mean that municipal law serves such a limiting function.

Article 4(2) does not, however, resolve certain issues. Interpretive problems may arise when the relevant municipal law is unclear on an organ's status or does not specify that the body acts on the State's behalf. Additionally, although municipal law does not have any impact on the 'scope' of international law[35] and 'international responsibility is by definition attracted exclusively for a breach of international law',[36] municipal law may still be relevant in determining the content of an international obligation.[37]

---

30. Report of the International Law Commission on the work of its Fiftieth Session, 20 Apr. 1988 to 12 Jun. 1988 and 27 Jul. 1988 to 14 Aug. 1998, A/53/10, ILC *Yearbook* 1998, vol. II (2), 17, para. 35; *see also* the Sixth Committee website at www.un.org/law/fiftythr.htm at 8, and ILC's 2555th meeting of 4 Aug. 1998, the summary of which is recorded in the ILC *Yearbook* 1998, vol. I, 241–247. One of the comments made by the United Kingdom was that 'principles developed in the context of State immunity are not necessarily applicable in the context of State responsibility'. *See*, Comments and Observations of Governments on Part One of the Draft Articles on State Responsibility for Internationally Wrongful Acts, doc.A/CN.4/488 and Add.1-3, ILC *Yearbook* 1988, vol. II (1), 37.
31. *See* Crawford, *The ILC's Articles on State Responsibility*, 96.
32. *Id.*, 98.
33. *Ibid.*
34. *Eureko v. Poland*, Ad hoc Arbitration, Partial Award, 19 Aug. 2005, *ICSID Reports*, 12 (2007), 331. A judgment of Court of First Instance of Brussels of 23 Nov. 2006 dismissed the application to set aside the award and a judgment of Court of First Instance of Brussels of 22 Dec. 2006 dismissed the challenge to an arbitrator. Both judgments are available on the Investment Treaty Arbitration website: http://ita.law.uvic.ca/documents/Eureko-awardchallenge.pdf, and http://ita.law.uvic.ca/documents/Eureko-arbitratorchallenge.pdf.
35. Bishop, Crawford and Reisman, *Foreign Investment Disputes* (The Hague, 2014), 541.
36. *Ibid.*
37. The ICJ has explained that a municipal authority's interpretation of municipal authority may assist an international tribunal's assessment of a claim under international law (*ELSI*, Judgment, 20 Jul. 1989, *ICJ Reports* (1989), 15, para. 124).

It is at least clear that municipal law cannot be the only source for determining whether an entity is a State organ. The ILC debated this extensively before adopting the formulation set out in Article 4. The governments[38] expressed:

> concern that the basis of attribution should be sufficiently broad to ensure that States could not escape responsibility based on a formal definition of their constitutive organs, particularly in the view of the recent developments concerning the increasing delegation of public functions to the private sector, such as maintenance of prison facilities. On the other hand, no Government had so far argued that the conditions for attribution should be more restrictively defined.[39]

The ILC considered whether to delete the reference to municipal law, in order to prevent any undermining of international law's role in determining the structure of the State.[40] There was concern that such a reference to municipal law would be invoked by States to avoid their international responsibility, in particular when there had been *ex post facto* changes to the relevant municipal law. The example of 'Bantustans' was mentioned; these were considered independent entities under the law in force under South Africa's former apartheid regime, but qualified as organs by the international community and national courts of other States.

Several members of the ILC's Committee, however, resisted deleting the reference to municipal law, because it is inevitably involved in determining whether an entity is an organ of the State. Furthermore, the reference to municipal law was considered 'the *raison d'être* for that article [Article 4], which was consistent with the right of States to determine their own internal structure in the absence of any a priori definition of State structure under international law'.[41] It was for the States to decide their internal organization and they could not be deprived of this sovereign right, even though international law had to play a role in the attribution process.

The ILC concluded the debate on Article 4 by using the word 'includes' to address the relevance of municipal law. As was to be explained further in the Commentary:

> While noting that internal law was of primary relevance in determining whether a person or entity was to be classified as an organ, the Special Rapporteur agreed

---

38. Comments and Observations of Governments on part one of the Draft Articles on State Responsibility for Internationally Wrongful Acts, doc.A/CN.4/488 and Add. 1-3, ILC *Yearbook* 1988, vol. II (1).
39. *See* Report of the International Law Commission on the work of its Fiftieth Session, 20 Apr. 1988 to 12 Jun. 1988 and 27 Jul. 1988 to 14 Aug. 1998, A/53/10, ILC *Yearbook* 1998, vol. II (2), 80, para. 363; and, ILC's 2553rd meeting of 31 Jul. 1998, the summary of which is recorded in the ILC *Yearbook* 1998, vol. I, 228.
40. *See* ILC's 2553rd meeting of 31 Jul. 1998, the summary of which is recorded in the ILC *Yearbook* 1998, vol. I, 228–233; ILC's 2554th meeting of 3 Aug. 1998, the summary of which is recorded in the ILC *Yearbook* 1998, vol. I, 236–241; ILC's 2555th meeting of 4 Aug. 1998, the summary of which is recorded in the ILC *Yearbook* 1998, vol. I, 241–247; ILC's 2562nd meeting of 13 Aug. 1998, the summary of which is recorded in the ILC *Yearbook* 1998, vol. I, 284–292; Report of the International Law Commission on the work of its Fiftieth Session, 20 Apr. 1988 to 12 Jun. 1988 and 27 Jul. 1988 to 14 Aug. 1998, A/53/10, ILC *Yearbook* 1998, vol. II (2), 82, paras 383–385.
41. Report of the International Law Commission on the work of its Fiftieth Session, 20 Apr. 1988 to 12 Jun. 1988 and 27 Jul. 1988 to 14 Aug. 1998, A/53/10, ILC *Yearbook* 1998, vol. II (2), 81, para. 384, and ILC's 2553rd meeting of 31 Jul. 1998, the summary of which is recorded in the ILC *Yearbook* 1998, vol. I, 232.

with a number of Governments that had suggested deleting the reference to internal law to avoid creating the impression that it was necessarily the decisive criterion. There were several reasons for doing so. First, internal law considered in isolation could be misleading, since practice and convention also played an important role in many legal systems. Secondly, internal law might not provide an exhaustive classification of State organs and indeed that law might not use the term 'organ' in the same sense as international law for the purposes of State responsibility. Thirdly, in some cases, narrow classifications of 'organs' under internal law might amount to an attempt to evade responsibility, which under the principle in article 4 a State should not be able to do. The relevance of internal law as an important criterion could be explained in the commentary.[42]

The use of 'includes' therefore preserves the delicate balance between a State's freedom to organize itself as it wishes and the 'complementary'[43] role of international law to prevent States from relying on their municipal law to escape their international responsibility. The ILC thereby intended to convey the point that municipal law was relevant to the extent that it was not inconsistent with international law.

One arbitration practitioner has suggested that the 'domestic law of a State is inherently unlikely to provide a comprehensive definition of who can engage its responsibility on the international plane'.[44] He explains that the 'position in domestic law may well be utterly irrelevant in international law',[45] and further states that domestic law provides the factual foundation for the assessment carried out under international law of whether an organ should be characterized as a State organ. The conclusion is that even if domestic law expressly classifies an entity as an organ 'it will not be dispositive'.[46] However, the same practitioner acknowledges that the legislative intent behind Article 4(2) was to recognize the significant role of domestic law in determining the status of a person or an entity within the State. This role was recognized as 'decisive' when domestic law deems a person or an entity to be an organ of the State. The role of domestic law is different in the event that a person or an entity is not classified as an organ. The Commentary clarifies that when municipal law characterizes an entity as a State organ, there is of course no difficulty with the characterization – international law simply accepts it.[47]

---

42. Report of the International Law Commission on the work of its Fiftieth Session, 20 Apr. 1988 to 12 Jun. 1988 and 27 Jul. 1988 to 14 Aug. 1998, A/53/10, ILC *Yearbook* 1998, vol. II (2), 81, para. 369.
43. ILC's 2553rd meeting of 31 Jul. 1998, the summary of which is recorded in the ILC *Yearbook* 1998, vol. I, 233.
44. Petrochilos, 'Attribution', in *Arbitration under International Investment Agreements* (Oxford, 2010), 287–322 at 292.
45. Ibid.
46. Id., 293.
47. Ibid. *See also* Crawford and Mertenskötter, 'The Use of the ILC's Attribution Rules in Investment Arbitration', in *Building International Investment Law, The First 50 Years of ICSID*, eds Kinnear et al. (Kluwer Law International, 2015), 27–42, at 28–29.

[B] The *Genocide Case*, *De Facto* State Organ and the Role of Municipal Law

In a context different from investment treaty disputes, the ICJ was called on to apply ILC Article 4 to determine whether the acts of genocide committed in Srebrenica were committed by individuals or entities having the 'status of organ of the Federal Republic of Yugoslavia (as the Respondent was known at the time) under its internal law, as then in force'.[48] Despite the different circumstances in which this case arose, the principles enunciated by the ICJ are relevant to investment treaty cases. The ICJ itself stated that the customary rules on attribution in the case of genocide do not depart from the rules considered in other situations, and remain the same across public international law. These rules may not be rendered irrelevant by a particular type of dispute, but can be overridden only when there is a provision in a treaty that would direct a tribunal to depart from the customary rules encapsulated in the ILC Articles.[49]

In the *Genocide* case, the ICJ first examined whether the individuals who perpetrated the massacre at Srebenica were de jure organs of the Respondent. The analysis was based on the Respondent's internal law; the conclusion reached was that the officers responsible for the massacre were not officers of the Respondent's army. The fact that the Respondent was providing financial support and paying salaries and other benefits to some of these officers was not deemed to 'automatically make them organs'.[50] The elements the ICJ considered relevant were: (a) who appointed the individuals; and (b) to whom they were subordinated. The expression 'State organ' was intended to be 'applied to one or other of the individual or collective entities which make up the organization of the State and act on its behalf'.[51]

The ICJ then addressed the issue of whether the officers were *de facto* organs of the Respondent. The concept of a *de facto* organ is a corollary of the principle that 'reality must prevail over appearances'. On this point, the ICJ held that 'persons, groups of persons or entities may, for purposes of international responsibility, be equated with State organs even if that status does not follow from internal law, provided that in fact the persons, groups or entities act in complete dependence on the State, of which they are ultimately merely the instrument'.[52] In such a case, the ICJ commented, the inquiry had to go beyond legal status alone 'in order to grasp the reality of the relationship between the person taking action, and the State to which he is so closely attached as to appear to be nothing more than its agent: any other solution would allow States to escape their international responsibility by choosing to act through persons or entities whose supposed independence would be purely fictitious'.[53]

---

48. The *Genocide* case, 138.
49. *Ibid.*
50. *Id.*, 139.
51. *Id.*, which refers to the ILC Commentary to Art. 4, para. 1, 94.
52. *Id.*, 140 referring to the case concerning *Military and Paramilitary Activities in and against Nicaragua (Nicaragua v. United States)*, Judgment of 27 Jun. 1986, *ICJ Reports* (1986), 62–64.
53. *Id.*, 140–141.

In summary, the *Genocide* case teaches that the analysis of whether an entity or a person is a State organ must start with the State's municipal law. A tribunal must first determine whether that municipal law defines the organ as such. If no definition exists, the tribunal must determine the degree of control and dependence that the State imposes on this 'organ'. If the degree of control and dependence is of such a degree to justify equating the entity or the person to an organ acting on the State's behalf, the organ's conduct can be attributed to the State. The ICJ emphasized that the *de facto* concept is exceptional, 'for it requires proof of a particularly great degree of State control over them, a relationship which the Court's Judgment quoted above expressly described as complete dependence'.[54] This means that the ties between the purported organ and the State must demonstrate a complete subordination and the lack of any autonomy. Powerful ties alone would not suffice to equate an entity/person with a State organ. Although the ILC Articles do not expressly deal with *de facto* organs in terms of attribution, the formulation of Article 4(2) and the principle that a State includes any entity or individual with a status of organ as a matter of municipal law does not preclude the attribution of acts of *de facto* organs.[55]

Scrutiny of the ILC's Articles on State Responsibility and the ICJ's judgment in the *Genocide* case thus show: (a) customary international law refers to municipal law for the definition of State organ; and (b) there is an exception to reliance on the municipal law categorization when the facts show that the entity is totally dependent on and controlled by the State.

[C] Investment Treaty Awards

The following investment treaty cases illustrate how ILC Article 4 and the principles stated in the *Genocide* case have been applied (or in certain instances should have been applied), and how the definition of State organ under municipal law may be understood in the investment treaty context. Issues such as 'separate personality' of putative State entities and *de facto* organs are also examined below.

[1] Eureko v. Poland *and the Question of Separate Personality*

Eureko purchased 20% of a large, State-owned Polish insurance company (PZU) from the Polish State Treasury. The purchase agreement and subsequent agreements provided that the State Treasury and PZU intended to carry out an Initial Public Offering (IPO) of PZU's shares. The State Treasury failed to carry out the IPO. The main issue for the arbitral tribunal was whether the State Treasury had an obligation to do so. Eureko argued that because of the failure to carry out the IPO, Poland frustrated its investment. Poland contended, *inter alia*, that the purchase agreement and subsequent agreements could not be attributed to Poland because they were agreements between

---

54. *Id.*, 141.
55. Crawford and Olleson, 'The Application of the Rules of State Responsibility', 424–432.

two business partners and were unrelated to the State Treasury's exercise of governmental powers.

The tribunal majority explained that it was a well-settled rule of international law that the conduct of a State organ was considered an act of that State, and such organ includes any person or entity holding that status in accordance with the State's internal law. When the Minister of the State Treasury sold PZU's shares and agreed to carry out an IPO, he acted pursuant to clear authority conferred on him by the Council of Ministers of the Government of Poland. The tribunal majority held that Poland was therefore responsible to Eureko for the State Treasury's actions.[56]

In a Dissenting Opinion, Rajski stated that under Polish law the State Treasury was a juridical entity separate from the State and therefore was not a State organ. Rajski considered that Article 4(2) should be read to mean that if under municipal law an entity does not have the status of a State organ, no State responsibility could arise from that entity's act.[57] He further commented that, at the very least, municipal law must be considered in determining the threshold question of whether, under international law, the wrongful act alleged by the foreign investor can be attributed to the State.

Rajski's position is consistent with the view Poland expressed in the ILC's drafting sessions for the Articles on State Responsibility. Poland's position was that the definition of a State organ 'should be governed exclusively by the domestic (constitutional) law of the State concerned'.[58] But Rajski's position is inconsistent with the principles actually adopted in the ILC Articles on State Responsibility and endorsed by the ICJ in the *Genocide* case. The Commentary to Article 4 explains that 'a State cannot avoid responsibility for a conduct of a body which does in truth act as one of its organs merely by denying it that status under its own law'.[59] Rajski appears to ignore this principle by interpreting the word 'includes' in Article 4(2) in a way that, while not wholly implausible as a matter of textual comprehension, clearly conflicts with basic international law principles. The State is responsible for the acts of State organs 'whether or not they have separate legal personality' under the State's municipal law.[60] Rajski's Dissenting Opinion also fails to accept that distinguishing the conduct of State organs on the basis of the criterion *acta iure imperii* versus *acta iure gestionis* would not apply here.[61]

While the State is responsible for acts of State organs regardless of whether they have separate legal personality under the State's municipal law, this does not mean

---

56. *Eureko v. Poland, supra,* paras 129–134.
57. *Id.*, Dissenting Opinion, paras 8–9.
58. Comments and Observations of Governments on part one of the ILC's Articles on State Responsibility for Internationally Wrongful Acts, A/CN.4/515/Add.2, Fifty-Third Session, 23 Apr. 2001 to 1 Jun. 2001 and 2 Jun. 2001 to 10 Aug. 2001, 6.
59. Crawford, *The ILC's Articles on State Responsibility*, 98.
60. ILC's Report, A/56/0 on the Responsibility of States for Internationally Wrongful Acts, Fifty-Third Session, 23 Apr. 2001 to 1 Jun. 2001 and 2 Jun. 2001 to 10 Aug. 2001, 83. *See also* the Commentaries on Draft Art. 2(b)(i) of the International Law Commission Draft Articles on Jurisdictional Immunities of States, 15; and Art. 3 of the Resolution adopted by the Institut de Droit International, during the Session of Basel, 2 Sep. 1991, concerning *Contemporary Problems Concerning the Immunity of States in Relation to Questions of Jurisdiction and Enforcement*.
61. Crawford, *The ILC's Articles on State Responsibility*, 96.

Chapter 1: Attribution under the Law of State Responsibility §1.02[C]

that the State is responsible for any conduct carried out by a State organ. A State organ's breach of contract is not automatically a breach of international law.[62] The *Eureko* tribunal, having first attributed the conduct of the State Treasury to the Republic of Poland, 'substituted the Republic of Poland for the State Treasury as the counterparty to Eureko's contractual relationship'.[63] Municipal law was not relevant in determining the State Treasury's status, because international law defined the State Treasury as a State organ. On this point the tribunal majority ruled correctly. But this does not mean that *any* conduct carried out by this State organ was an internationally wrongful act. In this respect, the majority's reasoning was defective.

Some arbitrators argue that an organ is an entity belonging to the State if: (i) it has been created by the State; and (ii) the functions assigned to the entity are State's functions rather than the entity's own functions.[64] From this perspective, institutional purpose is the key consideration; if the entity is separate from the State but does not have an independent purpose, the entity may be characterized as an organ. This approach seems to have been endorsed in *Edf v. Romania*,[65] where the tribunal determined that entities with separate legal personalities from the State were not State organs, since municipal law did not grant them that status, which suggests that institutional purpose is the chief analytical concern. But municipal law is only dispositive in the event that it declares the entity to be a State organ. On this point, as well, the *Edf* decision is unclear. In considering ILC Article 4(2) and the role of municipal law, the tribunal quoted a statement by the State's international law expert: 'once it is established that an entity is an organ of the State, the presumption is that all of its acts are attributable to the State unless the contrary is proven'.[66] Municipal law is then viewed as establishing only a presumption when it qualifies an entity as a State organ. However, the ILC commentary clearly indicates that when an organ is identified as such, no difficulty arises.[67] When municipal law determines that the entity is a State organ, any further enquiry on how it has been created and the functions assigned should stop.[68]

---

62. Ibid.
63. Douglas, 'Nothing If Not Critical for Investment Treaty Arbitration: *Occidental, Eureko* and *Methanex*', Arb. Int. 22 (2006), 27, at 43. See Ch. 6.
64. Petrochilos, 'Attribution', 296.
65. *Edf v. Romania*, Award, 8 Oct. 2009, available on the Investment Treaty Arbitration website: http://www.italaw.com/sites/default/files/case-documents/ita0267.pdf.
66. Id., para. 188.
67. Crawford, *The ILC's Articles on State Responsibility*, at 98 and also Crawford and Mertenskötter, 'The Use of the ILC's Attribution Rules in Investment Arbitration', at 28–29. *See also*, see Crawford and Olleson 'The Application of the Rules of State Responsibility', 425.
68. This ILC principle was clearly expressed by the *Toto Costruzioni Generali v. Lebanon* tribunal, which noted that in the event that the municipal law of Lebanon would have considered the relevant entities State organs 'they would unquestionably have the status of State organs under international law', *Toto Costruzioni Generali v. Lebanon*, Decision on Jurisdiction, 11 Sep. 2009, available on the Investment Treaty Arbitration website: http://www.italaw.com/sites/default/files/case-documents/ita0869.pdf, para. 45.

[2] Bosh International et al. v. Ukraine[69] and the Attribution of Obligations Stemming from Undertakings

In *Bosh v. Ukraine*, the dispute arose in connection with the Claimants' investment in Kiev, consisting of a contract to perform a two-stage renovation and redevelopment of a property. The project involved the creation of facilities to accommodate academic symposia, seminars and conferences. The Claimants alleged that the contract was terminated and that Ukraine, Ukrainian courts, the Ministry of Justice, the university and another entity breached the BIT. The tribunal rejected the claim on the grounds that the acts were not attributable to the State.

The *Bosh* tribunal first examined whether the disputed acts were attributable to the university (the Ukrainian courts and the Ministry of Justice were clearly state organs). The tribunal analysed the relevant municipal law and concluded that the university was not a State organ, since it was a separate entity with a high degree of autonomy.[70] The tribunal recognized that the university was an entity empowered by municipal law to exercise elements of governmental authority,[71] but determined that the conduct in dispute could not be characterized as an exercise of governmental authority and therefore was not attributable to Ukraine.[72]

Based on this finding, the tribunal rejected the claim that the breach of the contract between the university and the Claimants violated the BIT's umbrella clause. First, the tribunal reiterated that the conduct of the university was not attributable to Ukraine. Then, it examined whether Ukraine had undertaken any obligation *vis-à-vis* the Claimants by virtue of the umbrella clause, which imposed an obligation incumbent on 'each Party' to the BIT to observe undertakings. The issue was whether the definition of 'Party' included entities controlled by the State, since the contract was entered only with the university and not by a State organ.[73]

The tribunal noted that the BIT defined the term State enterprise, but that this term was distinct from the term 'Party' to the BIT. Thus, Ukraine and the university were two separate entities. The umbrella clause[74] referred to obligations entered into by the State or an entity which conduct was attributable to the State.[75] The umbrella clause was therefore not breached, because the university was not a 'Party' on which it was incumbent not to breach its undertakings and the term 'Party' referred only to the State. Further, since the university's conduct was not attributable to the State, the State was neither bound by the contract nor responsible for its alleged breach.

Bosh v. Ukraine has been cited to support the thesis that the ILC Articles contain the rules of attribution that apply to determine whether a State has entered into a

---

69. *Bosh International et al. v. Ukraine*, Award, 25 Oct. 2012, available on the Investment Treaty Arbitration website: http://www.italaw.com/sites/default/files/case-documents/italaw1118.pdf.
70. *Id.*, para. 172.
71. *Id.*, para. 173.
72. *Id.*, para. 178.
73. *Id.*, para. 243.
74. *Id.*, para. 242: the umbrella clause provided: [e]ach Party shall observe any obligation it may have entered into with regard to investments.
75. *Id.*, para. 246.

Chapter 1: Attribution under the Law of State Responsibility §1.02[C]

contract for umbrella clause purposes.[76] When the contract has been entered into by the government or an entity authorized by the government to do so, it is obvious that the State is bound. However, when the signatory party has a separate personality under domestic law, the question becomes whether 'by operation of international law a State can become Party to a contract that in the domestic law sphere binds only its signatory (…). If so contractual breaches could potentially engage the international responsibility of the State in an action under an umbrella clause'.[77]

The counterargument to the proposition that contractual obligations of entities separate from the State do not bind the State on the international plane are: (i) the breach of an umbrella clause is not a breach of the underlying undertaking, but the breach of the umbrella clause itself; (ii) for the purposes of umbrella clauses, the relevant obligation is imposed on the "contracting State", which is a notion of international law; (iii) under municipal law the concept of State is not unitary, which would make the umbrella clause meaningless if rules on attribution could not be evoked; and (iv) it is difficult to accept that a breach of an agreement signed by an agency would not give rise to a breach of an umbrella clause on the theory that that the agency has a separate legal personality. Pursuant to these counterarguments, determining whether a State has entered into a contract would call for an analysis under international law and an application of the rules of attribution.[78] Interpretation of an umbrella clause must resort to the rules on attribution, because otherwise the scope would remain unsettled.[79]

However, this position is at odds with the ILC Commentary, in the comments to Chapter II on the attribution of conduct to the State. The ILC distinguishes (a) the question of attribution of conduct to the State for the purposes of responsibility, from (b) the rules that govern how organs are authorized to enter into commitments on the State's behalf. The Commentary clarifies that the rules concerning attribution are formulated for the purpose of establishing State responsibility for conduct incompatible with its international obligations. Therefore, the rules on attribution are not formulated for other purposes, such as the ones that regulate how to define the State or its government and how they operate.[80]

Some authors have suggested applying international law to determine whether a contract has been entered on the State's behalf and discuss piercing the corporate veil or international rules on representation. This Chapter does not examine these theories since they venture into a domain different from the question of how the ILC Articles affect the interaction of municipal law and international law in investment dispute.

---

76. Petrochilos, Case *Comment: Bosh International, Inc and B&P Ltd Foreign Investment Enterprise v. Ukraine* – When is Conduct by a University Attributable to the State, ICSID Rev. F.I.L.J 28(2) (2013), 262–272. *see also* Crawford and Mertenskötter, 'The Use of the ILC's Attribution Rules in Investment Arbitration', in *Building International Investment Law, The First 50 Years of ICSID*, 31.
77. Petrochilos, 'Attribution', in *Arbitration Under International Investment Agreements*, 317.
78. *Id.*, 318.
79. *Id.*, 319.
80. Crawford, *The ILC's Articles on State Responsibility*, 92.

It has also been suggested that the question of whether a State has entered into a contract has to be resolved in accordance with the proper law of the contract.[81] Umbrella clauses will be examined in detail in Chapter 6, where the various schools of thought will be discussed. For the purposes of this Chapter, I would simply note that arbitrators who invoke the rules of attribution to determine the party to a contract in order then to apply an umbrella clause are misguided: the purpose of such rules is to determine State's responsibility for violating an international obligation, and not to determine whether a contract has been entered on behalf of the State.

[3] Salini Costruttori S.p.A. and Italstrade v. Morocco[82] and Noble Ventures v. Romania:[83] The Notion of De Facto Organ

The *Salini v. Morocco* tribunal reached a conclusion opposite to that of the *Eureko* tribunal: *Salini* held that not all conduct arising from a contractual relationship with a *de facto* State organ can be attributed to the State.

The dispute in *Salini* arose in connection with a contract concerning the construction of a highway joining two Moroccan cities. The works were substantially delayed, and Salini Costruttori S.p.A. and Italstrade ('Salini') commenced arbitration proceedings against Morocco. Morocco contended, *inter alia*, that Salini's contracting party was a private legal entity with its own assets.

The tribunal rejected Morocco's argument and found that the entity was State-owned, since it was predominantly controlled by the State. To reach this determination, the tribunal examined the company's structure and objectives.[84] The tribunal first considered whether the State actually controlled and managed the entity, and second, whether the entity's role and functions were under State control or were normally reserved to the State, or were not usually carried out by the State.[85] Although this structural-functional assessment was not strictly a matter of municipal law, it nonetheless involved an examination of the State's activities in relation to its municipal, as opposed to international, relations.

The tribunal held that the company's structure showed that the State-owned entity was 'controlled and managed by the Moroccan state through the medium of the Minister of Infrastructure and various political organs'.[86] Among the tribunal's key factual findings were that the Moroccan State held the majority stake; several ministers sat on the board of directors; and the Minister for Infrastructure was president of the board of directors. This translated into *de facto* control over the company. As for the

---

81. Crawford and Mertenskötter, 'The Use of the ILC's Attribution Rules in Investment Arbitration', in *Building International Investment Law, The First 50 Years of ICSID*, 32–35.
82. *Salini Costruttori S.p.A. and Italstrade v. Morocco*, Decision on Jurisdiction, 23 Jul. 2001, ILM 42 (2003), 609.
83. *Noble Ventures v. Romania*, Award, 12 Oct. 2005, available on the Investment Treaty Arbitration website: http://ita.law.uvic.ca/documents/Noble.pdf.
84. *Salini v. Morocco*, paras 32–33.
85. *Ibid*. See also *Maffezini v. Spain*, Award on Jurisdiction, 25 Jan. 2000, para. 77.
86. *Salini v. Morocco*, para. 32.

functional criterion, the entity's main objective was 'to accomplish tasks that are under State control'.[87]

The tribunal concluded, for these reasons, that the State-owned entity was acting on Morocco's behalf. However, the tribunal also affirmed that it did not have jurisdiction over mere breaches of contract by the separate legal entity in a dispute that did not also involve a breach of a treaty.[88]

The *Salini* decision is consistent with the guidance on *de facto* organs contained in the *Genocide* case. In particular, the decision reflects the significance, for attribution purposes, of the circumstance under which the State used its ownership interest in the entity to achieve a specific result and to carry out a public function. The State-owned entity was a *de facto* organ, notwithstanding that Moroccan law considered it a legally separate entity. The definition of an organ had to take into account factual realities. The ties between the purported entity and the State showed a complete subordination and lack of any autonomy, which justified the tribunal's disregard of its formal categorization under Moroccan law.

Salini addressed the issues of the existence of *de facto* State control. A different question was raised in *Noble Ventures:* as a matter of international law, if there is no stated finding of *de facto* control, can a tribunal nonetheless rely on municipal law to conclude that there is attribution?

The *Noble Ventures* dispute arose out of a privatization agreement concerning the acquisition and management and operation of a steel mill, Combinatul Siderurgic Resita (CRS), located in Romania. This agreement was entered into between Noble Ventures, an American corporation, and a Romanian entity, State Ownership Fund (SOF), created for the purpose of privatizing Romanian State-owned entities.[89] Pursuant to the agreement, Noble Ventures purchased SOF's shares in CRS. A few months after the privatization a number of problems emerged, and Noble Ventures claimed, *inter alia*, that SOF had misrepresented key assets of CRS, violated the duty of full protection and security during a labour unrest, and that the State's failure to renegotiate debt rescheduling led to a financial crisis in Romania.

Was the conduct of SOF and the Authority for Privatization and Management of the State Ownership (APAPS) attributable to Romania because these entities were State organs? Noble Ventures contended that since these entities were owned by the government, the Prime Minister appointed the board of directors, and their mandate was to carry out a governmental function (that is, the privatization of State-owned entities), SOF and APAPS were State organs; attribution therefore applied. Romania argued that these entities were separate bodies from the State; accordingly, the State was not a party to the disputed privatization agreement. Romania also submitted that even if these entities were carrying out governmental functions, the disputed acts were *acta iure gestionis*.

---

87. *Id.*, para. 33.
88. *Id.*, para. 61.
89. SOF was subsequently replaced by the Authority for the Privatisation and Management of the State Ownership – APAPS (para. 6).

The tribunal held that the relevant BIT did not address the issue of attribution, which meant that customary international law, as codified in the 2001 ILC Articles on State Responsibility, governed this issue. The tribunal referred to Article 4, and concluded that '[s]ince SOF and APAPS were legal entities separate from the Respondent, it is not possible to regard them as *de iure* organs'.[90] The tribunal also found, however, that SOF and APAPS were acting as governmental agencies, and, given that the ILC Articles did not support a distinction between *acta iure gestionis* and *acta iure imperii*, held that their conduct was attributable to Romania.

The *Noble Ventures* decision, even if it appears to be based on the ILC Articles, and even if it ultimately reaches the correct result, contradicts the rationale behind ILC Article 4; municipal law is relevant, but one cannot assess whether an entity is a State organ solely on the basis of what municipal law enunciates. In the course of the ILC debate concerning municipal law's role in attributing to a State conduct carried out by an organ, delegates emphasized that the existence of legal personality under municipal law 'was not decisive',[91] because there are many States (such as the United Kingdom) that have ministries with a legal personality distinct from the State. The existence of a separate personality was insufficient for determining whether an entity was a State organ. For the attribution purposes, it is irrelevant if a State is organized as an ensemble of legal entities that may be separate for different purposes. What is relevant is whether: (a) the separate entities are so closely connected and controlled by the State that they must be considered an organ; or (b) they are clearly independent from the State and simply exercise some functions delegated by the State. The label given by the State cannot be dispositive; the issue is whether the entity acted in the capacity of a State organ and exercised some State functions. This principle is confirmed by the *Genocide* case, where the analysis was based on whether the individuals were de jure or *de facto* organs, since for the purpose of international responsibility, individuals or entities can 'be equated with State organs even if that status does not follow from internal law, provided that the persons, groups or entities act in complete dependence on the State, of which they are ultimately merely the instrument'.[92]

The determination of whether an individual or an entity is a State organ must start with an analysis of municipal law, but cannot be confined to it. The entity may properly be considered a State organ if its relationship with the State is so close that the entity is nothing more than the State's agent; whether the State itself regards the entity as its agent is irrelevant.[93]

---

90. *Noble Ventures v. Romania*, para. 69.
91. ILC's 2555th meeting of 4 Aug. 1998, the summary of which is recorded in the ILC *Yearbook* (1998), vol. I, 242, para. 8.
92. *Genocide* case, para. 392, 140.
93. *See*, more recently, the analysis carried out with regard to the determination of whether an entity was a *de facto* organ in *Hamester v. Ghana* where the tribunal examined the relevant municipal law to determine whether the entity was independent from the State. *Ulysseas v. Ecuador*, Final Award, 12 Jun. 2012 available on the Investment Treaty Arbitration website: http://www.italaw.com/sites/default/files/case-documents/ita1019.pdf focused on the degree of independence, distinct personality and separate assets, which meant economic independence. In *Jan de Nul v. Egypt*, Award, 6 Nov. 2008, available on the Investment Treaty Arbitration website: http://www

However, the *Noble Ventures* tribunal did correctly point to the irrelevance of the distinction between *acta iure gestonis* and *acta iure imperii:* '[t]he ILC draft does not maintain or support such a distinction. Apart from the fact that there is no reason why one should not regard commercial acts as being in principle also attributable, it is difficult to define whether a particular act is governmental'.[94] As discussed above, this distinction is irrelevant for the purposes of ILC Article 4.[95] However, assessing an act's nature and determining whether it is governmental is crucial to applying the rule of attribution provided by ILC Article 5, to which this Chapter now turns.

§1.03 PARA-STATAL ENTITIES AND THE ROLE OF MUNICIPAL LAW

Article 5 of the ILC's Articles on State Responsibility states that the conduct of an individual or an entity that is not a State organ but exercises elements of governmental authority is considered an act of the State under international law. Under this article, a para-statal entity's act can be attributed to the State only if the entity is engaged in 'governmental activity'.[96] The term 'entity' is broadly defined and may even include private companies, if they are exercising elements of governmental authority.[97] Exercise of a governmental function is the main criterion for determining whether the person's or entity's disputed act should be attributed to the State.

Under ILC Article 5, then, 'the conduct of an entity must accordingly concern governmental activity and not other private or commercial activity in which the entity may engage'.[98] The entity's activity cannot be attributed to the State if it is related, for example, to a contract in which there is no exercise of governmental power.

In some investment treaty cases, the relevant BIT contains a provision on State-owned entities and attribution. For example in *Genin v. Estonia*[99] the tribunal held that the Bank of Estonia was an agency of a Contracting State:

> The Estonian central bank is a 'state agency', as defined by the BIT, which stipulates in Article II 2(b) that 'Each Party shall ensure that any state enterprise that it maintains or establishes acts in a manner that is not inconsistent with the Party's obligations under this Treaty wherever such enterprise exercises any regulatory, administrative or other governmental authority that the Party has delegated to it, such as the power to expropriate, grant licenses ...'. The Republic of Estonia is therefore the appropriate Respondent to a complaint relating to the conduct of the Bank of Estonia.

.italaw.com/sites/default/files/case-documents/ita0440.pdf; the emphasis was on the fact that the entity was not part of the State, but was carrying out commercial activities and had an autonomous budget.
94. *Noble Ventures v. Romania*, para. 82, 74.
95. Crawford, *The ILC's Articles on State Responsibility*, 96; and Dolzer and Schreuer, *Principles of International Investment Law*, 203.
96. Crawford, *The ILC's Articles on State Responsibility*, 100.
97. Ibid.
98. *Id.*, 101.
99. *Genin v. Estonia*, Award, 25 Jun. 2001, *ICSID Reports* 6 (2003), 241, para. 327.

Some scholars view this ruling as an exceptional case in which investment treaty provisions 'provide for the responsibility of states for action of their entities'.[100] However, this BIT does not appear to contain provisions different from the customary international law rule encapsulated in ILC Article 5: if the State-owned entity performs a governmental function, then its conduct is attributable to the State.

Although ILC Article 5 does not define the scope of governmental activity (the ILC Commentary indicated that this term must be interpreted by taking into account a particular society, its history and traditions[101]), this category is intended to be narrow: '[t]he formulation of Article 5 clearly limits it to entities which are empowered by internal law to exercise governmental authority'.[102] It has been argued that the term 'governmental' should be interpreted in a comparative manner, in an attempt to identify an objective definition of what is governmental.[103] Alternatively, the term 'governmental' can be interpreted in the same way as 'organ', following the ICJ ruling in the *Genocide* case: the starting point is the relevant municipal law provision, but if the facts point to a *de facto* governmental function, the municipal law definition must be displaced. The *de facto* governmental function must take into account what is considered a public function in a particular State, as advised in the ILC Commentary, which focuses on how governmental authority is conferred to the State entities, the purpose of the authority and the extent to which such entities are accountable to the State.[104]

The 'objective' definition of what is 'governmental' may lead to a violation of the State's sovereign rights and its freedom to organize its structure and identify what is public and what is private. For example, in certain States, railway companies or postal service companies can be considered companies exercising governmental authority, while in other States these companies are only carrying out private functions. The definition of what is governmental at a municipal level may conflict with what is governmental at an international level. A balance must be struck between: (a) not attributing to a State the type of conduct that its 'society, its history and traditions' determines to be non-governmental;[105] and (b) not remitting to a State's sovereign will the determination of international responsibility.

Under ILC Article 5, municipal law must characterize the para-statal entity's conduct 'as involving the exercise of public authority'.[106] However, this characterization does not require proof that the conduct was carried out at the State's direction. Assuming that the point at issue is whether the para-statal entity is exercising its governmental powers or merely engaging in private or commercial activities, a tribunal must first look to municipal law to determine whether the para-statal entity has been authorized to carry out an activity that involves the exercise of public authority.

---

100. Dolzer and Schreuer, *Principles of International Investment Law*, 220.
101. Crawford, *The ILC's Articles on State Responsibility*, 101.
102. *Ibid.*
103. Dolzer and Schreuer, *Principles of International Investment Law*, 221–222.
104. Crawford, *The ILC's Articles on State Responsibility*, 101.
105. *Ibid.*
106. *Id.*, 102.

Moreover, municipal law is relevant in determining the scope of the para-statal entity's activity.

The question then becomes whether there are any international standards applicable to the para-statal entity, as in the case of a State organ. Can a State avoid responsibility for the conduct of a body carrying out governmental activity merely by using its own law to deny that such activity is governmental?

ILC Article 5 may only be invoked, and the conduct of the entity exercising governmental activity attributed to the State, when the relevant municipal law specifically empowers the entity to exercise a governmental activity. But this is inevitably a very narrow category, especially given the restriction that a general authorization to carry out an 'activity as part of the general regulation of the affairs of the community' does not trigger ILC Article 5 protection.[107] If municipal law does not consider the activity as governmental, the activity must nonetheless be tested against a *de facto* criterion, which takes into account the content of the powers, the way they are conferred, their purpose, and the entity's accountability. International law governs the characterization of an internationally wrongful act, and therefore ultimately determines whether a governmental activity took place. Municipal law is the first step, but is not necessarily conclusive.

Article 2(b)(iii) of the 2004 United Nations Conventions on Jurisdictional Immunities of States and their Properties defines the term 'State' to include 'agencies or instrumentalities of the State or other entities, to the extent that they are entitled to perform and are actually performing acts in the exercise of sovereign authority of the State'. The Commentary to Draft Article 2(b)(iv)[108] of the ILC's Draft Articles on Jurisdictional Immunities of States explains that 'State enterprises or other entities are presumed not to be entitled to perform governmental functions and accordingly, as a rule, are not entitled to invoke immunity from jurisdiction of the courts of another State'.[109] Thus, although the State immunity context is not broad enough to cover the definition of State organ (ILC Article 4) that is applicable in investment treaty cases, the narrowness of State immunity is directly relevant to the definition of para-statal entity (ILC Article 5) and leads to the appropriate presumption that clear and precise evidence is required to identify entities that exercise a State's sovereign authority.[110]

Investment treaty awards concerning para-statal entities are discussed below. These cases indicate the complexities of the municipal law role in determining 'governmental activities'.

---

107. *Ibid.*
108. ILC Draft Art. 2(b)(iii) is almost identical to Art. 2(b)(iii) of the United Nations Conventions on Jurisdictional Immunities of States and their Properties.
109. Commentaries on Draft Art. 2(b)(iv) of the International Law Commission Draft Articles on Jurisdictional Immunities of States, 17.
110. Article 5 was mentioned in the *Genocide* case, but the ICJ did not take a position on whether it reflects customary international law. The provision did not apply to the facts of the case (*Genocide* case, para. 414, 149).

[A] *Maffezini v. Spain:*[111] The Structural and Functional Tests

The dispute in *Maffezini* arose in connection with the Claimant's investment in a company that produced and distributed chemical products in Spain. Spain challenged jurisdiction on, *inter alia*, the ground that acts affecting the Claimant's investment were not attributable to Spain because Maffezini's contractual counterpart was a commercial entity.

In deciding whether the entity in question was actually a State entity, the tribunal first examined the issue from a 'formal or structural point of view',[112] by reviewing the entity's ownership and purpose or objective. In particular, the tribunal examined the decree that incorporated the entity and the background to its creation. The tribunal then applied a 'functional test', taking into account whether the activities carried out by the State entity actually involved discharging governmental functions.[113] The tribunal noted that a determination reached at the municipal level that the entity performed governmental functions, 'while it is to be given considerable weight, is not necessarily binding on an international tribunal'.[114]

The tribunal concluded that the entity was created to carry out governmental activities.[115] It held that the Claimant showed that the entity was prima facie acting on Spain's behalf because it met 'both the structural test of State creation and capital ownership and the functional test of performing activities of public nature'.[116] The tribunal reserved for the merits stage the issue whether the entity was responsible for the acts alleged by the Claimant, and whether such acts were governmental as opposed to commercial, and thus attributable to Spain.

At the merits stage, the *Maffezini* tribunal confirmed the prima facie determination that the State entity was acting on behalf of Spain.[117] The tribunal then considered whether the specific acts in dispute were governmental and could be attributed to Spain.[118] The tribunal observed that when the entity was created, many of its functions were governmental, but that it later developed into a more market-oriented entity and many of its functions became commercial.[119] The tribunal then examined whether the entity discharged a public function when it performed the disputed acts or omissions, and therefore whether Spain was responsible for these acts. On the facts before it, the tribunal concluded that the entity had discharged a public function, and that Spain was liable to the Claimant.

The *Maffezini* decision establishes a very cumbersome, though not incorrect, framework for assessing whether the conduct carried out by a State-owned entity is attributable to the State. This first step is to determine whether the entity is under the

---

111. *Maffezini v. Spain*, Decision on Objections to Jurisdictions, 25 Jan. 2000, *ICSID Reports 5.* (2002), 396; Award, 13 Nov. 2000, *ICSID Reports 5.* (2002), 419.
112. *Maffezini v. Spain*, Decision on Objections to Jurisdiction, para. 77.
113. *Id.*, para. 80.
114. *Id.*, para. 82.
115. *Id.*, para. 85.
116. *Id.*, para. 89.
117. *Maffezini v. Spain*, Award, para. 47.
118. *Id.*, para. 52.
119. *Id.*, para. 57.

State's direction or control by applying 'structural' and 'functional' tests. This step is necessary to assess the entity's independence and possible status as a *de jure* or *de facto* organ. The entity can be under the State's strict control without being a State organ. If the entity is independent from the State and ILC Article 5 applies, the fact that this entity is 'public or private ... the existence of a greater or lesser State participation in its capital, ... the ownership of its assets, ... subject to executive control – these are not decisive criteria for the purpose of attribution of the entity's conduct to the State'.[120] The only relevant criterion for applying Article 5 is that the entity is 'empowered, if only to a limited extent or in a specific context, to exercise specified elements of governmental authority'.[121]

The second step in the *Maffezini* framework is to determine whether the acts or omissions complained of by the investor are commercial or governmental. Only if the act is considered to have been carried out while the entity was discharging public functions may the State be held responsible. In *Maffezini*, the tribunal looked to Spanish law and its definition of governmental acts to decide whether the State entity exercised elements of governmental authority. Although the entity's activities had shifted in a commercial direction over the years, the key consideration was whether a public function was being performed in giving rise to the investor's claim.

The *Edf v. Romania* tribunal also investigated the applicability of ILC Article 5, having determined that the relevant entities in the case before it were not State organs. It held that two cumulative conditions had to be fulfilled: (i) the act must be performed by an entity authorized to exercise elements of governmental authority, and (ii) the act must be performed in the exercise of the delegated governmental authority.[122] Although the relevant entities were not agents of the State and did not exercise governmental functions when they performed the acts that were claimed to have breached the BIT, the question nonetheless remained whether attribution was available under ILC Article 8: the tribunal answered yes, since the corporate bodies of the relevant entities acted under the direction of State organs.

The *Edf* tribunal's attribution analysis is, if anything, even more cumbersome than that of *Maffezini*. *Edf* distinguished between a 'structural' basis (attribution in accordance to ILC Article 4), a 'functional' basis (ILC Article 5) and 'control' basis (ILC Article 8).[123] The tribunal stated that while the conduct of an organ is always attributable to the State, the conduct of an entity that is separate from the State, will be attributable in accordance under ILC Article 5 or Article 8 only if the entity was exercising governmental authority.[124] Therefore, there is an inherent limitation in the

---

120. Crawford, *The ILC's Articles on State Responsibility*, 100.
121. *Ibid.*
122. *Edf v. Romania*, para. 191.
123. *Id.*, para. 187. *See Hamester v. Ghana*, para. 172: '[i]n order for an act to be attributed to a State, it must have a close link to the State. This close link can result from the fact that the person performing the act is part of the State's organic structure (Article 4); or is utilising the State's specific governmental powers to perform such act, even if it is a separate entity (Article 5); or is acting under the effective control (on the instructions, or under the direction or control) of the State, even if it is a private or public party (Article 8)'.
124. *Edf v. Romania*, para. 187. *See also* Crawford and Olleson 'The Application of the Rules of State Responsibility', at 433–434.

attribution of an act under ILC Article 5 (and Article 8): the relevant act must be exercised as a result of the exercise of governmental authority.[125] Municipal law determines whether an act is attributable to an entity that is not a State organ under ILC Article 4, when it empowers such entity to carry out an act that entails governmental authority.[126]

A question may arise as to whether the act attributed to the entity is considered *ultra vires* in accordance with municipal law. ILC Article 7 clarifies that the conduct of an organ or an entity empowered to exercise governmental authority 'shall be considered an act of the State under international law if the organ, person or entity, acts in that capacity, even if it exceeds its authority or contravenes instructions'.[127]

[B]   *Encana Corporation v. Ecuador*[128] and 'Governmental Nature'

The *Encana* claim was brought under the Canada-Ecuador BIT and concerned Ecuador's denial of refunds of value-added taxes. The tribunal had to determine whether the conduct of Petroecuador, a State-owned entity, was attributable to Ecuador.

The tribunal considered the following evidence to be relevant in this regard: (i) Petroecuador was 'subject to instructions from the President'; (ii) 'the Attorney-General, pursuant to Ecuadorian law, had authority and exercised authority to supervise the performance of ... contracts and to propose or adopt for this purpose the judicial actions necessary for the defence of the national assets and public interest'; and (iii) the Attorney-General's powers 'extended to supervision and control of Petroecuador's performance of the participation contracts and to their potential renegotiation'.[129] The tribunal concluded that Petroecuador's conduct was attributable to Ecuador, and ILC Articles 5 and 8, led to the same result.

The key to the finding of attribution in this case was the fact that the State-owned company was subject to instructions from the State's president, and the denial of VAT refunds was undertaken at the president's direction and control. Moreover, because Petroecuador was dealing with natural resources, it was arguably acting on Ecuador's behalf and exercising governmental functions.

In *Encana* there was no mention of the 'structural' and/or 'functional' criteria that the *Maffezini* tribunal considered. Rather, the tribunal's focus was on the role of the State-owned company *vis-à-vis* the State in relation to the performance of the disputed contracts. The tribunal conducted this analysis, with regard to the specific act to be attributed. The *Encana* award preceded the *Genocide* case, but applied the

---

125. Crawford and Olleson 'The Application of the Rules of State Responsibility', 434. See also *Hamester v. Ghana*, para. 197: 'only the acts of Cocobod [the entity] utilising State prerogatives are attributable to the State for the purpose of international responsibility, and that the Tribunal therefore only has jurisdiction over acts of Cocobod that would have been performed in the exercise of elements of governmental authority. This, in turn, requires an inquiry into the nature of each and every act of which the Claimant complains'.
126. Ibid.
127. Ibid. See also Crawford, *The ILC's Articles on State Responsibility*, 106.
128. *Encana Corporation v. Republic of Ecuador*, Partial Award on Jurisdiction, 27 Feb. 2004, Award, 3 Feb. 2006, ICSID Reports 12 (2007), 400.
129. *Encana Corporation v. Ecuador*, Award, 3 Feb. 2006, para. 154, 44.

customary international law rules on attribution in a manner consistent with the ICJ's subsequent approach, and provides a cogent example of when the presumption of separate personality is rebuttable.[130]

§1.04 INVESTMENT TREATY PROVISIONS ON ATTRIBUTION: *LEX SPECIALIS* AND THE ROLE OF MUNICIPAL LAW

As explained above, investment treaties may contain provisions on attribution that either displace or restate the ILC Articles. The two cases discussed below in this section illustrate the treatment of municipal law when provisions on attribution are contained in an investment treaty as *lex specialis*, and where, depending on the treaty language, municipal law may have, (a) no role or (b) must be examined because a *renvoi* is called for.

[A] *United Parcel Service of America v. Canada*[131]

In this dispute under the North American Free Trade Agreement (NAFTA),[132] United Parcel Service of America (UPS) claimed, *inter alia*, that Canada was unfairly enforcing its customs laws and Canada Post benefitted from preferential use of infrastructures and network.

One issue before the tribunal was whether Canada Post's conduct was attributable to Canada. Under Canadian law, Canada Post is a Crown Corporation, 'agent of Her Majesty in right of Canada' and an 'institution of the Government of Canada',[133] with the exclusive privilege of collecting, transmitting, and delivering first- class mail letters to addresses in Canada. Canada argued that Canada Post's conduct could not be attributed to the State because the rules of customary international law on State responsibility were displaced by the specific terms of NAFTA, which did not permit attribution in these circumstances.

The tribunal agreed with Canada, holding that the rules stated in NAFTA Chapters 11 and 15 governed the issue of attribution, and precluded the application of ILC Article 4. The tribunal observed that Chapters 11 and 15 clearly distinguish between the 'parties' on one side and government, monopolies, and State enterprises on the other. Chapter 15 contains detailed provisions on competition, monopolies, and State enterprises[134] that identify State parties' obligations in relation to monopolies and State enterprises. The tribunal concluded that Chapter 15:

---

130. *See*, for a useful account of the factors bearing on the rebuttable presumption, Petrochilos, 'Attribution', *supra*, 297–298.
131. *United Parcel Service of America v. Canada*, Award on Jurisdiction, 22 Nov. 2002, *ICSID Reports*, 7 (2005), 285; and Award on the Merits, 24 May 2007, available on the Investment Treaty Arbitration website: http://ita.law.uvic.ca/documents/UPS-Merits.pdf.
132. NAFTA, *ILM* 32 (1993), 612.
133. *United Parcel Service of America v. Canada*, Award on Jurisdiction, 22 Nov. 2002, para. 9.
134. *Id.*, 58–63.

provided for a *lex specialis* regime in relation to attribution of acts of monopolies and state enterprises, to the content of the obligations and to the method of implementation. It follows that the customary international law rules reflected in article 4 of the ILC text do not apply in this case.[135]

According to *UPS v. Canada*, then NAFTA is in this respect a self-contained regime that defines State organ and its attributable conduct, though NAFTA does not address attribution of acts carried out by para-statal entities exercising governmental power.[136]

If the relevant acts fall under NAFTA's detailed provisions, municipal law has no role to play. If the definition of monopoly under Canadian municipal law were different from that in Article 1505, the detailed treaty definition would supersede the municipal law provision. If, however, the relevant acts involved the exercise of governmental authority, customary international law would regulate the attribution of such acts (*see* the discussion above on para-statal entities), because the NAFTA provisions do not provide for a special regime in relation to such acts. In this particular case, the tribunal determined that in certain significant respects NAFTA did apply, and there was no attribution.

UPS v. Canada represents a situation where no *renvoi* to municipal law is called for. The special regime provided by NAFTA regulated the State's conduct because the treaty's specific wording replaces customary international law on attribution. NAFTA exhaustively defines the attribution of acts of monopolies and State enterprises, at least to the extent that they do not exercise governmental activities.

A similar approach (though leading to a largely different attribution result) appears in *Mesa Power Group LLC. v. Canada*.[137] There the question was whether the Ontario Power Authority (OPA) and other entities were organs of Canada. The tribunal first rejected the characterization that OPA and the other entities were organs pursuant to the definition in ILC Article 4, since they were corporations with separate juridical personalities and were not defined as organs by Canadian law.[138] The tribunal also stated that the WTO Panel's characterization of these entities as public bodies was irrelevant, since that characterization was carried out within the meaning of the Agreement on Subsidies and Countervailing Measures and the General Agreement on Tariffs and Trade (GATT) – provisions that do not distinguish between organs and state enterprises, as does NAFTA (the tribunal referenced *UPS* on this point).[139]

The *Mesa Power* tribunal reiterated that Chapters 11 and 15 of NAFTA distinguished between the obligations of a NAFTA Party itself (specified in Chapter 11), and the obligations of a NAFTA Party in respect of its state enterprises (specified in Chapter 15). A NAFTA Party was not responsible for every act of its enterprises; rather, Articles

---

135. *Id.*, 63.
136. *Id.*, 63, 34.
137. *Mesa Power Group LLC. v. Canada*, Award, 24 Mar. 2016, available on the Investment Treaty Arbitration website: http://www.italaw.com/sites/default/files/case-documents/italaw7240.pdf. Decision adopted by a concurring and dissenting opinion, although this opinion did not concern whether the entities in question were State organs/*de facto* organs.
138. *Id.*, paras 342–345.
139. *Id.*, paras 346–347.

1503(2) and 1503(3) circumscribed its responsibility.[140] NAFTA also detailed the 'control' obligations a NAFTA Party has over its enterprises, and thus specified a NAFTA Party's responsibility for acts of its enterprises.

Consequently, the *Mesa Power* tribunal concluded that Article 1503(2) constituted a *lex specialis* that excluded the application of Article 5 of the ILC Articles. However, on the basis of Article 1503(2), the tribunal concluded that the acts of OPA and other entities were attributable to Canada, since these enterprises exercised regulatory, administrative or other governmental authority when they carried out the relevant acts.[141]

[B] *Metalclad Corporation v. United Mexican States*[142]

Metalclad illustrates the interpretation of investment treaty provisions when they are deemed to coexist with customary international law, instead of constituting a *lex specialis*. The dispute in *Metalclad* arose in connection with the corporation's attempts to develop and operate a hazardous-waste landfill. Metalclad claimed that Mexico interfered with its activities through administrative measures and legal actions taken by State municipalities, and filed a request for arbitration under NAFTA, claiming violation of the fair and equitable treatment standard and the expropriation of its business.

The arbitral tribunal had to determine, *inter alia*, whether Mexico was responsible for the acts committed by local municipalities. The tribunal concluded that Mexico was responsible, and observed that a reference to a State or province in NAFTA includes local governments. The tribunal considered this to be consistent with customary law as well as supported by the ILC's Draft Articles of 1975.[143]

The *Metalclad* tribunal thus read NAFTA Articles 105[144] and 201 as being in full accord with customary law rules. In this case, unlike *UPS v. Canada*, the NAFTA provisions were not considered to constitute a special regime. These provisions concerning attribution and local municipalities were drafted in a general manner, and did not contain a rule different from the customary international law rule as expressed in ILC Article 4.

It is clear from *Metalclad* that a State can be internationally responsible for the acts of a State organ at any level of government, including local municipalities, even if municipal law distinguishes between these levels and the State is not responsible under municipal law for the acts of municipal entities.[145] *Metalclad* also demonstrates that a

---

140. *Id.*, paras 361–365.
141. *Id.*, paras 364–377.
142. *Metalclad Corporation v. United Mexican States*, Award, 30 Aug. 2000, *ICSID Reports*, 5 (2002), 209.
143. *Metalclad*, para. 73.
144. Article 105, *Extent of Obligations*: 'The Parties shall ensure that all necessary measures are taken in order to give effect to the provisions of this Agreement, including their observance, except as otherwise provided in this Agreement, by state and provincial governments.'
145. *See also Texaco Overseas Petroleum Company and California Asiatic Oil Company v. The Government of the Libyan Arab Republic*, Preliminary Award, 27 Nov. 1975, *ILR* 53 (1977), 389,

State cannot evade international liability on the ground that no liability exists at a municipal level due to autonomy under municipal law for a local entity. In *Metalclad*, then, international law plays a self-contained role: regardless of what municipal law provides as to the attribution to the State of local entities' conduct, the conduct may be relevant at an international level. Municipal law's role is also limited in the definition of a local municipality. Although the NAFTA provision does not define 'local municipality', and therefore the initial step is to refer to municipal law for such a definition, the municipal law definition is not dispositive; an entity can be considered a *de facto* local municipality at an international level if it satisfies certain requirements.

§1.05 CONCLUSIONS

[A] State Organs

This Chapter's analysis of international law principles and investment treaty awards leads to the following conclusions regarding municipal law's role in the definition of 'State organ' for the purpose of assessing State responsibility.

The first step is to determine whether the investment treaty at issue contains a provision on attribution of conduct to the State.[146] The ILC Articles on State Responsibility have a 'residual character' under Article 55; they are applied only in the absence of a *lex specialis*. Some international investment treaties provide a *lex specialis* provision on attribution which may replace, coexist with, or restate customary international law. Analysis and interpretation of the relevant treaty is therefore the initial task in determining the rules governing attribution.

In the absence of a treaty provision, ILC Article 4 applies.[147] ILC Article 4 codifies customary international rules. 'Organ' has a broad meaning under customary international law; it comprises any entity or individual exercising legislative, executive, judicial, or any other governmental function. The focus is on the State's structure rather than the organ's function. If the individual or the entity is under the State's control or is dependent on the State, it qualifies as a State organ.

---

para. 23, invoking the principle of 'the unity of that State', pursuant to which 'conduct of any State organ having that status under the internal law of the State shall be considered as an act of the State concerned under international law, provided that organ was acting in that capacity in the case in question'; and *Vivendi*, Award, 21 Nov. 2000, *ICSID Reports* 5 (2002), 296 para. 49: '[A]ctions of a political subdivision of a federal state, such as the Province of Tucumán in the federal state of the Argentine Republic are attributable to the central government.... [T]he internal constitutional structure of a country cannot alter these obligations.' (This decision was later annulled; however, the Annulment Committee did not comment on the tribunal's discussion of the concept of attribution and apparently accepted the tribunal's position on this issue).

146. *See*, on State Responsibility and attribution in the investment treaty context, Dolzer and Schreuer, *Principles of International Investment Law*, 195–206; and Cohen Smutny, 'State Responsibility and Attribution: When Is a State Responsible for the Acts of State Enterprises? *Emilio Agustín Maffezini v. The Kingdom of Spain'*, 17.

147. While it is doubtful whether Part II and Part III of the ILC's Articles apply in the investment treaty context, Part I of the articles unquestionably does: *see* Douglas, *The International Law of Investment Claims*, 96–98.

Within these broad Article 4-customary international law categories, municipal law is relevant in that it supplies: (i) the content of the 'State organ' categories; and (ii) the required elements of the conduct of a *de facto* State organ for the purpose of attribution of State responsibility. In this respect, international law must refer to municipal law to an important extent, at the same time that municipal law cannot dictate the conclusions reached under international law in the event that the State under scrutiny seeks to avoid attribution.

Guided by ILC Article 4 and the *Genocide* case, an investment treaty tribunal should therefore refer to municipal law for the substance of the definition of organ: if an individual or an entity is an organ under municipal law, then it is automatically an organ on the international plane.

If the entity or the individual is not a *de jure* organ, this entity or individual may still be considered an organ under international law, if it is controlled by and dependent on the State. The purported organ must be completely subordinate to the State and lack any autonomy. Powerful ties alone would not suffice to equate an entity or individual with a State organ. Functions carried out by the purported organ or the fact that it is formally distinct from the State are irrelevant in determining the existence of a *de facto* organ.

[B] Para-Statal Entities

The question of attribution also requires analysing the regime of State-owned entities, and understanding how tribunals should apply municipal law to determine the scope of a para-statal entity's activity. A central issue is how to characterize an entity exercising 'governmental' activities.

The general rule is that corporate entities, even if they are owned by the State, are separate from the State, and their internationally wrongful acts or omissions cannot be attributed to the State unless there is fraud or evasion and the corporate veil can be pierced. Again, the text of the relevant treaty must be analysed first, to determine whether it contains a rule on attribution. In the absence of such a rule, ILC Article 5 provides the exceptions to the principle of separateness between a State and State-owned entities; namely, internationally wrongful acts of a separate entity that is exercising 'elements of governmental authority' are attributable to the State. This is a narrow category. Attribution may occur, however, even though the exercise of such an authority implies a discretionary power. Moreover, there is no need to show that the State has specifically authorized the conduct.

Determining attribution under this approach requires examining whether the conduct is 'governmental'. The focus here is on the functions carried out by the entity rather than on the structure of the State. The distinction between *acta iure imperii* and *acta iure gestionis* is relevant, but only in the sense that *acta iure imperii* are considered to be those acts covered by the governmental activity umbrella and *acta iure gestionis* are acts outside of it; i.e., the distinction does not assist in the process of assessing the functions carried out by the entity, but is simply the ultimate characterization after the assessment has been made. Only those acts and omissions related to a breach of an international obligation – *not* to a breach of a contract – can be attributed. Municipal law plays a role in the sense that it must authorize the entity's conduct as 'involving the exercise of public authority'.[148]

It has been proposed that an objective definition of 'governmental' may be achieved through a comparative analysis of municipal legal systems.[149] However, this proposal does not take into account a particular system's cultural peculiarities and a State's freedom to determine what is a public or private function. Applying by analogy the principles regarding State organs, this Chapter submits that the following approach is the soundest. A tribunal should first review the relevant municipal law and determine whether the purported organ's activity is a public function. If the analysis of the relevant municipal law leads to a formalistic definition of public function, the tribunal should then consider the State's history and practices in deciding whether the disputed activity is a *de facto* governmental activity. The interests protected, how the population perceives these interests, whether the State delegates to the entity powers regarding this activity, and whether the State ultimately remains in charge of this activity by monitoring and controlling how it is carried out are all relevant factors. Bearing in mind that the ICJ has cautioned against an expansion of the rules on attribution, a restrictive approach must govern the determination of whether certain conduct is governmental.

The inapplicability of the attribution principles to breach of contract cases should not imply that a State can avoid liability for undertakings given by the State itself in contracts between a State-owned entity and an investor, in the event that the breach of such an undertaking is an internationally wrongful act. Here the State would be responsible for its own acts, even though they were carried out in the context of a contract between a State-owned entity and an investor.

In summary, investment treaty tribunals must achieve a balance between: (a) the State's potentially avoiding its responsibility by relying on its municipal law; and (b) the risks inherent in exclusively applying international law, with the potential broadening of State responsibility to include the conduct of entities that do not exercise governmental authority. To achieve this balance, tribunals cannot treat municipal law as irrelevant. Rather, municipal law is the first step in the proper application of international law. As Dupuy explains, international law 'remains free in its treatment' of facts provided by domestic law, but owns up to the relative dependence in which domestic law keeps it.[150]

---

148. Crawford, *The ILC's Articles on State Responsibility*, 102.
149. Dolzer and Schreuer, *Principles of International Investment Law*, 221–222.
150. Dupuy, 'Relations Between the International Law of Responsibility and Responsibility in Municipal Law', Ch. 15 in *The Law of International Responsibility*, 183.

CHAPTER 2
Article 42 of the ICSID Convention and the Relationship Between International Law and Municipal Law

§2.01 INTRODUCTION

This chapter[1] analyses the law applicable to the merits of a dispute under an ICSID treaty arbitration, i.e., the substantive law as opposed to the procedural law, and the interplay between international law and municipal law.[2] While Article 25 of the ICSID

---

1. Chapter 2 is a revision of a chapter previously published in 'The Applicable Law and the ICSID Convention', Ch. 10 in *ICSID Convention after 50 Years, Unsettled Issues*, ed. Baltag (Kluwer, 2017), 273–300.
2. See, generally, on Art. 42 of the ICSID Convention: Kjos, *Applicable Law in Investor-State Arbitration, The Interplay Between National and International Law* (Oxford, 2013); Broches, 'The Convention on the Settlement of Investment Disputes Between States and Nationals of Other States: Applicable Law and Default Procedure', in *International Arbitration Liber Amicorum for Martin Domke*, ed. Sanders (Martinus Nijhoff, 1967), 12–22; Kreindler, 'The Law Applicable to International Investment Disputes', in *Arbitrating Foreign Investment Disputes: Procedural and Substantive Legal Aspects*, eds. Kröll and Hom (Kluwer, 2004), 401–424; Newcombe and Paradell, Ch. 2, 'Applicable Substantive Law and Interpretation', in *Law and Practice of Investment Treaties: Standards of Treatment*' (Kluwer, 2009), 75–120; Schreuer, Malintoppi, Reinisch and Sinclair, *The ICSID Convention* (Cambridge, 2009), 545–639; Parra, *The History of ICSID* (Oxford, 2010), 85–86, 178–184, 231–233 and 303–306; Banifatemi, Ch. 9, 'The Law Applicable in Investment Treaty Arbitration', in *Arbitration under International Investment Agreements: A Guide to the Key Issues*, ed. K. Yannaca-Small (Oxford, 2010), 191–210; Douglas, Ch. 54.1, 'Other Specific Regimes of Responsibility: Investment Treaty Arbitration and ICSID', in *The Law of International Responsibility*, eds. Crawford, Pellet and Olleson (Oxford, 2010), 832–839; Bjorklund, Ch. 9, 'Applicable Law in International Investment Disputes', in *Litigating International Investment Disputes, A Practitioner's Guide*, ed. Giorgetti (Brill Nijoff, 2014), 260–286; Reisman and Arsanjani, Ch. 1, 'Applicable Law under the ICSID Convention: The Tortured History of the Interpretation of Article 42', in *Building International Investment Law, The First 50 Years of ICSID*, eds. Kinnear et al. (Kluwer, 2015), 3–11; Reisman, 'The Regime for *Lacunae* in the ICSID Choice of Law Provision and Question of Its Threshold', *ICSID Review* (2000) 15, 362–381; Parra, 'Applicable Substantive Law in ICSID Arbitrations Initiated under Investment Treaties', *ICSID*

Convention considers jurisdiction without a specific provision on applicable law, Article 42 of the ICSID Convention expressly addresses the law applicable to the merits. Article 42 states as follows:

> (1) The Tribunal shall decide a dispute in accordance with such rules of law as may be agreed by the parties. In the absence of such agreement, the Tribunal shall apply the law of the Contracting State party to the dispute (including its rules on the conflict of laws) and such rules of international law as may be applicable.
> (2) The Tribunal may not bring in a finding of *non liquet* on the ground of silence or obscurity of the law.
> (3) The provisions of paragraphs (1) and (2) shall not prejudice the power of the Tribunal to decide a dispute *ex aequo et bono* if the parties so agree.

The first sentence of Article 42(1) emphasizes party autonomy and the power of the contracting parties to choose any 'rules of law'. Investment tribunals have commonly referred to and relied upon this sentence when construing an investment treaty, or a contract, with an ICSID arbitration provision that expressly states the applicable law. In such treaty cases, the investor's acceptance of the offer to arbitrate contained in the BIT from the host State constitutes the consent to, *inter alia*, the applicable law provision contained in the BIT.[3] However, only some bilateral investment treaties contain an express applicable law provision;[4] many others do not include such a provision.

In the event that the investment treaty does *not* include a provision on applicable law, the second sentence of Article 42(1) becomes relevant. It is this part of Article 42 that has been the focus of a vigorous debate on the question of the centrality of municipal law[5] and the limits, if any, to the application of international law in treaty arbitration. (Articles 42(2) and 42(3) have not given rise to comparable controversy.[6])

Article 42(1)'s second sentence calls for a mandatory ('shall') application of the law of the host State and the 'rules of international law as may be applicable'. The issue

---

Review (2001) 16, 20–24, and 'Applicable Law in Investor-State Arbitration', *TDM* 1 (2009); Gaillard and Banifatemi, 'The Meaning of "and" in Article 42(1), Second Sentence, of the Washington Convention: The Role of International Law in the ICSID Choice of Law Process', *ICSID Review* (2003) 18, 375–411; Gaillard, 'The Extent of Review of the Applicable Law in Investment Treaty Arbitration', in *Annulment of ICSID Awards*, eds Gaillard and Banifatemi (Juris, 2004), 223–241; Thomas and Dhillon 'Applicable Law under International Investment Treaties', *SAcLJ* 26 (2014): 973–998.

3. *See* Gaillard and Banifatemi, 'The Meaning of "and" in Art. 42(1), Second Sentence, of the Washington Convention: The Role of International Law in the ICSID Choice of Law Process', *supra*, 375–379.
4. *See*, e.g., Art. 8 of the BIT between Argentina and the UK, 11 Dec. 1990: 'The arbitral tribunal shall decide the dispute in accordance with the provisions of this Agreement, the laws of the Contracting Party involved in the dispute, including its rules on conflict of laws, the terms of any specific agreement concluded in relation to such an investment and the applicable principles of international law. The arbitration decision shall be final and binding on both Parties.'
5. The terms 'municipal law', 'domestic law', and 'national law' are used as synonyms in this chapter.
6. Article 42(2): 'The Tribunal may not bring in a finding of *non liquet* on the ground of silence or obscurity of the law.' Article 42 (3): 'The provisions of paragraphs (1) and (2) shall not prejudice the power of the Tribunal to decide a dispute ex aequo et bono if the parties so agree'.

is, therefore, when international law 'may be applicable'. Applicability initially depends on whether the case has come to ICSID through an investment *contract* or an investment *treaty*.

Early jurisprudence on investment *contracts* offered an interpretation aimed to limit the application of international law to a complementary and corrective role (*see* below the discussion of *Klöckner v. Cameroon* and *Amco v. Indonesia*). In these cases, international law would be applicable only if there were a *lacuna* in national law or if international law was somehow inconsistent with national law.

Reisman rejected this interpretation. The *lacunae* identified in the earlier contract cases did not exist, in his view, since the relevant question should be whether the law of the host State directly addressed the issue at hand: if it did, then there should be no recourse to international law. Or, if national law regulated the issue in a manner different from of international law, the national law regulation would be the rule that prevails. An arbitral tribunal should analyse national law as a general framework and infer the specific rule from that framework. Thus, Reisman contested the application of international law in contract cases when national law provided a rule, directly or indirectly.[7] Moreover, he considered that only a very few cases of 'genuine' *lacunae* and inconsistencies between national and international law would preclude the application of national law – when, for example, there would otherwise be a violation of a fundamental principle such as *pacta sunt servanda* or a peremptory international human rights norm.[8]

According to the Reisman view, then, there are four situations in which an ICSID tribunal can apply international law: (i) where the parties so agree; (ii) where the law of the host State calls for the application of international law, including customary international law; (iii) where international law directly regulates the subject matter or issue, such as a treaty between the state parties to the dispute – i.e., the non-contract or bilateral or multilateral investment treaties' referral to ICSID; and (iv) where the law of the host State violates a fundamental principle of international law, including a peremptory international human rights norm.[9] As to point (iii), investment treaties, Reisman and Arsanjani emphasized in a subsequent article that international law applies to an investor-state dispute: 'a BIT, even if it does not contain an explicit provision on the applicable law, constitutes the *eo ipso* applicable law to claims for the breaches of the protection contained therein'.[10] In their opinion, therefore, the second sentence of Article 42(1) does not apply when a BIT governs a dispute – 'a treaty would have to be interpreted in accordance with international law'.[11] Pursuant to the

---

7. Reisman, 'The Regime for *Lacunae* in the ICSID Choice of Law Provision and Question of Its Threshold', *supra*, 371–375. Reisman stated that only if there were a 'genuine *lacuna*, i.e., one for which host State law does not provide a method for filling, the Tribunal may turn to international law' (375). As for inconsistency with international law, Reisman required a 'veritable collision', a 'violation of something fundamental to international law' (375).
8. *Id.*, 368.
9. *Id.*, 380.
10. Reisman and Arsanjani, Ch. 1 'Applicable Law under the ICSID Convention: The Tortured History of the Interpretation of Article 42', *supra*, 10.
11. *Ibid.*

Reisman/Arsanjani thesis, the second sentence of Article 42(1) has a limited application, since it has no relevance in cases where the dispute arises out of a BIT.

Gaillard and Banifatemi take a different position on applicable law. They opine that under Article 42(1) an investment treaty tribunal is free to adopt the rules of law that the tribunal deems applicable, whether national or international.[12] They endorse jurisprudence that is aligned with *Wena Hotels v. Egypt*, under which an investor-state tribunal has complete discretion to choose the law, national or international, that it wishes to adopt for each issue in dispute.

Thus, there are three important interpretations of Article 42(1)'s approach to the applicability of municipal law and potential limits on the application of international law:

(i) *Klöckner/Amco* on investment agreements – municipal law unless *lacunae* or inconsistency).
(ii) Reisman/Aransanjani – if investment agreement, almost always national law; if investment treaty, always international law, and
(iii) Gaillard/Banifatemi – complete tribunal discretion.

This chapter argues that none of the three standard interpretations is satisfactory and proposes that a fourth approach be adopted – the 'Broches approach'. This approach is what Aron Broches proposed, and is, unsurprisingly, closest to the intent of the Contracting Parties to ICSID. As in many aspects of ICSID, the most solid interpretive foundation is supplied by Broches; Article 42(1)'s uncertainties are most effectively resolved through the Broches approach. As explained below, pursuant to Broches, a tribunal should apply international law only when (a) national law provides for the application of international law, (b) where the subject matter is regulated directly by international law, and (c) when national law violates international law. That is the intended meaning of Article 42(1), and that is the meaning that makes sense, as a matter of international law.

§2.02 THE RELEVANCE OF THE HISTORICAL BACKGROUND OF ARTICLE 42(1)

An understanding of the historical background is necessary to appreciate the difference, and the importance of the difference, between Article 42(1)'s second sentence and the relevant provisions in antecedent draft conventions. The draft conventions are more aligned with the *initial* draft provision of Article 42(1), and offer a different pattern from the current Article 42.

From the ICSID *travaux préparatoires*, it is clear that once the question of applicable law was brought to the attention of the State delegates, and in particular to the delegates of capital-importing countries, there was a significant shift towards enhancing the role of municipal law; the antecedent draft conventions and the initial

---

12. Gaillard and Banifatemi, 'The Meaning of "and" in Article 42(1), Second Sentence, of the Washington Convention: The Role of International Law in the ICSID Choice of Law Process', *supra*, 411 (Gaillard represented Wena Hotels in *Wena Hotels Ltd v. Arab Republic of Egypt*).

preliminary draft of Article 42(1) had relegated municipal law to a marginal role. Under these drafts, municipal law could only be applied if more favourable to foreign investors than international law or, as in the initial draft of Article 42, as an alternative to international law, but the tribunal would in any event decide which law would be deemed applicable.

It has been suggested that the *ordinary meaning* of Article 42(1)'s second sentence, per Article 31 of the Vienna Convention of 1969 on the Law of the Treaties (Vienna Convention), is clear and there should be no reference to the ICSID *travaux préparatoires*.[13] However, it is difficult to accept this suggestion: the lack of clarity is apparent on a first reading: the Tribunal is to apply the host State's national law *and* (not *or*) international law rules 'as may be applicable'. What law then prevails, and how are the international law rules to be deemed applicable? What is the relationship between applicable national law and applicable international law rules? Article 42(1) is the very definition of a compromise, with an ambiguity at its heart. History helps to explicate and resolve the ambiguity.

[A]   **The Vienna Convention, Articles 31 and 32, and the Principles of Treaty Interpretation**

The interpretation of the ICSID Convention is governed by the rules of interpretation of treaties set out in Articles 31 and 32 of the Vienna Convention.[14] Interpretation begins with the ordinary meaning of the terms of the treaty, in their context and in light of the treaty's object and purpose. It is important to recognize that the Vienna Convention does not 'privilege' any of the three aspects of the Article 31(1) interpretation method.[15] Each aspect must be considered fully.

---

13. *Id.*, 382–383.
14. 'Article 31, GENERAL RULE OF INTERPRETATION:
    1. A treaty shall be interpreted in good faith in accordance with the ordinary meaning to be given to the terms of the treaty in their context and in the light of its object and purpose.
    2. The context for the purpose of the interpretation of a treaty shall comprise, in addition to the text, including its preamble and annexes:
        (a) Any agreement relating to the treaty which was made between all the parties in connection with the conclusion of the treaty;
        (b) Any instrument which was made by one or more parties in connection with the conclusion of the treaty and accepted by the other parties as an instrument related to the treaty.
    3. There shall be taken into account, together with the context:
        (a) Any subsequent agreement between the parties regarding the interpretation of the treaty or the application of its provisions;
        (b) Any subsequent practice in the application of the treaty which establishes the agreement of the parties regarding its interpretation;
        (c) Any relevant rules of international law applicable in the relations between the parties.
    4. A special meaning shall be given to a term if it is established that the parties so intended.'
15. *See Aguas del Tunari v. Bolivia*, Award, 21 Oct. 2005, para. 91 ('the Vienna Convention does not privilege any one of these three aspects of the interpretation method. The meaning of a word or phrase is not solely a matter of dictionaries and linguistics ... Rather, the interpretation of a word or phrase involves a complex task of considering the ordinary meaning of a word or phrase in the

Tribunals and courts have also emphasized the importance under Article 31(1) of interpreting treaties in good faith.[16] The principle of 'good faith' may be applied to assess the reasonableness of an interpretation, or to support an assessment of the parties' common intention (as opposed to their motives), or to prefer an interpretation that attributes a meaning to a term rather than one that does not (*effet utile*).[17] Tribunals and courts also have invoked good faith to limit the scope of a power asserted by a State or to balance the elements of a treaty so that no party faces too great a burden in demonstrating its position.[18]

The consideration of 'ordinary meaning' is not to be undertaken separately from consideration of context and treaty purpose. Article 31(1) of the Vienna Convention, clearly provides that the meaning of a word or phrase is not simply a matter of dictionaries and linguistics; rather, 'the interpretation of a word or phrase involves a complex task of considering the ordinary meaning of a word or phrase in the context in which that word or phrase is found and in light of the object and purpose of the document'.[19]

The ILC Commentary advised, on an earlier draft of Article 32 (supplementary recourse to, e.g., *travaux préparatoires*),[20] that this Article serves to emphasize the centrality of Article 31: 'that the text of the treaty must be presumed to be the authentic expression of the intentions of the parties, and that the elucidation of the meaning of the text rather than an investigation *ab initio* of the supposed intentions of the parties constitutes the object of interpretation'.[21]

In general, the ICJ has declined to use supplementary means of interpretation under Article 32 where the treaty text is sufficiently clear. However, in some cases the ICJ has used a treaty's *travaux préparatoires* to confirm the interpretation that it reached in applying Article 31.[22]

As indicated above, in the second sentence of Article 42(1), where the 'shall' that accompanies the application of the host State law is mirrored with 'rules of international law as may be applicable', there is an immediate uncertainty. The ordinary

---

context in which that word or phrase is found and in light of the object and purpose of the document'); *See, generally*, Gardiner, *Treaty Interpretation* (Oxford, 2011), 141 et seq. Ordinary meaning, context, and object/purpose of the treaty are an integrated whole in the interpretive process.
16. Gardiner, *supra*, 147 et seq.
17. *Id.*, 148.
18. *Id.*, 157–158.
19. *Aguas del Tunari v. Bolivia*, para. 91.
20. Article 32 of the Vienna Convention reads as follows: 'Article 32. SUPPLEMENTARY MEANS OF INTERPRETATION Recourse may be had to supplementary means of interpretation, including the preparatory work of the treaty and the circumstances of its conclusion, in order to confirm the meaning resulting from the application of article 31, or to determine the meaning when the interpretation according to article 31:

  (a) Leaves the meaning ambiguous or obscure; or
  (b) Leads to a result which is manifestly absurd or unreasonable.'
21. *Aguas del Tunari v. Bolivia*, para. 92.
22. *See* Brownlie, Brownlie's *Principles of Public International Law*, 8th ed., ed. Crawford (Oxford, 2012), 383–384.

meaning of the words does not shed sufficient light (or any light) on the interplay between the application of national and international law.

Examination of the two direct antecedent draft conventions to the ICSID Convention assists in understanding Article 42. These draft conventions, as well as the *travaux préparatoires* of the ICSID Convention, not only provide important context, but also reveal the approach to applicable substantive law in treaty arbitration that Broches ultimately designed, when all the States were brought into the discussion. The approach ultimately adopted in Article 42 places particular emphasis on the role of municipal law as substantive law.

[B] The Two Antecedent Draft Conventions

(i) *Abs-Shawcross Draft Convention on Investment Abroad* (1959)[23]

The Abs-Shawcross Draft Convention provides, *inter alia*, that (a) each contracting party should ensure fair and equitable treatment to the property of nationals of the other parties; (b) the undertakings given in relations to investment have to be observed; and (c) the contracting parties agree not to adopt any measure against nationals of another contracting party aimed to deprive them directly or indirectly of their property. Further, a national injured by measures in violation of the Draft Convention could institute an arbitral proceeding against the host State party, assuming that the State accepted the jurisdiction of the arbitral tribunal.

Article VI of the Draft Convention states that the 'provisions of the Convention shall not prejudice the application of any present or future treaty *or municipal law* under which more favourable treatment is accorded to nationals of any of the Parties' [emphasis added]. Thus, although the Draft Convention does not define the law applicable to the merits, Article VI clearly provides that any treaty or any provision of municipal law would be automatically applicable *if* more favourable to the investor. The applicability of municipal law only to the extent that it is more favourable than customary international law or treaty law is in significant contrast with the role of municipal law in the subsequent ICSID Convention.

(ii) Harvard Draft Convention on the International Responsibility of States for Injuries to Aliens (1961)[24] ('Harvard Convention')

Article 1 of the Harvard Convention states the 'basic principles of State responsibility', and Article 2 provides for the primacy of international law:

> responsibility of a State [...] is to be determined according to this Convention and international law, by application of the sources and subsidiary means set forth in paragraph 1 of Article 38 of the Statute of the International Court of Justice. A State

---

23. Hermann Abs and Lord Shawcross, 'Draft Convention on Investment Abroad', 9 *J.Pub.L.* 116 (1960).
24. 'Harvard Draft Convention on the International Responsibility of States for Injuries to Aliens', *American Journal of International Law* 55 (1961): 545–551.

cannot avoid international responsibility by invoking its municipal law. Nothing in this Convention shall adversely affect any right which an alien enjoys under the municipal law of the State against which the claim is made if that law is more favorable to him than this Convention.

Thus, the Harvard Convention, though it does not expressly identify the law applicable to the merits, states that with regard to the determination of State responsibility, international law must prevail. These articles echo principles later incorporated in the International Law Commission's Articles on State Responsibility. Again, municipal law cannot be invoked unless it is more favourable to the investor.

(iii) Organisation for Economic Cooperation and Development (OECD), Draft Convention on the Protection of Foreign Property (1967)

One year after ICSID entered into force, the OECD adopted a Draft Convention on the Protection of Foreign Property.[25] Article 8 provides that: '[w]here a matter is covered both by the provisions of this Convention and any other international agreement nothing in this Convention shall prevent a national of one Party who holds property in the territory of another Party from benefitting by the provisions that are most favourable to him'. Like the previous draft conventions, there is no provision on applicable law, though the OECD Draft clarifies that if there are provisions more favourable to the investor/national, these should apply, without any mention of whether they are national or international rules. Still, municipal law again does not play any role unless it is more favourable than international law.

[C] ICSID Convention: *Travaux Préparatoires*

The ICSID Convention, unlike the predecessor draft conventions and the OECD Draft, contains a provision on the law applicable to the merits that (a) expressly remits the issue to party autonomy, and (b) as a default rule, prescribes *renvoi* to municipal law and international law, to the extent that the latter is relevant. *Renvoi* to municipal law is *not* limited to circumstances where municipal law is more favourable to the investor. But the questions remain (i) what is the municipal/international law relationship, given the terseness – and vagueness – of the one-sentence provision; and (ii) do the *travaux préparatoires* assist in defining the relationship? The answer to the second question is affirmative, and is discussed in this subsection.

Paragraph 40 of the Report of the Executive Directors of the International Bank for Reconstruction and Development on the ICSID Convention explains that:

> Under the Convention an Arbitral Tribunal is required to apply the law agreed by the parties. Failing such agreement, the Tribunal *must apply the law of the State party* to the dispute (unless that law calls for the application of some other law), *as well as such rules of international law as may be applicable*. The term 'international law' as used in this context should be understood in the sense given to it by Article

---

25. Organization for Economic Cooperation and Development, Draft Convention on the Protection of Foreign Property (1967), 7 *ILM* 117 (1968).

38(1) of the Statute of the International Court of Justice[26], allowance being made for the fact that Article 38 was designed to apply to inter-State disputes'. [emphasis added]

As it will be seen below, the pillars of Article 42 that emerge from the *travaux préparatoires* are: (i) autonomy of the parties; (ii) relevance of municipal law and, to a certain indeterminate extent, international law; and (iii) narrowing the scope of arbitrators' discretion to determine applicable law. The ICSID *travaux préparatoires* clearly indicate that Article 42(1) awards priority to party autonomy and then municipal law; international law applies only if relevant as an additional element. This is apparent in large part because the initial drafts were transformed in the course of the debate.

As set out in the initial working drafts, the provision that subsequently became Article 42 articulated that '[i]n the absence of any agreement between the parties concerning the law to be applied ... the Arbitral Tribunal shall decide the dispute submitted to it in accordance with such rules of law, whether national or international, as it shall determine to be applicable'.[27] This draft provision left the determination of whether to apply international or national law entirely to the discretion of investment tribunal, and was the centre of a heated debate.

In one of the drafting sessions taking place in March 1962, the Contracting Parties' delegates started exploring the issue of applicable law, and noted that it could be possible for the countries to decide the applicable law in bilateral agreements or to reach *ad hoc* agreements.[28] In December 1962, during the meeting to discuss the salient features of the proposed convention, it was acknowledged that the parties had to select

---

26. Article 38(1) of the Statute of the International Court of Justice states:
    1. The Court, whose function it is to decide in accordance with international law such disputes as are submitted to it, shall apply:
        a. international conventions, whether general or particular, establishing rules expressly recognized by the contesting states;
        b. international custom, as evidence of a general practice accepted as law;
        c. the general principles of law recognized by civilized nations;
        d. subject to the provisions of Article 59, judicial decisions and the teachings of the most highly qualified publicists of the various nations, as subsidiary means for the determination of rules of law.
27. The preliminary draft stated: '[i]n the absence of agreement between the parties concerning the law to be applied . . . the Tribunal shall decide the dispute submitted to it in accordance with such rules of law, whether national or international, as it shall determine to be applicable.' The first draft stated, however: 'In the absence of agreement between the parties concerning the law to be applied, the Tribunal shall decide the dispute submitted to it in accordance with such rules of national and international law as it shall determine to be applicable. The term "international law" shall be understood in the sense given to it by Article 38 of the Statute of the International Court of Justice.'
28. *History of the ICSID Convention*, Vol II 1, available online on the ICSID website, https://icsid.worldbank.org/en/Pages/resources/The-History-of-the-ICSID-Convention.aspx: '[q]uestions of jurisdiction, procedure and applicable law might be dealt with in bilateral agreements between interested countries (or in the absence of such bilateral agreements it could be decided *ad hoc*)' (Memorandum Of Meeting Of Executive Directors On The Subject Of 'Settlement Of Investment Disputes', Tuesday 13 Mar. 1962).

the applicable law, and that the default rule remitted this decision to the arbitral tribunal.[29]

However, one year later, in December 1963, the Chairman, Broches clarified that under the preliminary draft, unless the parties provided a different rule, the tribunal had to examine the dispute from several angles and apply both national law and international law in relation to the specific issue to be resolved. The delegate from Cameroon raised the example of an act of nationalization: to what system of law would the tribunal apply in order to decide its legality? Broches replied that 'unless parties specifically restricted the tribunal, it would look into all the legal aspects of any dispute brought before it from the standpoint not only of domestic, but also of international law, to see if the rights of either party had been infringed. The tribunal would be in the same position as any international tribunal before which, say, the investor's State had brought a claim based on the expropriation of its national's property.'[30]

In February 1964, the Chairman again emphasized that in the absence of a choice of law (applicable to the merits), the arbitral tribunal would decide whether international law applied and had been breached. If, for example, there were provisions in a concession agreement for the submission of any dispute, after exhaustion of local remedies, to the Center, but there was no provision on applicable law, then the investor could still argue that despite there being no violation of national law, there was a violation of international law, which was the applicable law.[31]

In April 1964,[32] the discussion again emphasized the importance and centrality of party autonomy. The Chairman also stated that the local law of a host State was not always applicable, in reply to a question from the delegate from China, who assumed that municipal law was always applicable by virtue of the fact of an investment being made in a State.[33] The delegate from China argued that when a foreign investor made an investment, it seemed obvious to assume that the investor had consented to the jurisdiction and application of the law of the host State in all respects, unless there was a written and explicit declaration to the contrary. He suggested that the proper rule of interpretation regarding to the applicable law would not permit the application of

---

29. *Id.*, 79: '[a]nother rule would concern the law to be applied by the arbitral tribunal. The Convention would leave that primarily to the agreement of the parties, but would give the arbitral tribunal the power to determine the applicable law if the parties had left the matter open'.
30. *Id.*, 267. It is also interesting to note, that when the delegate from Cameroon was listing possible sources of agreements on applicable law between the parties included BIT ('Either stipulation could be included in an agreement with an investor, in a bilateral agreement with another State, or even in a unilateral offer to all investors, such as might be made through investment legislation').
31. *Id.*, 322.
32. *Id.*, 502. The Chairman suggested that '[t]he Convention did not call for the application of any specific law. It left the determination of the applicable law up to the tribunal in the absence of an agreement between the parties. A State when entering into an investment agreement could well provide that the agreement would be governed by its own laws as they prevailed from time to time. In that case, no other law could be applied and no complaint could be made of changes in that law. In many cases, however, States gave specific undertakings in offering incentives to investors. In that case, of course, the investor had a right to ask for, but would not necessarily obtain, assurances that those incentives would not be changed'.
33. *Id.*, 513–514.

international law without an agreement to the contrary. Broches contested this assumption, although he agreed that the entry into a country in general implied submission to local law, and that, in the absence of an agreement on a special position for the investor, most disputes regarding actions of the government would be decided under local law. However, Broches referred to two cases where the proposed language aimed at having national law alone as the applicable law would not help solve the problem of applicable law. The first was when there was a special agreement between investors and governments, which, in accordance with the laws of those governments, gave special treatment to the investor not provided by local law. In such cases, the contractual choice of law agreement should prevail.

Broches also pointed to the example of a public bond issue placed abroad. Bond issues sometimes did not contain an applicable law clause, but there was general agreement that in the case of a bond issue made in, e.g., Switzerland, where all the aspects of the transaction were linked with Switzerland (where the contract was signed, where the underwriting bankers were located, and where the bonds were payable), even in the absence of a governing law clause, Swiss law would apply.

The Chairman's Report on these issues was presented on 9 July 1964.[34] It emphasized that the article on applicable law was based on the principle that the parties could control the rules used by the arbitral tribunal to decide the case; this would be consistent with the consensual character of the ICSID Convention and of international arbitration in general. The Report then stated that the tribunal had to apply the applicable law selected by the parties or decide the dispute *ex aequo et bono*, if so chosen by the parties. If these agreements were absent, the tribunal would have to decide the dispute in accordance with national or international law. If the tribunal was confronted with more than one national law, 'it will choose the "proper one" by the application of generally accepted principles of the Conflict of Laws or Private International Law'.[35] The Report acknowledged that the tribunal might be confronted with a claim that international law should prevail over national law when, for example, a provision of municipal law violated international law.

The Report then summarized the views of some delegations, several of which supported the preliminary draft text as it then was. Two delegations asked whether the agreement on the applicable law could be deduced from an implicit agreement between the parties (in the absence of an express agreement), and it was acknowledged that an implicit agreement deduced from the facts and circumstances of the relationship between the parties would be considered an agreement on the applicable law.[36] As for requests to include the application of basic rules of international law (such as the prohibition of discriminatory treatment, the obligation to act in good faith, or the prohibition of measures contrary to international public policy or general principles of law), Broches expressed his doubts, since the ICSID Convention was a procedural

---

34. *Id.*, 569–571.
35. *Id.*, 570.
36. *Ibid.*

document and should not have substantive provisions; instead, he opined, it should be kept flexible to meet the need of a great variety of cases.[37]

A few delegations raised the issue of international law and whether a tribunal, in the event of the parties being unable to reach an agreement on applicable law, could test the legality of sovereign acts against international law standards. The Chairman replied that the tribunal would be free to apply international law in such circumstances. One delegation suggested inserting a provision in the Article that regardless of the agreement between the parties a tribunal should apply international law to the international aspects of the dispute. However, this suggestion was not implemented.

One delegation supported the view that the act of making an investment is per se an act of consent to apply the law of the host State in all respects – therefore the tribunal should apply the law of the host State and should not be permitted to apply international law in the absence of a specific agreement expressly providing that international law is applicable.[38] Another delegation agreed, and stated that the ICSID Convention should contain provisions to cover the majority of the cases and that in the majority of the cases municipal law of the host State should govern the investment. Broches pointed out that in some circumstances other national laws may govern the dispute, and the law of the host State could not be considered the exclusive national law to be applicable.

Broches clarified that: (i) there are rules of law that allow arbitral tribunals to choose between different laws, and there is no reason to require the parties to authorize the arbitral tribunal to do something tribunals are already accustomed to doing in cases concerning international transactions; and (ii) as to the issue of national *versus* international law:

(a) the ICSID convention is establishing an international tribunal and 'it is reasonable to provide that an international tribunal will have the power to apply international law' unless there is a specific provision excluding it; and
(b) 'even an *international tribunal would in the first place have to look to national law*, since the relationship between the investor and the host State is governed in *the first instance by national law*, and it would only be in those instances in which national law was in violation of international law that the tribunal would, in the application of international law, set aside national law'.[39] [emphasis added].

On 7 December 1964 the Legal Committee voted on what is now Article 42. Broches first mentioned that the reference to national law was not restricted to the municipal law of the host State since conflict of laws rules may introduce different applicable laws. A delegate attempted to limit the application of international law to the cases of discrimination, but Broches invited the delegates not to qualify 'international

---

37. Ibid.
38. Id., 571.
39. Ibid.

law'[40] in order to avoid the risk of not covering all potential situations where international law should be applied.

The delegate from China reiterated his objections; he stated that only the national law of the host State should apply. He argued that the preamble of the Convention should state that 'a foreign investment implies reliance by the investor on the laws of the host State'.[41] The Chairman responded[42] that national law had 'primary' importance and international law would refer to municipal law in the first place; he emphasized that the relevant principle of international law would be *pacta sunt servanda*. Tellingly, he added that the wording of the Article 42(1), second sentence, had the word 'and' between national and international law in order to indicate that the application of international law was not an alternative to the application of national law (the previous version contained the word 'or'). The delegate from China rebutted that he was aiming to have national law applicable first, in the event there was no agreement on applicable law.

The discussion continued with several delegates contending that the applicable law should be that of the host State, and that the reference to international law should be omitted.[43] To these contentions, the Chairman replied, 'whether there was a challenge to the validity of the local law would depend on what question was submitted to arbitration. For example, a concession agreement might be terminated by a law of the host State and not by action under the concession itself. In that case the issue in dispute would be whether a State was acting in good faith, and the question of *pacta sunt servanda* would arise.' Other delegates agreed with Broches, and posited that there were many countries in which the national courts apply national law as well as international law, and it would seem strange if a tribunal that was admittedly international would be precluded from applying international law.

However, some delegates supported China's position, arguing that the draft of Article 42 radically departed from existing principles of law. Contracts between private persons and States had not been governed by customary international law. Some delegates were concerned that this provision could result in purely domestic or internal actions of a State being tested by an uncertain set of principles. This would run counter to the doctrine of State sovereignty. ('The *newly* independent States of Asia and Africa

---

40. *History of the ICSID Convention*, Volume II 2, 800: '[Chairman] pointed out that as one could not foresee all the cases in which international law might be applicable the citation of examples such as "discrimination" might not be very useful. He thought the provision was an accurate reflection of the considerations an arbitral tribunal would have to go through where the parties failed to make a specific agreement on the choice of law and at one of the regional consultative meetings he had been supported in this view by a member of the International Law Commission'.
41. *Ibid.*
42. *Ibid.*: 'Mr. BROCHES (Chairman) thought there was some inconsistency in the various proposals just made. It was quite clear that the laws of the host country would be of primary importance and that international law itself would in the first place refer to them. The principles of international law which might be brought into play would be such as *pacta sunt servanda*. He further wished to point out that the earlier draft of the Convention referred to "national or international law". The present draft uses the word "and" so as to avoid the impression that international law would always apply or that it was necessarily a question of alternatives.'
43. *Id.*, 801.

were always willing to accept and abide by the principles of public international law, but were not in favour of expanding the scope of their application'.)[44] Delegates from emerging States saw the provision as containing principles created solely to protect the interests of the industrial and colonial powers.

Broches explained that many arbitral tribunals applied both national and international law, and that in the ordinary case the parties will have chosen the applicable law to the dispute.[45] He then modified the text of Article 42(1) and called for a vote.[46] In the *travaux préparatoires* the vote is reported as: 'The first sentence dealing with an express choice of law agreement was approved by a majority of 35 to one. The first part of the second sentence referring to the 'national' law applicable was adopted by a majority of 31 to one. The final provision relating to international law *(which would bring it into play both in the case of a lacuna in domestic law as well as in the case of inconsistency between the two)* was adopted by a majority of 24 to 6'.[47] [emphasis added].

In February 1965, Broches explained why certain delegates felt that the discretion conferred to the arbitrators by Article 42 had to be narrow, and, why on the issue of national versus international law, 'the vote in the Legal Committee had been very clearly in favour of permitting the tribunal to apply international law, particularly in order to take into account of cases where a State changed its own law to the detriment of an investor and in violation of an agreement not to do so. In such a case, international law would not question the power of the sovereign State to change its law, but could hold that State liable in damages to the investor whose rights it had violated through an act inconsistent with international law'.[48] Faced with the question as to whether Article 42(1) would create confusion between the application of national and international law, *Broches stated that one should start with national law.*[49] From

---

44. *Ibid.*
45. *Id.*, 803, Mr Broches also stated that: '[he] thought that the misapprehension with respect to the power of foreign investors might have been justified in the past but he was doubtful whether it was justified under present conditions. He thought the parties should be free to tell the Tribunal which issues required its solution and which had already been solved by agreement between them. He thought the text might be improved so as to convey this idea and he would propose that the first part of the first sentence of paragraph (1) be replaced by the following sentence: "The Tribunal shall decide disputes submitted to it in accordance with such rules of law as shall have been agreed upon between the parties". That would indicate that in the normal case one would expect the parties to choose the applicable law and would reflect the normal practice in the field of foreign investment agreements.'
46. *Id.*, 803-804: 'Mr. BROCHES(Chairman) noting that the meeting appeared to be concerned with two problems, said the first one was which was the applicable national law' and the second, under what circumstances, if any, should international law be applicable. Taking these views into consideration, he would propose that the provisions following that dealing with an express choice of law agreement be redrafted to read as follows: 'Failing such agreement, the Tribunal shall apply the law of the State party to the dispute (including its rules on the conflict of laws) and such principles of international law as may be applicable'.
47. *Id.*, 804.
48. *Id.*, 985-986.
49. *Id.*, 986: 'Mr. Broches replied that Article 42 intentionally referred to domestic law and international law since a tribunal might be called upon to determine whether standards set by both systems of law had been respected by the host State. As a practical matter, in the case of expropriation for instance, the expropriated investor might complain that the amount of

the discussion, it also emerged that a number of delegates did not oppose the application international law in the event of municipal law's silence on an issue or inconsistency between municipal and international law.

From the *travaux préparatoires,* it is clear that the initial draft conferring unbounded discretion to investment tribunals to apply either international or national law was unacceptable. The role of municipal law was deemed to be so central that the application of municipal law was mandatory ('shall'). The application of international law was more tentative ('may', and to the extent that it was applicable). Although the *travaux préparatoires* refer to the application of international law in the event of *lacunae* in or inconsistency with municipal law, it is unclear whether the delegates had these two situations in mind when they voted for the Article.

[D] ICSID Convention: Article 42

In 1967, shortly following the adoption of the ICSID Convention,[50] Broches wrote an article[51] discussing, *inter alia*, Article 42 and summarizing the delegates' views during the debate (at the time, the *travaux préparatoires* were not yet available). Broches discussed the criticism raised by a minority of the delegates who had objected to the freedom conferred to the tribunal to apply international law, and their assumption that the act of making an investment implied that the investor consented to the law of the host State in all respects. Broches summarised the arguments in reply to these points: (i) the basic purpose of the proposed Convention was the establishment of an international tribunal with the power to apply international law; and (ii) the tribunal will look first to national law, and only when a provision of a national law violated international law would the tribunal apply international law. He also wrote that a tribunal was authorized to apply the proper law, whether or not this was the national law of the host State.

As for modifications made to Article 42 during the course of discussions, Broches explained that the replacement of the words 'such rules of law, whether national or international', by 'such rules of international law', was intended to exclude any need by the arbitral tribunal to choose between national and international law. Broches concluded by stating that the first sentence of Article 42, reiterating party autonomy, was adopted with only one vote against, and that the most important point was to preserve the tribunal's freedom to apply international law and to prescribe as 'mandatory the application of the host State's law, unless the law calls for the application of

---

compensation he actually received was insufficient under the host State's own laws or was insufficient under some minimum standard of international law, if such standard existed. Conceivably a claim of that kind could be submitted to the tribunal in an alternative form, the investor claiming that his compensation was insufficient under the domestic law of the host State and, if the tribunal did not so find, was insufficient under international law'. Although it is impossible to foresee how the parties would plead their cases, Mr Broches thought that, in general, one would have to start with the domestic law of the host State.
50. The ICSID Convention entered into force on 14 Oct. 1966.
51. Broches, 'The Convention on the Settlement of Investment Disputes between States and Nationals of Other States: Applicable Law and Default Procedure', *supra*, 13–17.

some other law'.[52] Broches then listed the objectives that this provision sought to implement:

(1) party autonomy as the 'basic principle governing the law to be applied by the tribunal';[53] and
(2) the tribunal 'may' apply international law when:
   (i) national law calls for its application;
   (ii) where the subject matter is directly regulated by international law; and
   (iii) where national law or action taken under such law violates international law.[54]

In his recollection of the discussions on Article 42(1)'s second sentence and the application of international law, Broches did not consider national and international law to be equal alternatives (national law clearly was the primary one), but he also did not want to confine the application of international law to the existence of 'genuine' *lacunae* or inconsistency with fundamental provisions of international law. The approach he succeeded in implementing in Article 42(1) was nuanced and clear and persuasive – and there is every reason for his approach to be followed by ICSID tribunals. Unfortunately, the Broches approach has largely been ignored, and the misinterpretations of Article 42(1) have grown.

The following subsections consider how Article 42(1) has been interpreted in investment treaty arbitration decisions, and, specifically, the roles that tribunals have accorded to national law and to international law.

§2.03 JURISPRUDENCE FROM *KLÖCKNER/AMCO* TO *WENA*

[A] *Klöckner v. Cameroon*

In early cases, arbitral tribunals tended to apply international law in the event of an inconsistency with national law or to fill a *lacuna*. I assess below whether this application is consistent with the Broches approach on how to interpret Article 42(1).

Klöckner v. Cameroon is one of the earliest ICSID cases, decided in 1983.[55] The dispute arose in relation to the construction of a fertilizer factory, which was shut down after several months of unprofitability and sub-capacity operation. There were several attempts to re-open the factory, but the factory failed to reach a stage of economic viability. The government decided to close it in 1981. Klöckner filed a request for arbitration, claiming the outstanding balance of the price for supplying the factory.

---

52. *Id.*,16.
53. *Id.*,17.
54. *Ibid.*
55. *Klöckner Industrie-Anlagen GmbH v. Cameroon*, Award, 21 Oct. 1983, 2 ICSID Rep. 9, 59 (1994). See also Parra, History of ICSID, *supra*, 179–181; and Paulsson, 'The ICSID *Klöckner v. Cameroon* Award: the Duties of Partners in North-South Economic Development Agreements', *J. Int'l Arb.* 1984, Vol. 1, issue 2, 145–168 (Paulsson represented Cameroon).

Some of the contractual arrangements between the parties contained an ICSID arbitration clause, and a management contract contained an ICC clause. The ICSID award declared that the outstanding debt was cancelled by virtue of Klöckner's breach of the management contract.[56]

The relevant part of the award for present purposes is the section on applicable law. The tribunal acknowledged that in Cameroon both French civil law and British common law are applied; specifically, French law was applicable in the former Republic of Cameroon and common law in the former British Cameroon. The factory was located in the former Republic of Cameroon.[57]

The tribunal stated that '[w]e have not established that there is a law applicable to such contracts. We do not intend to apply new or exceptional legal principles to turn-key operations only because they concern projects affecting the economic and social development of a given country',[58] and then referred to a 'duty of full disclosure to a partner', and asserted that this was a basic principle of French law. The tribunal concluded that Klöckner did not manifest frankness and loyalty towards its Cameroonian partner, as would have been required in these types of contracts.[59]

Klöckner sought to annul the award, alleging, *inter alia*, that the tribunal based its award on purportedly universal principles, rather than on principles of French law. The application was successful. The ICSID *Ad Hoc* Committee analysed the 'duty of full disclosure to a partner', and whether this principle was based on Cameroonian law via French law pursuant to the second sentence of Article 42(1).[60] The Committee noted that the tribunal 'asserts or postulates the existence of such a "principle" which (after having postulated its existence) the Tribunal *assumes* or takes for granted that it "is a basic principle of French civil law"'.[61]

The Committee also observed that the tribunal was convinced that the universal requirements of frankness and loyalty ought to be applied in cases similar to the one in dispute. The Committee considered this interpretation to be contrary to the requirements of Article 42(1). The Committee attributed to international law a dual role: '*complementary* (in the case of a "*lacuna*" in the law of the State), or *corrective*, should the State's law not conform on all points to the principles of international law. *In both cases*, the arbitrators may have recourse to the "principles of international law" only *after* having inquired into and established the content of the law of the State party to the dispute (which cannot be reduced to *one* principle, even a basic one) and *after* having applied the relevant rules of the State's law'[62] [emphasis added]. The Committee

---

56. For an extensive recapitulation of the facts and a detailed analysis of the award, *see* Paulsson, 'The ICSID *Klöckner v. Cameroon* Award: the Duties of Partners in North-South Economic Development Agreements', *supra*.
57. Paulsson, 'The ICSID *Klöckner v. Cameroon* Award: the Duties of Partners in North-South Economic Development Agreements', *supra*, 152–153.
58. *Klöckner v. Cameroon*, Award, 59–60; and Parra, *History of ICSID*, *supra*, 180.
59. *Klöckner v. Cameroon*, 105 and Paulsson 'The ICSID *Klöckner v. Cameroon* Award: the Duties of Partners in North-South Economic Development Agreements', *supra*, 152.
60. *Klöckner v. Cameroon*, Ad Hoc Committee decision, 3rd May 1985, 2 *ICSID Review* (1994), 95–144.
61. *Id.*, 111.
62. *Id.*, 112.

determined that Article 42(1) does not permit the arbitrators to ground their decision solely on the 'rules' or 'principles of international law'.[63] The award did not refer to legislative texts, to judgments, or to scholarly opinions, and even though the principle of full disclosure can be implied from the general principle of good faith, the award did not discuss the rules of the obligation of frankness and loyalty, its conditions, limits, and how this principle was applied.

The Committee stated that it could not insert, *a posteriori*, rules of French civil law that supported the existence of these principles, because it had to evaluate the award as it stood. The Committee underlined the importance of attributing emphasis on loyalty in dealings especially in international contracts, but this importance could not exempt it from ascertaining whether the conditions of Article 42(1) had been met. In the absence of any information, evidence or citation in the award, the Committee found it impossible to presume that there was a general duty under French civil law to make a full disclosure to business partners. The award appeared to have referred to equity and to universal principles, postulating rules and not applying the law of the Contracting State. The Committee concluded that:

> "arbitrators may have recourse to the "principles of international law" only *after* having inquired into and established the content of the law of the State party to the dispute (which cannot be reduced to *one* principle, even a basic one) and *after* having applied the relevant rules of the State's law. Article 42(1) therefore clearly does not allow the arbitrator to base his decision *solely* on the "rules" or "principles of international law"'.[64]

The Committee's interpretation of Article 42(1) diverged from Broches's approach. As set out above, Broches explained that a tribunal 'may' apply international law when: (i) national law calls for its application; (ii) where the subject matter is directly regulated by international law; and (iii) where national law or action taken under such law violates international law. Broches never proposed a mechanical process whereby a preliminary investigation of the content of municipal law is necessary to apply international law. The Committee therefore made a cogent legal analysis in one respect, but it was an analysis that misunderstood the analytical process that the ICSID Convention prescribes.

[B]   *Amco Asia Corp. v. Indonesia (Amco Asia)*

The Ad Hoc Committee in *Amco Asia* took an approach similar to that of the *Klöckner v. Cameroon* Committee.[65] The dispute arose in connection with an agreement for the construction and management of a hotel in Indonesia. In 1980 the hotel was allegedly seized in an armed military action; subsequently, Amco's lease and management agreement was rescinded and the investment license was revoked. In 1981, Amco

---

63. *Ibid.*
64. *Id.*, 112.
65. *Republic of Indonesia v. Amco Asia Corp., and others*, Annulment Decision, 16 May 1986, *Yearbook Commercial Arbitration* 1987, Volume XII, 129–148. A portion of the Award on the merits of 20 Nov. 1984 is published in 24 *ILM* (1985), 1022–1039.

initiated ICSID proceedings against Indonesia for unlawful seizure of the investment and revocation of the license. In 1984, the arbitral tribunal awarded damages to Amco. Two years later, the Ad Hoc Committee annulled the award, stating, *inter alia*, that the tribunal failed to apply the relevant provisions of Indonesian law and to provide reasons when the tribunal credited loan funds to the amount of the investment in dispute.[66]

In particular, the Committee determined that the second sentence of Article 42(1) authorizes an ICSID tribunal to apply rules of international law *only* to fill lacunae in the applicable domestic law and to ensure precedence to international law norms where the rules of the applicable domestic law collide with such norms:

> The above view of the role or relationship of international law norms vis-à-vis the law of the host State, in the context of Art. 42(1) of the Convention, is suggested by an overall evaluation of the system established by the Convention. The law of the host State is, in principle, the law to be applied in resolving the dispute. At the same time, applicable norms of international law must be complied with since every ICSID award has to be recognized, and pecuniary obligations imposed by such award enforced, by every Contracting State of the Convention (Art. 54(1), Convention). Moreover, the national State of the investor is precluded from exercising its normal right of diplomatic protection during the pendency of the ICSID proceedings and even after such proceedings, in respect of a Contracting State which complies with the ICSID award (Art. 27, Convention). The thrust of Art. 54(1) and of Art. 27 of the Convention makes sense only under the supposition that the award involved is not violative of applicable principles and rules of international law.[67]

The *Amco Asia* Committee referred to *Klöckner*, scholarly articles, and the drafting history of the ICSID Convention to support its view on the supplemental and corrective role of international law. The Committee's research into the Convention's *travaux*, however, was flawed.

It is sometimes cautioned that these two cases, *Amco Asia* and *Klöckne*, are contract cases, not BIT cases, and therefore the role of international law is different: according to these commentators, international law in BIT cases is relevant since each violation of the investment treaty would be asserted under international law (although domestic law may also be relevant in a number of circumstances[68]). This apparent difference led Reisman and Arsanjani to conclude that the second sentence in Article 42(1) is not applicable if a BIT is at issue, since the BIT is, by definition, an indication that the parties have chosen international law as the law applicable to the dispute. Along these lines, an important BIT case, *Wena Hotels Ltd v. Egypt*,[69] expanded

---

66. Parra, *The History of ICSID, supra*, 186.
67. *Republic of Indonesia v. Amco Asia Corp., and others*, Annulment Decision, *supra*, 131–132.
68. Parra, *The History of ICSID, supra*, 303; Douglas, *The International Law of Investment Claims* (Cambridge, 2009).
69. *Wena Hotels Ltd v. Arab Republic of Egypt*, Award, 8 Dec. 2000 in 41 *ILM*, 896–932 (2002); *Wena Hotels Ltd v. Arab Republic of Egypt*, Ad Hoc Committee decision, 5 Feb. 2002, in 41 *ILM*, 933–953 (2002). *See also* Reisman and Arsanjani, Ch. 1, 'Applicable Law under the ICSID Convention: The Tortured History of the Interpretation of Article 42', *supra* (Reisman appeared as an expert instructed by Egypt in *Wena Hotels*).

significantly the role of international law, and 'launched a new approach to choice of law under Article 42(1) of the ICSID Convention'.[70] The new approach was the tribunal's unfettered discretion to apply international law.

[C] Wena Hotels Ltd v. Egypt

This dispute arose out of long-term agreements to lease and develop two hotels, one located in Luxor and the other in Cairo. In 1989, Wena and an Egyptian public sector company entered into a lease and development agreement for the Egyptian company to develop and upgrade the hotel in Luxor hotel, and a year later Wena and the same Egyptian company entered into a similar agreement for the hotel in Cairo.

Shortly after the agreements were executed, differences arose between Wena and the Egyptian company regarding their respective obligations under the leases. Wena contended that the conditions of the hotels were below what was stipulated, and the Egyptian company complained about Wena's failure to pay the rent. Subsequently, Wena initiated arbitration and court proceedings. In 1991 the Egyptian company seized the two hotels. In 1992, Egypt's Chief Prosecutor ruled that the seizure of the hotel in Cairo was illegal and that Wena was entitled to repossess the hotel. Shortly afterwards, Wena's demand for a permanent license was denied, and Wena was later evicted from the hotel.

With regard to applicable law,[71] the *Wena* arbitral tribunal first acknowledged that the UK –Egypt Agreement for the Promotion and Protection of Investments was the primary source of applicable law for the arbitration. However, this treaty was a 'fairly terse agreement of only seven pages containing thirteen articles', and neither the tribunal nor the parties considered that the treaty contained all the rules of law applicable to the dispute. The tribunal further stated that 'beyond the provisions of the [UK-Egypt BIT] there is no special agreement between the parties on the rules of law applicable to the dispute. Rather, the pleadings of both parties indicate that, aside from the provisions of the [UK-Egypt BIT], the tribunal should apply both Egyptian law' (i.e., 'the law of the Contracting State party to the dispute') and 'such rules of international law as may be applicable'. Further, the tribunal stated that the provisions of the BIT 'would in any event be the first rules of law to be applied by the Tribunal, both on the basis of the agreement of the parties and as mandated by Egyptian law as well as international law'.

Following an award granting damages to Wena, Egypt filed an application for annulment, alleging that the tribunal failed to apply Egyptian law in violation of ICSID Article 42(1). Although the tribunal referred to the law of the host State, it had failed – according to Egypt – to apply Egyptian law because the tribunal relied on the provisions of the UK-Egypt BIT as the primary source of rules of law.[72]

The *Wena* Ad Hoc Committee stated that the although the contracts were subject to Egyptian law, the dispute before the ICSID tribunal involved parties different from

---

70. Parra, *The History of ICSID, supra,* 231.
71. *Wena Hotels Ltd v. Arab Republic of Egypt,* Award, 8 Dec. 2000, 910–911.
72. *Wena Hotels Ltd v. Arab Republic of Egypt,* Ad Hoc Committee decision, 5 Feb. 2002, *supra,* 939.

the parties to the contracts (namely the Egyptian State rather than the Egyptian company), and concerned a subject matter entirely different from that underlying the contracts. Despite the connection between the contracts and the BIT, the contracts were a 'condition precedent' to the operation of the BIT, and these were different legal instruments with different dispute settlement arrangements.[73] The issues concerning the contracts were of a commercial nature, while the BIT raised questions of a governmental nature concerning the standard of treatment accorded by the State to foreign investors. The Committee found that the choice of law in the contracts was different from a choice of law agreement in accordance with the first sentence of Article 42(1), under the BIT.

Having established that the applicable law issue had to be resolved in accordance with the second sentence of Article 42(1), the *Wena* Ad Hoc Committee next considered the relation between municipal and international law in the context of Article 42(1). The Committee entertained arguments in favour of (i) a broad interpretation of international law, (ii) a position that would limit international law to supplement municipal law in the event of a *lacuna* and to correct municipal law if it did not conform with international law, and (iii) yet another position whereby international law would only be adopted in the event of a collision with fundamental norms of international law, such as *jus cogens*.[74]

The *Wena* Ad Hoc Committee concluded that:

> There seems not to be a single answer as to which of these approaches is the correct one. The circumstances of each case may justify one or another solution. However, this Committee's task is not to elaborate precise conclusions on this matter, but only to decide whether the Tribunal manifestly exceeded its powers with respect to Article 42(1) of the ICSID Convention. Further, the use of the word 'may' in the second sentence of this provision indicates that the Convention does not draw a sharp line for the distinction of the respective scope of international and of domestic law and, correspondingly, that this has the effect to confer on to the Tribunal a certain margin and power for interpretation.[75]

The Committee further commented that municipal law and international law both played a role: '[t]he law of the host State can indeed be applied in conjunction with international law if this is justified. So too international law can be applied by itself if the appropriate rule is found in this other ambit.'[76] The Committee observed that Egyptian law fully supported of the investors' rights contained in the BIT, and held that the tribunal's reliance on the BIT was not an excess of power. Egypt's annulment application was dismissed.

Thus, *Wena Hotels v. Egypt* held that the second sentence of Article 42(1) grants an arbitral tribunal complete discretion as to the choice of the applicable law. Tribunals would choose to apply international law if this is, simply, the 'appropriate' law, and the

---

73. *Id.*, 940.
74. *Ibid.*
75. *Id.*, 941.
76. *Ibid.*

Ad Hoc Committee suggests, at the very least, that because BITs are international law instruments, application of international law would be an understandable choice.

Several cases after *Wena Hotels v. Egypt* followed the interpretation of Article 42(1) adopted by the *Wena* Committee, e.g., *CMS v. Argentina*[77] and *Sempra v. Argentina*.[78] This sequence led Parra to conclude, correctly, that this jurisprudence 'is difficult to reconcile' with the ICSID *travaux préparatoires*, which required both national and international law to be applicable.[79] Indeed, none of the major interpretations of Article 42(1) – major in the sense of frequently discussed – are consistent with the actual intention of Article 42(1)'s second sentence, and none of them reach the soundness of Broches's explanation of how Article 42(1) is meant to operate in practice.

§2.04 THE THREE SCHOOLS OF THOUGHT IN LIGHT OF THE ICSID TRAVAUX

[A] The Complementary/Corrective Interpretation

As discussed above, *Klöckner v. Cameroon* and *Amco v. Indonesia*, among the earliest ICSID cases, interpreted Article 42(1) to limit the application of international law to a complementary and corrective role. That is, international law would be applicable only if there were a *lacuna* in national law or if international law were somehow inconsistent with national law.

This interpretation finds some support in the *travaux préparatoires* and the delegates' vote on Article 42(1): 'The first sentence dealing with an express choice of law agreement was approved by a majority of 35 to one. The first part of the second sentence referring to the "national" law applicable was adopted by a majority of 31 to

---

77. *CMS v. Argentina*, Award, 12 May 2005, available on the Investment Treaty Arbitration website: http://www.italaw.com/cases/288, 34–35: 'More recently, however, a more pragmatic and less doctrinaire approach has emerged, allowing for the application of both domestic law and international law if the specific facts of the dispute so justifies. It is no longer the case of one prevailing over the other and excluding it altogether. Rather, both sources have a role to play. The Annulment Committee in *Wena v. Egypt* held in this respect (...). This is the approach this Tribunal considers justified when taking the facts of the case and the arguments of the parties into account. Indeed, there is here a close interaction between the legislation and the regulations governing the gas privatization, the License and international law, as embodied both in the Treaty and in customary international law. All of these rules are inseparable and will, to the extent justified, be applied by the Tribunal'. (Argentina's application for annulment was upheld only as far as the umbrella clause was concerned.)
78. *Sempra v. Argentina*, Award, 28 Sep. 2007, available on the Investment Treaty Arbitration website: http://www.italaw.com/cases/1002, 70: 'the Tribunal will consider both Argentine law and international law to the extent each is relevant to a determination on liability' (this award was annulled on the basis of manifest excess of powers in respect of failure to apply Art. XI of the relevant BIT): '[o]n the basis of the above, the Committee considers that it is obvious from a simple reading of the reasons of the Tribunal that it did not identify or apply Article XI of the BIT as the applicable law, and that it failed to do so on the assumption that the language of this provision was somehow not legitimated by the dictates of customary international law'). *See also* Parra, *The History of ICSID*, supra, 305–306.
79. Parra, *The History of ICSID*, supra, 306.

one. The final provision relating to international law *(which would bring it into play both in the case of a lacuna in domestic law as well as in the case of inconsistency between the two)* was adopted by a majority of 24 to 6'.[80] [emphasis added]. However, these two qualifications do not clearly emerge from the text of Article 42(1); the fact that they were discussed at such a length and not inserted in the text also signifies that there was no intention to limit the application of international law to only these two situations.

It is necessary to consider the text in the context of the *travaux*. The argument that in the case of Article 42(1) it is doubtful that there is a need to consider the *travaux*[81] is unpersuasive, since the ordinary meaning of the second sentence of Article 42 is in fact obscure in that it does not identify *when* municipal law or international law applies. Thus, the *travaux préparatoires* are needed to shed light on vague terminology. One concern in doing so is that upon review of the *travaux préparatoires*, it appears that the second sentence of Article 42 is purposely vague, because the delegates differed as to the role of international law and the automatic applicability of municipal law.[82] However, Broches's Report clarifies the result and resolves the vagueness. Moreover, to confine international law's applicability to *lacunae* in or inconsistencies with municipal law as *Klöckner* and *Amco* indicate is to virtually eliminate an international law role, since *lacunae* in municipal law are very few, and inconsistencies are also infrequent. As Gaillard and Banifatemi correctly observe, national law 'may not address a particular issue directly, but this by no means implies that it provides no response or legal framework for that issue'.[83] As for possible inconsistencies between national and international law, these may be mere differences or they may constitute a violation of fundamental rules of international law. In the first situation, it is unclear, under the *Klockner/Amco* approach, if any differences would allow international law to trump national law, and on what basis a tribunal would decide that the differences are such as to require international law, rather than national law, to regulate the issue in dispute.[84]

A final problem with the *Klöckner/Amco* approach to Article 42(1), when applied to treaties instead of investment contracts, is that treaties often do not contain any substantive rules on the subject matter of their protection, and simply rely on references to municipal law. Accordingly, conflicts between municipal law and investment treaties are very infrequent (though the possibility cannot be excluded). Investment treaties lay down international standards of protection; the beneficiaries of the protections are entities or individuals – the investors – in relation to their individual investments. These beneficiaries are subject to municipal law, which governs the

---

80. *History of the ICSID Convention*, Volume II 2, 804.
81. Gaillard and Banifatemi, 'The Meaning of "and" in Article 42(1), Second Sentence, of the Washington Convention: The Role of International Law in the ICSID Choice of Law Process', *supra*, 382–383.
82. *Id.*, 383–387 and *History of the ICSID Convention*, Volume II 2, 804. *See also* the above discussion of the ICSID *travaux*.
83. *Id.*, 394.
84. *Id.*, 398.

underlying investment that such treaties address.[85] Thus, few inconsistencies between international and municipal law would be manifested because of the very nature of investment protection.

[B] The Reisman Interpretation: BITs Require Application of International Law

According to Reisman, as noted above, there are four situations in which an ICSID tribunal should apply international law: (i) where the parties so agree; (ii) where the law of the host State calls for the application of international law, including customary international law; (iii) where the subject matter or issue is directly regulated by international law, such as a treaty between the state parties to the dispute; and (iv) where the law of the host State violates a fundamental principle of international law, including a peremptory international human rights norm.[86]

This approach is problematic in both the non-BIT and BIT situations. For example, in relation to point (ii), Reisman attributes relevance only to 'genuine' *lacunae*, i.e., where inconsistencies between national and international law *preclude* the application of national law. This would be a very small subset of cases – when, for example, there would be a violation of a fundamental principle such as *pacta sunt servanda* or a peremptory international human rights norm.[87] However, it is difficult to identify a 'genuine' lacuna ('one for which host State law does not provide a method for filling, the Tribunal may turn to international law'[88]). As for inconsistencies with fundamental principles, if these principles were fundamental they would apply even without the provision contained in Article 42(1), whereby international law 'may' be applicable. If there is a violation of *jus cogens*, by definition municipal law is inapplicable, whether or not there is a provision stating so. Therefore, this approach would deprive Article 42(1) of its *effet utile*.

In their subsequent article, Reisman and Arsanjani explained that international law applies where there is a treaty between the state parties to the dispute (Reisman's 'third situation'): 'a BIT, even if it does not contain an explicit provision on the applicable law, constitutes the *eo ipso* applicable law to claims for the breaches of the protection contained therein'.[89]

In their view, the second sentence of Article 42(1) does not apply in the event that a BIT governs the dispute: 'a treaty would have to be interpreted in accordance with

---

85. *See also* on this subject, Douglas, *The International Law of Investment Claims* (Cambridge, 2009).
86. Reisman, 'The Regime for *Lacunae* in the ICSID Choice of Law Provision and Question of Its Threshold', *supra*, 380.
87. Reisman, 'The Regime for *Lacunae* in the ICSID Choice of Law Provision and Question of Its Threshold', *supra*, 368.
88. *Id.*, 375.
89. Reisman and Arsanjani, Ch. 1 'Applicable Law under the ICSID Convention: The Tortured History of the Interpretation of Article 42', *supra*, 10.

international law'.[90] Article 42(1), second sentence, would thus have a very limited application since it would be excluded in all the cases where the dispute arose out of a BIT.

However, the flaw here is that the second sentence of Article 42(1) is not restricted to contractual disputes. The Reisman/Arsanjani approach ignores the reality that investment treaties protect foreign investors and their investments by setting *independent* standards: for example, fair and equitable treatment, and prohibition against expropriation without compensation. International law often does not regulate the rights that it protects. Therefore, the determination of whether a contractual right constitutes an investment first requires an analysis under the relevant municipal law to determine whether the right exists, and any limits to which it may be subject to.[91]

International law is not insulated from national law. As the tribunal observed in *Asian Agricultural Products Ltd (AAPL) v. Republic of Sri Lanka*[92] (*Asian Agricultural Products*), albeit in a context where the BIT contained an express provision on applicable law, a BIT is 'not a self-contained closed legal system limited to provide for substantive material rules of direct applicability, but it has to be envisaged within a wider juridical context in which rules from other sources are integrated through implied incorporation methods, or by direct reference to certain supplementary rules, whether of international law character or of domestic law nature.'[93] The Reisman/Arsanjani approach suggests that international law and municipal law exist in entirely distinct spheres, such that a BIT, an international law instrument, can only concern international law. However, this misses the point that international law, in the BIT context, must draw much of its content from the Host State's municipal law (and on certain issues from the Home State's municipal law).

The *Asian Agricultural Products* explanation prompted a public international law scholar to conclude that in investment disputes there is a 'mosaic of applicable laws',[94] contrary to the traditional view in public international law whereby international law plays an exclusive role and municipal law is merely treated as a question of fact.[95] As Judge Morelli stated, in his *Barcelona Traction* opinion: '[n]o subordination of international responsibility, as such, to the provisions of municipal law involved: the point is rather that the very existence of the international obligations depends on a state of affairs created in municipal law, though this is so not by virtue of municipal law but, on the contrary by virtue of the international rule itself'.[96]

---

90. *Ibid.*
91. *See* Chapter 4.
92. *Asian Agricultural Products Ltd (AAPL) v. Republic of Sri Lanka*, Award, 27 Jun. 1990, available on the Investment Treaty Arbitration website: http://www.italaw.com/cases/96.
93. *Id.*, 533.
94. Douglas, *The International Law of Investment Claims, supra*, 40.
95. Thomas and Dhillon 'Applicable law under International Investment Treaties', *supra*, at 979; Douglas, *The International Law of Investment Claims, supra*, 40; Schreuer, 'International domestic Law in Investment Disputes: The Case of ICSID' (1996) 1 *Austrian Rev of Int and Eur L*, 89.
96. *Barcelona Traction, Light and Power Company, Limited,* Judgment, *ICJ Reports* (5 Feb. 1970), Separate Opinion of Judge Morelli, 234–235, paras 4 and 5.

Thus, it is unclear on what basis the second sentence of Article 42(1) can be deemed irrelevant to disputes originating from BITs. Even if treaties and contracts are 'different things (...) they are part of the same one world with many legal systems that international arbitrators have long inhabited'.[97]

The *travaux préparatoires* also do not support an approach that limits the applicability of the second sentence of Article 42 solely to contractual disputes. Broches faced a challenge from one of the delegates, who said that while 'he understood the reference in Article 42(1) to "rules of international law" as including the rules of law set down in bilateral investment treaties between the State party to the dispute and the State whose national was a party to the dispute',[98] an earlier draft more clearly indicated that 'international law' was understood in the sense given to it by Article 38 of the Statute of the ICJ. The delegate said that the draft that they were discussing gave rise to doubts as to whether the rules of law set down in bilateral investment treaties would or would not apply to disputes under the terms of Article 42(1). Broches replied that 'there could be *no doubt* whatever that the term "international law" in Article 42(1) did in fact *include rules set out in bilateral agreements* between the States concerned. The fact that the interpretative clause in the original version of the Article had been transferred to the Report of the Executive Directors did not imply any change in the substance of the provision'.[99] [emphasis added].

[C] The 'Tribunal Discretion' Interpretation

Gaillard and Banifatemi have taken a position on applicable law that differs from *Klöckner v. Cameroon* and *Amco v. Indonesia*, and the early Reisman and later Reisman/Aransanjani positions. They advocate for an investment treaty tribunal's freedom to adopt the rules of law that the tribunal deems applicable, whether national or international.[100] They endorse the jurisprudence of the *Wena Hotels v. Egypt* line of cases that confers complete discretion to the tribunal to choose the law, national or international, that it wishes to adopt for each issue in dispute. Gaillard/Banifatemi have emphasized that 'arbitrators today are increasingly called upon to assess the validity of acts of States, who, on the basis of those treaties, undertake to ensure the promotion and protection of foreign investments'.[101] In other words, there cannot be a restriction on the role played by international law in ICSID arbitration, particularly since arbitrators may need to use international law to protect foreign investments.

---

97. Crawford, 'Treaty and Contract in Investment Arbitration', in *Arb. Int.*, Vol. 24, No 3, 351–374, at 374.
98. *History of the ICSID Convention*, Volume II 2, *supra*, 984.
99. *Ibid.*
100. Gaillard and Banifatemi, 'The Meaning of "and" in Article 42(1), Second Sentence, of the Washington Convention: The Role of International Law in the ICSID Choice of Law Process', *supra*, 411.
101. *Ibid.*

This approach, however, carries some significant negative consequences. One example of the negatives appears in *Venezuela Holdings BV. et al. v. Venezuela*.[102] This tribunal held that, pursuant to Article 42 of the ICSID Convention, the Contracting States of the BIT made their choice of law in the BIT by including a governing law provision. This provision[103] listed several sources, including general principles of international law and municipal law. The tribunal members held that it was for them 'to determine whether an issue is subject to national or international law'.[104] The Annulment Committee upheld the request for annulment[105] of, among other portions, this paragraph of the Award, stating that the tribunal did not indicate from where it derived the authority to decide whether to apply international or municipal law and also failed to disclose the criterion it would have used to make such a decision.[106] The Committee held that (i) in investment disputes, it cannot merely be assumed that the State used municipal law to evade the State's obligations under the BIT, and (ii) the resolution of a disputed issue under international law can itself entail the application of municipal law 'simply because that is what the international rule requires'.[107] The Committee rejected the tribunal's ruling that international law imposed a quantum of compensation, and noted that in 'its anxiety to dismiss any thought that national law can be invoked as a defence to the breach of an international obligation, the Tribunal ended up falling into an another version of exactly the same type of proposition, i.e., that some alternative source of international obligation can be invoked to displace

---

102. *Venezuela Holdings BV, Mobil Cerro Negro Holding, Ltd, Mobil Venezolana De Petroleos Holding Inc., Mobil Cerro Negro Ltd and Mobil Venezolana De Petroleos Inc v. Venezuela*, Award, 9 Oct. 2014 available on Investment Treaty Arbitration website: http://www.italaw.com/sites/default/files/case-documents/italaw4011.pdf. (para. 223: '[a]ccordingly, the Tribunal will apply the BIT and the other agreed sources of law where appropriate. Article 9(5) of the Treaty does not allocate matters to any of those laws. Accordingly, it is for the Tribunal to determine whether an issue is subject to national or international law. Further, if and when an issue arises, the Tribunal will determine whether the applicable international law should be limited to general principles of international law under Article 9(5) of the BIT or whether it includes customary international law').
103. *Id.*, para. 222: Art. 9(5) of the Treaty designates the following sources of law to govern disputes under the Treaty:

    The arbitral award shall be based on: the law of the Contracting Party concerned; the provisions of this Agreement and other relevant Agreements between the Contracting Parties; the provisions of special agreements relating to the investments; the general principles of international law; and such rules of law as may be agreed by the parties to the dispute.

104. *Id.*, para. 223: '[a]ccordingly, the Tribunal will apply the BIT and the other agreed sources of law where appropriate. Article 9(5) of the Treaty does not allocate matters to any of those laws. Accordingly, it is for the Tribunal to determine whether an issue is subject to national or international law. Further, if and when an issue arises, the Tribunal will determine whether the applicable international law should be limited to general principles of international law under Article 9(5) of the BIT or whether it includes customary international law'.
105. *Venezuela Holdings BV, Mobil Cerro Negro Holding, Ltd, Mobil Venezolana De Petroleos Holding Inc., Mobil Cerro Negro Ltd and Mobil Venezolana De Petroleos Inc v. Venezuela*, Decision on Annulment, 9 Mar. 2017 available on Investment Treaty Arbitration website: http://www.italaw.com/sites/default/files/case-documents/italaw8536.pdf.
106. *Id.*, paras 155, 159–160.
107. *Id.*, para. 181.

particular rights and obligations established by treaty'.[108] The Committee ruled that the tribunal exceeded its powers by failing to apply the proper law, and the 'manifest' nature of this failure was shown by the inadequacies in the tribunal's reasoning for the choice of applicable law. In particular, the tribunal exceeded its power to the extent that it held that general international law, and customary international law, regulated the determination and the assessment of the compensation due to the claimants.[109]

The *Venezuela Holdings* tribunal approach, remitting the choice of law to the arbitrators' discretion is misguided; it fails to take into account the relevance of the *travaux préparatoires*. Although the initial draft of Article 42(1) conferred to the arbitrators total freedom to apply international law, the ICSID delegates rejected that draft. The discussion that preceded the adoption of Article 42(1) shows very clearly that the States opposed according such freedom to arbitral tribunals. To enter into international treaties is an 'attribute of State sovereignty.'[110] In doing so, States submit themselves to a limitation of the exercise of their sovereign rights. However, this limitation must result from, and be limited to, the terms of the treaty itself. An individual investment tribunal lacks authority to freely regulate the subject matters of an investment treaty without an express provision contained in the treaty or to adopt an interpretation that was clearly rejected in the *travaux préparatoires*. To allow an arbitral tribunal to do so, as the Gaillard-Banifatemi approach advocates, would imply that a State waived its sovereign authority to regulate foreign investment in favour of arbitral tribunals constituted on an *ad hoc* basis, with virtually unbounded discretion. Such an approach has no foundation in international law. The term 'international law' indicates that rules pre-exist investments and apply to all the nationals of the State party to the investment treaty. Arbitral tribunals should not seek to create rules of international law.

§2.05 CONCLUSION

The second sentence of Article 42(1) must be interpreted in conformity with the text, and, to the extent that more clarity is needed to interpret the interplay between national and international law, the *travaux préparatoires*. On this basis, an arbitral tribunal may apply international law when national law provides for the application of international law, where the subject matter is regulated directly by international law, and when national law violates international law. That is the intended meaning of Article 42(1), and that is the meaning that makes sense, as a matter of international law. It is the approach supported by Broches in order to determine substantive law in an investment treaty arbitration under the ICSID Convention.

Douglas has suggested adopting a 'proper law of the issue approach'[111] to determine the applicable law: if the investor advances a case for a contractual breach,

---

108. *Id.*, para. 187.
109. *Id.*, para. 188–189.
110. *SS Wimbledon*, Judgment (17 Aug. 1923), PCIJ Series A No 1, 15, at 25.
111. Douglas, Ch. 54.1, 'Other Specific Regimes of Responsibility: Investment Treaty Arbitration and ICSID', in *The Law of International Responsibility, supra,* 833.

the proper law of the contract applies; if the investor pleads abuse of executive powers to frustrate the performance of a contract, the conduct of the State is to be determined in accordance with the standard of protection. Under this interpretation, a tribunal should apply international law when the issue to be determined is regulated by international law, for instance the standard of protection.[112] Douglas's approach is in line with the intention of the parties to the ICSID Convention and the Broches approach, and serves as a sounder guide for tribunals than any of the three schools of thought discussed in this chapter, which have gained prominence to date.

Each of those three views on the second sentence of Article 42(1) is at odds with the *travaux préparatoires*. The final text was adopted to encapsulate a delicate balance between national and international law – a balance that was not meant to be remitted to arbitral tribunals to ignore at their complete discretion.

Broches's guidance remains the appropriate framework for interpreting and applying Article 42(1), when investor-state arbitral tribunals must make the crucial decision of identifying the law applicable to the merits of the dispute:

(1) party autonomy is the 'basic principle governing the law to be applied by the tribunal';
(2) the tribunal 'may' apply international law when:
    (i) national law calls for its application;
    (ii) where the subject matter is directly regulated by international law; and
    (iii) where national law or action taken under such law violates international law.

Absent the circumstances set out in points (i) through (iii) above, and absent an agreement by the Contracting Parties to apply international law, ICSID tribunals should apply municipal law to the merits of the dispute. The Broches approach may seem uncomfortably non-international to arbitrators who view themselves as resolving weighty matters of international law, but it is what a treaty – the ICSID Convention – requires that they implement.

---

112. *Id.*, 835.

CHAPTER 3
Investor Nationality under Municipal and International Law

§3.01 INTRODUCTION

Investment treaties protect an investor, who may be an individual or an entity, with a link to one of the State parties to the treaty. This link is almost always represented by nationality, although there may be additional relevant criteria, for example, domicile, residence, or, in the case of legal entities, control. If the investor is an entity, municipal law may be relevant in answering the threshold question of whether the entity has a legal personality different from its participants before the question of nationality (and any other link required by the treaty) is reached. For an individual, there is no similar threshold question; nationality (plus any further link) is the matter to be determined. Municipal law therefore is directly relevant to the assessment of nationality for individuals and entities. Investment treaties often define investor nationality simply by referring to each Contracting State's legislation.

However, applying municipal law to establish the investor's nationality may raise difficulties when the connection to the home State is tenuous. Moreover, as discussed below, the applicability of municipal law does not mean that international law plays no role in the analysis. Customary international law may limit a State's designation of its nationals. Two international conventions, which are generally seen as expressing customary law, indicate both the centrality of municipal law and the boundaries placed by international law:

(a) Article 1 of The Hague Convention on Certain Questions relating to the Conflict of Nationality Laws (12 April 1930) states:

> It is for each State to determine under its own law who are its nationals. This law shall be recognised by other States in so far as it is consistent with

international conventions, international custom, and the principles of law generally recognised with regard to nationality.

(b) Article 3 of the European Convention on Nationality (Strasbourg 6 November 1997) similarly states:

1. Each State shall determine under its own law who are its nationals.
2. This law shall be accepted by other States *in so far as it is consistent with applicable international conventions, customary international law and the principles of law generally recognised with regard to nationality.* [emphasis added]

This chapter first considers the influence of the investment treaty background on the determination of nationality, followed by a discussion of the International Law Association's (ILA) Articles on Diplomatic Protection. The chapter then analyses several investment treaty awards bearing on the issue of investor nationality. The analysis focuses on the role of municipal law in determining the nationality of an individual or a corporation, and whether international law can override municipal law rules on the grounds that a company is not a 'genuine entity'[1] or that the individual does not have a substantive link with the home State. The chapter also considers the rules for determining the seat of a corporation, in the event that the seat is relevant for the purposes of nationality. The question of corporate seat and applicable law has arisen as a key point of dispute in several recent investment treaty arbitrations.

§3.02 INVESTOR NATIONALITY AND MUNICIPAL LAW

[A] The Investment Treaty Background

The 1959 Abs-Shawcross Draft Convention defined investors to include 'companies which under the municipal law of that Party are considered national companies of that Party and companies in which national companies of that Party have directly or indirectly a controlling interest' (Article IX). Companies are defined as 'juridical persons' by municipal law even if they do not 'possess legal personality' according to the relevant municipal law (Article IX). The 1967 OECD Draft Convention provides more specific guidance in certain respects on 'company', but omitted consideration of controlling interests. Article 9 of the OECD Draft Convention defined 'company' as an entity that is recognized under a Party's law as 'a legal person' or as an entity that through its members 'has the capacity to dispose of property or to institute legal proceedings'. However, no claim could be made in respect to the interest of a member of a company.[2]

---

1. *Tokios Tokeles v. Ukraine*, Decision on Jurisdiction, 29 Apr. 2004, *ICSID Rev. 20 – FILJ* (2005), 205; Dissenting Opinion of Prosper Weil (President), *ICSID Rev. 20 – FILJ* (2005): 245, para. 21.
2. OECD Draft Convention on the Protection of Foreign Property, 137, Appendix IV.

Chapter 3: Investor Nationality under Municipal and International Law §3.02[A]

The approach taken by the ICSID Convention (1965), just prior to the OECD Draft Convention, was to leave questions of nationality, including that of foreign control of companies, to the parties' Agreement. ICSID Article 25 provides that:

> National of another Contracting State' means:
>
> (a) any natural person who had the nationality of a Contracting State other than the State party to the dispute on the date on which the parties consented to submit such dispute to conciliation or arbitration as well as on the date on which the request was registered pursuant to paragraph (3) of Article 28 or paragraph (3) of Article 36, but does not include any person who on either date also had the nationality of the Contracting State party to the dispute; and
> (b) any juridical person which had the nationality of a Contracting State other than the State party to the dispute on the date on which the parties consented to submit such dispute to conciliation or arbitration and any juridical person which had the nationality of the Contracting State party to the dispute on that date and which, because of foreign control, the parties have agreed should be treated as a national of another Contracting State for the purposes of this Convention.

In the ICSID *travaux préparatoires*, the chairman, Aron Broches, noted that the arbitral tribunal would decide all questions of its competence, including the nationality of the parties. Further, the decision on the issue of nationality would be adopted by reference to the law governing that nationality – 'that is the national law claimed by the private individual or corporation'.[3] In the *travaux*, the delegates accorded municipal law pride of place, on the grounds that nationals of a State were those persons subject to its direct authority, and whose civil and political rights were recognized by the State that also undertook to protect them outside of its borders. The responsibility for establishing the rules relating to nationality lay with the internal legislation of each State, despite the fact that these rules had to be consonant with public international law, conventional or traditional, and with the general principles of law relating to the matter, in order that the standards set by each State in this matter would be recognized by the other States.[4]

Ten years later, Broches commented that the ICSID nationality requirement was designed to balance the interests of host States, on the one hand, and investors, on the other hand.[5] Thus, in the case of natural persons, a certificate of nationality should be no more than *prima facie* evidence, and ineligibility to be a Claimant was definitive in the event of double nationality of the State party to the proceeding and another State.[6] As for juridical entities, the delegates had abandoned attempts to define nationality and the ICSID Convention gave 'the greatest possible latitude to the parties to decide under what circumstances a company could be treated as a "national" of another Contracting State'.[7] Broches also indicated that the ICSID text implied that incorporation was a

---

3. *See* History of the ICSID Convention, vol. II (1), 67 available on the ICSID Convention website: https://icsid.worldbank.org/en/Pages/resources/The-History-of-the-ICSID-Convention.aspx
4. *See* History of the ICSID Convention, vol. II (2), 839.
5. *Id.*, 356.
6. *Id.*, 357–358.
7. *Id.*, 360.

criterion of nationality, but it was not the only criterion.[8] He stated that Article 25(1) of the ICSID Convention contained the 'outer limits within which disputes may be submitted to conciliation or arbitration under the auspices of the Centre with the consent of the parties thereto'.[9] The contracting States therefore could agree on the meaning of 'nationality', and any stipulation 'based on a reasonable criterion' should be accepted. Broches clearly supported giving effect to agreements between the contracting States, taking into account not only formal criteria such as incorporation, but also adhering to functional approaches that attributed relevance to ownership and control, if included in the treaty.[10]

BITs and other multilateral conventions usually provide that their protections are available if the individual investor has the nationality of the Home State, and the legal entity has been incorporated or has its seat in the Home State or is controlled by nationals of the Home State. However, certain BITs and multilateral conventions require a closer connection than incorporation, residence, or domicile.[11] An issue that occasionally arises in investment treaty disputes is whether the 'close connection' test should be applied, notwithstanding the absence of an express reference to this test in international investment treaties.[12] This issue is considered below; the consensus that has emerged, properly, is that absent a specific treaty directive to do so (or an applicable municipal law provision), an investment treaty tribunal should not insert the 'close-connection' test into its decision-making.

[B] Nationality and Diplomatic Protection

The issue of nationality has long been debated in diplomatic protection cases, where a State has espoused the claim of one of its nationals against another State. Nationality in the context of investment treaties is a relatively recent question. However, the conclusions reached pursuant to the law of diplomatic protection are not automatically applicable to investment treaty cases. Article 17 of the International Law Commission's Articles on Diplomatic Protection[13] (hereafter 'ILC Articles on Diplomatic Protection') states that the articles 'do not apply to the extent that they are inconsistent with special rules of international law, such as treaty provisions for the protection of investments'.

The investment treaty framework providing for direct action between investors and the host State distinguishes investment treaties from diplomatic protection, where

---

8. Ibid.
9. Id., 361.
10. Ibid.
11. See Dolzer and Stevens, *Bilateral Investment Treaties*, 31–42, and Schreuer et al., *The ICSID Convention: A Commentary*, 160–168 and 296–299. See also NAFTA, Art. 201; ECT, 17 Dec. 1994, 2080 UNTS 100, Arts 1(7) and 17; and Agreement for the Promotion and Protection of Investment, 15 Dec. 1987, Art. 1, in *ILM* 27 (1988): 612 (ASEAN).
12. *Tokios Tokeles v. Ukraine*.
13. Text adopted by the International Law Commission at its fifty-eighth session, in 2006, *Official Records of the General Assembly, Sixty-first Session* (A/61/10), ILC Yearbook 2006, Vol. II (2), available on the ILC website: http://untreaty.un.org/ilc/texts/instruments/english/draft%20articles/9_8_2006.pdf.

the parties are the two States.[14] The Commentaries to the ILC Articles on Diplomatic Protection explain that some investment treaties have departed from the rules governing diplomatic protection. For example, the diplomatic protection condition requiring exhaustion of local remedies does not apply to investment treaties. However, the Commentaries clarify that Article 17 is formulated so that the articles 'do not apply *"to the extent that"* they are inconsistent with the provisions of a BIT'. To the extent that the articles 'remain consistent with the BIT in question, they continue to apply'.[15]

The conclusions set out in the ILC Articles on Diplomatic Protection – to the further extent that they reflect customary international law – may therefore be relevant to certain investment treaty cases. For example, in *Société Générale in respect of DR Energy Holdings Ltd v. Dominican Republic*,[16] the tribunal acknowledged that although investment treaties represent a departure from the law governing diplomatic protection, 'this is correct largely to the extent that applicable treaties and conventions have so established by providing rules different from those of diplomatic protection'.[17] The tribunal observed that '[t]he rules governing issues not addressed by the specific language of the treaty may sometimes be provided by the law of diplomatic protection, which apply as customary international law, and thus, provides for a residual role for at least some aspects of the law of diplomatic protection'.[18]

Thus, the ILC Articles on Diplomatic Protection may have an 'authoritative influence on the development of the law and are a cogent material source of law'.[19] They stand as guidance in cases where investment treaty provisions are silent or unclear, and where the diplomatic protection principles appear to be consistent with the terms of the treaty or represent customary international law.

On the question of nationality, Article 4[20] of the ILC Articles on Diplomatic Protection provides that the State of nationality of a natural person is the State whose nationality that person has acquired 'in accordance with the law of that State, ... not inconsistent with international law'.[21] Article 9[22] concerns legal persons; it provides that the State of nationality means the State under whose law the legal entity has been incorporated. However, Article 9 contains an important *caveat*:

---

14. *Id.*, 89.
15. *Id.*, 90.
16. *Société Générale in respect of DR Energy Holdings Ltd et al. v. Dominican Republic,* Award on Preliminary Objections to Jurisdiction, 19 Sep. 2008, available on the Investment Treaty Arbitration website: http://www.italaw.com/sites/default/files/case-documents/ita0798.pdf.
17. *Id.*, para. 108.
18. *Ibid.*
19. *Oppenheim's International Law*, 9th edn, vol. 1 (London, 1996), 50.
20. Article 4: *State of nationality of a natural person,* 'For the purposes of the diplomatic protection of a natural person, a State of nationality means a State whose nationality that person has acquired, in accordance with the law of that State, by birth, descent, naturalization, succession of States or in any other manner, not inconsistent with international law.'
21. ILC Articles on Diplomatic Protection, 31.
22. Article 9, *State of nationality of a corporation,* reads in full: 'For the purposes of the diplomatic protection of a corporation, the State of nationality means the State under whose law the corporation was incorporated. However, when the corporation is controlled by nationals of another State or States and has no substantial business activities in the State of incorporation, and the seat of management and the financial control of the corporation are both located in another State, that State shall be regarded as the State of nationality.'

when the corporation is controlled by nationals of another State or States and has no substantial business activities in the State of incorporation, and the seat of the management and the financial control of the corporation are both located in another State, that State shall be regarded as the State of nationality.[23]

The Commentaries clarify that Article 9 does not allow multiple actions:

> [t]he State of nationality with the right to exercise diplomatic protection is *either* the State of incorporation *or*, if the required conditions are met, the State of the seat of management and financial control of the corporation. If the seat of management and the place of financial control are located in different States, the State of incorporation remains the State entitled to exercise diplomatic protection.[24] [emphasis in the original]

As the Commentaries note with regard to companies, the ILC Articles do not require a 'genuine' or 'close' connection between the company and its State of nationality. However, if a 'permanent and close connection' exists between the State exercising diplomatic protection and the corporation,[25] this connection is a point that may be taken into account when determining nationality that is otherwise uncertain. Still, it cannot be said that a 'close connection' test is an element of customary international law.

[C]   Arbitral Decisions on Investor Nationality

Several investment treaty arbitral decisions have been influential in guiding other tribunals on the issue of an investor's nationality under international investment law. The decisions analysed below concern the following issues: (i) effective nationality of individuals (*Fakes v. Turkey*[26]) and of corporations (*Tokios Tokeles v. Ukraine*[27]); (ii) denial of benefits (*Plama v. Bulgaria*[28]); (iii) the relevance, if any, of 'control' of corporations by States (*CSOB v. the Slovak Republic*[29]); (iv) the determination of the seat of a corporation (*Tenaris S.A et al. v. Venezuela*,[30] and *AFT v. Slovak Republic*[31]); cand (v) how to prove nationality (*Soufraki v. The United Arab Emirates*[32]). These

---

23. ILC Articles on Diplomatic Protection, 52.
24. *Id.*, 55.
25. *Id.*, 53–54.
26. *Saba Fakes v. Turkey*, Award, 14 Jul. 2010, available on the Investment Treaty Arbitration website: http://www.italaw.com/sites/default/files/case-documents/ita0314.pdf.
27. *Tokios Tokeles v. Ukraine*, Decision on Jurisdiction, 29 Apr. 2004, *ICSID Rev. – FILJ* 20 (2005): 205; Dissenting Opinion of Prosper Weil (President), *ICSID Rev. – FILJ* 20 (2005): 245, para. 21.
28. *Plama Consortium v. Bulgaria*, Decision on Jurisdiction, 8 Feb. 2005, *ICSID Reports* (2008): 13, 268.
29. *Ceskoslovenska Obchodni Banka A.S. v. Slovak Republic*, Decision on Jurisdiction, 24 May 1999, ICSID Reports 13 (2008): 178.
30. *Tenaris SA and Talta-Trading E Marketing Sociedade Unipessonl LDA v. Venezuela*, Award, 29 Jan. 2016, available on the Investment Treaty Arbitration website: http://www.italaw.com/sites/default/files/case-documents/italaw7098.pdf.
31. *AFT v. Slovakia*, UNCITRAL, 5 Mar. 2011, available on Investment Treaty Arbitration website: https://www.italaw.com/sites/default/files/case-documents/ita0027.pdf.
32. *Soufraki v. The United Arab Emirates*, Award, 7 Jul. 2004, *ICSID Reports* 12 (2007): 156 and Decision of the *Ad Hoc* Committee on the Application for Annulment of Mr Soufraki, 5 Jun. 2007,

Chapter 3: Investor Nationality under Municipal and International Law   §3.02[C]

decisions elucidate the relationship between international and municipal law in determining an investor's nationality (though a few do so negatively, e.g., *CSOB v. the Slovak Republic* and *AFT v. Slovak Republic*, by failing to consider municipal law).

[1] Fakes v. Turkey *and Effective Nationality of Individuals*

Fakes v. Turkey considered the issue of dual nationality of individuals, and the consequences, if any, of lack of effective home State nationality in an investment arbitration dispute.[33] Fakes alleged breaches of the Netherlands-Turkey BIT in connection with Turkey's failure to provide fair and equitable treatment to him, and the expropriation of his investment in a telecommunications company.

Turkey countered that Fakes was a dual Dutch and Jordanian national, and on that basis, challenged the effectiveness of Fakes's Dutch nationality. The tribunal rejected this challenge (though it ruled that it did not have jurisdiction on the grounds that Fakes had not made an investment in accordance with ICSID Convention Article 25(1).

The nationality question was whether the express exclusion from jurisdiction in ICSID Article 25(2)(a) of dual nationals who hold the nationality of the host State was applicable to dual nationals who (a) hold the nationality of a Contracting State, and (b) do not hold the nationality of the host State, but (c) hold a nationality of a third State. Fakes was Jordanian and Dutch. If he had been Jordanian and Turkish, his dual nationality clearly would have made him ineligible for BIT protection.[34]

The tribunal observed that during the negotiation of the ICSID Convention, a delegate from Guatemala suggested including the requirement of effective nationality, but this suggestion was not adopted.[35] Thus, the ICSID drafters did not subject access to the ICSID jurisdiction to the effective nationality test.[36] Additionally, the text of the relevant BIT did not require an investor's nationality to be effective.[37] Contracting States are free to require elements in addition to municipal law, but in the absence of such elements, nationality is determined in accordance with municipal law.[38]

The effective nationality argument had been articulated in the *Nottebohm*[39] case and in *Decision A/18* of the Iran-US Claims Tribunal. In *Nottebohm*, the ICJ declared Liechtenstein's application against Guatemala inadmissible stating that nationality is determined within the domestic jurisdiction of the State, but when two States conferred their nationality upon the same individual, the conflict has to be resolved. To do so, the

---

available on the Investment Treaty Arbitration website: http://ita.law.uvic.ca/documents/SoufrakiAnnulment.pdf. This decision was adopted by the majority of the panel.
33. *See* on effective nationality and the ICSID Convention, Reed and Davis, Ch. 6, III, A, in *International Investment Law*, eds M. Bungenberg et al. (C.H. Beck-Hart-Nomos, 2015), 614–637 at 626.
34. *Saba Fakes v. Turkey*, Award, para. 62.
35. Report of the Executive Directors on the ICSID Convention in *ILM* 4 (1965), 524, para.29.
36. *Saba Fakes v. Turkey*, Award, para. 63.
37. *Saba Fakes v. Turkey*, Award, para. 64.
38. *Ibid.*
39. *Nottebohm Case (second phase)*, Judgment of 6 Apr. 1955, *I.C.J. Reports* 1955, p. 4.

ICJ chose 'real and effective nationality' as the test, which meant determining the State to which the individual had the stronger ties. Conferring relevance to effective nationality did not undermine the municipal law determination, the ICJ noted. Since Nottebohm had stronger ties to Guatemala the application failed.

It is important to keep in mind, as indicated above, that the test articulated in *Nottebohm* has not been retained in the ILC Articles on Diplomatic Protection, where Article 4 does not require a state to prove an effective or genuine link between the State and the individual.[40] The *Fakes* tribunal noted that in *Nottebohm* the issue was whether a State with no 'genuine link' with a person could exercise diplomatic protection on behalf of such individual, which was different from the question whether an individual can bring a direct claim against a State notwithstanding that the individual has two nationalities.[41] Moreover, in the context of investment treaty protection, the States waived their right to diplomatic protection and therefore the rules of customary international law applicable in diplomatic protection are not applicable in investment disputes.[42] Similarly, the *Siag*[43] and *Champion Trading*[44] tribunals had previously held that Article 25 of the ICSID Convention does not permit a test of effective nationality.[45] They did so on the grounds that the ICSID Convention expressly excludes the operation of rules that may be relevant in the context of diplomatic protection.

The distinction between ICSID nationality and diplomatic protection nationality that the *Fakes*, *Siag*, and *Champion Trading* tribunals emphasized is also consistent with Broches's description, in 1972, of the protections for States associated with nationality under the ICSID Convention. Broches pointed to Article 27 of the ICSID Convention, which suspends the right of diplomatic protection of the home State whose national is submitting an investment arbitration dispute. Further, Article 54 of the ICSID convention requires the Contracting States to recognize an ICSID award as binding and to enforce it as if it were a final judgment of their national court. Therefore, the ICSID nationality element ensures that the host State is able to enforce an award in its favour on the assumption that the investor's home State, where presumably the majority of the investor's assets are, is a Contracting State.[46]

---

40. The ILC Articles on Diplomatic Protection contain a provision on multiple nationalities, Art. 7 states: 'A State of nationality may not exercise diplomatic protection in respect of a person against a State of which that person is also a national unless the nationality of the former State is predominant, both at the date of injury and at the date of the official presentation of the claim'. However, this Article does not concern multiple nationalities with third States.
41. *Saba Fakes v. Turkey*, Award, para. 68.
42. *Id.*, para. 69, quoting Sinclair, 'ICSID's Nationality Requirement', in *Investment Treaty Arbitration and International Law*, ed. Weiler (Juris, 2008), 86–88.
43. *Siag and Vecchi v. Egypt*, Decision on jurisdiction, 11 Apr. 2007, available on the Investment Treaty Arbitration website http://www.italaw.com/sites/default/files/case-documents/ita0785.pdf. This decision was adopted by the majority of the panel.
44. *Champion Trading company et al v. Egypt*, Decision on Jurisdiction, 21 Oct. 2003, available on the Investment Treaty Arbitration website: http://www.italaw.com/sites/default/files/case-documents/ita0147.pdf.
45. *Id.*, p. 16 and *Siag and Vecchi v. Egypt* paras 198–201.
46. Broches, 'The Convention on the Settlement of Investment Disputes Between States and Nationals of other States', *supra*, at 356.

Broches also commented that the ICSID Convention excluded the possibility of a confrontation between a State and an investor who holds the nationality of that State. On the other hand, 'no concern was expressed'[47] in the case where one of the nationalities of a dual national was that of a State not party to the Convention or of a third Contracting State. However, he concluded that investment tribunals might have to decide whether a nationality of convenience or a nationality acquired involuntarily by an investor should be disregarded.[48]

The *Fakes* tribunal stated that a nationality of convenience acquired for the purposes of bringing an investment claim or a nationality passed over several generations with no ties with the home State should be disregarded for the purposes of Article 25 of the ICSID Convention. In the case in dispute, however, these elements were not present, and thus the effective condition of the nationality that Fakes claimed was considered immaterial.

Fakes, then, stands in a line of cases that confirms that the nationality of an investor is determined in accordance with municipal law, which may only be disregarded in very exceptional cases. Article 25 of the ICSID Convention excludes from jurisdiction investors with dual nationality (home State and host State), but other dual or multiple nationalities are acceptable, unless there is a provision to the contrary in the relevant BIT. Moreover, the principle of effective nationality is inapplicable in the ICSID context.

[2]   Tokios Tokeles v. Ukraine *and the Question of Tenuous Links to the State of Incorporation*

In *Tokios Tokeles v. Ukraine* the Claimant, an advertising, publishing, and printing company incorporated in Lithuania, claimed a breach of the Lithuania-Ukraine BIT. Ukraine objected to jurisdiction, arguing that the Claimant was not a 'genuine entity' of Lithuania because it was owned and controlled by Ukrainian nationals and had its administrative headquarters in Ukraine.[49] Ukraine requested that the tribunal pierce the corporate veil and determine nationality according to the location of the Claimant's shareholders and headquarters. Ukraine further argued that the Claimant had not made a foreign investment in Ukraine because the origin of its funds was Ukrainian.[50]

The tribunal majority rejected the State's jurisdictional challenge. It reasoned as follows:

---

47. *Id.*, at p. 357.
48. *Id.*, at p. 358.
49. *Tokios Tokeles v. Ukraine*, Decision on Jurisdiction, para. 21. *See*, among several commentaries concerning this decision, Tercier and Tran Thang, *Criteria to Determine Investor Nationality (Juridical Persons)*, in *Building International Investment Law, The First 50 Years of ICSID*, eds Kinnear et al. (Kluwer, 2015).
50. *Id.*, para. 72.

(i) 'The use of a control test to define the nationality of a corporation to *restrict* the jurisdiction of the Centre would be inconsistent with the object and purpose of Article 25(2)(b)', which is to expand ICSID jurisdiction.[51]
(ii) The Contracting Parties were free to define their consent to jurisdiction and could have invoked different tests to identify the investor's nationality. However, once consent to ICSID is given, the tribunal must implement it and identify the investor's nationality on the basis of the criterion that the Contracting Parties put into place in the BIT.[52]
(iii) The BIT defined investors as 'any entity established' in Lithuania.[53] Therefore the Contracting States selected the State of incorporation and not the State of location of the headquarters or the nationality of the shareholders as the relevant criterion to establish investors' nationality. It was not for the tribunal to impose limits on the scope of protection that were not set out expressly in the BIT.[54] The BIT's approach to nationality was 'consistent with the predominant approach in international law'.[55]

The dissenting opinion of the tribunal president, Weil, posited a different understanding of substantive law relating to the definition of 'investment' and 'investor' in ICSID cases. Weil stated that the ICSID mechanism encourages *international* investment and therefore its scope and application could not be extended beyond the limits contained in the Convention: it 'is only the *international* investment that the Convention governs, that is to say, an investment implying a transborder flux of capital'.[56] He further stated that 'when it comes to ascertaining the *international* character of an investment, the origin of the capital *is* relevant, and even decisive' [emphasis in the original].[57] According to this reasoning, each individual ICSID tribunal must determine whether the facts of the case support a finding of 'international investment',[58] since ICISD procedures are applicable '*only* to genuinely international investment'.[59]

Weil agreed with the tribunal majority that the ICSID Convention does not define corporate nationality. However, he contended that 'it cannot be the case that this definition is left to the discretion of the Parties, because it is not for the Parties to extend the jurisdiction of ICSID beyond what the Convention provides for'.[60] The ICSID settlement dispute mechanism is 'not meant for investments made in a State by its own citizens'.[61]

---

51. *Id.*, para. 46.
52. *Id.*, paras 25–26, 39.
53. *Id.*, para. 28.
54. *Id.*, para. 36.
55. *Id.*, para. 70.
56. *Id.*, Dissenting Opinion, paras. 19, 30.
57. *Id.*, para. 20.
58. *Ibid.*
59. *Id.*, paras 19, 24.
60. *Id.*, para. 16.
61. *Id.*, para. 19.

The dissent sought to create an objective notion of investor that overrides the consent of the Contracting Parties and their reference to municipal law. However, as a matter of international law, this attempt at 'objectivity' is misguided when States do not narrow the definition of the investor's nationality. In the absence of such limitation there is no basis under international law for an arbitral tribunal to determine that an objective notion should be implied, and thereby insert elements that the BIT does not contain.

The central flaw in Weil's reasoning is his failure to recognize that there is no *a priori* category of 'international' investor. The ICSID Convention refers to the Agreement of the Contracting Parties in defining the concept of investor, and an arbitral tribunal cannot (or at least should not) override the parties' discretion by determining jurisdiction on the basis of flexible and autonomous criteria that identify an investor's nationality. The application by tribunals of so-called objective criteria that conflict with the provisions of the relevant investment treaty renders jurisdictional determinations under the ICSID Convention and Rules unpredictable, and improperly remits to a tribunal's discretion the ability to override the plain meaning of international treaties.

Moreover, the Weil approach to investor nationality would not even have found support in the ILC Articles on Diplomatic Protection, which uphold the criterion of incorporation, and only provide for consideration of other links where the seat and controlling shareholders point to a *third* State. In any event, the ILC Articles could not have assisted the *Tokios Tokeles* tribunal, since they are inconsistent with the Lithuania-Ukraine BIT and the ICSID Convention. The BIT was neither silent nor unclear on the question of nationality; therefore, there was no room to apply other criteria inconsistent with those expressly started in the BIT. The BIT specified incorporation as the relevant criterion, and did not refer to a control test. This criterion was satisfied in accordance with the relevant municipal law. Further, on the issue of nationality the ILC Articles on Diplomatic Protection do not themselves necessarily reflect customary law, and instead adopt a criterion *de lege ferenda*, on which, as the ICJ recognized in the *Barcelona Traction* case, no broad consensus exists.

Subsequent cases have confirmed the *Tokios Tokeles* majority's approach to the determination of a corporation's nationality. For example, in *KT Asia Investment Group BV v. Kazakhstan*,[62] the tribunal observed that the ICSID Convention does not impose any particular test for the nationality of juridical persons, giving Contracting States

---

62. *KT Asia Investment Group BV v. Kazakhstan*, Award, 17 Oct. 2013, available on the Investment Treaty Arbitration website: http://www.italaw.com/sites/default/files/case-documents/italaw 3006.pdf. *See* recently *Gold Reserve v. Venezuela*, Award, 22 Sep. 2014, available on the Investment Treaty Arbitration website: http://www.italaw.com/sites/default/files/case-documents/italaw4009.pdf and *Rompetrol Group v. Romania*, Decision on Respondent's Preliminary Objection on Jurisdiction and Admissibility, 18 Apr. 2008, available on the Investment Treaty Arbitration website: http://www.italaw.com/sites/default/files/case-documents/ita0717.pdf. See *contra*, *Venoklim Holding BV v. Venezuela*, Award, 3 Apr. 2015, available on the Investment Treaty Arbitration website: http://www.italaw.com/sites/default/files/case-documents/italaw4229.pdf. *See also TSA v. Argentina*, Award, 19 Dec. 2008, available on the Investment Treaty Arbitration website: http://www.italaw.com/sites/default/files/case-documents/ita0874.pdf. The latter case, although with a different factual matrix, endorsed Professor Weil's Dissenting Opinion.

broad discretion to define nationality in accordance with the relevant investment treaty.[63] The tribunal rejected the application of the principle of 'real and effective nationality', since the ordinary meaning – pursuant to Article 31(1) of the Vienna Convention on the Law of the Treaties – of the words contained in the relevant BIT was clear and indicated that the place of incorporation would establish the nationality of legal persons.[64] The *KT Asia* tribunal further stated that there was no basis for applying the rules of diplomatic protection in order to trump the regime created by the investment treaty: 'the nationality of a corporation is a legal construct and that in the absence of any obligatory test for the nationality of corporations in international law, it falls to the Contracting States of the relevant investment treaty to define the nationality of a corporation as they see fit'.[65] In *KT Asia* the relevant treaty referred to municipal law. No piercing of the veil is permitted, and no diplomatic protection principles apply.

[3] Plama Consortium v. Bulgaria, *Corporate 'Control', and Denial of Benefits Clauses*

Soon after the *Tokios Tokeles* decision, the *Plama Consortium v. Bulgaria* tribunal[66] issued a decision concerning the 'control test' for corporate nationality under the ECT, which expressly provides for such a test.[67] Article 17 of the ECT states that a Contracting State may 'deny the advantages' of Part III (which provides that the Contracting States undertake to accord fair and equitable treatment and 'constant protection and security' to investments) to legal entities if nationals of a third State own or control that entity and the entity has no substantial business activities in the Contracting State in which it is organized.[68]

---

63. *Id.*, para. 113.
64. *Id.*, paras 114–116.
65. *Id.*, para. 128.
66. *Plama Consortium v. Bulgaria*, Decision on Jurisdiction. *See also Aguas del Tunari v. Bolivia*, Decision on Jurisdiction, 21 Oct. 2005, *ICSID Rev. – FILJ* 20 (2005): 450, where the disputed question was whether the concept of control required (a) the legal potential to control or (b) the actual exercise of control. The tribunal majority opted for the concept of legal control.
67. *Id.*, *Plama Consortium v. Bulgaria*, para. 1.
68. ECT Art. 17:

> Each Contracting Party reserves the right to deny the advantages of this Part to: (1) a legal entity if citizens or nationals of a third state own or control such entity and if that entity has no substantial business activities in the Area of the Contracting Party in which it is organized; or
> (2) an Investment, if the denying Contracting Party establishes that such Investment is an Investment of an Investor of a third state as to which the denying Contracting Party:
>   (a) does not maintain a diplomatic relationship; or
>   (b) adopts or maintain measures that: (i)prohibit transactions with Investors of that state; or(ii)would be violated or circumvented if the benefits of this Part were accorded to Investors of that state or to their Investments'.
>   (i) prohibit transactions with Investors of that state; or
>   (ii) would be violated or circumvented if the benefits of this Part were accorded to Investors of that state or to their Investments.

The ECT control test is in effect a denial of benefits clause, which aims to exclude from investment treaty protection nationals, and in particular legal entities, with substantial connections to a third State not party to the investment arbitration dispute.[69] These clauses often require an economic link between the company and its home State represented by 'substantial business activities' or, as in the 2012 US Model BIT, exclude companies owned or controlled by investors from a country that a Contracting State does not entertain diplomatic relations with, or that a Contracting State prohibits transactions with.

Denial of benefits clauses, originally developed to deny diplomatic protection and exclude from protection 'enemy companies',[70] were imported into the investment protection arena to exclude investors without an economic link to their State of incorporation. Prominent examples of such clauses are in, as indicated above, the 2012 US Model BIT (Article 17) and Article 17 of the ECT.[71] Although these clauses share the same general purpose of ensuring that the home State national actually has a connection to the home State beyond mere incorporation or citizenship, the wording of the clauses may vary substantially, leading to varying interpretations.[72] For example, the Central American Free Trade Agreement (CAFTA-DR), Article 10.12.2,[73] contains a denial of benefits clause that the *Pac Rim v. El Salvador* tribunal interpreted as placing a heavy burden on the Respondent State to establish: (i) that the US Claimant had no substantial business activities in US territory (beyond mere form); and (ii) either

---

69. *See inter alia*: Gastrell and Le Cannu, 'Procedural Requirements of "Denial-of-Benefits" Clauses in Investment Treaties: A Review of Arbitral Decisions', ICSID *Review* 30(1) (2015), 78–97; Feldman, *Denial of Benefits after* Plama v. Bulgaria, in *Building International Investment Law, The First 50 Years of ICSID*, eds Kinnear et al. (Kluwer Law International, 2015), 477–494; Mistelis and Baltag, 'Denial of Benefits and Article 17 of the Energy Charter Treaty' in *Penn. State L. Rev.* 113(4) (2009), 1301–1321; Hoffmann, 'Denial of Benefits' Ch. 6 G, in *International Investment Law*, eds M. Bungenberg et al. (C.H. Beck-Hart-Nomos, 2015), 598–613; Douglas, *The International Law of Investment Claims* (Cambridge, 2009), 468–472.
70. Mistelis and Baltag, *supra*, p. 1302.
71. Article 17:

    Each Contracting Party reserves the right to deny the advantages of this Part to:
    1. (1) a legal entity if citizens or nationals of a third state own or control such entity and if that entity has no substantial business activities in the Area of the Contracting Party in which it is organised; or
    2. (2) an Investment, if the denying Contracting Party establishes that such Investment is an Investment of an Investor of a third state with or as to which the denying Contracting Party:
        (a) does not maintain a diplomatic relationship; or
        (b) adopts or maintains measures that:
            (i) prohibit transactions with Investors of that state; or
            (ii) would be violated or circumvented if the benefits of this Part were accorded to Investors of that state or to their Investments.

72. *See* on the differences between the wordings: *Plama v. Bulgaria*, Decision on Jurisdiction *supra*, para. 156.
73. Article 10.12.2: 'deny the benefits of [Chapter 10 of CAFTA] to an investor of another Party that is an enterprise of such other Party and to investments of that investor if the enterprise has no substantial business activities in the territory of any Party, other than the denying Party and persons of a non-Party, or of the denying Party, own or control the enterprise'.

(a) that the Claimant was owned by persons of a non-CAFTA-DR Party or (b) that the Claimant was controlled by persons of a non-CAFTA-DR Party.[74]

A number of investment treaty tribunals have considered denial of benefits clauses.[75] Among the most substantial significant issues determined in these cases, discussed below, are notification requirements that the host State must satisfy as well as the link between the legal entity and the third State that must be shown to obtain protection of the clause. In each instance, the wording of the particular clause is of course the interpretive starting point, which is a matter of international law pursuant to the Vienna Convention on the Law of Treaties. However, determination of notice and links should involve application of municipal law, although a number of decisions do not expressly undertake a municipal law analysis.

Plama remains an important interpretation of the ECT notification requirement. Plama Consortium (Plama), a Cyprus company, purchased the shares of Plama AD, a Bulgarian company that owned an oil refinery in Bulgaria. Plama filed a request for arbitration with ICSID, alleging that the Bulgarian government deliberately created serious difficulties for the refinery and refused to adopt or unreasonably delayed the adoption of adequate corrective measures. Jurisdiction was founded on the ECT and ICSID Convention.

---

74. *Pac Rim Cayman LLC v. Republic of El Salvador*, para. 4.61.
75. *See*, among others, *Generation Ukraine v. Ukraine*, Award 16 Sep. 2003 available on the Investment Treaty Arbitration website: http://www.italaw.com/sites/default/files/case-documents/ita0358.pdf; *Petrobart v. Kyrgyz Republic*, Award 29 Mar. 2005 available on the Investment Treaty Arbitration website: http://www.italaw.com/sites/default/files/case-documents/ita0628.pdf; *Pan American v. Argentina*, Decision on Preliminary Objections, 27 Jul. 2006, available on the Investment Treaty Arbitration website: http://www.italaw.com/sites/default/files/case-documents/ita0616.pdf; *Plama v. Bulgaria*, Decision on Jurisdiction, 8 Feb. 2005, and Award, 27 Aug. 2008; *AMTO v. Ukraine*, Award, 26 Mar. 2008, available on the Investment Treaty Arbitration website: https://www.italaw.com/sites/default/files/case-documents/ita0030.pdf; *Empresa Electrica del Ecuador v. Ecuador*, Award 2 Jun. 2009, available on the Investment Treaty Arbitration website: https://www.italaw.com/sites/default/files/case-documents/ita0274.pdf; *Hulley Enterprises Limited (Cyprus) v. The Russian Federation*, Interim Award on Jurisdiction and Admissibility, 30 Nov. 2009, available on the Investment Treaty Arbitration website: https://www.italaw.com/sites/default/files/case-documents/ita0411.pdf; *Veteran Petroleum Limited (Cyprus) v. The Russian Federation*, Interim Award on Jurisdiction and Admissibility 30 Nov. 2009, available on the Investment Treaty Arbitration website: https://www.italaw.com/sites/default/files/case-documents/ita0891.pdf; *Yukos Universal Limited (Isle of Man) v. The Russian Federation*, Interim Award on Jurisdiction and Admissibility, 30 Nov. 2009, available on the Investment Treaty Arbitration website: https://www.italaw.com/sites/default/files/case-documents/ita0910.pdf; *Liman Caspian Oil BV and NCL Dutch Investment BV v. Republic of Kazakhstan*, Award 22 Jun. 2010, available on the Investment Treaty Arbitration website: https://www.italaw.com/sites/default/files/case-documents/italaw1429.pdf; *Ulysseas Inc v. The Republic of Ecuador*, Interim Award 28 Sep. 2010, available on the Investment Treaty Arbitration website: https://www.italaw.com/sites/default/files/case-documents/ita1045.pdf; *Pac Rim Cayman LLC v. Republic of El Salvador*, Decision on Respondent's Jurisdictional Objections, 1 Jun. 2012, available on the Investment Treaty Arbitration website, https://www.italaw.com/sites/default/files/case-documents/ita0935.pdf; *Anatolie Stati, Gabriel Stati, Ascom Group SA and Terra Raf Trans Trading Ltd v. Kazakhstan*, Award 19 Dec. 2013, available on the Investment Treaty Arbitration website: http://www.italaw.com/sites/default/files/case-documents/italaw3083.pdf; *Guaracachi America, Inc and Rurelec PLC v. The Plurinational State of Bolivia*, Award 31 Jan. 2014, available on the Investment Treaty Arbitration website: http://www.italaw.com/sites/default/files/case-documents/italaw3293.pdf.

After receiving the request for arbitration, Bulgaria sent a letter in which it exercised its rights under Article 17(1) of the ECT, the denial of benefits provision, on the ground that Plama was a 'mailbox company'. The State then asserted that, because Article 17 of the ECT did not protect Plama, there was no consent to submit disputes concerning alleged breaches of the ECT to ICSID, and consequently no basis for the arbitral tribunal's jurisdiction.

The tribunal rejected Bulgaria's argument, and found as follows:

(i) The Contracting State's exercise of its right of denial under Article 17(1) operated with prospective effect only.[76]

(ii) Since Plama had no substantial business activities in Cyprus, the second limb of Article 17(1) favoured of the State's position. However, given its ruling on the perspective effect of Article 17, the tribunal's finding on this issue did not alter its jurisdictional decision.

(iii) The tribunal declined to make findings regarding the first limb of Article 17(1) (i.e., whether Plama was owned or controlled by nationals of a third State not party to the ECT), and reserved its decision on this point for a later stage of the proceedings[77] – although even this reservation provided no support for the defence of the State on liability.

Although ECT Article 17(1) attributes relevance to the control exercised by the investor and to the location of the entity's exercise of its 'substantial activity', under the *Plama* tribunal's ruling the State must nonetheless notify the investor that it will exercise its right of denial of treaty benefits, and this notice will not have retroactive effect. The tribunal considered prospective notification necessary because the State's exercise of its Article 17 rights must be made known to investors. The tribunal therefore suggested that a Contracting State should make a general declaration of exercise of its right under Article 17(1) in an official gazette, in an investment law, or in an exchange of letters with a particular investor or class of investor.[78]

The *Plama* tribunal's Article 17 'prospective effect' determination was based on its interpretation of the Article's wording, pursuant to the Vienna Convention. This interpretation took into account a putative investor's expectations of enjoying the advantages of Part III of the ECT *unless* the State exercises its right under Article 17(1).

The *Waste Management* tribunal characterized denial of benefits clauses (specifically referring to NAFTA Article 1113) as possible 'protection shopping' – that is, these clauses are the States' counter to investors' 'treaty shopping' efforts, whereby investors restructure their investments to incorporate in a State in which they have no other interest but to derive treaty protection from the host State (assuming that a specific dispute has not already arisen, in which case restructuring may constitute an abuse of rights). As the *Waste Management* tribunal explained, protection shopping includes situations where the substantial control or ownership of an enterprise of a Party lies with an investor of a non-Party State, and the enterprise has no substantial

---

76. *Plama Consortium v. Bulgaria*, Decision on Jurisdiction, paras 162, 165, 179, and 240.
77. *Id.*, paras 179 and 240.
78. *Id.*, para. 157.

business activities in the territory of the Party under whose law it is constituted or organized. Denial of benefits clauses address situations where the investor is simply an intermediary for interests substantially foreign, and it allows investment protections to be withdrawn in such cases (subject to prior notification and consultation).[79]

In *Hulley Enterprises Limited (Cyprus) v. The Russian Federation*, the tribunal commented on the reasoning behind notification, in stating that ECT Article 17(1) does not deny *simpliciter* the advantages of Part III of the ECT to a legal entity if the citizens or nationals of a third State own or control such entity and if that entity has no substantial business in the Contracting Party in which it is organized. Rather, it reserves the right of each Contracting Party to deny the advantages of that Part III of the treaty to such an entity. That is why, to effect denial, the Contracting Party must exercise the right through notification (and in this case, the tribunal held that the Russian Federation had not done so).[80] Similarly, the *Liman v. Kazakhstan* tribunal ruled that ECT Article 17(1) had to be interpreted as conferring to the Contracting State the right of denial of benefits only when the right was exercised in an explicit way; thus, the notification had a prospective and not retroactive effect.[81] Retroactive notification was incompatible with the object and purpose of the ECT to promote long-term cooperation in the energy field, which required that an investor must be able to rely on the advantages under the ECT, as long as the host State had not explicitly invoked the right to deny such advantages.

However, the tribunal in *Ulysseas v. Ecuador* reached the opposite conclusion in interpreting a denial of benefits clause in a BIT. The tribunal stated that it saw no valid reasons to exclude retrospective effects. The tribunal found that this would not cause uncertainties as to the legal relations under the BIT, since the investor knew from the time it made its investment that the State may operate the clause. The tribunal concluded that the protection afforded by the BIT is subject during the life of the investment to the possibility of a denial of the BIT's advantages by the host State.[82] Similarly, in *Pac Rim v. El Salvador*, discussed above, the tribunal held that CAFTA-DR does not provide a time limit for a Contracting Party to deny benefits under the Agreement.[83]

The tribunal in *Rurelec v. Bolivia* provided further background on why States should not be held to a notification requirement. The tribunal observed that the consent by the host State to arbitration itself is conditional and thus may be denied by it, provided that the State can demonstrate certain objective requirements concerning the putative investor. All investors are aware of the possibility of a denial of benefits,

---

79. *Waste Management, Inc v. United Mexican States*, Award, 30 Apr. 2004 available on the Investment Treaty Arbitration website: http://www.italaw.com/sites/default/files/case-documents/ita0900.pdf.
80. *Hulley Enterprises Limited (Cyprus) v. The Russian Federation*, para. 455. Similar conclusions were reached in *Veteran Petroleum Limited (Cyprus) v. The Russian Federation, cit.* and *Yukos Universal Limited (Isle of Man) v. The Russian Federation, cit.*
81. *Liman Caspian Oil BV and NCL Dutch Investment BV v. Republic of Kazakhstan*, paras 224 and 225.
82. *Ulysseas Inc v. The Republic of Ecuador*, para. 172.
83. *Pac Rim Cayman LLC v. Republic of El Salvador*, para. 4.83.

Chapter 3: Investor Nationality under Municipal and International Law §3.02[C]

such that no legitimate expectations can be frustrated by its exercise.[84] In *Rurelec*, the investment predated the entry into force of the BIT, which, the tribunal noted, showed that the investor did not invest in Bolivia with an investment treaty protection in mind. The tribunal acknowledged that this approach places the investor in an uncertain position, since the investor will not know if there will be a denial of benefits until the investor triggers a legal proceeding. At the same time, however, a denial should not ever come as a surprise, since the BIT is not secret and the investor opted to use an investment vehicle controlled by a company of a third country, which had no substantial business activities in the territory of the Contracting Party under whose laws it was constituted or organized.[85]

Apart from the issue of notification and timing, there have been several significant decisions interpreting denial of benefits clauses where the text is unclear or is worded very generally. For example, in *Generation Ukraine v. Ukraine*, the tribunal confronted a clause (in the US-Ukraine BIT) containing an ambiguity, which allowed the State to argue that the right to deny the benefits could extend to companies without substantial activities in the place of incorporation regardless of whether they were subject to 'third country control'. The issue, therefore, was whether Ukraine could deny benefits simply by showing the absence of substantial activities or whether the State also had to show that the Claimant-US company was subject to third country control. The tribunal interpreted the clause in the light of the US letter of submittal from the Department of State to the President, which indicated that third party control was a condition precedent to exercising the right of denial (Ukraine did not produce any evidence to the contrary). On this basis, and since the State could not show third country control, the denial of benefits clause was not triggered (and there was no need to consider whether the Claimant in fact conducted substantial business activities in the US).[86]

In interpreting the term 'substantial business activity' (ECT Article 17 (1)), the *Amto* tribunal held that the 'ECT does not contain a definition of "substantial"', nor does the Final Act of the European Energy Charter Conference, which could otherwise serve as guidance. The tribunal reasoned that since the purpose of Article 17(1) is to exclude from ECT protection investors adopting a nationality of convenience, 'substantial' in this context means 'of substance, and not merely of form'. But it does not mean 'large', and the materiality rather than the magnitude of the business activity is the decisive question. The tribunal was satisfied that the Claimant had substantial business activity in Latvia, on the basis of 'its investment related activities conducted from premises in Latvia, and involving the employment of a small but permanent staff'.[87]

The above review of decisions on denial of benefits clauses indicates a weak basis for any emerging *jurisprudence constante*. The jurisprudence on notification is divided between an approach that requires notice (albeit without any express requirement in

---

84. *Guaracachi America, Inc and Rurelec PLC v. The Plurinational State of Bolivia, cit.*, paras 372 and 388.
85. *Id.*, para. 388.
86. *Id.*, p. 48.
87. *AMTO v. Ukraine*, para. 69.

the clause) and attributes to such notice only prospective effects (*Plama, Yukos, Liman*), and more recent cases (*Ulysseas, Rurelac and Pac Rim*) that accept retrospective effects in an attempt to take into account the difficulty for the State to issue any notice before a dispute arises. States should be prompted from these cases to adopt general notices of denial of benefits in order to derive retrospective protection.

It is noteworthy that tribunals' interpretation of these clauses (particularly interpretations that have taken into account the right of denial from the State's perspective) do not seek (at least not expressly) to examine whether municipal law might be relevant. However, considering whether, as a factual matter, 'substantial business activity' exists in the home State or whether 'control' is exerted from a third State, tribunals are applying municipal law and should acknowledge that they are doing so – their decisions will be more soundly reasoned.

[4] Ceskoslovenska Obchodni Banka A.S. v. The Slovak Republic ('CSOB v. Slovakia') *and the Question of State Control of Corporations*

In *CSOB v. Slovakia*, Slovakia argued that since 99% of CSOB's shares were owned by the Czech and Slovak Republic, it was a state agency of the Czech Republic and therefore did not qualify as an independent commercial entity.

The tribunal rejected this jurisdictional challenge on three grounds:

(i) The concept of nationality was 'not intended to be limited to privately owned companies, but to embrace also wholly or partially government owned companies'.[88]

(ii) The determinative test to disqualify a company wholly or partially owned by a government was whether such company was 'acting as an agent for the government or is discharging an essentially governmental function'.[89]

(iii) The determination of whether a company discharges governmental functions is based on 'the nature of [its] activities and not their purpose'. Because CSOB was performing international banking activities, even though it was 'promoting the governmental policies or purposes', these activities were deemed commercial.[90]

The tribunal achieved the correct result in denying Slovakia's jurisdictional objection. However, its analysis was flawed. The tribunal failed to apply Czech law to determine whether CSOB was a Czech entity or a Czech governmental agent. Indeed, the tribunal did not mention municipal law; it simply relied on a criterion that applies in the context of State Responsibility.[91] In this case, however, there was no basis for

---

88. *Ceskoslovenska Obchodni Banka A.S. v. The Slovak Republic*, Decision on Objections to Jurisdiction, para. 16.
89. *Id.*, para. 17.
90. *Id.*, para. 20.
91. *See* Crawford, *The International Law Commission's Articles on State Responsibility*, 5, Art. 100.

any reliance on the doctrine of State Responsibility: there was no wrongful act to be attributed to the Czech Republic, and ILC Article 5 on State Responsibility was therefore irrelevant. [92] The question was whether the tribunal had jurisdiction under Article 25 of the ICSID Convention, and whether CSOB was a national of a Contracting State. This question had to be answered by addressing whether CSOB was a Czech legal entity under Czech internal law.

[5] AFT v. Slovak Republic and Tenaris S.A v. Venezuela: *The Concept of Corporate 'Seat'*

A number of investment treaties require both that the putative legal entity-investor be incorporated in the home Contracting State and have its 'seat' or 'headquarters' in the home State. Some treaties contain the further requirement that the company have substantial business activities in the home State.[93]

The issue that tribunals face is how to determine the concept of 'seat', i.e., whether the definition of this term is to be found in international law or in municipal law. This determination becomes even more intricate when the home Contracting State does not define seat in its municipal law. Significant rulings on this issue were made in *AFT v. Slovak Republic*[94] and with *Tenaris v. Venezuela*.[95]

In *AFT*, an *ad hoc* tribunal constituted under the UNCITRAL Arbitration Rules considered whether the Claimant had demonstrated that it was constituted or otherwise organized under the laws of Switzerland, had its seat in Switzerland, and performed real economic activities in Switzerland, pursuant to Article 1(1)(b) and (c) of the Czech and Slovak Federal Republic-Swiss BIT.[96] The tribunal determined that the existence of the Swiss seat had to be established pursuant to 'the meaning of

---

92. *Id.*, 92. The Commentary clarifies that '[t]he question of attribution of conduct to the State for the purposes of responsibility is to be distinguished from other international law processes by which particular organs are authorized to enter into commitments on behalf of the State'.
93. *See*, e.g., the BIT between the United Kingdom and Cameroon, dated 4 Jun. 1982, which differentiated companies incorporated in the UK from Companies incorporated in Cameron and defined legal entities: '(i) in respect of the United Kingdom: corporations, firms or associations incorporated or constituted under the law in force in any part of the United Kingdom or in any territory to which this Agreement is extended in accordance with the provisions 01 Article II; (ii) in respect of the United Republic of Cameroon: corporations firms or associations incorporated or constituted under the law in force in any part of Cameroon which have their *headquarters* in the territory of Cameroon.' [*emphasis added*] or the BIT between Switzerland and Georgia, dated 3 Jun. 2014, which requires *tout court* that legal entities organized under the law of a Contracting Party would have their seat together with substantial business activities in the territory of that contracting Party (Art. 1 (1) b).
94. *AFT v. Slovakia*, UNCITRAL, 5 Mar. 2011, available on Investment Treaty Arbitration website: https://www.italaw.com/sites/default/files/case-documents/ita0027.pdf.
95. *Tenaris SA et al. v. Venezuela*, Award, 29 Jan. 2016, available on the Investment Treaty Arbitration website: http://www.italaw.com/sites/default/files/case-documents/italaw7098.pdf.
96. *AFT v. Slovak Republic*, para. 213, quoting part of Art. 1(1)(b) and (c) of the 'Agreement between the Czech and Slovak Federal Republic and the Swiss Confederation on the Promotion of Reciprocal Protection of Investments', entered into force on 7 Aug. 1991. *See* on the protection of legal persons, Perkams, Ch. 6, III, B, in *International Investment Law*, eds M. Bungenberg et al. (C.H. Beck-Hart-Nomos, 2015), 638–652.

international business law'.⁹⁷ But the tribunal did not discuss (a) why a *renvoi* to Swiss law should not be used to determine the applicable definition of seat, or (b) how the meaning of 'international business law' should be ascertained (assuming there was any basis to look beyond Swiss law for the determination of 'Swiss seat'). On the latter point, the tribunal simply relied on a single article, by Schlemmer.⁹⁸ On the basis of that article, the tribunal held, first, that a 'business seat' means an effective centre of administration of the business operation, and then listed several elements to identify the seat: (a) the place where the company's board of directors regularly meets or the shareholders' meetings are held; (b) the place where the management of the company is sitting; (c) a certain number of employees; (d) an address with a phone and fax number for third parties to contact the company; and (e) certain expenses or overhead costs incurred for the maintenance of the physical location of the seat to indicate that a business entity is organized in a certain place.⁹⁹

Given this list of elements, it is unexplained how the definition of seat would differ from the performance of 'real economic activities', also expressly required under the Swiss-Czech Republic BIT. For the 'real economic activities' requirement, the *AFT* tribunal looked to tax returns, type of clients, and contracts entered into. But in defining the concept of seat, the tribunal also looked at contracts and turnover. For the *AFT* tribunal, it seems that the concept of 'seat' and 'real economic activities' overlapped, although it is clear from the text of the treaty that the Contracting Parties understood that 'seat' and 'real economic activities' entailed two different meanings, with seat not necessarily involving 'real economic activities'.

It should also be noted that the *AFT* tribunal's interpretation of 'seat' is at odds with the interpretation of the same term in *an obiter* by the tribunal in *Tokios Tokeles v. Ukraine*, where the term is understood to comprise statute of incorporation, registered address, and address for payment of taxes in the home State.¹⁰⁰ Consistent with the view of the *Tokios Tokeles* tribunal, the arbitrators in *Lanco v. Argentina* also referred to both the place of incorporation and seat, and did not require the extensive 'real economic activity' elements identified in *AFT v. Slovak*.¹⁰¹

---

97. *AFT v. Slovak Republic*, para. 216.
98. Schlemmer, 'Investment, Investor, Nationality and Shareholders', Ch. 2 in *International Investment Law*, eds. Muchlinski, Ortino and Schreuer (Oxford, 2008), 49, and in particular, 75.
99. *AFT v. Slovak Republic*, para. 217.
100. *Tokios Tokeles v. Ukraine*, ICSID ARB/02/18, Decision on Jurisdiction and Dissent, para. 43. 'As discussed above, the Claimant is an "investor" of Lithuania under Article 1(2)(b) of the Ukraine-Lithuania BIT based on its state of incorporation. Although not required by the text of the Treaty, an assessment of the siege social of the Claimant leads to the same conclusion. (...) Among the relevant evidence of siege social, the Claimant's registration certificate (issued by the Ministry of the Economy of Lithuania), its statute of incorporation, and each of the Claimant's "Information Notices of Payment of Foreign Investment" (registered by Ukrainian governmental authorities), all record the Claimant's address as Vilnius, Lithuania. Contrary to the assertion of the Respondent, a nationality test of siege social leads to the same result as one based on state of incorporation.' [footnotes omitted] *See generally* on incorporation and seat: Schreuer et al., *The ICSID Convention* (Cambridge University Press, 2009), 279–283.
101. *Lanco International v. Argentina*, ICSID ARB/97/6, Decision on Jurisdiction 8 Dec. 1998, ILM, Vol. 40, p. 457, at p. 472, para. 46: 'As for the nationality of the investor company, and as

Perhaps most troubling, the *AFT* tribunal interpreted the term 'seat' by adopting an alleged meaning in 'international business law', even though there is no rule of 'international business law' that defines such a term. Schlemmer's article does not identify a definition of seat in accordance with international business law. Instead, Schlemmer *advocates* requiring a real link between a corporation and the State wholly apart from the concept of seat in order to assess nationality, and also advocates lifting the corporate veil,[102] – none of which has any basis in ICSID arbitration, except when an Article 25(2)(b) (second limb) 'because of foreign control' corporation is a putative Claimant.

In short, regrettably, the *AFT* tribunal invented an 'international business law' rule – and should not have gone looking for one in the first place. Instead, it should have analysed the concept of corporate seat under Swiss law. Moreover, if the criteria of seat listed in *AFT* are always to be applicable, as one would expect from an alleged general international business law rule, this would discourage investments by small companies, which would be unable to qualify as 'investors', because of lack of extensive economic activities. By focusing on large companies, the *AFT* approach also runs counter to the well-established position in treaty cases that a company whose sole function is to own an investment can be a viable Claimant. As Vandevelde has pointed out, a seat for these companies may consist of little more than a small office.[103]

In the subsequent *Tenaris* decision, the issue was whether the Claimants' definition of seat as 'registered office' or 'statutory seat' would be accepted, thereby enabling them to establish that they had a seat in their home States (Luxembourg for one company and Portugal for the other). They argued that the seat ought to be interpreted in accordance with international law because the investment treaty did not refer to domestic law, and it would be 'inappropriate'[104] to do so, since the term seat appears with reference to the definition of investor, which is not related to a State's

---

observed by the arbitral tribunal called on to decide the case of *SocieteOuest-Africaine des Betons Industriels (SOABI) v. Republic of Senegal*, in the Decision on Jurisdiction, the ICSID Convention does not define the term "nationality", which leaves in the hands of each State the power to determine whether a company does or does not have its nationality.' As a general principle, to this end, the States use as criteria the principal place of business or where the company is established. Thus, 'a juridical person which has the nationality of the Contracting State party to the dispute, being the expression used in Article 25(2)(b) of the Convention, is a juridical person which, under the legal system of the State in question, has its principal place of business in such State or has been established under its legislation concerning company law'. *See also* two arbitral decisions where the tribunals looked at municipal law to determine whether the Claimant was an investor: *Renta 4 S.V.S.A., et al v. The Russian Federation*, Stockholm Chamber of Commerce, Case No. 024/2007, Award on Preliminary Objections, 20 Mar. 2009, available on Investment Treaty Arbitration website: https://www.italaw.com/sites/default/files/case-documents/ita1075.pdf, and *Sanum Investments Limited v. Lao People's Democratic Republic*, PCA Case No. 2013-13, UNCITRAL, Award on Jurisdiction, 13 Dec. 2013, available on Investment Treaty Arbitration website: https://www.italaw.com/sites/default/files/case-documents/italaw3322.pdf.

102. Schlemmer, *supra*, p. 79.
103. Vandevelde, *Bilateral Investment Treaties, History, Policy and Interpretation* (Oxford, 2010), 163-164: it 'may require more of an economic link than mere incorporation, but not always a great deal more'. *See also* Douglas, *The International Law of Investment Claims* (Cambridge, 2009), 314–318.
104. *Tenaris SA et al. v. Venezuela*, para. 125.

domestic provisions. Further, the Claimants contended that Venezuela's municipal law conception of seat differs from that of Luxembourg and Portugal, which would preclude the Tribunal from referring to municipal law: 'there is no concept of *"siège social"* or *"sede"* in Venezuelan law and it would be wrong to interpret a Treaty provision by reference to the domestic law of only one of the parties to the Treaty'.[105]

The *Tenaris* tribunal dismissed the potential guidance provided by the *AFT* decision on the basis that the *AFT* BIT required both seat and real economic activities, while in *Tenaris* the BIT required only seat. The tribunal defined seat as a 'legal term of art'[106] with two possible meanings: one formal and one substantial. The task was to examine the context and object and the purpose of the treaty to determine which one of the possible meanings of the term seat was applicable.[107] Since a company incorporated in Luxembourg or in Portugal had to have a registered seat, the term could not be interpreted in accordance with a formal and narrow meaning, because the term would be redundant (i.e., it would not add anything to the incorporation requirement). The term seat had to have a different meaning from the statutory seat that was necessary for the purposes of incorporation. This led the tribunal to conclude that the term meant 'effective management'.[108]

The *Tenaris* tribunal concluded with an analysis of municipal law as a 'background of its interpretation'.[109] Although it stated that it had interpreted the term under international law, the tribunal admitted that the requirements in question are 'in substance, nationality requirements. The criteria of *"siège social"* and *"sede"* are both mechanisms to determine the nationality of a company, and as such whether or not the company qualifies for coverage by a Treaty. And nationality requirements are frequently (though not exclusively) applied in light of relevant domestic law'.[110] The tribunal quickly added that the analysis of municipal law did not 'cause it to re-consider the interpretation of *"siège social"* and *"sede"*'.[111]

The problem here is that the *Tenaris* tribunal adopted the meaning of 'actual or effective management' without identifying the authority on which it relied. The 'formal' versus 'substantial' meaning choice in the decision is an academic debate, lacking precise formulation of the meaning of 'formal' and 'substantial' and omitting any sustained legal analysis. If the definition of 'seat' is to be found in international law, there must be a precise source and formulation; otherwise, every investment

---

105. *Ibid.*
106. *Id.*, para. 144.
107. *Ibid.*
108. *Id.*, paras 150–154. Para. 154: '[i]n conclusion, in order to make sense of each provision, and ensure that each term is given meaning, the tribunal determines that both *"siège social"* and *"sede"* in the Treaties in issue in this case mean the place of actual or effective management'.
109. *Id.*, para. 169.
110. *Id.*, para. 167. The tribunal quoted Douglas: 'The tribunal's jurisdiction *ratione personae* extends ... to an individual or legal entity ... which has the nationality of another of the contracting state parties in accordance with the relevant provision in the investment treaty and the municipal law of that contracting state party and, where applicable, Article 25 of the ICSID Convention.' (emphasis added) (Douglas, The International Law of Investment Claims (2009), p. 284).
111. *Id.*, para. 171.

tribunal would be able to establish its jurisdiction on the basis of unpredictable, unclear, and invented criteria.

The legal reality is that there is no definition of 'seat' in international law. Tribunals should define the term in accordance with municipal law. Failure to do so is not only incorrect as a matter of international law, but will also bring treaty tribunals into disrepute as unregulated bodies that simply make up the law as they wish it to be in an individual case.

[6]   Soufraki v. United Arab Emirates[112] *and Proof of Nationality*

In *Soufraki*, the Respondent State challenged the individual investor's Italian nationality, and the tribunal had to examine Italian law to decide the challenge. The tribunal stated that nationality was within 'the domestic jurisdiction of the State, which settles by its own legislation the rules relating to the acquisition (and loss) of its nationality'.[113] As to *how* to apply the relevant municipal law, the tribunal emphasized that it 'will accord great weight to the nationality law of the State in question and to the interpretation and application of that law by its authorities'.[114] However, great weight does not mean complete deference.

The ICSID Convention's *travaux préperatoires* contain a lengthy debate as to how to determine nationality.[115] The Preliminary Draft referred to a certificate of nationality granted by the home State, but this reference was dropped.[116] Delegates pointed out that a certificate of nationality should not be more than *prima facie* evidence, which became the prevailing view.[117] That, in fact, is how the *Soufraki* tribunal proceeded in analysing the challenge before it.

The *Soufraki* tribunal held that the Claimant failed to discharge his burden of proof, because he did not demonstrate that he was an Italian national under Italian law.[118] The conclusion of the Italian authorities that he was an Italian national was not dispositive. Annulment proceedings upheld the award.[119] This case provides clear guidance on the issue of how a tribunal should apply municipal law: the tribunal is to avail itself of the interpretation and application of the relevant provisions by the relevant State authorities, but then must make its own decision.

---

112. *Soufraki v. United Arab Emirates*, Award, 7 Jul. 2004, available on Investment Treaty Arbitration website at https://www.italaw.com/sites/default/files/case-documents/ita0799.pdf.
113. *Id.*, para. 55.
114. *Ibid.*
115. Tercier and Tran Thang, 'Criteria to Determine Investor Nationality (Juridical Persons)', in *Building International Investment Law, The First 50 Years of ICSID*, eds Kinnear et al., 153–161.
116. *Id.*, pp. 153–154.
117. Broches, 'The Convention on the Settlement of Investment Disputes Between States and Nationals of other States' at 357.
118. *Soufraki v. United Arab Emirates*, para. 81.
119. *Soufraki v. United Arab Emirates*, Decision of the *Ad Hoc* Committee, 5 Jun. 2007, available on Investment Treaty Arbitration website at https://www.italaw.com/sites/default/files/case-documents/ita0800.pdf.

However, the applicability of municipal law does not imply that international law has no role.[120] Precisely because the home State's certificate is only *prima facie* evidence of nationality in the investment treaty context, it is clear that international law retains investigative 'oversight'. The Annulment Committee in *Soufraki* observed that the ICSID tribunal could make an independent determination of the nationality of the Claimant, and was not bound by the determination of the Italian municipal and consular authorities.[121] But the Committee distinguished the act of granting nationality at a domestic level from the act of recognizing nationality on an international level:

> 'Summarizing, the Tribunal had the power to determine whether it had jurisdiction to hear the dispute. In determining whether the jurisdictional requirements of the ICSID Convention and the BIT have been satisfied, the Tribunal is empowered to make its own investigation into the nationality of parties regardless of the presence of official government nationality documents. Certificates of nationality constitute prima facie – not conclusive – evidence, and are subject to rebuttal. In fine, the Tribunal did not manifestly exceed its powers in deciding that it had to determine for itself Mr. Soufraki's nationality.
>
> (…) Meantime, prudential considerations require that the ad hoc Committee make crystal clear that it is addressing a very specific and limited situation: that is, the situation of an international Tribunal vested with competence-competence, which must verify the reality of the claimed nationality of a natural person who is a party to a proceeding before it, if the Tribunal is to determine its own jurisdiction to go forward with that proceeding, when its jurisdiction is contingent upon that nationality. (…) The rulings of the ad hoc Committee should not be read as relating to other situations'.

It is important to note that the *Soufraki* tribunal applied substantive Italian law to the issues of nationality raised in the case, and did not create its own rules to establish whether Mr Soufraki was an Italian citizen. This is an important example of a *renvoi* to municipal law to meet international law requirements. The tribunal referred to three provisions of Italian law, which it considered relevant to the facts of the present case.[122]

The *Soufraki* Annulment Committee concluded that the tribunal did *in reality* apply Italian law. The tribunal's statement that it 'will in the end decide for itself whether, on the facts and the law before it, [Mr Soufraki] was or was not a national of [Italy]' must be considered in the context in which that statement was made. The Committee reads the tribunal's statement as effectively saying that 'it will in the end decide for itself whether Mr Soufraki can or cannot be considered a national of Italy *for ICSID arbitration purposes*'.[123] The Committee explained that an international tribunal's duty to apply Italian law is a duty to endeavour to apply that law in good faith and

---

120. *See*, above in the discussion of the ILC Articles on Diplomatic Protection and Art. 1 of The Hague Convention on Certain Questions relating to the Conflict of Nationality Laws (12 Apr. 1930), and Art. 3 of the European Convention on Nationality (Strasbourg, 6 Nov. 1997). For example, a tribunal could not properly decline jurisdiction in the case of a female national who lost her nationality because the relevant municipal law prescribed a loss of nationality when a female national marries an alien.
121. *Soufraki v. United Arab Emirates*, Decision of the *Ad Hoc* Committee, para. 18.
122. *Id.*, para. 90.
123. *Id.*, para. 93.

Chapter 3: Investor Nationality under Municipal and International Law   §3.03

in conformity with national jurisprudence and the prevailing interpretations given by the State's judicial authorities.[124] On that basis, the Committee rejected the position that the certificates of nationality were conclusive in Italian law. Even the Italian Supreme Court declared that an Italian passport is only 'presumptive evidence of Italian nationality'.[125]

Should the *Soufraki* ruling, which was rendered in the context of nationality of natural persons, be extended to juridical persons? Broches, commented that Article 25 of the ICSID Convention implicitly assumed that incorporation is a criterion of nationality, that the parties had the widest possible latitude to agree on the meaning of nationality, and that the tightness of the bond of nationality between a State and its nationals is different (and presumably looser) for juridical persons.[126] If the bond of nationality differs for natural and juridical persons, it is not clear if the conclusions reached in *Soufraki* can be extended to juridical entities. That is, for corporations the certificate of incorporation – if that is all that the relevant treaty requires – should be sufficient to prove nationality.

§3.03 CONCLUSION

This Chapter's analysis of treaties, awards, and other international law sources suggests the following framework for assessing investor nationality questions under international investment law.

The starting point is the treaty provision that states a nationality requirement. Article 25 of the ICSID Convention, for example, remits the definition of an investor's nationality to the parties' consent. Therefore the agreement between the parties (the BIT or the host State's investment law) is of primary relevance in determining an investor's nationality. The principles of diplomatic protection, to the extent that they represent customary international law, do not apply if they are inconsistent with the terms of the relevant investment treaty. A 'control' test should not be imported into an investment treaty dispute unless such a test explicitly appears in the relevant investment treaty.

Once the treaty criteria have been established, they must be applied pursuant to the relevant municipal law. In certain, limited circumstances, municipal law should be disregarded if the investment treaty refers to specific criteria to determine corporate nationality (such as Article 17 of the ECT). Absent such circumstances, a natural person's nationality is assessed under municipal law to the extent that municipal law is consistent with international conventions, international custom and the principles of law generally recognized with regard to nationality (such as the 1930 Hague Convention, the European Convention on Nationality). As decided in *Soufraki*, investment tribunals may need to decide whether consular or other municipally issued certificates were obtained by fraud or perhaps even error. Investment treaty tribunals are not bound by the municipal authorities' determination of nationality. Incorporation, unless

---

124. *Id.*, para. 96.
125. *Id.*, para. 104.
126. *Id.*, at pp. 360–361.

the relevant treaty requires more, should be the beginning and end of the assessment of corporate nationality.

To the extent that municipal clashes with principles of international law, international law must prevail. But on certain issues, such as the meaning of 'seat', where there is no international law definition whatsoever, the tribunal's international law obligation is to apply the municipal law conception of seat of the relevant home Contracting State.

CHAPTER 4
From Property to Investment

§4.01 INTRODUCTION

When the concept of investment protection treaties emerged with clarity in the aftermath of World War II, the term 'property' appeared together with 'investment', the latter term having previously been a feature of economic analysis rather than treaties. The first modern BIT[1] marked the new approach to broadening investor protection under international law in several respects, in particular by redirecting the focus of international protection from property to investment, though without jettisoning the concept of property rights. The Germany–Pakistan BIT expressly granted protection to 'investments' by nationals or companies of either party. Article 8 defined the term as comprising 'capital brought into the territory of the other Party for investment in various forms in the shape of assets such as foreign exchange, goods, *property rights*, patents and technical knowledge' [emphasis added]. This BIT's expropriation clause also refers to investments, rather than property, as being the subject of protection (Article 3(2)). This means, for example, that a foreign-owned expropriated immovable asset, which would otherwise attract protection as a property right, triggers the BIT protection only if it constitutes an investment, as defined by the BIT. In this respect, one can appreciate a legal irony: while the ambit of investor protection is broadened, satisfying a new – and often imprecise – definition is necessary to qualify for protection.

The existence of an 'investment' under the relevant investment protection treaty is fundamental to a foreign investor's claim against the State. The term 'investment' is usually defined broadly and in general terms, by considering the economic activity being carried out. This can entail the financial or know-how commitment of investors, a certain duration, economic risk, and the investment's contribution to the host State's

---

1. Germany – Pakistan BIT (1959), 1963 UNTS 24.

economic development.[2] Investment is one of the elements that define the jurisdiction of investment arbitral tribunals. The intentional absence of a precise definition has triggered a debate among and arbitrators and commentators regarding the interpretation of this elusive term.

A treaty may identify various types of economic activities as 'investment'. A treaty may also refer to the host State's laws and regulations concerning the concept of 'investment'; this reference may not necessarily be used to define 'investment', but may be intended to regulate the validity of the investments protected by the treaty.[3] Thus, municipal law may, in certain respects, limit the types of investment attracting treaty protection, because treaty protection should not be granted for unlawful investments. Douglas explains that investments *are, therefore, given an 'objective' treaty definition. But this definition does not in some way detach the rights in rem that underlie those investments from municipal law that creates and gives recognition to those rights. Investment treaties do not contain substantive rules of property law. There must be a renvoi to a municipal property law*.[4] Moreover, under a particular treaty the role of municipal law may vary according to the type of investment that is protected. For example, if the investment is characterized by contractual rights, municipal law will play a different role than if the investment is characterized by property rights.[5]

International and municipal law do not often define the term 'investment', and any treaty definition is, as indicated above, usually a list of underlying rights[6] without substantive content. However, the concept of investment 'consists of legal entitlements and does not extend to mere expectations'.[7] Given this overarching limitation of 'legal entitlement', the roles and relationship of international and municipal law are crucial. Yet, they remain largely unexplored by arbitral tribunals and commentators.

Almost fifty years ago one scholar asserted that 'the terms *investments* and *property* are treated as synonyms and cover all types of interests and rights in property'.[8] He contended that the terms 'property' or 'investment' include any right or interest 'in anything owned or possessed, whether movable or immovable, tangible or intangible'.[9] But this approach does not address the clear intention in investment treaties to make property a subset of investment. Others have suggested that replacing property with investment:

---

2. *See, e.g., Mitchell v. the Democratic Republic of Congo*, Decision on the Application for the Annulment of the Award issued on 1 Nov. 2006, para. 27, available on the Investment Claim website: www.investmentclaims.com/decisions/Mitchell-Congo-Annulment_Decision.pdf.
3. *See, e.g., Salini Costruttori S.p.A. and Italstrade v. Morocco*, Decision on Jurisdiction, 23 Jul. 2001, *ILM* 42 (2003), 609, paras 43–46.
4. Douglas, 'The Hybrid Foundations of Investment Treaty Arbitration', at 198.
5. *See infra*.
6. *See* United Nations Conference on Trade and Development, United Nations '*International Investment Agreements: Key Issues*', vol. I (New York and Geneva, 2004), 119.
7. Brownlie, Separate Opinion, in *CME Czech Republic SA v. Czech Republic*, Final Award, para. 20, available on the Investment Treaty Arbitration website: http://ita.law.uvic.ca/documents/CME2003-SeparateOpinion_001.pdf.
8. Schwarzenberger, *Foreign Investments and International Law* (London, 1969), 17.
9. *Ibid*.

must lie in the intervening developments, in particular with respect to the Cold War, later decolonisation and emergence of 'development economics'. It was no longer sufficient to say that a 'rule of law' protecting the property of foreigners was conducive to economic development, wherever. The State-oriented and socialist colours of the economic development theory of that time required that purchasing and managing assets in another country was no longer enough to justify protection. It needed to be clothed in the form of 'foreign investment' conveying a much more pro-active, development oriented activity that was justified because it filled an investment gap.[10]

However, this historical explanation fails to take into account that (a) the ICSID *travaux préparatoires* do not mention this social function of investment, and (b) BITs typically provide for a definition of investment that includes property.

It is not feasible to extract a general principle regarding the relationship of 'property' and 'investment'. Municipal law of the host State determines if a property right exists, but international law determines if the investment treaty protects that property right.[11] If, for example, a BIT lists bonds and loans as property rights, this does not necessarily make every loan or bond a protected asset, since a bond or loan will still have to qualify as an investment under the treaty. This Chapter considers the following topics, which broadly parallel the steps that an investment treaty arbitral tribunal should take in determining whether an asserted property right may qualify as an investment.

First, given the absence of a definition of property under international law, it will usually be the case that municipal law regulates the substantive aspects of property. As this Chapter section will show, arbitral tribunals that attempt to define property exclusively and directly by international law will have gone astray from proper legal analysis at the outset.

Second, the Chapter then focuses on whether to characterize intangible rights and contracts as property rights, and whether 'legitimate expectations' may constitute a property right. If, for example, municipal law governs a contract, what is the meaning of the 'internationalization' of that contract: to what extent does municipal law define the rights arising from the contract, and what role is reserved to international law? Some international investment tribunals have stated that foreign investors may rely on rights that, while null and void in an arguably relevant municipal system, can serve as an autonomous source of rights in investment treaty disputes.[12] Similarly, some tribunals have found foreign investors' 'expectations' to be property rights independently from any finding that such expectations constitute rights under the applicable municipal law.[13]

---

10. *New Aspects of International Investment Law, Recueils Des Cours*, eds. Khan and Wälde (The Hague, 2004), 99.
11. *Id.*, 73.
12. *See*, e.g., the discussion *infra* of *Eureko v. Poland*.
13. *See* the discussion below of *Tecnicas Medioambientales Tecmed SA v. Mexico*, Award, 29 May 2003, *ILM* 43 (2004), 133, and the comments of the Annulment Committee, paras 67–69, in *MTD Equity Sdn Bhd. & MTD Chile S.A v. Republic of Chile*, Decision on Annulment, 21 Mar. 2007, available on Investment Claims website: www.investmentclaims.com/decisions/MTD-Chile_Ad_Hoc_Committee_Decision-21-03-07.pdf.

Third, the Chapter examines the concept of investment. 'Property' does not suffice for treaty protection. In the absence of a uniformly accepted legal definition of 'investment', it is useful to consider the historical background in interpreting this concept.

Fourth, the Chapter discusses the relevance, to investment treaty claims, of a Claimant's violation of the host State's law in carrying out an investment. Broches emphasized that there is no shortage of definitions of investment. However, a Claimant filing an ICSID arbitration can bring only a 'legal dispute'; this expression was used in the ICSID Executive Directors' Report to make sure that only conflicts of rights were within the ICSID jurisdiction, and not conflicts of interest.[14] This explains why, despite many definitions of investment, the existence of an underlying property right must be the foundation of any definition. This foundation inevitably implicates municipal law.

§4.02 THE ROLE OF INTERNATIONAL LAW IN DEFINING PROPERTY

Although considerable authority supports the position that international law protects both tangibles and intangibles as property rights,[15] international law does not provide for any substantive definition of these rights.[16] The following discussion of several international law instruments shows that while international law protects 'property rights', it does not define their content. This is the foundational point for the justification – and need – for *renvoi* to municipal law.

[A] European Convention on Human Rights

The European Convention on Human Rights ('European Convention') refers to the peaceful enjoyment of any 'possession' rather than 'property', the former concept being broader than the latter.[17] This Convention is significant in that it demonstrates how international law, while considering the concept of 'possession' as autonomously

---

14. Broches, 'The Convention on the Settlement of Investment Disputes Between States and Nationals of other States', *Recueil des Cours* (1972), 331–410 at 362.
15. *See, inter alia,* Shaw, *International Law* (Cambridge, 2008), 830; and Brownlie, *Principles of Public International Law* (Cambridge, 2008), 531–533.
16. Sacerdoti, writing on expropriation, has stated that international protection covers 'all rights and interests having an economic content come into play, including immaterial and contractual rights': 'Bilateral Treaties and Multilateral Instruments on Investment Protection', *Recueil des Cours* 269 (1997), 251, at 381.
17. *See Djidrovski v. The Former Yugoslav Republic of Macedonia*, Judgment of 24 Feb. 2005, para 80, available on the Council of Europe website: http://cmiskp.echr.coe.int////tkp197/viewhbkm.asp?action=open&table=F69A27FD8FB86142BF01C1166DEA398649&key=9961&sessionId=7975326&skin=hudoc-en&attachment=true: 'The Court reiterates that the concept of "possessions" in Article 1 of Protocol No. 1 has an autonomous meaning and that Article 1 of Protocol No. 1 in substance guarantees the right of property (*see Marckx v. Belgium*, judgment of 13 Jun. 1979, Series A no. 31, 27–28, § 63). A "possession" within the meaning of the above provision may be either an "existing possession" or a claim, in respect of which the applicant can argue that he has at least a "legitimate expectation" of obtaining effective enjoyment of a property right' (*see* the *Pine Valley Developments v. Ireland* judgment of 29 Nov. 1991, Series A no. 222, 23, § 51). *See also* Kriebaum and Schreuer, 'The Concept of Property in Human Rights Law and International Investment Law', in *Human Rights, Democracy and the Rule of Law*, ed. S.

defined, nonetheless refers to a municipal legal system for certain purposes, such as the existence of a disputed right and whether it was violated.

Article 1 of the First Additional Protocol to the European Convention, signed in Paris on 20 March 1952 (currently ratified by forty-six European States), provides that:

> Every natural or legal person is entitled to the peaceful enjoyment of his possessions. No one shall be deprived of his possessions except in the public interest and subject to the conditions provided for by law and by the general principles of international law.
>
> The preceding provisions shall not, however, in any way impair the right of a State to enforce such laws as it deems necessary to control the use of property in accordance with the general interest or to secure the payment of taxes or other contributions or penalties.

The European Court of Human Rights (ECHR) has held that the concept of 'possessions' (in French: *biens*) in Article 1 'has an autonomous meaning which is certainly not limited to ownership of physical goods: certain other rights and interests constituting assets can also be regarded as "property rights", and thus as "possessions" for the purposes of this provision (...)'.[18] The ECHR has thus adopted a broad approach to the concept of 'possessions'. For example, denial of inheritance of property situated abroad due to alleged absence of reciprocity has been deemed a violation of Article 1 of Protocol No. 1.[19] Moreover, the ECHR has determined that denial of the ability to be affiliated with a farmers' social security scheme on account of nationality violates the same provision.[20] Still, the ECHR does not define of the rights or interests protected as possessions. The classification of rights as property rights for the purpose of applying Article 1 of Protocol No. 1 is autonomous, but this does not mean that the *content* of these rights is also autonomous. Municipal law still regulates the content of these rights.

This enduring role of municipal law is apparent from ECHR's *Apostolidi v. Turkey* decision. In this denial of inheritance case, the Greek applicants registered a flat and a piece of land in a Turkish town after being issued an inheritance certificate. The Turkish courts subsequently annulled this certificate after another heir, of Turkish nationality, claimed title to the property. The annulment was on the grounds that

---

Breitenmoser (Zurich/Baden-Baden, 2007), 743–762, available online: www.univie.ac.at/intlaw/concept_property.pdf at 3.

18. *Case of Fleri Soler and Camileri v. Malta*, Judgment, 26 Sep. 2006, para. 57, available on the Council of Europe website: http://cmiskp.echr.coe.int////tkp197/viewhbkm.asp?action = open&table = F69A27FD8FB86142BF01C1166DEA398649&key = 58321&sessionId = 5054724&skin = hudoc-en&attachment = true. See also *Gasus Dosier- und Fördertechnik GmbH v. the Netherlands*, Judgment of 23 Feb. 1995, Series A no. 306-B (1999), 46, § 53, and *Iatridis v. Greece* [GC], Judgment 25 Mar. 1999, no. 31107/96, § 54, ECHR 1999-II.
19. *Case of Apostolidi and others v. Turkey*, Judgment of 27 Mar. 2007, available on the Council of Europe website: http://cmiskp.echr.coe.int/tkp197/viewhbkm.asp?action = open&table = F69A27FD8FB86142BF01C1166DEA398649&key = 61437&sessionId = 5055316&skin = hudoc-en&attachment = true.
20. *Case of Luczak v. Poland*, Judgment of 27 Nov. 2007, available on the Council of Europe website: http://cmiskp.echr.coe.int////tkp197/viewhbkm.asp?action = open&table = F69A27FD8FB86142BF01C1166DEA398649&key = 66341&sessionId = 5055269&skin = hudoc-en&attachment = true.

Turkish nationals could not acquire property in Greece by inheritance, and therefore the condition of reciprocity provided for in Article 35 of the Turkish Land Code had not been met. The ECHR held that the annulment of the inheritance certificate concerning the flat violated, *inter alia*, Article 1 of Protocol No. 1, but that there had been no breach regarding the piece of land because the applicants had not owned a possession within the meaning of the Convention. The ECHR defined the ability to inherit as an interest in possession, despite such an interest not being classified as a property right under Turkish law – but Turkish law nonetheless provided the content of this interest, the entitlement to inherit.

The ECHR expressed a similar approach in its decision on membership in a social security scheme. The applicant, a French national, alleged a violation of Article 14 (prohibition of discrimination) and Article 1 of Protocol 1 when Polish authorities' refused to admit him to the Polish farmers' social security scheme because he was not Polish. The ECHR held that there had been a violation of Article 14 and Article 1 of Protocol 1. The analysis of the individual's right to join the scheme was considered under municipal (Polish) law, even though the right to join was considered an interest in property protected under international law in accordance with an autonomous classification contained in Article 1 of Protocol No. 1. Again, the analysis of whether the right to join was protected under Article 1 of Protocol 1 was conducted pursuant to the autonomous definition of possession, but the content of the right at issue was established pursuant to municipal law.[21]

The ECHR has also held that goodwill in a business, a license to serve alcoholic beverages, fishing rights, and planning permission are all possessions under Article 1 of Protocol 1.[22] In all these instances, the classification of the concept of possession is autonomous, but the substance of the right or interest is considered in accordance with the relevant municipal law. As discussed below, even when the ECHR has protected certain 'expectations', the standard is that the expectation is sufficiently established in the relevant national legal system to constitute an asset for the applicant.[23]

[B] Inter-American Convention on Human Rights

Article 21 of the Inter-American Convention on Human Rights ('Inter-American Convention')[24] provides that:

> Everyone has the right to the use and enjoyment of his property. The law may subordinate such use and enjoyment to the interest of society.

---

21. *Luczak v. Poland*, decision on admissibility, 27 Mar. 2007, available on the Council of Europe website: http://cmiskp.echr.coe.int////tkp197/viewhbkm.asp?action=open&table=F69A27 FD8FB86142BF01C1166DEA398649&key=61948&sessionId=5513414&skin=hudoc-en&attachment=true.
22. Jacobs and White, *The European Convention on Human Rights* (Oxford, 2006), 350.
23. *Gratzinger and Gratzingerova v. Czech Republic*, Admissibility Decision of 10 Jul. 2002, para. 69.
24. This Convention entered into force on 18 Jul. 1978, and has been ratified by twenty-five States (http://www.oas.org/en/sla/dil/treaties_agreements.asp).

> No one shall be deprived of his property except upon payment of just compensation, for reasons of public utility or social interest, and in the cases and according to the forms established by law.
>
> Usury and any other form of exploitation of man by man shall be prohibited by law.

The Inter-American Convention does not define property. However, the Inter-American Court of Human Rights (IACHR) has determined the boundaries of the concept. In particular, the IACHR has adopted:

> a broad concept of property that includes, among other matters, the use and enjoyment of property, defined as material goods that can be possessed, as well as any right that may form part of a person's patrimony. This concept includes all movables and immovables, corporeal and incorporeal elements, and any other immaterial object which may have a value. Also, under Article 21 of the Convention, the Court has protected acquired rights, understood as rights that have been incorporated into a person's patrimony.[25]

Property is thus defined under the Inter-American Convention as any corporeal and incorporeal element with an economic value, but there is no explanation of what it means to be 'incorporated' into a person's patrimony or of the rules that determine whether an element is corporeal or incorporeal. Instead, the relevant municipal law provides the content of these elements. This framework was demonstrated in the *Case of Chaparro Álvarez y Lapo Íñiguez v. Ecuador*, where the content of property rights at issue was supplied in accordance with Ecuadorian law.[26]

[C] The 1959 Abs-Shawcross Draft Convention on Foreign Investments

A review of draft multilateral investment treaties reveals a common pattern: they adopt a broad notion of 'property', but provide no substantive definition of the concept.

The 1959 Abs-Shawcross Draft Convention ('Abs-Shawcross Draft') requires fair and equitable treatment, and protection from expropriation without compensation, of the property of foreign nationals (Articles I and III). It defines the term 'property' to include 'property, rights and interests' (members of a company being deemed to have an 'interest').[27] In one of the Commentaries, the drafters clarified that:

---

25. *Case of Chaparro Álvarez y Lapo Íñiguez v. Ecuador*. Judgment of 21 Nov. 2007, Series C No. 170, para 174. *See also Case of Palamara Iribarne*, Judgment of 22 Nov. 2005. Series C No. 135, para. 102; *Case of the Yakye Axa Indigenous Community*, Judgment of 17 Jun. 2005. Series C No. 125, para. 137; *Case of the Moiwana Community, Preliminary objections, merits, reparations, and costs*. Judgment of 15 Jun. 2005. Series C No. 124, para. 129. 'Property' can be defined as 'those material things which can be possessed, as well as any right which may be part of a person's patrimony; that concept includes all movables and immovables, corporeal and incorporeal elements and any other intangible object capable of having value': para. 144 of I/A Court H.R., *Case of the Mayagna (Sumo) Awas Tingni Community v. Nicaragua*. Merits, Reparations and Costs, Judgment of 31 Aug. 2001, Series C No. 79, para 144. *See also Ivcher Bronstein Case*. Judgment of 6 Feb. 2001. C Series No. 74, para. 122.
26. *Case of Chaparro Álvarez y Lapo Íñiguez v. Ecuador*, para 174.
27. 'Draft Convention on Investment Abroad', 'The Proposed Convention to protect private foreign investment: around table', *J. Pub. L.* 9 (currently *Emory Law Journal*) (1960), 115. *See also*

The wide formulation in the Draft Convention of property rights as including proprietary interests is in conformity with international law on the international judicial level. Yet, whether, under customary international law, the interests of the members of a company in a company's property can be equated so generally as is done in this clause with those of the members of the company may well be doubted.[28]

The Abs-Shawcross Draft adopts a broad preliminary classification of what is included in the phrase 'property rights', but fails to define the content of such rights. The drafters certainly were aware that customary international law did not define such content, but they did not provide further guidance or comment on municipal law, though it is unlikely that they had an alternative to municipal law in mind as supplying such content.

[D] Harvard Draft Convention on International Responsibility of States for Injuries to Aliens

The Harvard Draft Convention ('Harvard Draft')[29] sought to protect against, *inter alia*, any taking of foreign property. Property is used in a wide sense, 'comprising all movables and immovable property [...], whether tangible or intangible, including industrial, literary and artistic property as well as all rights or interests, whether legal or equitable, in any kind of property. [...]'. This Draft Convention further states that 'what sort of interest is so remote, uncertain or contingent as not to constitute "property" within the meaning of this article must be left to judicial determination, for it would be impossible to draw any precise line of demarcation for the purposes of this Convention'.[30]

The Harvard Draft also addresses contracts and concessions. The Commentary states that:

> No contract or concession exists in a legal vacuum. It draws its binding force, its meaning and its effectiveness from a legal system, which must be so developed and refined as to be capable of dealing with the great range of problems to which the performance and violation of promises gives rise. [...] In determining whether there has been a violation of a contract or concession between the central government of a State and an alien, two extremes must be avoided. The first of these would be to test every breach of a contract concession immediately and directly by an international standard, notwithstanding any choice of law which the parties might have been incorporated in the agreement. [...] The opposite extreme would be to treat a contract or a concession as being governed exclusively by the

---

Appendix 1. *See* Schwarzenberger, 'The Abs-Shawcross Draft Convention on Investment Abroad: A Critical Commentary', *J. Pub. L.* 9 (1960), 147 and Seidl-Hohenveldern, 'The Abs-Shawcross Draft Convention to Protect Private Foreign Investment: Comments on the Round Table.', *J. Pub. L.* 10 (1961), 100.
28. *See* Schwarzenberger, 'The Abs-Shawcross Draft Convention on Investment Abroad: A Critical Commentary', at 152.
29. 'Draft Convention on the International Responsibility of States for Injuries to Aliens', by Sohn and Baxter, in 'Responsibility of States for Injuries to the Economic Interests of Aliens', *AJIL* 55 (1961), 545. *See* Appendix 3.
30. *Id.*, 563.

municipal law of the contacting State. [...] This view would leave the alien contractor defenceless against any modification or termination of the contract by the State.[31]

This Commentary considers a contract governed exclusively by municipal law to be 'extreme', because this would automatically leave the alien 'defenceless' against modification or termination. However, there was no explanation of why a contract governed by its applicable law, albeit municipal law, would be incompatible with international law principles. International law already governs the issue of whether certain conduct violates the standard of protection granted by a treaty.[32]

To be sure, some arbitral awards had determined that contracts or concessions cannot be construed according to municipal law, but instead must be construed under general principles of law.[33] For example, in the earlier *Abu Dhabi*[34] case, Lord Asquith held that the proper law applicable to a contract made in Abu Dhabi and to be performed in that country could not be Abu Dhabi, because 'no such law can reasonably be said to exist'.[35] Accordingly, he applied 'principles rooted in the good sense and common practice of the generality of civilized nations – a sort of "modern law of nature"'.[36] The Commentary did not address this case. The pertinent point here is that while these draft conventions acknowledged that neither international nor municipal law could exclusively govern contracts or concessions, the drafters offered no framework for determining the relationship between international and municipal law. As with other draft conventions, they define the term 'property' broadly, but remit the content to another, undefined source – in the example of the Harvard Draft, 'judicial determination'.

[E] The OECD Draft Convention on the Protection of Foreign Property

The OECD Draft Convention of 12 October 1967 ('OECD Draft')[37] provides for fair and equitable treatment and protection from takings in respect of property owned by

---

31. *Id.*, 569–570.
32. Douglas, 'Nothing If Not Critical for Investment Treaty Arbitration: *Occidental, Eureko* and *Methanex*', 45.
33. *See*, e.g., Mann, 'The Law Governing State Contracts', *BYIL* 21 (1944), 11; Delaume, 'The Proper Law of State Contracts Revisited', *ICSID Rev. – Foreign Inv. L.J.* 12 (1997), 128; Weil, 'The State, the Foreign Investors and International Law: The No Longer Stormy Relationship of a Ménage à Trois', *ICSID Rev. – Foreign Inv. L.J.* 15 (2000), 401; *Government of Saudi Arabia v. The Arabian American Oil Company (ARAMCO)*, Award, 23 Aug. 1958, ILR 27 (1958), 117; *Sapphire International Petroleum v. National Iranian Oil Company*, Award, 15 Mar. 1963, ILR 35 (1963), 136; *Texaco Overseas Petroleum Company & Californian Asiatic Oil Company v. Government of the Libyan Arab Republic*, Award, 19 Jan. 1977, ILR 53 (1977), 389; *Government of Kuwait v. American Independent Oil Company* (AMINOIL), Award, 24 Mar. 1982, ILR 66 (1982), 518.
34. *Petroleum Development Ltd v. Sheikh of Abu Dhabi* (*Abu Dhabi* case), September 1951, ILR 18 (1951), 144.
35. *Id.*, 149.
36. *Ibid.*
37. OECD Draft Convention, with Notes and Comments, in *ILM* 7 (1968), 117.

nationals of other parties. Article I identifies the 'object of protection' to be any type of property. Further, Article 9 defines 'property' to be all:

> property, rights and interest, whether held directly or indirectly, including the interest which a member of a company is deemed to have in the property of the company. However, no claim shall be made under this Convention in respect of a member of a company: i) if the company is a national of a Party other than the Party which has taken the measures affecting the property of the company; or ii) in the case of a company which is a national of a Party by whose measures its property is affected, if the interest of the member of the company does not arise out of and, at the time of such measures, does not represent either an investment of foreign funds made by him or his predecessor in title or an investment of compensation or damages paid in accordance with the provisions of this Convention.[38]

The term 'property' is deliberately used in the 'widest sense and includes contractual rights',[39] which 'must be lawfully acquired or invested by the foreign national or his predecessor in title'.[40] Property includes any 'interest' – a term not defined in the OECD Draft.

The OECD Commentary, in remarking that the Draft contains a definition of property 'which is in conformity with international judicial practice' and is 'meant to be used in its widest sense which includes, but it is not limited to, investments',[41] indicated that the drafters were comfortable with breadth and vagueness. The inclusion of the term 'interest' highlighted the definition's breadth and vagueness. The drafters' focus was on 'property' owned by aliens; their intention was to rely on a liberal interpretation of the customary international law definition of 'property'. Property had to be lawfully acquired, but neither the OECD Draft nor its Commentary indicated *how* to establish whether such property was lawfully acquired or *how* to identify the provisions that regulate the substantive aspects of the 'property rights' subject to the Convention.

The OECD Draft then, like the preceding draft Conventions, classified rights and interests broadly. The classification could be detailed in a non-exhaustive list of direct and indirect, tangible and intangible holdings. However, the drafters also recognized that however broad the classification might be, it was also shallow in the sense that international law could not, or at any rate did not, establish the content of the elements that 'property' comprised. For the OECD Draft, facing a situation where the municipal law providing such content could not be clearly analysed or described, the solution was simply to leave the content undefined. However, that solution was and is clearly unsatisfactory. One needs to consult case authorities to begin to develop a usable relationship between international law and municipal law regarding treaty protection of 'property'.

---

38. *Id.*, 137.
39. *Id.*, 125.
40. *Id.*, 120. The absence of a more circumscribed clause has been criticized by Schwarzenberger, *Foreign Investments and International Law*, at 157.
41. *Id.*, 139.

§4.03 THE ROLE OF MUNICIPAL LAW IN DEFINING PROPERTY

[A] The PCIJ and the ICJ

Several important decisions by the PCIJ and the ICJ have addressed the role of municipal law in defining the concept of property. These cases point to the need to refer to municipal law in assessing whether there has been an international law violation.

In *Certain German Interests in Polish Upper Silesia* (Merits),[42] the PCIJ had to decide whether the Polish government's taking of the property of the Chorzów factory breached the Geneva Convention. The Court stated that it would not examine, save as an incidental or preliminary point, the possible existence of rights under German municipal law'.[43] But this preliminary point was crucial to the outcome of the case. In order to determine whether the Polish government's application of Polish law violated Articles 6 et seq. of the Convention, the Court had to decide whether two companies (Oberschlesische and the Bayerische) were really the owners of the rights that together constituted the Chorzów enterprise: 'if this point is established, it automatically follows that these rights are protected by Article 6 of the Geneva Convention, the other conditions required by the article being fulfilled in the present case'.[44] In short, did the German company own the Chorzów factory under German law?

To decide this question, the PCIJ had to analyse the contracts in view of the structure of the German companies and the transfer of the factory from the Reich to the two companies. The PCIJ concluded that the Reich intended to transfer the right of ownership of the Chorzów factory. Under German municipal law this transaction was valid.[45] Further, the ownership was duly recorded in the land registry and the registration had not been challenged, which meant that the companies' rights were vested.

In *Certain German Interests*, then, determining whether an international obligation had been violated depended on the validity of the proprietary interest in the Chorzów factory under municipal law. If the transfer had been invalid under German law, the PCIJ would have reached the opposite conclusion, that is, there was no violation of an international obligation because there was no underlying right in municipal law.

The PCIJ subsequently placed an express and dispositive weight on municipal law in the *Panevezys-Saldutiskis Railway* case, where it held that 'the property rights and the contractual rights of individuals depend in every state on municipal law and fall therefore more particularly within the jurisdiction of municipal tribunals'.[46] Not only would municipal law control, but the rule of the exhaustion of local remedies also returned the rights at issue to the jurisdiction of the Lithuanian courts; the PCI therefore could not hear the claim.

---

42. *Certain German Interests in Polish Upper Silesia* (Merits), Judgment no. 7 of 25 May 1926, PCIJ, Series A, 7, 1.
43. *Id.*, para. 42.
44. *Id.*, para. 35.
45. *Id.*, para. 42.
46. *Panevezys-Saldutiskis Railway* case, Judgment of 28 Feb. 1939, PCIJ, Series A/B, No. 76, 4, at 18.

In *Barcelona Traction* the ICJ took a similar approach, in a diplomatic protection case, regarding the significance of municipal law. The ICJ recognized that:

> [In the field of diplomatic protection] international law is called upon to recognize institutions of municipal law that have an important and extensive role in the international field. This does not necessarily imply drawing any analogy between its own institutions and those of municipal law, nor does it amount to making rules of international law dependent upon categories of municipal law. All it means is that international law has had to recognize the corporate entity as an institution created by States in a domain essentially within their domestic jurisdiction. This in turn requires that, whenever legal issues arise concerning the rights of States with regard to the treatment of companies and shareholders, as to which rights international law has not established its own rules, it has to refer to the relevant rules of municipal law. Consequently, in view of the relevance to the present case of the rights of the corporate entity and its shareholders under municipal law, the Court must devote attention to the nature and interrelation of those rights.[47]

In 2007, in *Diallo*, another case concerning diplomatic protection, the ICJ reiterated that where an internationally wrongful act consists of a violation of shareholders' rights, such rights are 'defined by the domestic law of that State'.[48]

From these decisions, it is clear that the PCIJ and, subsequently, the ICJ have viewed the roles of international law and municipal law as separate and different in scope when defining property claims. These decisions also demonstrate that proper application of international law may require applying rights defined under municipal law. Although certain investment treaty decisions have maintained this dichotomy, a number of others have blurred the distinction.

[B] Investment Treaty Tribunals

The investment treaty decisions analysed below concern the characterization of intangible rights. If the issue in dispute concerns contractual rights, municipal law will arguably be more significant than if the investment is characterized by tangible assets. The nationalization of a manufacturing facility, for example, would not likely require any close examination of municipal law.

This section analyses intangible rights generally, and then considers the following question: if municipal law governs a State contract and under this law a particular contractual right does not exist, how can an investor claim the existence of this 'right'? The section concludes by addressing the situation where foreign investors rely on their expectations as an autonomous source of rights independent from those under the contract's governing law. The threshold question in this line of cases is to determine whether international law includes the concept of legitimate expectations as a *property*

---

47. *Barcelona Traction* case, para. 38.
48. *Diallo (Republic of Guinea v. Democratic Republic of the Congo)*, Preliminary Objections 24 May 2007, para. 64, available on the ICJ website: www.icj-cij.org/docket/files/103/13856.pdf#view = FitH&pagemode = none&search = %22diallo%22 .

right. Property law and contract law are different; property law concerns rights in rem as opposed to contract law's focus on rights in personam.[49]

[1] Intangible Rights

In the first case discussed below, the tribunal disregarded municipal law's role in defining the underlying right, leading to a flawed decision whereby mere economic interests are treated as property rights. The second case, however, properly dismisses an attempt to treat an economic interest as a property right.

[a] Pope & Talbot Inc. v. Canada[50]

This NAFTA dispute concerned an alleged regulatory expropriation of right of access to the US market. The tribunal held, *inter alia*, that NAFTA protected this right, but that Canada's conduct did not amount to expropriation. Canada argued that the property claimed to have been expropriated, 'ability to alienate its products to [the U.S.] market', was not a property right because it was neither a tangible nor intangible form of property, nor was it a right that can be acquired or alienated.[51] The investor submitted that 'access to the U.S. market is the means by which the Investment generates cash flow that comprises its value, therefore, interference with the access to the U.S. market has a direct effect on the value of its Investment'.[52]

The tribunal reasoned that access to the US market is a property interest protected by NAFTA Article 1110,[53] even though it did not consider the disputed regulatory measures 'tantamount to nationalization or expropriation'.[54] The tribunal determined that the 'true interests at stake are the Investment's asset base, the value of which is largely dependent on its export business'.[55]

The *Pope & Talbot* tribunal blurred the distinction between legal interest and commercial interest, and elevated the latter to a property right that can be expropriated. The tribunal attributed no relevance to the question whether the interest was a legal one governed by a municipal law. The approach taken in *Pope & Talbot* is so broad as to comprise virtually any interest'. There is no reference in the NAFTA definition of investment[56] to the 'true interest at stake.' The notion of investment of course introduces an economic factor, but this does not mean that any economic interest is relevant. The definition in NAFTA clearly identifies the legal interest embedded in the definition of investment (such as an enterprise, a debt security in certain circumstances, an interest in an enterprise, etc.), and limits such interests in order to exclude

---

49. Douglas, *The International Law of Investment Claims*, 202.
50. *Pope & Talbot Inc. v. Canada*, Interim Award, 26 Jun. 2000, *ILR* 122 (2002), 293.
51. *Id.*, para. 87.
52. *Id.*, para. 95.
53. *Id.*, para. 96.
54. *Ibid.*
55. *Id.*, para. 98.
56. The NAFTA definition of 'investment' is contained in NAFTA Art. 1139.

claims to money arising from contracts for the sale of goods or services or the extension of credit in connection with a commercial transaction.

[b] Encana Corporation v. Republic of Ecuador[57]

Unlike *Pope & Talbot*, several investment treaty arbitration cases have recognized municipal law's role in assessing the existence of a property right. For example, in *Encana Corporation v. Republic of Ecuador*, the tribunal held that 'for there to have been an expropriation of an investment or return (in a situation involving legal rights or claims as distinct from the seizure of physical assets) the rights affected must exist under the law which creates them, in this case the law of Ecuador'.[58] The dispute in *Encana* turned on whether the State's denial of tax refunds to the Claimant's subsidiaries was expropriation, in violation of the Canada-Ecuador BIT. The tribunal majority decided that it had to consider whether Ecuadorian law granted a right to value-added tax (VAT) refunds and, if so, whether such a right had been expropriated. The majority ruled that the Ecuadorian policy on tax refunds 'never rose to the level of the repudiation of an Ecuadorian legal right'[59] and rejected the claim for expropriation.

The dissenting tribunal member stated that examining Encana's legal entitlement to VAT refunds under Ecuadorian law was 'of little practical significance'[60] since it would evoke the requirement of 'substantive exhaustion of local remedies'.[61] That is, the assessment of such a right would require analysing Ecuadorian law and precedent to determine whether such a right to refunds existed. The dissent characterized the majority's approach as a '*renvoi* from international law to domestic law'.[62] He contended that municipal laws and acts are 'facts to be freely evaluated by arbitrators to determine if the foreign investor's entitlement to protection under international law has been infringed at a specific moment in time or not',[63] and that arbitral discretion is unbounded by 'determinations of local courts under their own laws'.[64] In this dissenting perspective, municipal law becomes a background factual matrix in investment treaty arbitration cases, and an investor's legal entitlement must be determined by the investment treaty and by public international law, which are 'inextricably linked'[65] with 'foreign legitimate return expectation'.[66] The dissent concluded that such expectations represent a relevant interest under international law because they have an economic value, and are not premised on any municipal law.

The dissent inferred, from the requirement that expropriated rights must exist under the laws of the State creating them, that any claim first had to be brought before

---

57. *Encana v. Ecuador*, Award, 3 Feb. 2006, *ICSID* 12 (2007), 400.
58. *Encana v. Ecuador*, cit., para. 184.
59. *Id.*, para. 197.
60. *Id.* Horacio Grigera Naón, Dissenting Opinion, 30 Dec. 2005, *ICSID Reports*, 12 (2007), para. 8.
61. *Ibid.*
62. *Id.*, para. 9.
63. *Id.*, para. 12.
64. *Ibid.*
65. *Id.*, para. 17.
66. *Ibid.*

the State's courts. But exhaustion of local remedies, does not necessarily flow from the principle that a right must exist under municipal law. A treaty may require such exhaustion as a prerequisite to a certain action, but this is not linked to the applicability of municipal law to define the content of a right. A tribunal should apply municipal law to identify the content. An investor's legal entitlement is based on a 'legal' interest, which must be assessed under a set of rules. International law does not provide such rules.

To equate property rights with any interest with an economic value would render property a subjective concept and attribute relevance to interests that fall short of being legally protected interests. For some individuals, the right to VAT refunds would have an economic value, because they may wish to use them to win an arbitration; for others, this right would have no economic value if they had no access to arbitration proceedings. To elevate an interest to the protection of international law on the mere basis of its potential economic value as it is perceived by a foreigner would open the door to an indistinct 'hope' with an economic value. The difference between a legal interest and a mere interest is then hopelessly blurred.

[2]   Contracts

The cases analysed below concern contracts governed by a specific municipal law. The first case is an example of the so-called 'internationalization' of contracts, and highlights the dangers in applying international law to questions such as contract breach and termination. The second case concerns the characterization of certain rights purportedly arising from a contract in accordance with general principles. The third and fourth cases show how a breach of contract may amount to an expropriation.

[a]   In the matter of Revere Copper and Brass Inc. and Overseas Private Investment Corporation[67]

In *Revere Copper* the tribunal confused the relationship between municipal and international law. The Claimant and the Jamaican government entered into an agreement containing a tax stabilization clause. A few years later, the government stated that it was not bound by the agreement and increased taxes. The Claimant submitted a claim for expropriation, contending that a series of governmental acts 'abrogated the 1967 Agreement between the Government and RJA'.[68] The government claimed that the disputed measures did not deprive the Claimant of control over its investment, and that the stabilization clause was void *ab initio*.[69] The tribunal majority held that the Jamaican government's conduct amounted to expropriation.[70]

---

67. *In the Matter of Revere Copper and Brass Inc. and Overseas Private Investment Corporation*, in *ILR* 56 (1980), 258.
68. *Id.*, 270.
69. *Ibid.*
70. *Id.*, 290.

The majority concluded that the government had abrogated the contract in dispute and was bound by the stabilization clause.[71] In reaching this decision, it considered not only the law of Jamaica but also international law as the law applicable to the agreement, and stated that the question of a breach of contract could not be determined only under Jamaican law.

This is a flawed decision. The question for the tribunal was whether the measures adopted by the government in alleged breach of the stabilization clause amounted to an indirect expropriation and entitled the Claimant to compensation. There was no need to qualify the contract as 'transnational' or to refer to international law on the question of breach of contract. International law does not provide any rule concerning termination or breach of a contract when the proper law of the contract is not international law. The tribunal should have analysed the agreement to be regulated under its own municipal law, while international law should have been invoked to determine whether an expropriation had occurred. It did not matter if the contract was 'internationalized'; international law has nothing to add if there are no international law rules governing the performance of the contract in question.

[b] Eureko v. Poland[72]

Other investment treaty arbitral tribunals have also erroneously disregarded the law applicable to property rights. In *Eureko* the Claimant purchased 20% of a State-owned company (PZU) from the Polish State Treasury.[73] The purchase agreement provided that the State Treasury and PZU intended to carry out an IPO of a part or all of PZU's shares, unless the State Treasury believed market conditions to be unsatisfactory. The purchase agreement also contained a clause providing for the jurisdiction of the Polish courts. The parties subsequently entered into further agreements, which provided that the parties should 'exercise due care and diligence in order to have the IPO concluded before 31 December 2001' (Article 5).

Eureko alleged that a few months after the purchase agreement was executed, the privatization of PZU had become a political issue. It argued that as a result of its investment it acquired rights pertaining to the company's governance and to the holding of the IPO. It claimed that the State had frustrated these rights.

The main issue for the tribunal to resolve was whether the State Treasury was obliged to carry out the IPO. Poland argued that under the express terms of the agreements the Polish courts were exclusively competent to resolve any disputes between the parties. The tribunal rejected Poland's position, holding that it had jurisdiction over the dispute, and finding that Poland had breached the BIT.

On the question of liability, the *Eureko* majority held, in particular that Eureko acquired rights with respect to holding of the IPO, and these rights were assets.

---

71. *Id.*, 290 and 296.
72. *Eureko v. Poland*, Partial Award, 19 Aug. 2005, available on Investment Treaty Arbitration website at https://www.italaw.com/sites/default/files/case-documents/ita0854.pdf.
73. *See* Douglas, 'Nothing if not critical for Investment Treaty Arbitration: *Occidental, Eureko* and *Methanex*', 45.

Poland's actions were discriminatory and deprived Eureko of those assets in violation of the BIT, i.e., the acts constituted an expropriation. [74]

While the *Eureko* majority concluded that Poland's breach of Eureko's contractual corporate governance rights violated the BIT, it did *not* examine these rights under Polish law. The majority failed to establish whether these 'rights' were actually rights under Polish or any other law, including international law. The majority did not explore whether Polish law required the State Treasury to conduct an IPO, and if Eureko was entitled to additional shares once an IPO was carried out. Nor did it explain on which grounds the State Treasury's duty to exercise due care and diligence should be interpreted as a firm commitment under Polish law, and, accordingly, a right relating to the conduct of the IPO, thereby entitled to protection under the BIT.[75]

The dissenting member of the Eureko tribunal stated that the only enforceable right under Polish law was the initial purchase of the shares, not the IPO or the rights to obtain additional shares. As noted above, as a matter of international law, municipal law can either be 'relevant as facts in applying the applicable international standard, or else that they are actually incorporated in some form, conditionally or unconditionally, into that standard'.[76] The dissenting opinion was attentive to this principle of international law; the tribunal majority was not. The tribunal majority failed to perform the relevant municipal law analysis, and failed to establish whether the disputed interests were legal interests or mere economic interests.

[c]   Waste Management Inc v. Mexico[77]

The dispute in *Waste Management* arose in connection with a concession for the provision of waste disposal services in Acapulco. The Claimant encountered difficulties in enforcing the concession's exclusivity provision, as well as in obtaining the payment for its waste collection services from the city of Acapulco.

The tribunal, constituted in accordance with NAFTA Chapter 11, determined that persistent non-payment of debts assumed by a State organ in breach of a contract cannot be equated with a violation of an investment treaty provision, including expropriation, provided that it does 'not amount to an outright and unjustified repudiation of the transaction and provided that some remedy is open to the creditor to address the problem'.[78] The tribunal concluded that 'an enterprise is not expropriated just because its debts are not paid or other contractual obligations towards it are breached. ... It is not a function of Article 1110 to compensate for failed business venture, absent any arbitrary intervention by the State amounting to a virtual taking or sterilizing of the enterprise'.[79]

---

74. *Eureko v. Poland*, paras 240–243.
75. *Id.*, paras 152, 157–158.
76. ILC Art. 3; *see* Crawford, *The International Law Commission's Articles on State Responsibility*, 89.
77. *Waste Management Inc v. United Mexican States*, Decision on Jurisdiction, 26 Jun. 2002, *ILM* 41 (2002), 1315; Award of 30 Apr. 2004, *ILM* 43 (2004), 967.
78. *Waste Management*, Award, para. 115.
79. *Id.*, para. 160.

The *Waste Management* tribunal reiterated that the 'mere non-performance of a contractual obligation is not to be equated with a taking of property nor (unless accompanied by other elements) is it tantamount to expropriation'.[80] On the basis of this distinction, the tribunal concluded that the Claimant 'did not lose its contractual rights, which it was free to pursue before the contractually chosen forum'.[81]

The *Waste Management* tribunal thus properly distinguished specific property rights that can be expropriated from loss of expectation. Its definition of property rights under international investment law attributes no relevance to normal commercial risks or failures of a business plan due to outstanding debts. A right must be defined by municipal law, and this definition must take into account the existence, if any, of other 'available legal avenues for redress', unless these are 'futile in face of governmental intransigence'.[82]

[d] Emmis International Holding B.V. et al. v. Hungary[83]

An important recent decision concerning the role of municipal law in the determination of property rights is *Emmis International et al. v. Hungary*. The dispute concerned the alleged unlawful expropriation by Hungary of Claimants' investments in a national FM-radio frequency broadcasting licensee, Sláger Rádió Műsorszolgáltató Zrt. (Sláger). Sláger, a Hungarian company 100% owned by the Claimants, was the previous successful bidder of one of two frequencies in 1997. Sláger's broadcasting license ended in November 2009. Accordingly, in 2009 the National Radio and Television Broadcasting Board conducted a call for tenders to award broadcasting rights over two national FM frequencies, one of which was held by Sláger. Sláger submitted a bid, but lost.

The Claimants alleged that the 2009 tender process was unlawful and claimed that Hungary indirectly expropriated its assets, including *inter alia* the shares in Sláger and tangible and intangible rights held by an investment vehicle. Hungary asserted that the tribunal lacked jurisdiction to hear the present dispute because only proprietary rights can be expropriated, and the Claimants failed to demonstrate the existence of such rights or a dispute arising directly out of an investment in relation to the 2009 tender. The Claimants replied that shares in Sláger, were assets that qualified as a covered investment or, alternatively, the investment was their interest in Sláger as a business operation, comprising all of its value, including their indirect interest in the legal rights and assets held by Sláger under Hungarian law.

The tribunal dismissed the case for lack of jurisdiction. It held that the only proprietary right capable of protection from expropriation was the broadcasting right

---

80. *Id.*, para. 174.
81. *Id.*, para. 175.
82. *Id.*, para. 177.
83. *Emmis International Holding B.V, et al. v. Hungary*, Award, 16 Apr. 2014, available on the International Treaty Arbitration website: http://www.italaw.com/sites/default/files/case-documents/italaw3143.pdf. *See also* Douglas, 'Property Rights as the Object of an Expropriation', in *The First 50 Years of ICSID*, eds Kinnear et al. (Kluwer, 2016), 331–348.

that Sláger acquired in 1997. However, this right expired in 2009, and therefore Claimants did not have any property right subject to BIT protection.

The *Emmis* tribunal reached its decision by first noting the need to identify a proprietary interest, which was confirmed by the definition of 'investment' – every kind of assets – in the relevant BIT. The tribunal commented that:

> In order to determine whether an investor/claimant holds property or assets capable of constituting an investment it is necessary in the first place to refer to host State law. Public international law does not create property rights. Rather, it accords certain protections to property rights created according to municipal law.[84]

Having determined that property rights must be created under municipal law, the tribunal explained that the notion of property is not to be narrowly construed, emphasizing that the BIT referred to tangible and intangible rights.[85] Rights conferred by contract 'may (…) constitute an asset',[86] but protection from expropriation of such rights still requires the identification of a property interest or asset.[87] As seen above in *Waste Management*, non-compliance with a contractual obligation by a State does not amount to an expropriation.[88]

In summary, at one end of the spectrum there is the *Eureko* majority, and its finding that expectations are entitled to protection under investment treaties. At the other end, there are the *Waste Management* and *Emmis* tribunals, and their refusal to equate expectations and protected legal entitlements. The *Eureko* majority, this Chapter argues, unjustifiably broadens the jurisdiction of investment tribunals beyond the offer to arbitrate contained in investment treaties.

[3]   Legitimate Expectations

Although the definition of property rights in investment treaties is often very broad, this does not mean that such rights should encompass interests or expectations. The cases discussed below show that if legitimate expectations are considered a property right, the result is that any interest amounts to a property right under an international investment treaty, regardless of the presumption that international law protects legal interests and not expectations.

To indicate how legitimate expectations can and should be circumscribed, the concluding sub-section analyses the ECHR jurisprudence that has considered whether a possession exists in accordance with Article 1 of Protocol 1 of the ECHR Convention.

---

84. *Emmis International Holding B.V, et al. v. Hungary, cit.*, paras 161–162.
85. *Id.*, para. 163.
86. *Id.*, para. 164.
87. *Id.*, para. 165.
88. *Waste Management II*, paras 174–175.

[a] Tecnicas Medioambientales Tecmed SA v. Mexico[89]

Tecmed is often cited as a precedent for the formulation of the concept of legitimate expectations.[90] The Claimant was awarded the operation of a hazardous waste landfill through bidding held in Mexico. The dispute concerned the denial of a license renewal and alleged breach of the investment treaty provisions on expropriation, fair and equitable treatment, and full protection and security.

The *Tecmed* tribunal held that a permanent and irreversible measure adopted by the State that prevented the exploitation of assets and rights and deprived them of any economic value was an expropriatory measure. The tribunal did not consider whether the Claimant was legally entitled to the license renewal under Mexican law, it focused only on the fact that the denial was unreasonable. Moreover, it did not test reasonableness against Mexican law. This decision on expropriation disregarded the concept of property and did not analyse or explain on which ground the right to seek a renewal was considered a property right. The mere expectation of obtaining renewal was deemed a legal entitlement that was indirectly expropriated.

The *Tecmed* tribunal also considered the fair and equitable treatment standard and concluded that Mexico violated this protection by reassuring the Claimant that it could operate the landfill before its relocation, but then denying the license renewal. The tribunal stated that the commitment of fair and equitable treatment required 'the Contracting Parties to provide to international investments treatment that does not affect the basic expectations that were taken into account by foreign investor to make the investment'.[91] *Tecmed's* obiter dictum referring to 'basic expectations' is often quoted as support for the position that in investment treaty disputes, legal entitlements are basic expectations.[92] However, the concept of legitimate expectations is not an autonomous legal entitlement, and cannot be understood as such from the *Tecmed* decision. *Tecmed* did not adopt a broad definition of expectations and did not reach its decision based on the Claimant's mere hopes of license renewal.

[b] Metalclad Corporation v. Mexico[93]

This decision, which preceded *Tecmed*, is another example of how arbitral tribunals have improperly relied on the concept of investment in order to disregard the requirement of the existence of a legal entitlement.

Metalclad purchased a Mexican company in order to acquire and operate the company's hazardous waste transfer station and landfill. It made the purchase after it received a federal permit to build the landfill, but while waiting for another permit from

---

89. *Tecnicas Medioambientales Tecmed SA v. Mexico*, Award, 29 May 2003, available on Investment Treaty Arbitration website: https://www.italaw.com/sites/default/files/case-documents/ita0854.pdf.
90. McLachlan, 'Investment Treaties and General International Law', *ICLQ*, 2008, 361 at 376.
91. *Tecmed*, para. 154.
92. Douglas, 'Nothing if not critical for Investment Treaty Arbitration: *Occidental, Eureko* and *Methanex*', 28.
93. *Metalclad Corporation v. Mexico*, Award, 30 Aug. 2000, *ICSID Reports* 5 (2002), 212.

the municipal authorities. After the purchase, the municipal authorities prevented the landfill operation. Metalclad continued construction for several months before the municipal authorities ordered it to cease; the authorities later denied Metalclad's permit application.

The tribunal found that Mexico failed to ensure a transparent and predictable framework for Metalclad's investment,[94] breached the standard of fair and equitable treatment in violating NAFTA Article 1105,[95] and indirectly expropriated Metalclad's investment without providing for compensation in violation of NAFTA Article 1110.[96] The tribunal held that the municipality took measures that were outside its authority, which bundled with the representations of the Mexican federal government on which Metalclad relied, amounted to indirect expropriation.[97]

---

94. *Id.*, para. 99.
95. *Id.*, para. 74. Art. 105: *Extent of Obligations*, 'The Parties shall ensure that all necessary measures are taken in order to give effect to the provisions of this Agreement, including their observance, except as otherwise provided in this Agreement, by state and provincial governments.'
96. *Id.*, para. 112. Art. 1110: *Expropriation and Compensation*:
    1. No Party may directly or indirectly nationalize or expropriate an investment of an investor of another Party in its territory or take a measure tantamount to nationalization or expropriation of such an investment ('expropriation'), except:
       (a) for a public purpose;
       (b) on a non-discriminatory basis;
       (c) in accordance with due process of law and Art. 1105(1); and
       (d) on payment of compensation in accordance with paras 2 through 6.
    2. Compensation shall be equivalent to the fair market value of the expropriated investment immediately before the expropriation took place ('date of expropriation'), and shall not reflect any change in value occurring because the intended expropriation had become known earlier. Valuation criteria shall include going concern value, asset value including declared tax value of tangible property, and other criteria, as appropriate, to determine fair market value.
    3. Compensation shall be paid without delay and be fully realizable.
    4. If payment is made in a G7 currency, compensation shall include interest at a commercially reasonable rate for that currency from the date of expropriation until the date of actual payment.
    5. If a Party elects to pay in a currency other than a G7 currency, the amount paid on the date of payment, if converted into a G7 currency at the market rate of exchange prevailing on that date, shall be no less than if the amount of compensation owed on the date of expropriation had been converted into that G7 currency at the market rate of exchange prevailing on that date, and interest had accrued at a commercially reasonable rate for that G7 currency from the date of expropriation until the date of payment.
    6. On payment, compensation shall be freely transferable as provided in Art. 1109.
    7. This article does not apply to the issuance of compulsory licenses granted in relation to intellectual property rights, or to the revocation, limitation or creation of intellectual property rights, to the extent that such issuance, revocation, limitation or creation is consistent with Chapter Seventeen (Intellectual Property).
    8. For purposes of this article and for greater certainty, a non-discriminatory measure of general application shall not be considered a measure tantamount to an expropriation of a debt security or loan covered by this Chapter solely on the ground that the measure imposes costs on the debtor that cause it to default on the debt.
97. *Id.*, para. 107.

The British Columbia Supreme Court[98] set the award partially aside on the ground that the tribunal misstated the applicable law to include obligations of transparency, which were found to be outside the scope of the submission to arbitration. However, the Court did not analyse the definition of property rights underlying the tribunal's finding concerning expropriation.

The tribunal's award equated Metalclad's legitimate expectations with a property right and held that Mexico had expropriated its legitimate expectation to obtain a municipal permit. The tribunal did not analyse whether case law supported its ruling, even though the dispute concerned whether the municipality acted within its authority.

The issue in *Metalclad* was how broadly investment treaty tribunals should treat the concept of a proprietary right, and to what extent this concept can encompass a legitimate expectation. If investment treaty disputes concern legal interests, then the answer would be negative, and legitimate expectations should not be considered property rights. If, on the other hand, tribunals must look to the concept of economic interests for the reason that investment treaties refer to the concept of 'investment', the answer must be affirmative. However, there is no basis for the position that the concept of investment displaces the requirement that violation of a legal right triggers a dispute. Legitimate expectations cannot be characterized as a legal right for purposes of investment treaty disputes unless the treaty expressly refers to them.

[c]   Biloune and Marine Drive Complex v. Ghana Investment Centre *(and the Government of Ghana)*[99]

The *Biloune* tribunal reached conclusions similar to *Metalclad*. The dispute arose out of the construction of a hotel resort complex in Ghana. The investment was made under the framework created by the Ghana Investment Centre, a State entity in charge of foreign investments. When the construction was almost completed, the governmental authorities issued a stop order because of the lack of a building permit and started demolishing the complex. The stop order was issued notwithstanding previous assurances from governmental authorities that construction could proceed. The government arrested and deported Biloune.

The United Nations Commission on International Trade Law (UNCITRAL) tribunal held that although the investment contract referred to the laws of Ghana as applicable law, the parties did not plead these laws and therefore the principles of customary international law were to be applied.[100] The tribunal deemed the need for a building permit to be a formality; the Claimants were 'entitled to rely on the indications of ... the long-term leaseholder of the premises, as well as an experienced government-affiliated entity, and to proceed with the work despite the absence of a permit.'[101] On

---

98. *Mexico v. Metalclad*, British Columbia Supreme Court, 2 May 2001, 2001 BCSC 664, and British Columbia Supreme Court Supplementary Reasons, 31 Oct. 2001, 2001 BCSC 1529.
99. *Biloune v. Ghana Investment Centre*, ILR, 95 (1994), 183.
100. *Id.*, 207.
101. *Id.*, 208.

this basis, the tribunal held that Ghana had expropriated the Claimant's assets. In so doing, the tribunal elevated the mere expectation to obtain a building permit to a right, and did so in the absence of any analysis of the applicable municipal law provisions.[102]

[d] Other Investment Treaty Tribunal Decisions and the ECHR

Not all investor-State tribunals have embraced this broadened concept of expectations. Some have cautioned against the dangerous consequences of applying such a concept. For example, the Annulment Committee in *MTD v. Chile*[103] considered 'questionable'[104] the 'reliance on the foreign investor's expectations as the source of the host State's obligations'. The *Saluka Investment BV v. Czech Republic*[105] tribunal warned against according relevance to 'subjective motivations and considerations'.[106]

The ECHR, in a different framework, also has declined to adopt a broad 'expectations' concept. The Court has clarified that 'possession' within the meaning of Article 1 of Protocol 1 can be assets or legal claims 'in respect of which [the applicant] has at least a "legitimate expectation" that they will be realized'.[107] The standard is not expansive: what is required is that such a claim is 'sufficiently established in the national legal order to constitute an asset for the applicant'.

The ECHR judgments exemplify how 'legitimate expectations' can be rigorously applied, albeit in a possessions instead of property rights context. The ECHR has held that an applicant can allege a violation of Article 1 of Protocol No. 1 only in so far as the claim is related to his 'possessions' within the meaning of this provision:

> 'Possessions' ... can be either 'existing possessions' ... or assets, including claims, in respect of which an applicant can argue that he or she has at least a 'legitimate expectation' that they will be realized.... On the other hand, the hope that a long-extinguished property right may be revived cannot be regarded as a 'possession' within the meaning of Article 1 of Protocol No 1.[108]

The ECHR first developed the notion of 'legitimate expectation' in the context of Article 1 of Protocol No. 1 in *Pine Valley Developments Ltd and Others v. Ireland*.[109] There, the Court found that a 'legitimate expectation' arose when outline planning permission had been granted, in reliance on which the applicant companies had

---

102. In the absence of any pleading on municipal law, the tribunal could not decide these issues under the laws of Ghana.
103. *MTD Equity Sdn BHd and MTD Chile v. Chile*, Decision on Annulment, 21 Mar. 2007, available on the Investment Treaty Arbitration website at https://www.italaw.com/sites/default/files/case-documents/ita0546.pdf.
104. *Id.*, para. 67.
105. *Saluka Investment BV v. Czech Republic*, Partial Award of 17 Mar. 2006, available on the Investment Treaty Arbitration website: http://ita.law.uvic.ca/documents/Saluka-Partialaward Final.pdf.
106. *Id.*, para. 304.
107. *Gratzinger and Gratzingerova v. Czech Republic*, Admissibility Decision of 10 Jul. 2002, para. 69.
108. *Ibid.*
109. *Pine Valley Developments Ltd and Others v. Ireland*, 29 Nov. 1991, Series A no. 222.

purchased land with a view to its development. The outline planning permission was considered 'a component part of the applicant companies' property'.[110]

Another aspect of the notion of 'legitimate expectation' arose in *Pressos Compania Naviera S.A. and Others v. Belgium*,[111] where the issue concerned claims for damages. The 'legitimate expectation' did not in itself constitute a proprietary interest; rather, it related to the way in which the claim qualifying as an 'asset' would be treated under domestic law. In particular, the ECHR relied on the fact that the established case law of the national courts would continue to be applied in respect to damage that had already occurred. In an additional line of cases, the ECHR has found that the applicants did not have a 'legitimate expectation' where it could not be said that they had sufficiently established a currently enforceable claim. In these cases, the ECHR distinguished between legitimate expectations and mere hopes.[112]

The ECHR has stated that its precedents 'do not contemplate the existence of a "genuine dispute" or an "arguable claim" as a criterion for determining whether there is a "legitimate expectation" protected by Article 1 of Protocol No. 1'.[113] Instead, it has taken the view that where the proprietary interest is in the nature of a claim, it may be regarded as an 'asset' only where it has a sufficient basis in national law, for example, 'where there is settled case-law of the domestic courts confirming it'.[114]

In summary, then, under ECHR jurisprudence:

(i) a 'legitimate expectation' is not an autonomous right or interest under Article 1 of Protocol 1. Instead, a legitimate expectation must be related to a right or interest that already falls within the definition provided by Article 1 of Protocol No. 1;
(ii) the expectation of an asset is legitimate only where there is a sufficient basis in national law – for example, where there is settled case-law of the domestic courts confirming it; and
(iii) an arguable case is not enough to establish a legitimate expectation.

The concept of legitimate expectations in the investment treaty context should not be considered identical to the treatment of the concept adopted by the ECHR. The former includes specific representations made to investors and may also refer to the legal framework in place at the time the investment is made. The latter considers legitimate expectations as an interest confirmed by settled case law. However, in either context, the notion of 'legitimate expectation' should exclude subjective motives of individuals. This is clearly the case with the ECHR. ECHR jurisprudence, for example, has confined the concept to a legitimate expectation of a right that is well-settled under

---

110. *Id.*, 52.
111. *Pressos Compania Naviera S.A. and Others v. Belgium*, 20 Nov. 1995, Series A no. 332.
112. *Gratzinger and Gratzingerova v. Czech Republic* (Dec.) [GC], no. 39794/98, ECHR 2002-VII, para. 73.
113. *Kopecky v. Slovakia*, [GC], no. 44912/98, ECHR 2004-IX, para. 52.
114. *Ibid.*

Chapter 4: From Property to Investment §4.04

national law. The Ad Hoc Committee in *CMS Gas Transmission Company v. Argentina*[115] and a number of investment treaty tribunals have similarly pointed to the narrowness of the concept: '[a]lthough legitimate expectations might arise by reason of a course of dealing between the investor and the host State, these are not, as such, legal obligations, though they may be relevant to the application of the fair and equitable treatment clause contained in the BIT'. Legitimate expectations are not legal obligations and do not represent a new category of property right at an international level, and should not be classified as such. They do not represent a separate set of property rights that may be expropriated. They may constitute a proprietary right if the investor can express the expectation in contractual terms, but without that aspect they are not legal obligations. Instead, they may be relevant to determining whether the standard of fair and equitable treatment has been breached.

The role of international law, then, is to classify the type of property it protects, while municipal law defines the substantive rules of property. The general reference contained in international treaties to property rights should not be construed to include legitimate expectations to the extent that they do not constitute a property right under municipal law.

§4.04 DEFINITION OF 'INVESTMENT'

From an international law perspective, the concept of investment is relatively recent and has yet to be defined in substantive terms.[116] As described above, many investment treaties provide an illustrative list of what can constitute an investment, but the list is usually non-exhaustive and does not attempt to define the concept generally.[117] The emergence of the concept of 'investment' is linked to the rise of modern BITs and,

---

115. *CMS Gas Transmission Company v. Argentina*, Decision of the *Ad Hoc* Committee on the application for annulment dated 25 Sep. 2007, available on the ICSID website: http://icsid.worldbank.org/ICSID/FrontServlet?requestType = CasesRH&actionVal = showDoc&docId = D C687_En&caseId = C4, para. 89.
116. *See, generally*, Dolzer and Schreuer, *Principles of International Investment Law*, 60; McLachlan, Shore and Weiniger, *International Investment Arbitration: Substantive Principles* (Oxford, 2017), 217; and Krishan, 'A Notion of ICSID Investment', *Transnational Dispute Management* 6(1) (March 2009).
117. *See*, e.g., Art. I of the BIT concluded in 1984 between the United States of America and the Democratic Republic of Congo (formerly the Republic of Zaïre): 'Definitions. For the purposes of this Treaty: [...]

   (c) 'Investment' means every kind of investment, owned or controlled directly or indirectly, including equity, debt, and service and investment contracts; and includes:
      (i) tangible and intangible property, including all property rights, such as liens, mortgages, pledges, and real security;
      (ii) a company or shares of stock or other interests in a company or interests in the assets thereof;
      (iii) a claim to money or a claim to performance having economic value, and associated with an investment;
      (iv) intellectual and industrial property rights, including rights with respect to copyrights, patents, trademarks, trade names, industrial designs, trades secrets and know-how, and goodwill;
      (v) licenses and permits issued pursuant to law, including those issued for manufacture and sale of products;

in particular, to the 1965 ICSID Convention. Customary law, as well as earlier international agreements or draft conventions, commonly referred to 'property' of aliens as the subject of protection under international law. In view of the absence of a uniformly accepted legal definition of investment, this section examines the historical background of the concept, which is also needed for an understanding of whether and how municipal law should play a role in the legal interpretation of the concept. To a large extent, this examination covers most of the instruments discussed above in considering the treatment of property.

[A] Early Investment Treaties: Multilateral and Bilateral

Although the 1959 Abs-Shawcross Draft defined 'property' to include 'property, rights and interests', it did not define 'investment'. The term 'investment' appears only with regard to undertakings; the term used in relation to the standard of fair and equitable treatment and to expropriation was 'property'.[118] The text of the OECD Draft[119] did not advance the use of the term 'investment' much further than the Abs-Shawcross Draft. The OECD Draft referred to property, and only once to 'investment of capital'. The provision concerning the observance of undertakings did not mention the term 'investment'. The notes and comments to Article 1 ('Treatment of Foreign Property'), however, identified the Draft Convention's 'object of protection' to be any type of property, and the commentary clarified that 'in international law the rules contained in this Convention – and therefore in Article 1 – apply to property in the widest sense of the term which includes, but is not limited to, investments'.[120] The same comment appeared in connection with Article 2, regarding the observance of undertakings, and with Article 3, concerning the taking of property. The commentary to Article 9, which defined 'property' as all 'property, rights and interest' but did not define 'investment of capital', reiterated that the property is understood 'in conformity with international judicial practice' and is 'meant to be used in its widest sense which includes, but is not limited to, investments'.[121]

Thus, from the perspective of the legal scholars responsible for the emergence of these draft conventions, 'investment' was a subset of property, and no attempt was made to specify the dimensions or nature of the subset. The focus was on 'property'

      (vi) any right conferred by law or contract, including rights to search for or utilize natural resources, and rights to manufacture, use and sell products; and
      (vii) returns which are reinvested.

    Any alteration of the form in which assets are invested or reinvested shall not affect their character as investment.

118. See Schwarzenberger, 'The Abs-Shawcross Draft Convention on Investment Abroad: A Critical Commentary', *J. Pub. L.* 9 (1960), 147, and Seidl-Hohenveldern, 'The Abs-Shawcross Draft Convention to Protect Private Foreign Investment: Comments on the Round Table', *J. Pub. L.* 10 (1961), 100. The Harvard Draft Convention similarly eschews a consideration of 'investment': see Appendix 3.
119. Draft Convention with notes and comments in *ILM* 7 (1968), 117. See Appendix 4.
120. OECD Draft Convention, 119.
121. *Id.*, 139.

Chapter 4: From Property to Investment §4.04[A]

owned by aliens, and the intention was to rely on a liberal interpretation of the customary international law definition of 'property'.[122]

With the first modern BIT between Germany and Pakistan (1959),[123] 'investment' and 'property' changed places. This BIT not only expressly protected 'investments' by nationals or companies of either Party, but also offered a description of the overarching category: 'capital brought into the territory of the other Party for investment in various forms in the shape of assets such as foreign exchange, goods, property rights, patents and technical knowledge'. Article 8 added that the 'term "investment" shall also include the returns derived from and ploughed back into such investment', and 'partnerships, companies or assets of similar kind, created by the utilization of the above mentioned assets shall be regarded as "investment"' (Article 8(1)(b)).[124]

Unlike the draft multilateral conventions from a similar timeframe, then, the first modern BIT was founded on 'investment' rather than 'property'. It also appears that, in contrast to the draft multilateral conventions, 'investment' is intended to be a broader term than 'property rights'. The approach followed by many subsequent BITs is to refer generically to the term 'investment' and to list several categories of investment in a non-exhaustive manner.[125] It is also apparent that in the vast majority of BITs, 'investment' comprises 'property'.

If the term 'investment' includes property, there are two aspects that have to be taken into consideration: the economic nature of the investment *and* the existence of underlying rights.[126] The literature on 'investment' examines, for the most part, the economic aspects[127] and the application of the so-called 'Salini test',[128] while discussion of the existence of underlying rights is often left aside. The following Chapter sections consider: (i) in the absence of a generally accepted international law definition of investment, how investment may be defined; (ii) how registration requirements for foreign investment, a frequent aspect of municipal law, should be interpreted in investment disputes; and (iii) if municipal law determines the lawfulness of the rights

---

122. *See* above.
123. 1963 UNTS 24. Germany and Pakistan entered into a new BIT in December 2009. *See* Appendix 2.
124. *Id.*, Art. 8(2).
125. *See* Schlemmer, 'Investment, Investor, Nationality and Shareholders', in *The Oxford Handbook of International Investment Law*, eds Muchlinski, Ortino and Schreuer (Oxford, 2008) 49 at 57; Dolzer and Stevens, *Bilateral Investment Treaties* (The Netherlands, 1995), 25–31; Dolzer and Schreuer, *Principles of International Investment Law*, 60; and McLachlan, Shore and Weiniger, *International Investment Arbitration*, 218. The same approach has been adopted in Art. 2 of the draft Multilateral Agreement on Investment, available on the OECD website: (Daffe/MAI(98)/Rev1, 22 Apr. 1998), and Art. 1(6) of the Energy Charter Treaty. But, *see* Art. 1139 of the NAFTA, which offers a definition of investment narrower than that adopted by most BITs.
126. Douglas, *The International Law of Investment Claims*, 163: 'an investment, in order to qualify for investment treaty protection, must incorporate certain legal and economic characteristics'.
127. *See*, e.g., Krishan, 'A Notion of ICSID Investment'; and Gaillard, 'Identify or Define? Reflections on the Evolution of the Concept of Investment in ICSID Practice', *International Investment Law for the 21st Century, Essays in Honour of Christoph Schreuer*, eds. Binder, Kriebaum, Reinisch and Wittich (Oxford, 2009), 403.
128. *Salini v. Morocco*, paras 39–58.

underlying the investment, are these internal rules relevant in investment treaty arbitration?

[B] The ICSID Convention

The term 'investment' is central to the ICSID Convention. Article 25(1) provides that:

> The jurisdiction of the Centre shall extend to any legal dispute arising directly out of an investment, between a Contracting State (or any constituent subdivision or agency of a Contracting State designated to the Centre by that State) and a national of another Contracting State, which the parties to the dispute consent in writing to submit to the Centre. When the parties have given their consent, no party may withdraw its consent unilaterally.

Article 25(4) further states that:

> Any Contracting State may, at the time of ratification, acceptance or approval of this Convention or at any time thereafter, notify the Centre of the class or classes of disputes which it would or would not consider submitting to the jurisdiction of the Centre. The Secretary-General shall forthwith transmit such notification to all Contracting States. Such notification shall not constitute the consent required by paragraph (1).[129]

The ICSID Convention therefore anchors its jurisdiction, and its applicability, to the concept of investment, and yet makes no attempt to define the term. A key issue in ICSID arbitration is whether the 'investment' condition is satisfied by only taking into account Article 25, such that any *renvoi* to municipal law contained in a BIT, for example, is excluded *a priori*:

> The Report of the Executive Directors on the ICSID Convention explains that:
> No attempt was made to define the term 'investment' given the essential requirement of consent by the parties, and the mechanism through which Contracting States can make known in advance, if they so desire, the classes of disputes which they would or would not consider submitting to the Centre (Article 25(4)).[130]

From the notes of the discussions of the ICSID Convention's various drafts, it appears that delegates made several attempts to define the term 'investment' and failed because of inability to formulate a precise definition or because the proposals were otherwise unacceptable to other delegates.[131]

Although the ICSID Convention itself does not define 'investment', the flexibility of its meaning of the term is at least constrained by the requirement of consent to establish jurisdiction. In one of the last meetings before the Convention was executed, Aron Broches, in reply to a request for an approach to define 'investment' in a more precise manner, stated:

---

129. *ICSID Convention*, Art. 25.
130. *ILM* 4 (1965) 524, para. 27.
131. *See* Schreuer, Malintoppi, Reinisch and Sinclair, *The ICSID Convention: A Commentary* (Cambridge, 2009), 114–117.

Chapter 4: From Property to Investment §4.04[B]

the staff had prepared a definition of 'investment' and had also brought to the attention of the Legal Committee a number of examples of definitions of that term taken from the legislation and bilateral agreements. None of these had proved acceptable. The large majority had, moreover, agreed that while it might be difficult to define 'investment', an investment was in fact readily recognizable. The Report would say that the Executive Directors did not think it necessary or desirable to attempt to define 'investment' given the essential requirement of consent of the parties and the fact that the Contracting States could make known in advance within what limits they would consider making use of the facilities of the Centre. Thus each Contracting State could, in effect, write its own definition.[132]

In summary, during the Convention's negotiation, the lengthy discussion on the definition of investment reached the following conclusions: (i) there was no generally acceptable definition; (ii) jurisdiction pursuant to Article 25 was based on consent, and each Contracting State could 'write its own definition' of investment through Article 25(4) and the possibility of notifying the class of disputes excluded or included; and (iii) emphasis should be placed on the existence of a 'legal dispute' – the term that expressly appears in Article 25(1) – and legal rights rather than 'interests'.[133] This final, crucial point was set out in the Memorandum prepared by the General Counsel to the ICSID Convention:

> the dispute must be a 'legal dispute arising out of an investment'. The expression 'legal dispute' has been used to make clear that while conflicts of rights are within the jurisdiction of the Centre, mere conflicts of interests are not. The dispute must concern the existence or scope of a legal right or obligation, or the nature or extent of the reparation to be made for breach of a legal obligation. The Executive Directors did not think it necessary or desirable to attempt to define the term 'investment', given the essential requirement of consent by the parties, and the mechanism through which Contracting States can make known in advance, if they so desire, the classes of disputes which they would or would not consider submitting to the Centre (Article 25(4)).[134]

The Report of the Executive Directors also underlined the crucial role of the parties' consent, together with the opportunity for Contracting States to notify the classes of disputes that they could accept or decline to submit to the jurisdiction of the Centre. The parties' consent could be granted in four ways: (i) an agreement between the parties; (ii) host State legislation (representing an open offer by the State and acceptance by the investor when it commences arbitral proceedings); (iii) BITs (offer by the State and acceptance by the investor through its Contracting home State); and (iv) Multilateral Instruments (e.g., NAFTA or the ECT).[135] However, as Broches later clarified, although the term investment confers a broad discretion to the parties, 'this

---

132. Memorandum of the Meeting of the Committee of the Whole, 16 Feb. 1965 (Discussion of Chs I and II of the Draft Convention, SID/65-2 (17 Feb. 1965), in History of the ICSID Convention, vol. II (2), 965 at 972.
133. *See* History of the ICSID Convention, vol. II (1), 54, 57, 83, 149, 322, 395, 493, 537, 564, and 565.
134. Memorandum from the General Counsel, R 65-11 (19 Jan. 1965), in History of the ICSID Convention, vol. II (2), 957.
135. Schreuer et al., *The ICSID Convention: A Commentary*, 190–217.

discretion is not unlimited and cannot be exercised to the point of being clearly inconsistent with the purposes of the Convention'.[136]

Thus, Article 25 does not create an autonomous and self-contained concept of 'investment' that somehow floats apart from the underlying rights that may exist under municipal law in relation to 'investment'. Article 25 defines the nature of the disputes referable to the Centre as any *'legal dispute'* arising from an *'investment'*. These two terms require, in the absence of an express definition in an investment treaty, a *renvoi* to the substantive regulation contained in municipal law. If not, the term 'legal dispute' becomes a nullity and the ordinary meaning of the words of Article 25(1) are ignored, which is not permitted under the Vienna Convention on the Law of Treaties.

If two countries are signatories to the ICSID Convention and their municipal laws define investment, the definitions are relevant since the *travaux préparatoires* of the ICSID Convention point to States' freedom to define 'investment'. However, this does not mean that, for example, a host State's practice of denying admission to foreign investments of companies of a particular nationality would be consistent with the provisions of an investment treaty's. The State's freedom to define 'investment' does not remit the application of an international treaty to its sovereign will.

The scope of an investment treaty's protections may nonetheless be limited by municipal law of one of the State signatories, which may contain a definition of investment or some requirements that must be complied with to be considered an investment.[137] For example, the BIT between the UK and Indonesia[138] defines investment as 'every kind of asset' (Article 1), but Article 2 provides that the BIT is applicable only to the investments of British individuals or companies that 'have been granted admission in accordance with the Foreign Capital Investment Law No. 1 of 1967 or any law amending or replacing it'. Despite a broad definition of investment, the BIT's scope is limited to foreign investments complying with Indonesian law. In this situation, the definition of investment contained in a municipal law is directly relevant.

Some commentators and ICSID tribunals have suggested that the concept of investment under Article 25 has certain general characteristics applicable to all cases.[139] These characteristics are said to be: (i) duration; (ii) regularity of profit and return; (iii) risk; (iv) substantial financial know-how or commitment; and (v) significance for the host State's development.[140] However, it is unclear how and when these

---

136. Broches, 'The Convention on the Settlement of Investment Disputes Between States and Nationals of other States' (1972) *Recueil des Cours*, 331–410 at 362.
137. *See* Schlemmer, *supra* n. 173, 52–55.
138. Agreement for the Promotion and Protection of Investment, 27 Apr. 1976, available on the UNCTAD website: www.unctad.org/sections/dite/iia/docs/bits/uk_indonesia.pdf.
139. *See* Schreuer et al., *The ICSID Convention: A Commentary*, 128–134; *Fedax v. Venezuela*, Decision on Jurisdiction, 11 Jun. 1997, *ILM* 37 (1998), 1378; *Salini Costruttori S.p.A. and Italstrade v. Morocco; Mihaly International Corporation v. Democratic Socialist Republic of Sri Lanka*, Award, 15 Mar. 2002, *ILM* 41 (2002), 867; and *Mitchell v. the Democratic Republic of Congo*.
140. For the history of these features, *see*, e.g., Krishan, 'A Notion of ICSID Investment', and *Mitchell v. Congo*, Decision on the Application for Annulment, para. 27.

characteristics should actually be applied, and how they may help in distinguishing an investment from an 'ordinary commercial transaction'.[141]

For example, 'duration' is a variable factor in relation to different project types; some projects have a short life span, despite the fact that they may be considered an investment for the host State from an economic perspective. Duration therefore is a flawed basis for differentiating 'investment' and 'ordinary commercial transaction'. 'Regularity of profit and return' is a questionable distinguishing factor. A regular profit/return does not necessarily accompany a long-term, major investment, where there may be no profit or return for a substantial number of years, while an ordinary commercial transaction that is repeated over several years may provide a regular return. 'Risk' may be present in ordinary commercial transactions as well as in investments. 'Substantial commitment' may also be present in an ordinary commercial transaction if, for example, it involves the sale of expensive equipment. Finally, 'significance for the host State's development' can be an unsound predictive factor depending on the volatility of the host State's economic programmes. The construction of a nuclear plant may in one year be considered a significant contribution to the development of a State and in the next be regarded as detrimental because of environmental issues. On the other hand, the sale of machinery may contribute significantly to the host State's economic development.

In short, these five '*Salini*' characteristics are of limited usefulness in the identification of 'investment'. Their elasticity (and subjectivity) enable a moderately determined interpreter to stretch them to serve his purpose. They assist in the definition of the economic characteristics of an investment. But these characteristics are insufficient for defining 'investment': there is still the requirement under ICSID Article 25(1) to determine whether a legal dispute arises out of an investment and whether the investment is lawful.

Not every municipal law right constitutes an investment, however, because investment tribunals might then enjoy jurisdiction over a dispute concerning, e.g., a metro ticket, which could arguably constitute an investment. Definitions of the economic characteristics of an investment such as the one provided by the OECD[142] or the five criteria discussed above may provide an initial framework. Alternatively, Douglas, noting the subjectivity of some of these criteria, proposed three characteristics of an investment: '(i) commitment of resources to the economy of the host state;

---

141. *See*, e.g., *Mitchell v. Congo*.
142. 'Foreign direct investment reflects the objective of obtaining a lasting interest by a resident entity in one economy ('direct investor') in an entity resident in an economy other than that of the investor ('direct investment enterprise'). The lasting interest implies the existence of a long-term relationship between the direct investor and the enterprise and a significant degree of influence on the management of the enterprise. Direct investment involves both the initial transaction between the two entities and all subsequent capital transactions between them and among affiliated enterprises, both incorporated and unincorporated' (OECD Benchmark Definition of Foreign Direct Investment, 3rd edn, available from the OECD website: www.oecd.org/dataoecd/10/16/2090148.pdf).

(ii) assumption of risk; and (iii) expectation of a commercial return'.[143] The three Douglas criteria are arguably more objective and represent, this Chapter submits, a more useful framework to identify the economic characteristics of 'investment' – assuming the existence of a legal right pursuant to municipal law.

Gaillard has suggested two approaches to the definition of investment: deductive and intuitive.[144] The former method determines 'in the abstract the factors that are of the essence to an investment in order to then proceed in each case to a process of characterization', while the latter 'merely *identifies* features or "characteristics" that have already been observed'[145] in previous decisions on the notion of investments. These methods do not identify the characteristics of an investment, but only whether these characteristics are abstract factors or variable features: no role is left for municipal law. However, not every economic investment may entail an underlying legal right, and not every investment is protected under an investment treaty.[146]

Several conclusions may be drawn from this *excursus*:

(i) International law provides no general definition of 'investment'. The term may be described in a treaty by a non-exhaustive (or exhaustive) list of assets, but there is no accepted definition of this term.
(ii) The ICSID Convention refers to 'investment', but the term was not defined because of a lack of consensus among delegates. However, it is clear that an investment dispute must concern a dispute over legal rights – as conveyed by the words 'legal dispute' in Article 25(1).
(iii) BITs often identify 'investment' by means of a list (exhaustive or non-exhaustive) of the class of assets that are considered an 'investment' and do not address substantive regulation of an investment. In certain BITs, the scope is limited to foreign investments defined as such by the host State regulation on admission of foreign investments.
(iv) In the event of arbitral proceedings under the auspices of ICSID or to which the State consented in a BIT, once the types of economic activity that are considered an investment are identified under the relevant treaty, an arbitral tribunal *must* refer to municipal law to identify *in specie* what constitutes an 'investment'. Investment has a legal and an economic aspect. The role of municipal law is to determine whether there is an underlying right, and if the investment is lawful. However, this *renvoi* should not be understood as remitting the definition of investment entirely to the host State's sovereign will.

---

143. Douglas, *The International Law of Investment Claims*, 191.
144. Gaillard, 'Identify or Define? Reflections on the Evolution of the Concept of Investment in ICSID Practice', 407–411.
145. *Id.*, 407.
146. *See, infra, Mihaly International Corporation v. Sri Lanka*.

§4.05 THE ROLE OF MUNICIPAL LAW IN THE DEFINITION, REGISTRATION REQUIREMENTS, AND LEGAL VALIDITY OF INVESTMENTS

[A] Definition of an Investment

This section addresses the role of municipal law in determining whether an economic activity is to be considered an investment, and whether any right listed as an investment in a treaty is automatically an investment.

[1] Mihaly International Corporation v. Sri Lanka[147]

Investment treaty tribunals have to define investment in accordance with the definition contained in the relevant treaty. This definition must take into account whether there is an underlying right, and that assessment, properly conducted, must refer to municipal law. In *Mihaly International Corporation v. Sri Lanka*[148] the tribunal held that it lacked jurisdiction over a dispute concerning expenditure incurred in connection with a prospective investment that did not materialize. The tribunal ruled that its jurisdiction was 'based on the consent of the Parties to the dispute that have previously agreed to submit the dispute in question to the jurisdiction of ICSID'.[149] In particular, the tribunal stated that:

(i) In the absence of a generally accepted definition of investment, it was necessary to examine ICSID 'practice' and the practice of States as evidenced in multilateral and bilateral treaties.[150]
(ii) In this specific case, the Letters of Intent executed between the parties did not contemplate any obligation, and therefore Sri Lanka had never accepted that the Claimant's expenditures would have been considered an investment. In this case, there was no evidence of treaty interpretation or State practice that pre-investment and development expenditure 'could automatically be admitted as "investment" in the absence of the consent of the host State to the implementation of the project'.[151]

The *Mihaly v. Sri Lanka* tribunal's decision properly focused on the parties' consent and whether there was an underlying right. If the tribunal had considered whether an investment existed only on the basis of the five features applied in *Salini v.*

---

147. *Mihaly International Corporation v. Democratic Socialist Republic of Sri Lanka*, Award, 15 Mar. 2002, *ILM* 41 (2002), 867.
148. *See* Hamida, 'The Mihaly v. Sri Lanka case: Some Thoughts Relating to the Status of Pre-Investment Expenditures', in *International Investment Law and Arbitration: Leading Cases from the ICSID, NAFTA, Bilateral Treaties and Customary International Law*, 47. *See also Zhinvali Development Limited v. Republic of Georgia*, Award, 24 Jan. 2003, ICSID Reports 10 (2007), 3.
149. *Mihaly v. Sri Lanka*, para. 55.
150. *Id.*, para. 58.
151. *Id.*, paras 59–60.

Morocco and *Fedax v. Venezuela*, it might have reached a different – and incorrect – conclusion. Those features arguably were satisfied. Instead, the *Mihaly* tribunal disregarded the five features. It determined that the letters of intent conferred no rights upon the parties. Municipal law played its appropriate role of determining the substance of the rights stemming from the investment. The notion of investment was not tested under some vague criteria; instead, an analysis of the rights in dispute was carried out pursuant to the applicable municipal law. There was a commitment of capital by the Claimant, but no *legal* commitment arose from the letters of intent.

Both terms, 'legal dispute' and 'investment', are relevant to establish ICSID jurisdiction. The 'notion of a "pre-investment" is meaningless':[152] either an investment exists and is protected under the relevant treaty or it is not. Even if an investment in the economic sense existed – which was questionable – the letters of intent did not confer any right under the relevant municipal law. The *Mihaly* tribunal rightly concluded that the investment made by Mihaly was therefore not an Article 25 investment. [153]

[2]   Fedax v. Venezuela[154]

An ICSID award often cited for the meaning of the term 'investment' is *Fedax v. Venezuela*.[155] It is the first award that considers at length the State's objection to jurisdiction on the ground of lack of an investment. In two earlier awards, *Kaiser Bauxite v. Jamaica*[156] and *Alcoa Minerals of Jamaica Inc. v. Jamaica*,[157] arbitral tribunals cursorily examined whether there was an investment, and briefly referred to the lack of a definition in Article 25 of the ICSID Convention. Both tribunals held that an investment existed, but they did not provide a substantive analysis.

Fedax provides an analysis; unfortunately it is misguided. The *Fedax* dispute concerned promissory notes that had been endorsed to the Claimant. Venezuela objected to the tribunal's jurisdiction on the ground that the promissory notes did not qualify as an investment under the ICSID Convention, because the Claimant had acquired, by way of endorsement, promissory notes issued by Venezuela in connection with a contract made with a Venezuelan corporation. This transaction (i.e., the endorsement) did not constitute a direct foreign investment involving (a) first, a long term transfer of financial resources – capital flow – from one country to another (the

---

152. Douglas, *The International Law of Investment Claims*, 187.
153. A different case is when the reimbursement of pre-investment expenses is claimed in connection of an investment that later materialized. *See* Malicorp v. Egypt, Award, 7 Feb. 2011, para 113, available on italaw.com website: http://www.italaw.com/sites/default/files/case-documents/ita0499.pdf.
154. *Fedax v. Venezuela*, Decision on Jurisdiction, 11 Jun. 1997, *ILM* 37 (1998), 1378; Award of 9 Mar. 1998, *ILM* 37 (1998), 1391.
155. This is the first award that considers the State's objection to jurisdiction on the ground of lack of an investment. In two previous awards, *Kaiser Bauxite v. Jamaica*, ICSID Reports 1, 1993, 296, and *Alcoa Minerals of Jamaica Inc. v. Jamaica*, Yearbook Commercial Arbitration, vol. IV (1979), 206, the tribunals examined whether there was an investment, and both ruled that an investment existed.
156. *Kaiser Bauxite v. Jamaica*, ICSID Reports 1, 1993, 296.
157. *Alcoa Minerals of Jamaica Inc. v. Jamaica*, in Yearbook Commercial Arbitration, vol. IV (1979), 206.

recipient of the investment) in order to acquire interests in a corporation, and (b) a transaction that would entail certain risks to the potential investor, which would normally be the case in any transaction. Venezuela characterized the disputed transaction as a portfolio investment to acquire titles to money, by an investor's acquisition of shares of a corporation through the Stock Exchange, whereas the definition of investment entailed laying out money or property in business ventures to produce a revenue or income.[158]

Venezuela's contentions were unavailing. The tribunal determined that the dispute was within its jurisdiction and stated that:

(i) The term 'investment' was to be 'broadly understood'[159] since: (a) Article 25 of the ICSID Convention left the definition of investment to the consent of the parties;[160] (b) commentators on the Convention have concluded that 'a broad approach to the interpretation of this term in Article 25 is warranted';[161] and, (c) it 'is within the sole discretion of the Contracting State to determine the type of investment disputes that it considers arbitrable in the context of ICSID'.[162]

(ii) The broad scope of Article 25(1) and the conclusions reached by previous tribunals were sufficient to ground its jurisdiction. Loans qualify as an investment within ICSID's jurisdiction as do, in certain circumstances, the purchase of bonds. Since promissory notes were evidence of a loan and constitute a typical financial and credit instrument, there was nothing to prevent their purchase from qualifying as an investment under the Convention. This conclusion, however, had to be tested in the context of the specific consent of the parties as contained in the BIT.[163]

(iii) The relevant BIT defined investment as 'every kind of asset', including rights derived from shares, bonds and other types of interests in companies and joint ventures and title to money, other assets or to 'any performance having an economic value'.[164] This provision evidenced a broad meaning for the term investment.[165] It was therefore left to the parties' discretion whether loans were considered an investment.[166] Venezuela had not notified any class of investment to be or not to be submitted to the tribunal's jurisdiction pursuant to Article 25(4) of the ICSID Convention.

---

158. *Fedax v. Venezuela*, Decision on Jurisdiction, paras 18, 19.
159. *Id*, para. 25.
160. *Id.*, para. 21.
161. *Id.*, para. 22.
162. *Ibid.*
163. *Id.*, para. 29.
164. *Id.*, para. 31.
165. *Id.*, para. 32.
166. *Id.*, paras 22–23.

(iv) In other investment treaties entered into by Venezuela, when Venezuela intended to exclude a transaction from the investment definition, it did so in unequivocal terms.[167]

(v) Promissory notes were evidence of a loan and therefore qualified as an investment.[168] As an 'additional element', the promissory notes were issued in compliance with the Law on Public Credit and the transaction therefore involved a fundamental public interest.[169] The status of the promissory notes showed that the type of investment was not a 'short-term occasional financial arrangement'.[170]

(vi) It was undisputed that the Government of Venezuela foresaw the possibility that the promissory notes would be transferred and endorsed to subsequent holders, since they explicitly allow for such a possibility. Thus, the investment itself remained constant.

(vii) The 'basic features of an investment have been described as involving a certain duration, a certain regularity of profit and return, assumption of risk, a substantial capital commitment and a significance for the host State's development': each of these features was present in this case. '[M]ost importantly', 'there is clearly a significant relationship between the transaction and the development of the host State as specifically required under the Law for issuing the pertinent financial instruments'.[171]

The *Fedax* decision has been rightly criticized as having broadened the definition of investment and, consequently, ICSID jurisdiction under Article 25 to the point where any financial transaction would constitute an investment.[172] The *Fedax* tribunal further failed to explain how the presence of a public interest, represented by the fact that the promissory notes were issued in compliance with a Venezuela's Law on Public Credit, transformed the notes into an investment. The notes existed under and were governed by Venezuelan law, but this did not convert the notes into an investment in Venezuela. If that were the case, investment treaty jurisdiction would arise every time Venezuelan law accorded a right to a foreigner. Indeed, it has been suggested that *Fedax* stretches ICSID jurisdiction to include any investments regardless of whether the dispute arises directly from the investment or represents an ancillary transaction. The conclusion reached by the *Fedax* tribunal simply does not accord with the *travaux préparatoires* of the ICSID Convention.[173]

---

167. *Id.*, para. 36.
168. *Id.*, para. 29.
169. *Id.*, para. 42.
170. *Id.*, para. 43.
171. *Id.*, para. 43.
172. *See* Waibel, 'Opening Pandora's Box: Sovereign Bonds in International Arbitration', *AJIL* 101 (2007), 711, at 722.
173. Furthermore, *Fedax* stretches ICSID jurisdiction to include any investments regardless of whether the dispute arises directly from the investment or represents an ancillary transaction: *see* Dolzer and Schreuer, *Principles of International Investment Law*, 231.

[3] Salini Costruttori S.p.A. and Italstrade v. Morocco[174] ('Salini v. Morocco')

The so-called five 'objective' features that define the concept of investment discussed above, are commonly referred to as the *'Salini'* factors. In this ICSID arbitration, the Claimants sought damages in connection with a highway construction contract. Morocco objected to jurisdiction on the grounds that, *inter alia*, no investment existed either under the relevant BIT or the ICSID Convention.

The *Salini* tribunal rejected the State's challenge. It commented that the investment requirement in Article 25 'must be respected as an objective condition of the jurisdiction of the Centre'.[175] The tribunal observed that the 'doctrine generally considers that investment infers: contributions, certain duration of performance of the contract and a participation in the risks of the transaction' and that 'one may add the contribution to the economic development of the host State'.[176] It assessed these criteria 'globally' and held that the Claimants made contributions 'in money, in kind and in industry'. The duration met the minimum length (from two to five years). The risk incurred by the Claimants 'flows from the nature of the contract at issue'. The contribution to the development of Morocco 'cannot seriously be questioned'.[177] The construction contract therefore constituted an investment under Article 25.

As for the relevant BIT, the *Salini* tribunal stated that it included within the term investment, 'any rights to any contractual benefit having an economic value' and 'any right of an economic nature conferred by law or by contract'.[178] The reference in the BIT to the law of the host State for the definition of investment concerned the validity and not the definition of investment.[179] The *Salini* tribunal considered that the construction contract created a right to a contractual benefit having an economic value, and the Claimants had benefited from a right of an economic nature conferred by contract.[180] The Claimants never violated Moroccan regulations during the pre-contractual stage or the performance stage.[181] The contract also approved by the competent authority, as Moroccan law required.[182] The contract therefore constituted an investment pursuant to the BIT.

The *Salini* jurisdictional decision thus placed in separate categories the definition of investment under Article 25 and the relevant BIT. Municipal law played a role because the investment concerned a contract that was valid under Moroccan law. The existence of the five features did not exclude the determination under municipal law of

---

174. *Salini Costruttori S.p.A. and Italstrade v. Morocco*, Decision on Jurisdiction, 23 Jul 2001, 42 ILM 609 (2003).
175. *Id.*, para. 52.
176. *Ibid.*
177. *Id.*, paras 52–57.
178. *Id.*, para. 45.
179. *Id.*, para. 46.
180. *Id.*, para. 45.
181. *Id.*, para. 46.
182. *Id.*, paras 47–48.

whether a legal and valid right arose from the investment.[183] Article 25 in the *Salini* interpretation contains an outer-boundary on investment and lists objective economic factors that must be present notwithstanding the definition contained in the relevant BIT. The flaw is that this interpretation of Article 25 omits to consider that the intention of the ICSID Contracting States was to leave the definition of investment open, with the only boundaries being those agreed by the parties *and* the existence of a legal dispute on rights, not on interests.[184]

[4]   Mitchell v. Congo[185]

The Annulment Decision in *Mitchell v. Congo* largely relies on *Salini v Morocco*[186] though in finding against the investor. This decision emphasizes that the notion of investment has to meet both the 'objective standard' set out in Article 25 of the ICSID Convention, and, separately, the BIT requirements. Based on this approach, the Ad Hoc Committee annulled the tribunal's award on the grounds of, *inter alia*, failure to state reasons as to the existence of an investment in accordance with Article 25 of the ICSID Convention.

The *Mitchell* dispute concerned a claim for expropriation in connection with legal services rendered by the Claimant. Congo argued that the Claimant's activity, a law firm, did not qualify as an investment. The Annulment Committee reasoned that the fact that a State has not made use of the notification option provided for under Article 25(4) of the ICSID Convention cannot be understood to mean that that State has taken a certain position regarding the concept of investment. It is necessary to verify whether the concept of investment as set out in the parties' agreement or in the BIT conforms with the concept of investment in the ICSID Convention, as well as from ICSID case law, to the extent the latter may contribute to defining the concept.[187] The concept in the Convention should 'prevail' over any other definition of investment in the parties' agreement or in the BIT.[188] The relevant BIT contained an enumerative and non-exhaustive approach to investment, which made it possible to apply the protection provided by the BIT to a range of rights and assets of the foreign investor.

The *Mitchell* Annulment Committee acknowledged that the BIT did not contain a definition of investment, as such.[189] However, the Committee considered that ICSID

---

183. The issue of the legality of the investment was also addressed in *Tradex Hellas SA v. Albania*, Decision on Jurisdiction, 24 Dec. 1996, *ICSID Reports 5* (2002), 47; Award, 29 Apr. 1999, *ICSID Reports 5* (2002), 70, and in *World Duty Free Company Limited v. Republic of Kenya* (Jurisdiction based on contract not BIT), Award, 4 Oct. 2006, available on the International Treaty Arbitration website: http://ita.law.uvic.ca/documents/WDFv.KenyaAward.pdf.
184. Report of the Executive Directors on the ICSID Convention, paras 25-28.
185. *Mitchell v. Congo*, Decision on the Application for Annulment, 1 Nov. 2006, available on Investment Treaty Arbitration website: https://www.italaw.com/sites/default/files/case-documents/ita0537.pdf.
186. *Id.*, para. 67.
187. *Id.*, para. 25.
188. *Ibid.*
189. *Id.*, para. 26.

decisions and 'legal doctrine' identified four characteristics of investment: the investor's commitment; duration; economic risk (i.e., 'uncertainty regarding [the investment's] successful outcome'); and contribution to economic development (although the contribution does not need to be 'sizeable or successful').[190] The Committee agreed with commentators – and *Salini* – that the contribution to the economic development of the host State was the only possible indication of an 'objective meaning' of the term 'investment'. The parties to a treaty cannot open the jurisdiction of the Centre to *any* operation they might arbitrarily qualify as an investment. Thus, the ICSID Convention has supremacy over an agreement between the parties or a BIT.[191]

The Committee concluded that the dispute in question 'did not involve a "readily recognizable" investment, as it concerned a legal counseling firm established by a U.S. citizen in [Congo]'.[192] Furthermore, the project (which, if it 'fulfils certain characteristics, becomes the investment') was distinct from all the rights protected by the BIT.[193] Since the arbitral award had not addressed the content of services rendered by the Claimant's firm that would 'justify the decision to qualify them as an investment',[194] annulment was appropriate.

The *Mitchell* Annulment Committee's decision is significant (albeit controversial) since it clarifies that 'investment' in ICSID cases does not necessarily coincide with the rights protected by investment treaties. Municipal law is relevant in determining whether a legal entitlement underlies the investment, though the existence of such entitlement is not sufficient: there is still the need to determine whether an investment exists. The *Mitchell* Annulment Committee relied on the *Salini* test to determine such existence, though the application of, for example, the three Douglas criteria[195] (see above) might have led to a different result.

The *Mitchell* Annulment Committee's reliance on *Salini* is at odds with the approach taken by the tribunal in *Biwater Gauff (Tanzania) Ltd v. Tanzania*.[196] The *Biwater* tribunal emphatically rejected a strict interpretation of the criteria identified in *Salini* and stated that 'these criteria are not fixed or mandatory as a matter of law. They do not appear in the ICSID Convention'.[197] The tribunal concluded by refusing to impose an objective definition of investment applicable in all cases, and instead adopted 'a more flexible and pragmatic approach' to its meaning, which considered the criteria identified in *Salini* and all the circumstances of the case, including the nature of the instrument containing the relevant consent to ICSID.[198] This approach was also

---

190. *Id.*, paras 27–33.
191. *Id.*, para. 31.
192. *Id.*, para. 34.
193. *Id.*, para. 38.
194. *Ibid.*
195. Douglas, *The International Law of Investment Claims*, 191.
196. *Biwater Gauff (Tanzania) Ltd v. Tanzania*, Award, 24 Jul. 2008, available on Investment Treaty Arbitration website: http://ita.law.uvic.ca/documents/Biwateraward.pdf.
197. *Id.*, para. 312.
198. *Id.*, para. 316.

adopted in *Malaysian Historical Salvors v. Malaysia* annulment proceedings,[199] which overturned the tribunal's finding that there had been no investment.

Collectively, these decisions (*Mitchell* Annulment, *Biwater*, *Malaysian Historical*) explain that the definition of 'investment' may consider economic features that cannot be regarded *numerus clausus*, but the term has an inherent limitation represented by the existence of a legal entitlement. This entitlement, in the absence of an express definition contained in the investment treaty, has to be defined in accordance with municipal law, with the *caveat* that any definition of legal entitlement aimed exclusively or substantially at preventing or circumventing investment protection must be disregarded.

[5] Pantechniki SA Contractors & Engineers v. Albania ('Pantechniki'[200]) and 'Inherent Meaning' of Investment

The Claimant in *Pantechniki* won a tender to carry out works on roads and bridges in Albania, and signed contracts in 1994. In 1997, after violent riots, the Claimant abandoned the work site. The State raised a jurisdictional challenge on the ground of lack of an investment. The sole arbitrator rejected the challenge (though he dismissed the claims on other grounds).

The arbitrator observed that while the alleged 'investment' clearly fell under the express terms of the relevant BIT, there were difficulties under ICSID Article 25, given the lack of a definition of 'investment' in the Convention. He declined to follow the *Salini* 'test', which it considered to be a list of characteristics rather than a proper test.[201] Instead, the arbitrator proceeded by addressing whether Article 25 contained a definition more restrictive than some BITs. He noted that the Report of the Executive Directors on the ICSID Convention[202] identifies the cornerstone role played by consent, but consent does not suffice to bring a dispute within ICSID. ICSID jurisdiction is limited by reference to the parties and to the nature of the dispute. The term 'investment', he concluded, carries an 'inherent meaning' that should be adopted to invalidate certain very broad definitions of investment contained in certain BITs. In the dispute before him, because the Claimant was in charge of building roads, there had been a qualifying investment under the BIT and under Article 25.[203]

The *Pantechniki* arbitrator's (a) 'inherent meaning' understanding of Article 25; (b) consideration of certain portions of the Report of the Executive Directors; and (c) view that the so-called 'objective' criteria promulgated in *Salini* contain unacceptably subjective elements are, in total, a useful approach to the problem posed by the

---

199. *Malaysian Historical Salvors v. Malaysia*, Decision on the Application for Annulment, 16 Apr. 2009, available on Investment Treaty Arbitration website: http://ita.law.uvic.ca/alphabetical_list.htm.
200. *Pantechniki SA Contractors & Engineers v. Albania*, ICSID Case No. ARB/07/21, Award 30 Jul. 2009, available on Investment Treaty Arbitration website: https://www.italaw.com/sites/default/files/case-documents/ita0618.pdf.
201. *Id.*, para. 36.
202. Report of the Executive Directors on the ICSID Convention: *ILM* 4 (1965), 524, para. 25.
203. *Id.*, para. 48.

relationship between Article 25 and the parties' 'consent' to refer disputes to ICSID. However, this approach might have been strengthened if it had expressly considered other aspects of the ICSID *travaux préparatoires* and how those might bear directly on the application of Article 25. In particular, the *Pantechniki* arbitrator could have pointed to paragraph 26 in the Report of the Executive Directors – "Article 25(1) requires that the dispute must be a 'legal dispute arising directly out of an investment'" – and explained that mere conflicts of interests are not within the Centre's jurisdiction.

Conclusions similar to those in *Pantechniki* were reached in *Philip Morris Brands Sarl v. Uruguay*[204] where the tribunal held that a more flexible approach than *Salini* to the definition of investment was warranted under Article 25: the consent of the Contracting Parties does 'not have an unfettered discretion to go beyond what have been called the "outer limits" set by the ICSID Convention'.[205] To establish these 'outer limits', the tribunal ruled that the concept of investment under Article 25 must be interpreted in accordance with the Vienna Convention on the Law of Treaties. When that task is undertaken, the term investment should be given a broad meaning.[206] The *Philip Morris* tribunal further concluded that the 'outer limits' would exclude from the notion of investment a single commercial transaction, such as mere delivery of goods against payment of the price, though this exclusion simply confirmed that the limits are indeed very expansive.[207] The *Philip Morris* tribunal commented that the characteristics of an investment defined in *Salini* do not constitute jurisdictional requirements and they are not a set of mandatory legal requirements.[208]

§4.06 REGISTRATION REQUIREMENTS

Many BITs require that foreign investors register their investments in the host State or impose other admission requirements for an investment to attract treaty protection. This section addresses the role of municipal law in the definition of registration requirements.[209]

The *Philippe Gruslin v. Malaysia*[210] case arose in relation to a purchase of securities listed on the Kuala Lumpur Stock Exchange through a fund registered in Luxembourg, and a loss suffered as a result of exchange controls. One of the issues was whether this transaction was an 'approved project by the appropriate Ministry in Malaysia, in accordance with the legislation and the administrative practice'.[211] Malaysia argued, *inter alia*, that a portfolio investment would not fall under the definition of 'approved projects'. The tribunal found that an investment in shares, even

---

204. *Philip Morris Brands Sarl v. Uruguay*, ICSID Case No ARB/10/7, Decision on Jurisdiction, 2 Jul. 2013, available on Investment Treaty Arbitration website: https://www.italaw.com/sites/default/files/case-documents/italaw1531.pdf.
205. *Id.*, para. 198.
206. *Id.*, para. 202.
207. *Id.*, para. 203.
208. *Id.*, para. 206.
209. Baltag, 'Admission of Investments and The ICSID Convention', *TDM*, vol. 6, 1 (2009).
210. *Philippe Gruslin v. Malaysia*, Award, 27 Nov. 2000, *ICSID Reports 5* (2002), 484.
211. Article 1 of the Intergovernmental Agreement of 22 Nov. 1979 between Malaysia and Belgium (acting on behalf of Luxembourg).

if in listed shares and therefore in compliance with the regulatory laws of Malaysia, was not approved in compliance with the Intergovernmental Agreement between Malaysia and Belgium-Luxembourg. Thus, even if an investment in shares did qualify as a protected investment under the Intergovernmental Agreement, the investment was not protected because it was not an 'approved project'.

The *Philippe Gruslin* decision underscores the point that municipal law has to be taken into account to establish if the investment fully complies with the rules identified in the investment treaty. However, this does not mean that municipal law's determination of the Claimant's compliance or non-compliance with the rules is dispositive. In *Desert Line Projects v. Yemen*[212] an issue arose over the lack of an investment certificate pursuant to Article 1 of the relevant BIT, and the Claimant's failure to register the investment in accordance with Yemeni Investment Law. The Claimant argued that Yemen had accepted the investment without the certificate, and that Yemen's position was therefore formalistic and lacked good faith. The Claimant further indicated that municipal law was relevant only to the extent that it determined the legality of the investment.

Having noted that the parties did not produce evidence on the meaning of the concept of investment certificate in Yemeni law 'that might deviate from the plain-language purport of the terms "accepted" and "certificate"',[213] the tribunal dismissed the State's objections on the following grounds:[214]

(i) The preamble of the BIT supported the view that municipal law was a 'support and not an impediment' to investments.
(ii) Yemeni law did not define 'investment' in a way that in that would override the definition of the BIT.
(iii) Neither the BIT nor the Yemeni investment law specified how the investment had to be 'accepted' and the Yemeni Investment Law did not require a particular form of acceptance.
(iv) The certificate requirement was not a mere formalism ('an artificial trap depriving investors of the very protection the BIT was intended to provide'[215]), but a substantive requirement. In this case, the investment was endorsed by the highest authorities and the Claimant would have obtained the certificate if it had believed that it was necessary to request it.
(v) Yemen was estopped from raising violation of its own law since it knowingly overlooked it and endorsed the investment.

Municipal law was relevant in both *Gruslin* and *Desert Line*. However, these cases also show that municipal law must not be interpreted in a formalistic manner. The host State cannot rely on its own law only to prevent an investor from benefiting from the BIT. The State cannot first endorse an investment and then refuse to accord

---

212. *Desert Line Projects v. Yemen*, Award, 6 Feb. 2008, available on Investment Treaty Arbitration website: http://ita.law.uvic.ca/documents/DesertLine.pdf.
213. *Id.*, para. 98, 23.
214. *Id.*, paras 99–123, 23–28.
215. *Id.*, para. 106, 24.

treaty protection on the basis of a certificate that was never previously requested before or deemed necessary to execute the investment. In short, municipal law cannot subordinate the concept of investment to the sovereign's will.

§4.07 LEGAL VALIDITY OF INVESTMENT

An investment must be lawful, and lawfulness must be determined by a *renvoi* to municipal law. In *Fraport AG Frankfurt Airport Services Worldwide v. Philippines*,[216] the Claimant invested in a company incorporated in the Philippines (PIATCO). The Claimant was a shareholder in and a lender to PIATCO, which had the concession rights for the construction and operation of a new airport in Manila. One of the allegations made by the Respondent, which became the dispositive issue in the case, was that the Claimant made the investment in violation of Philippines legislation concerning foreign ownership and control legislation, the Anti-Dummy Law (ADL). Specifically, the airport concession concerned a public utility and was therefore subject to the nationality restrictions set forth by the Philippines Constitution and the ADL. The Respondent argued that the Claimant tried to circumvent the 40% foreign ownership limitation through shareholder agreements and indirect ownership. The State also alleged fraud and corruption on the part of PIATCO shareholders as well as Philippines public officials.

The *Fraport* tribunal majority observed, first, that the BIT provided that 'the term "investment" shall mean any kind of asset *accepted in accordance with respective laws and regulations or either Contracting State*'[217] [emphasis in the Award]. The tribunal found that Fraport was 'consciously, intentionally and covertly structuring its investment in a way which it knew to be a violation of the ADL'. (...) Despite having been advised of and plainly understanding the law, 'Fraport secretly designed its investment in the project so as to have that prohibited management and control.'[218] Fraport's strategy was to 'conceal its illegal control from the Philippine authorities.'[219]

Given the violation of the ADL, the tribunal turned to Article 1 of the BIT and the other references in the treaty requiring that investments would be allowed by and in accordance with the Philippine Constitution and laws of the Contracting Parties. The tribunal interpreted these references to mean that 'economic transactions undertaken by a national of one of the parties to the BIT had to meet certain legal requirements of the host state in order to qualify as an "investment" and fall under the Treaty'.[220] Accordingly, the determination of the legality of the investment could be made only by

---

216. *Fraport AG Frankfurt Airport Services Worldwide v. Philippines*, Award, 16 Aug. 2007, available on Investment Treaty Arbitration website: http://ita.law.uvic.ca/documents/FraportAward.pdf. This award was later annulled for a violation of the right to be heard: Decision on the Application for Annulment, 23 Dec. 2010, available on Investment Treaty Arbitration website: https://www.italaw.com/sites/default/files/case-documents/ita0341.pdf.
217. *Id.*, paras 300, 138.
218. *Id.*, paras 323, 153.
219. *Id.*, paras 326, 155. *See also* paras 332, 159.
220. *Id.*, paras 340, 162. The issue of estoppel was dismissed since the arrangement to cover the management and control of PATCO was hidden to the Respondent.

the investment tribunal because such legality was 'a premise for this Tribunal's jurisdiction',[221] though the tribunal explained that, as a matter of international law, it had to consider municipal law:

> The Tribunal cannot agree, as a matter of law, with the Claimant's contention that '[e]ven if there could be said to be an issue as to whether the Philippine laws were complied with [...], it could be of only municipal, not international legal significance'. This interpretation, if accepted, would deprive a significant part of the ordinary words of a treaty of any meaning and effect. The BIT is, to be sure, an international instrument, but its Articles 1 and 2 and Article 2 of the Protocol effect a renvoi to national law, a mechanism which is hardly unusual in treaties and, indeed, occurs in the Washington Convention. A failure to comply with the national law to which a treaty refers will have an international legal effect.[222]

Even granting a presumption in favour of the investor, the tribunal found that the Claimant 'knowingly and intentionally circumvented the ADL'.[223] Therefore, the purchase of shares in the project was not an investment covered by the BIT.

There was a dissenting opinion in *Fraport*, which did not exclude the relevance of municipal law. Rather, the dissent stated that PIATCO was not a public utility franchise. Therefore, the ADL did not apply, and the issue of illegality of the investment had to be addressed in the merits stage; it was not a jurisdictional issue.

The *Fraport* decision was annulled for a violation of the right to be heard in relation to evidence produced by the Respondent. The arbitral tribunal's holding on the definition of investment was not reached on review.[224] The dispute was then submitted to a new tribunal, which rendered an award dismissing the claim for lack of jurisdiction.[225] This second tribunal concluded that the relevant BIT required that an investment comply with the laws of the host State at the time it was made in order to be protected.[226] This second tribunal reiterated that there was 'an increasingly well-established international principle which makes international legal remedies unavailable with respect to illegal investments, at least when such illegality goes to the essence of the investment'.[227]

The lucid reasoning demonstrated by the *Fraport* (I and II) tribunals in applying municipal law was not as apparent in an earlier case, in which the tribunal made its task easier by importing international law principles into the relevant municipal law. The disputed contract in *World Duty Free Company Ltd v. the Republic of Kenya*[228]

---

221. *Id.*, paras 391, 186.
222. *Id.*, paras 394, 187.
223. *Id.*, paras 401, 191.
224. *Fraport.*, Annulment Committee para. 118.
225. *Fraport AG Frankfurt Airport Services Worldwide v. Philippines* II, Award, 10 Dec. 2014, available on Investment Treaty Arbitration website: http://www.italaw.com/sites/default/files/case-documents/italaw4114.pdf.
226. *Id.*, para. 333.
227. *Id.*, para. 323.
228. *World Duty Free Company Ltd v. Republic of Kenya*, Award, 4 Oct. 2006, available on Investment Treaty Arbitration website: http://ita.law.uvic.ca/documents/WDFv.KenyaAward.pdf.

concerned the construction of duty-free complexes at Nairobi and Mombasa International Airports, and contained an arbitration clause providing for consent to ICSID jurisdiction. This provision stipulated that the contract was related to an investment but did not refer to any legality requirement. An issue in dispute concerned the legality of the contract, which allegedly had been procured by bribing the then president of Kenya. The tribunal held that the amount paid by the Claimant was a bribe made in order to obtain the contract,[229] and a claim based on a contract obtained by corruption could not be upheld by the tribunal.[230] The tribunal reached its conclusion by examining whether bribery contravened international, English, and Kenyan public policy.

In *Fraport* the legality of the investment was determined under municipal law pursuant to a *renvoi* from international law. In *World Duty Free*, however, the legality of an investment was determined under municipal law, but tested *vis-à-vis* some general principles of international law.[231] Are the general principles of international law (good faith, *nemo auditur propriam turpitudinem allegans*, international public policy, prohibition of unjust enrichment) redundant because municipal law rendered the investment unlawful? If the investment treaty provides that the investment must be validly made in accordance with the host State's law, these general principles of international law would seem inapposite. To be sure, the lawfulness of an investment cannot be entirely subject to the will of a sovereign State. *Fraport* emphasized that the host State could be prevented from relying on invalidity with its internal law in the event that it did not act in good faith and knowingly endorsed the investment in violation of its own law.

Finally, *Fraport* distinguished between illegality at the time of entry of the investment in the host State from subsequent illegality. Illegality *ab initio* prevents the economic transaction from qualifying as an investment protected by the investment treaty, while a subsequent violation is relevant as a defence for the host State. In both situations, municipal law remains a crucial element in a tribunal's determination of its own jurisdiction.

§4.08 UNCITRAL INVESTMENT ARBITRATION PROCEEDINGS

The distinction discussed above between Article 25 of the ICSID Convention and BIT provisions concerning 'investment' would not appear to be relevant in investment proceedings conducted pursuant to the UNCITRAL Arbitration Rules. There is only the definition in the BIT. However, the absence of a jurisdictional threshold such as ICSID Convention Article 25 does not mean that the inherent or 'underlying legal right' notion of investment is inapplicable in UNCITRAL cases.

---

229. *Id.*, para. 136, 41.
230. *Id.*, para. 157, 48.
231. *See Plama Consortium Ltd v. Republic of Bulgaria* Award, 27 Aug. 2008, para 140, where the tribunal considered both international law and municipal law in determining an investment's lawfulness, even though the relevant investment treaty did not mention its legal validity. Decision available on the Investment Treaty Arbitration website: http://ita.law.uvic.ca/documents/PlamaBulgariaAward.pdf.

In *Romak v. Uzbekistan*,[232] the tribunal held that it lacked jurisdiction since the Claimant did not own an 'investment' within the meaning of Article 1 of the Switzerland—Uzbekistan BIT. Romak's rights were embodied in a sales contract, a one-off commercial transaction pursuant to which the Claimant undertook to deliver wheat against a price to be paid by the Uzbek parties.[233] As a result of difficulties in obtaining payment for the wheat deliveries, Romak commenced arbitration proceedings against its Uzbek counterparty, under the auspices of the Grain and Feed Trade Association; Romak won an award, but unsuccessfully attempted to enforce it in several countries, including Uzbekistan.[234] Romak then commenced an investment arbitration proceeding, alleging violation of the BIT. Uzbekistan argued lack of an investment.[235]

The tribunal had to address the interpretation of the term 'investments' as found in Article 1(2) of the BIT. To do so, it resorted to the *'ordinary meaning'* of the terms of the BIT, *'in their context and in the light of its object and purpose'*.[236] The tribunal stated that the *'ordinary meaning'* of the term 'investments' was the commitment of funds or other assets with the purpose to receive a profit, or 'return', from that commitment of capital. The term 'asset' instead meant property of any kind.[237]

The tribunal rejected the Claimant's approach, which sought to demonstrate that its assets could fall within one or more of the categories listed in Article 1(2) of the BIT.[238] The tribunal stated that there ought to be a benchmark against which to assess those non-listed assets or categories of assets in order to determine whether they constituted an 'investment' under the BIT. The term 'investment' had a meaning in itself that could not be ignored when considering the list of assets contained in the BIT.[239] A mechanical application of the categories listed in the BIT could produce a result that was manifestly absurd or unreasonable,[240] rendering meaningless the distinction between investments, on the one hand, and purely commercial transactions, on the other. Under the Claimant's approach, every contract entered into between a Swiss national and a State entity of Uzbekistan would constitute an investment under the BIT.

The *Romak* tribunal concluded that 'investments' had a meaning independent of the categories enumerated in Article 1(2). However, since Contracting States were free to deem any kind of asset or economic transaction an investment attracting treaty protection, and could even go as far as stipulating that a 'pure' one-off sales contract may constitute an investment, such a transaction would in that event be covered.

---

232. *Romak v. Uzbekistan*, PCA No AA/280, UNCITRAL Rules, 26 Nov. 2009, available on Investment Treaty Arbitration website: https://www.italaw.com/sites/default/files/case-documents/ita0716.pdf.
233. *Id.*, paras 242, 243.
234. *Id.*, para. 13.
235. *Id.*, para. 93.
236. *Id.*, para. 176.
237. *Id.*, para. 177.
238. *Id.*, para. 178.
239. *Id.*, paras 179 and 180.
240. *Id.*, para. 184.

However, the tribunal determined that the wording of the Switzerland—Uzbekistan BIT did not permit the tribunal to infer such extraordinary intent in the present case.[241]

Thus, even in proceedings under the UNCITRAL Rules, where there is no Article 25 'outer limit' for 'investment', the term has been deemed to have an intrinsic meaning that encompasses the presence of economic features. A simple sale of goods cannot be qualified as an investment whether the proceedings are under ICISD or UNCITRAL Rules – unless, under UNCITRAL, the BIT states this possibility in clear and unmistakable language.

§4.09 CONCLUSION

International law classifies or identifies the property rights that fall under its umbrella of protection; municipal law governs the substantive aspects, including the existence and validity of a property right.

A tribunal must first determine whether the relevant treaty defines property right or provides for a *renvoi* to municipal law for the substantive regime of property rights. The treaty's wording is fundamental; although customary international law lacks a general definition of property, States are free to define the content of property rights for the purpose of a particular treaty.

The authorities supporting the proposition that international law protects tangibles and intangibles as property rights confirm that international law does not substantively defines these rights. Several examples are discussed in this Chapter: the European Convention on Human Rights, the Inter-American Convention on Human Rights, the 1959 Abs-Shawcross Draft Convention on Foreign Investment, the Harvard Draft Convention on International Responsibility of States for Injuries to Aliens, and the OECD Draft Convention on the Protection of Foreign Property. These conventions and draft conventions grant (or propose granting) international law protection to property rights, but none defines the substantive contents of these property rights.

As for contractual rights protected by international law, this Chapter has argued that, unless the parties adopt international law as the contractual governing law, municipal law must still apply, and reference to the contract's transnational character does not enhance or alter the solution that would have been reached under the governing law. Several investment treaty tribunals have nonetheless mistaken an economic interest for a legal interest, in the absence of any express provision in an international treaty.

The definition of a property right contained in BITs is often very broad, to the extent that it can be characterized as a right to a commercial return. However, this does not mean that legitimate expectations qualify automatically as *property* rights under international law, unless investment treaties expressly designate them as such. The concept of legitimate expectations and the misguided decisions formulated by several investment treaty tribunals suggest that legal categories have given way to protection

---

241. *Id.*, para. 205.

of economic interests. This approach contrasts with the sounder and more circumscribed position adopted in the 'possessions' context by the ECHR. Investment treaty tribunals should follow the ECHR approach. Legitimate expectations are economic interests rather than legal interests, and should not be characterized as a property right unless the relevant investment treaty characterizes them in that way.

The notion of 'investment' pursuant to Article 25 of the ICSID Convention was intended to be flexible and to be determined by the parties' consent. Consent can be given via a BIT. In these circumstances, the BIT identifies categories of investment, and municipal law is relevant to define the underlying right and the investment's legal validity. A number of ICSID decisions, however, have accorded relevance only to the existence of an investment in the sense of an economic transaction without enquiring as to the existence of a legal entitlement. These decisions focus on four or five elements of a so-called 'objective' notion of investment. Other tribunals have transformed the existence of the underlying right under the relevant municipal law into the existence of an investment. Both of these approaches have broadened the jurisdiction of investment tribunals well beyond the offer to arbitrate contained in investment treaties, and have fostered uncertainty concerning the proper test for ICSID jurisdiction.

The concept of investment comprehends an underlying legal requirement, and the determination of this requirement's existence is referred to municipal law. However, municipal law should not be interpreted in a formalistic way, and the host State cannot rely on its own law only to prevent an investor from benefiting from the bilateral protection. For example, the State cannot first endorse an investment and then refuse to accord protection on the basis of a certificate that was never requested before or deemed necessary to execute the investment. Municipal law cannot subordinate the concept of investment to the sovereign's will.

Finally, municipal law is also relevant to determine an investment's legality. A number of investment treaty tribunals have tested legality *vis-à-vis* municipal law *and* international law. However, testing against international law principles is often redundant, because international law refers to municipal law in the first place. Principles of international law become significant in this process only if municipal law circumvents or violates international law.

CHAPTER 5
Shareholders' Rights

§5.01 INTRODUCTION

International investment law protects shares and shareholders' rights.[1] Many BITs identify shares as one of the types of protected investment.[2] ICSID arbitral tribunals have recognized minority shareholders' treaty rights in a number of cases.[3] BITs do not, however, define 'shareholder' or 'share', and typically do not state whether

---

1. Schreuer, 'Shareholder Protection in International Investment Law', in *Essays in Honour of Christian Tomuschat*, eds. Dupuy et al. (Oxford, 2006), at 601–619; also in *Transnational Dispute Management*, vol. 2, no. 3 (2005).
2. *See*, e.g., the Argentina – US BIT; Estonia – US BIT; and the Czech Republic – US BIT.
3. *See*, e.g., *CMS Gas Transmission Company v. Argentina*, Decision of the Ad Hoc Committee on the Application for Annulment, 25 Sep. 2007, para. 73; *Camuzzi International S.A. v. Argentina*, Decision on Jurisdiction, 11 May 2005, para. 81 available on the ICSID website: http://icsid.worldbank.org/ICSID/FrontServlet?requestType = CasesRH&actionVal = showDoc&docId = DC5 10_En&caseId = C10; *Enron v. Argentina*, Decision on Jurisdiction, 2 Aug. 2004, para. 29 available on the ICSID website: http://icsid.worldbank.org/ICSID/FrontServlet?requestType = CasesRH& actionVal = showDoc&docId = DC502_En&caseId = C3 (the decision on the merits, 22 May 2007, was annulled in part, but the *Ad Hoc Committee* confirmed that the minority shareholders had *ius standi* to bring an investment claim – *see* para. 127 of the Decision on the Application for Annulment of the Argentine Republic, 30 Jul. 2010 available on the Investment Treaty Arbitration website: https://www.italaw.com/sites/default/files/case-documents/ita0299.pdf); *LG&E v. Argentina*, Decision on Liability, 3 Oct. 2006, *ICSID Rev. Foreign Inv. L. J.* 21 (2006), 203, para. 78; *Sempra Energy v. Argentina*, Decision on Jurisdiction, 11 May 2005, para. 93, available on the ICSID website: http://icsid.worldbank.org/ICSID/FrontServlet?requestType = CasesRH& actionVal = showDoc&docId = DC509_En&caseId = C8. The award on the merits was annulled by the Decision on the Argentina Republic's Application for Annulment of the Award, 29 Jun. 2010, available on the Investment Treaty Arbitration website: https://www.italaw.com/sites/default/files/case-documents/ita0776.pdf. However, the *Ad Hoc Committee* confirmed that Sempra was entitled to bring a claim under the ICSID Convention for damages from its investment represented by a minority shareholdings, *see* para. 103 of the Annulment Decision. But *see*, where only the majority shareholder had access, Feller, *The Mexican Claims Commissions* (New York, 1935), 113, 117.

shareholders must own a majority of the shares or control a company's administration to qualify for treaty protection.

There are three situations in which shareholders may bring a claim. The first relates to their 'direct rights', defined by the ICJ in *Barcelona Traction* as 'rights which municipal law confers upon the [shareholders] distinct from those of the company, including the right to any declared dividend, the right to attend and vote at general meetings, the right to share in the residual assets of the company on liquidation'.[4] Thus, a shareholder's claim concerning his right to dividends or his right to participate in the company's management would be examples of 'direct' claims.[5]

The second situation occurs when shareholders claim for a loss of value of their shares in connection with violations of international law obligations in relation to the company. This 'loss of value' situation has arisen with increasing frequency in investment treaty disputes; it includes claims for breaches of the fair and equitable treatment standard *vis-à-vis* the shareholders-investors while the host State conduct is addressed against the company.

Third, shareholders may bring a claim on behalf of the company if a treaty expressly provides that they can act in lieu of the company.[6] This would be an 'indirect claim'; NAFTA Article 1117, for example, expressly provides for such a claim.

Just as BITs generally refer to shares without defining them, international law outside the investment treaty context does not define shares or shareholders. The ICJ in *Barcelona Traction* stated that:

> [T]he Court must ... start from the fact that the present case essentially involves factors derived from municipal law – the distinction and the community between the company and the shareholder – which the Parties, however widely their interpretations may differ, each take as the point of departure of their reasoning. If the Court were to decide the case in disregard of the relevant institutions of municipal law it would, without justification, invite serious legal difficulties. It

---

4. *Barcelona Traction*, 36.
5. *See Foremost-McKesson HBOC Inc. & others v. Iran*, Award No. 220-37/231-1, 10 Iran-US Cl. Trib. Rep. 228 (1986), at 250. This case concerned an alleged expropriation of shares held by a US company in an Iranian dairy company. The US company argued that the Iranian company withheld dividends from the US company over a period of years while continuing to pay dividends to its Iranian shareholders. The Iran-US Claims Tribunal concluded that Iran's interference with McKesson's rights did not amount to an expropriation before 19 Jan. 1981, the 'cut-off' date of the Iran-US tribunal's jurisdiction. Foremost-McKesson issued proceedings in the United States District Court for the District of Columbia to challenge the expropriation of its shares. The Court held that the Treaty of Amity between Iran and the United States granted the corporation a cause of action and awarded damages for the expropriation of the shares, *McKesson Corp. v. Iran*, No. CIV A82-220(TAF) 1997 WL 361177 (D.D.C. 1997). It further held that the US corporation was not subject to any 'come to the company' requirement in order to receive dividends and that compliance with such a requirement would have been futile (*see* the decision of 18 Jul. 2007, recapitulating the case's long procedural history and affirming the decision to hold Iran liable and to award damages: 520 F. Supp. 2d. 38 (D.D.C. 2007). The 2007 decision was reversed on appeal, on the ground that McKesson had no cause of action under the Treaty of Amity, and was remitted to the District Court, Judgment, 26 Aug. 2008, *McKesson Corp. v. Iran*, 539 F.3d 485 (D.C.Cir. 2008).
6. *Diallo*, para. 88.

would lose touch with reality, for there are no corresponding institutions of international law to which the Court could resort. Thus the Court has, as indicated, not only to take cognizance of municipal law but also to refer to it. It is to rules generally accepted by municipal legal systems which recognize the limited company whose capital is represented by shares, and not to the municipal law of a particular State, that international law refers.[7]

The absence of a general international law definition of shares or shareholders leads to the need, as the ICJ explained, to refer to such concepts as they are generally accepted by municipal law by way of *renvoi* to municipal rules. However, this process must 'preserve the integrity of the concept';[8] tribunals and courts cannot modify or deform these concepts.[9]

If the shareholder is acting in relation to its direct rights, municipal law is required to identify the shareholder's rights and obligations. If the shareholder is acting in connection with violations *vis-à-vis* his company (the loss of value situation) or in lieu of his company (indirect claims), the relevant municipal law applicable to the company must be consulted.[10] The relationship between international law and municipal law also bears on the issue of whether the shareholders' right concerns the value of their shares or the company's assets and value. If a shareholder is acting on behalf of the company by virtue of a rule of international law which confers on him the right to act, is the shareholder entitled to a portion of the assets of the company or is he instead entitled to the value of his shares? Do the company's creditors have any right to obtain a portion of the damages paid directly to the shareholders as a result of a tort suffered by a company? How can multiple claims, from various creditors and shareholders, be reconciled and what rules apply to them? Investment treaty tribunals have generally ignored these fundamental questions.

In his separate opinion appended to *Barcelona Traction*, Judge Morelli stated:

> the fact that the rules of international law in question envisage solely such interests of foreigners as already constitute rights in the municipal order is but the necessary consequence of the very content of the obligations imposed by those rules; obligations which, precisely, presuppose rights conferred on foreigners by the legal order of the State in question.[11]

Municipal law frequently confers different protections on companies and their shareholders. The same distinction between rights and interests must be drawn at the international level. Judge Morelli clarified this in his separate opinion:

---

7. *Barcelona Traction*, 37, para. 50.
8. Watts, 'Nationality of Claims', in *Fifty Years of the International Court of Justice, Essays in Honour of Sir Robert Jennings* (Cambridge, 1996), 424 at 437.
9. *Barcelona Traction*, 37, para. 50.
10. *Id.*, 38 'International law may not, in some fields, provide specific rules in particular cases. In the concrete situation, the company against which allegedly unlawful acts were directed is expressly vested with a right, whereas no such right is specifically provided for the shareholder in respect of those acts. Thus, the position of the company rests on a positive rule of both municipal and international law.' (para. 52).
11. *Id.*, 233, para. 3.

The reference to the legal order of the State and to the rights which it confers constitutes merely the means whereby international law establishes what interests it is concerned to protect. International law protects, by laying certain obligations upon a State, solely such interests of the members as already enjoy protection within the municipal legal order of that State on account of the attribution to those members of rights or other personal legal situations.[12]

This principle – i.e., if the interest is not a right under municipal law, it is not protected under customary international law – does not necessarily apply in the investment treaty context. In some BITs there are interests that are not considered rights at a municipal level but are nonetheless protected under international law (*see*, for example, the concept of investment, discussed in Chapter 4). BITs set out the protection of certain rights under international law; if these rights have an equivalent at the municipal level but are not defined at an international level, there is then a *renvoi* to the municipal rules. If the rights do not have a municipal-level equivalent, these concepts have to be defined in accordance with the principles and purposes described in the BITs.

Assessment of damages has proved to be particularly problematic in shareholder cases. In *Vivendi v. Argentina (Vivendi II)*[13] and *Eastern Sugar v. Czech Republic*,[14] the shareholders were preferred to all the company's creditors. Moreover, the amounts they received would be taxed pursuant to the tax regime applicable to the shareholders, and the company would (presumably) be exempted from paying any amount to the tax authorities at the place of its incorporation, despite the fact that the damages represent its own assets. In a case concerning a violation of a concession, if the violation had not occurred, the company would have performed the concession and paid taxes under a certain tax regime. If the concession is not performed and damages are awarded instead to the company's shareholders, the payment of the relevant taxes occurs according to a different tax regime. The same problem occurs if the company is bankrupt; its shareholders can claim damages in relation to the concession and be paid in preference to the company's creditors, evading the municipal insolvency regime. These difficulties are avoided if a provision such as NAFTA Article 1117 applies, where damages suffered by the company are awarded to the company even if the shareholders have commenced proceedings on the company's behalf. But NAFTA Article 1117 stands, at least at this stage, as an exception to the rule in investment treaty arbitration.

The following points require emphasis in the investment treaty context:[15]

---

12. *Id.*, 236, para. 5.
13. *Vivendi v. Argentina*, Award of 20 Aug. 2007, available on Investment Treaty Arbitration website: http://ita.law.uvic.ca/documents/VivendiAwardEnglish.pdf. Annulment proceedings ended with the rejection of Argentina's application to annul the award (Decision on the Argentina Republic's Request for Annulment of the Award, 10 Aug. 2010, available on Investment Treaty Arbitration website: https://www.italaw.com/sites/default/files/case-documents/ita0221.pdf).
14. *Eastern Sugar v. Czech Republic*, Partial Award, 27 Mar. 2007, available on Investment Treaty Arbitration website: http://ita.law.uvic.ca/documents/EasternSugar.pdf.
15. Jones, 'Claims on behalf of Nationals who are Shareholders in Foreign Companies', *BYBIL* 26 (1949), 225, at 232.

(i) A corporation is a juridical person distinct from its members.[16]
(ii) An international wrong against the corporation does not translate automatically into an international wrong against its members.
(iii) Only the company may seek redress for an international wrong committed against it absent an express provision granting shareholders this right.

A further difficulty in allowing shareholders to act on the company's behalf is that there are often many shareholders from many countries, and if one adds the possibility of intermediate companies, this could lead to the practical problem of an exponential number of disputes arising from one contested act. For some scholars, international law does not expressly forbid this potential quagmire, and the quagmire should simply be accepted as a proper application of international law.[17] To be sure, an endless string of claims may encourage States to take various legislative steps to correct them, but an analysis is still needed to determine whether there is a principle of international law that somehow enables the shareholder to effectively pierce the corporate veil at will and independently of the conditions laid down by customary international law for that exceptional relief.

§5.02 SHAREHOLDERS' RIGHTS PRE-*BARCELONA TRACTION*

The ICJ addressed shareholders' rights in foreign companies for the first time in 1964–1970, during the *Barcelona Traction* proceedings. However, before the two *Barcelona Traction* judgments were issued, a number of cases addressed protection of shareholders' rights in foreign companies under international law.

In 1934, Sereni stated that two principles could be deduced from arbitral awards and judicial precedents: (i) the right to protect the company's interest belongs only to the State to which the company belongs and not to the State to which the shareholders belong; and (ii) the shareholders' State does not have a right to diplomatic protection to obtain the payment of pro rata damages if the company that suffered the loss belongs to another State.[18]

To derive these principles, Sereni relied on, *inter alia*, a precedent of the Washington Commission constituted on 31 December 1862, in connection with the damages suffered by American citizens during the civil wars in Costa Rica. The Commission rejected an American citizen's application for damages suffered by a Nicaraguan company: the damages were suffered entirely by the company, therefore only the company had *locus standi*. Additionally, because the company was not American, it could not seek redress before the Commission.[19] Sereni also relied on what

---

16. *See* Staker, 'Diplomatic Protection of Private Business Companies: Determining Corporate Personality for International Law Purpose', *BYBIL* 61 (1990), 155, at 173: 'the municipal concept of the incorporated company as a separate legal entity is one which commends itself to adoption on the international plane'.
17. Schreuer, 'Shareholder Protection in International Investment Law', at 612.
18. Sereni, 'La cittadinanza degli enti morali nel diritto internazionale', *RDI* (1934), 170 at 184.
19. *Id.*, 184–185.

he termed a 'leading case',[20] *Antioquia*, in which a ship was temporarily taken by the Colombian government and the US government refused to act on behalf of the shareholders of the company to which the ship belonged, on the ground that the company owning the ship was Colombian.

Several other frequently cited shareholder protection cases should be briefly reviewed. These decisions largely confirm Sereni's assessment and extend its application. They also provide background for more recent customary international law discussions of shareholders' rights. Although many of the earliest cases do not bear directly on the issue of shareholder versus company, it is noteworthy that they provide virtually no support for the notion that shareholders can stand in the shoes of their companies.

[A] Awards Pre-*Barcelona Traction*

[1] Ruden[21]

Ruden, in 1868, is one of the earliest decisions on the issue of shareholders' rights;[22] it concerns a US citizen's claim submitted on his and on his company's behalf in connection with damages incurred from the burning of plantations in Peru by rioters. The case arose under a Claims Convention between the United States and Peru. The umpire held that the only claim that could be considered was the one submitted by Mr Ruden on his own behalf; the umpire dismissed the claim presented by Mr Ruden on behalf of the company. But he did so on the ground that this company was Peruvian.[23] Since the company was not foreign, it lacked *locus standi*. The question of whether the shareholder could act on behalf of his company was not discussed.

[2] Delagoa Bay *and East African Railway Company*[24]

In 1887, the Portuguese government granted an American citizen, MacMurdo, a concession to construct a railway. MacMurdo incorporated a company under the laws of Portugal to which the concession was transferred. All the shares of the Portuguese company were then transferred to an English company, whose shares were owned by MacMurdo. The English company provided the funds to construct the railway. The Portuguese government asked for an extension of the railway and, after a dispute arose in this regard, cancelled the concession. MacMurdo was named in the concession, and he was personally liable to perform it.[25]

---

20. *Id.*, 185.
21. Cited in Jones, 'Claims on Behalf of Nationals who are Shareholders in Foreign Companies', 227.
22. *Ibid.*
23. *Ibid.*
24. Final award of the *Delagoa* arbitral tribunal, 29 Mar. 1890 (Berne 1890).
25. Mr Blaine, US Secretary of State, letter reported in Moore, *International Arbitration*, vol. II, 1866–1870, para. 1866, 237. Final award of the Delagoa arbitral tribunal, 8–18.

Chapter 5: Shareholders' Rights §5.02[A]

The dispute was submitted to arbitration and the tribunal was asked to decide:

> as it judges most fair, the sum of compensation due from Portugal to those entitled in the two other countries as a result of the revocation of the concession for the Lourenco Marques railway and the taking possession of the railway by the Portuguese Government.[26]

The tribunal stated that its mandate was simply a matter of fixing the sum to be awarded to the plaintiffs as compensation for the loss of their concession and their property,[27] and that it had to fix this amount 'as it judges most fair'.[28] In this case, then, the shareholder was compensated since the tribunal's mandate was the amount of compensation rather than who should receive it. The issue of the shareholder's rights *vis-à-vis* the company's rights was not raised because the revoked concession was granted to the shareholder and not to the company.

[3]   El Triunfo[29]

El Salvador cancelled a concession granted by it to certain individuals and further assigned to El Triunfo, a Salvadorian company with American shareholders. As soon as the success of the enterprise became apparent, a plan was put in place 'to oust the management and control of the American interests and to wrest the concession from their hands'.[30] A petition for bankruptcy was presented on behalf of the company; the Salvadorian Court granted the petition and appointed a receiver. Shortly afterward, the president of the Republic of El Salvador cancelled the concession, which was subsequently issued in favour of other Salvadorian individuals. By a Protocol signed in Washington on 19 December 1901, the dispute was referred by the United States and the Republic of El Salvador to an arbitral tribunal.[31]

The tribunal held that the shareholders were entitled to recover damages suffered as a result of the fraudulent bankruptcy. It did not discuss the issue of the right to 'make reclamation for these shareholders in El Triunfo company, a domestic corporation of Salvador, for the reason that the question of such right is fully settled by the conclusions reached in the frequently cited and well-understood *Delagoa Bay Railway* arbitration'.[32]

El Triunfo has often been cited[33] as support for the thesis that shareholders have an independent right to seek redress for damage suffered by their company. However, that reading fails to take into account that the case was essentially a denial of justice claim stemming from the fraudulent bankruptcy and San Salvador's conspiratorial

---

26. Final award of the *Delagoa* arbitral tribunal, 3.
27. *Id.*, 153.
28. *Id.*, 154.
29. Claim of the Salvador Commercial Company ('El Triunfo Company'), 8 May 1902, RIAA, vol. XV, 467–479.
30. *Id.*, 474.
31. Protocol signed in Washington on 19 Dec. 1901, RIAA, vol. XV, 459–461.
32. Claim of the Salvador Commercial Company ('El Triunfo Company'), 479.
33. *See*, e.g., Jones, 'Claims on behalf of Nationals who are Shareholders in Foreign Companies', 247.

involvement. The lack of judicial redress against the conspiracy, and in particular the concession's cancellation, constituted denial of justice. Moreover, the tribunal incorrectly relied on the *Delagoa Bay Railway* arbitration, which, as described above, cannot be considered as a precedent supporting the existence of shareholders' independent rights to recover damages suffered by the company.

[4] Kunhardt & Co.[34]

In 1897, the Minister of Public Works of Venezuela entered into a contract with certain individuals to construct certain works in the port of Encontrados. The payment for these works was represented by the right to collect tolls from vessels. These individuals assigned their rights arising out of the concession to a company called Compañia Anónima Transportes en Encontrados. Kunhardt & Co., a co-partnership composed of three US citizens, became the owner of the company in 1899. In 1900 the concession was declared void. The United States presented a claim on behalf of Kunhardt & Co., submitting that the concession was annulled without justification and that it deprived the shareholders in Compañia Anónima Transportes en Encontrados (of which Kunhardt & Co. held three-quarters) of their assets.

The Commissioners concluded that:

> the shareholders of a corporation are not co-owners of the property of the corporation during its existence; they only have in their possession a certificate which entitles them to participate in the profits and to become owners of proportional parts of the property of the corporation when the latter is by final adjudication dissolved or liquidated.[35]

Since the corporation was not liquidated in accordance with Venezuelan law, it was held that the shareholders had no standing before the Commission. However, the Commissioners further noted that the rights of the shareholders are 'equitable rights to proportionate shares of the corporate property after the payment of the debts'.[36] The claim was dismissed since 'no evidence of the amount of the corporate debts is presented, although the existence of corporate indebtedness is apparent'.[37] *Kunhardt & Co.* clearly supports the principle that shareholders do *not* have independent rights to claim damages for harm to their company.

[5] Baesch e Römer v. Venezuela[38]

Here the company that suffered the losses was Venezuelan. The Mixed Claims Commission concluded that it had no jurisdiction on an application submitted by the

---

34. *Id.*, 246.
35. Claim of Kunhardt & Co., Mixed Claim Commission United States-Venezuela, 17 Feb. 1903, RIAA, vol. IX, 171–180, at 172.
36. *Id.*, 175.
37. *Id.*, 176.
38. Baasch & Römer, 'Mixed Claims Commission Netherlands – Venezuela, constituted under the Protocol of 28 Feb. 1903', *RIAA*, vol. X, 723–727.

company's Dutch shareholders.[39] However, the umpire held that for the purpose of this particular case, the claim had to be allowed in proportion of the Dutch shareholders' interest on the ground that the company was defunct.

On the basis that there was 'no inequity or injustice, even if a technical mistake has been made',[40] judgment was entered for a certain amount. This case thus provides little substantive support for shareholders' individual right of protection. The separateness of a company and its shareholders was upheld, and the shareholders were allowed to present a claim only on an ad hoc basis.

[6] The Alsop Claim[41]

Two final pre-*Barcelona Traction* cases fit into the pattern discussed above: no support for shareholders acting on behalf of the company.
Alsop, a Chilean company with American shareholders, entered into a settlement agreement with the Government of Bolivia in relation to a previous transaction. This settlement provided for two charges: a charge on a custom-house and a share in some mines. The territory on which the firm held the security was transferred to Chile, which agreed to undertake Bolivia's liability to a limited extent and offered an amount that was refused.

This dispute was first referred to and rejected by the United States and the Chilean Claims Commission: it held that Alsop's shareholders were ineligible to seek damages suffered by their company because the company was Chilean. Subsequently, the United States and Chile referred the dispute to the King of Great Britain; he decided the case as an *amiable compositeur*, pursuant to a Protocol dated 1 December 1909. The Protocol stated that the dispute concerned the amount, if any, due under all the facts and circumstances of the case.[42] There was no decision on the rights of the shareholders *vis-à-vis* the company. However, the King determined that Chile considered the Alsop claim 'as part of the consideration for a permanent settlement between the two Governments',[43] which accelerated the signature of the Treaty of Peace. Impliedly, the issue of the shareholders' *locus standi* was irrelevant, because Chile was prepared to pay for the damage suffered. The issue in dispute was the amount payable rather than the shareholders' standing.

[7] The Shufeldt Claim[44]

Guatemala and the United States referred to arbitration Shufeldt's claim for indemnification for damages suffered as a result of the termination of a contract in Guatemala.

---

39. Id., 726.
40. Id., 727.
41. The Alsop Claim (Chile-United States), 5 Jul. 1911, RIAA, vol. XI, 349–375.
42. Id., 356.
43. Id., 369.
44. The Shufeldt Claim, Special Agreement, 2 Nov. 1929, between the United States and Guatemala, award, 24 Jul. 1930, RIAA, vol. II, 1079–1102.

Mr Shufeldt was a cessionary of the rights arising from the disputed contract. His rights were subsequently assigned to a partnership.

Guatemala argued that Mr Shufeldt divested himself of all these rights once they were assigned to the partnership created under Guatemalan law. The arbitrator held that 'it is not the rights of the partnership that are in question but the personal interest of Mr Shufeldt in the partnership'.[45] He interpreted the word 'right' contained in the Protocol of Arbitration to mean 'equitable right', and stated that:

> [i]f the point raised by the Guatemala Government was sound why should they have consented to arbitration? They referred to arbitration not the rights of Shufeldt & Co but those of Shufeldt and this notwithstanding the provision in the contract requiring the formation of a partnership[46]

The arbitrator found that Mr Shufeldt had a right to be indemnified based on the wording of the Protocol of Arbitration. The arbitrator did not consider the issue of a partnership because it was deemed irrelevant.[47] The *Shufeldt* claim is a case decided on the *ad hoc* wording of an arbitration agreement, and therefore does not stand for the proposition that shareholders can act on behalf of their company under customary international law, when municipal law does not provide for such *locus standi*.

[B] Treaties Pre-*Barcelona Traction*

Several treaties that preceded *Barcelona Traction* considered the rights of shareholders to claim damages suffered by their company. A brief review of these treaties establishes that while they recognise such rights, which generally do not find protection under municipal law, the treaties do so for specific situations. It cannot be said that 'international law' protects these rights.

[1] Treaty of Versailles (1919)

Article 297(e) of the Treaty of Versailles provided that:

> The nationals of Allied and Associated Powers shall be entitled to compensation in respect of damage or injury inflicted upon their property, rights, or interests including any company or association in which they are interested, in German territory as it existed on August 1, 1914, by the application either of the exceptional war measures or measures of transfer mentioned (...). The claims made in this

---

45. *Id.*, 1097.
46. *Id.*, 1098.
47. *Id.*: 'Any other view with regard to this question of partnership would be contrary to the provisions of the protocol of arbitration, which submits this question: 'Has P. W. Shufeldt ... the right to claim pecuniary indemnification ...?' What does the word 'right' in this question mean? It can only mean an equitable right of which international law takes cognizance. It cannot mean legal right enforceable only in keeping with Guatemalan law, for if that was so this case never would have been referred to an international tribunal which does not administer municipal law'.

respect by such nationals shall be investigated and the total of the compensation shall be determined by the Mixed Arbitral Tribunal (...)[48]

One suggested explanation for this provision was that it aimed 'to prevent the German government from evading liability to pay Allied nationals for compensation for war damage, merely on the ground that the Allied interest affected were owned through a German corporation'.[49] The claims made under this provision were decided on the basis that the company's nationality would be that of the majority of the shareholders or of the controlling interests.[50] This qualification, together with exceptional wartime circumstances, places the Versailles Treaty's shareholder protection in its proper context.

[2] The Mexican Claims Conventions

Further examples of treaties expressly providing for shareholders' right of intervention include the Mexican Claims Conventions of 1923-1926, between, on the one side, the United States, France, Germany, Italy, Spain, and the United Kingdom, with Mexico as the counterparty.

The United States-Mexico Convention applied to:

> all claims against Mexico of citizens of the United States, whether corporations, ..., for losses or damages suffered by persons or by their properties ... including losses or damages suffer by citizens of the United States by reason of losses or damages suffered by any corporation, company, association or partnership in which citizens of the United States have or have had a substantial and bona fide interest, provided an allotment to the American claimant by the corporation, company, association or partnership of his proportion of the loss or damage is presented by the claimant to the Commission hereinafter referred to.[51]

The France-Mexico Convention, as well as the Germany-Mexico Convention, the UK-Mexico Convention,[52] the Italy-Mexico Convention, and the Spain-Mexico Convention considered relevant only shareholders holding more than 50% of a company's shares. Moreover, these Conventions provided for the requirement of an 'allotment' to the Claimant by the corporation in proportion to his shares.[53] The Mexican Claims

---

48. Parry, *The Consolidated Treaty Series*, vol. 225, 1919, at 329.
49. Jones, 'Claims on Behalf of Nationals Who Are Shareholders in Foreign Companies', 251-252.
50. Ibid.
51. Art. 1, Convention of 8 Sep. 1923: Feller, The *Mexican Claims Commissions*, 386. *See also* Art. 1, Convention of 10 Sep. 1923.
52. This Convention referred expressly to interests which could pertain jointly to several British subjects.
53. Art. III, Convention of 25 Sep. 1924 between France and Mexico; Art. IV, Convention of 16 Mar. 1925 between Germany and Mexico; Art. 3, Convention of 19 Nov. 1926 between United Kingdom and Mexico: Art. III, Convention of 13 Jan. 1927 between Italy and Mexico; and Art. 3, Convention of 25 Nov. 1925 between Spain and Mexico; *see* Feller at 415, 445, 470, 504-505, and 522.

Conventions thus allowed shareholders to act on their own behalf in connection with damage suffered by their companies.[54]

The term 'allotment' in these Conventions seems to refer to an 'invention of the negotiators of the Convention'.[55] The requirement of the so-called 'allotment' ('cession', in French, or 'cesión' in Spanish) was intended to protect the respondent State against multiple claims by shareholders on behalf of the company. The allotment would guarantee that the company could not bring an analogous claim for the entire damage suffered while another award would grant a portion of the loss to the shareholders.[56]

Uncertainties arose as to whether a Claimant was entitled to a proportionate share of the damage suffered by the corporation or, as Mexico argued, only to a share of the company's assets in the event of liquidation. Mexico's position conflicted with the terms of the Conventions, which referred to an allotment of a proportionate share of the damage suffered.[57]

It was clear, at least to Feller, that a claim for damages sought by a shareholder could prejudice the company's creditors. Feller was certainly right about this in the event of the company's insolvency. He argued that the Commissions should have exercised greater caution and demanded the production of a balance sheet to determine whether the company was insolvent. If the company were indeed insolvent, the Commission should have awarded what 'it may believe the value of the shareholder's interest to be'.[58] However, Feller's position does not take into account that the award of a sum based on the value of the shareholders' interest rather than the damage suffered would have conflicted with the text of the Conventions, which referred to the damage suffered and the number of shares held by the shareholders. Further, in the event that the company had no recourse under the Convention because, for example, it was a Mexican company, that damage would not have been redressed if the company became insolvent. Feller's interpretation of the Claims Conventions runs against the plain meaning of their text. There are no cases based on the practice of the Mexican Claims Commissions on this point.

Collectively, these Conventions are an example of how treaty provisions can expressly enable shareholders to claim damages suffered by their companies (i.e., a claim for loss of value, the second situation identified above). The ICJ, as will be seen below, has stated that the Conventions cannot be generalized to support the proposition that shareholders can claim for such damages under customary international law.

[3] Treaty of Peace with Italy (1947)

Article 78(4)(b) of the Italian Peace Treaty provides that:

---

54. The United States Convention adopting a higher threshold for asserting this right ('substantial interest' instead of an interest of more than 50%).
55. Feller, *The Mexican Claims Commissions*, 119.
56. *Id.*, 119.
57. *Id.*, 120–121.
58. *Id.*, 121.

United Nations nationals who hold, directly or indirectly, ownership interests in corporations or associations which are not United Nations nationals within the meaning of paragraph 9 (a) of this Article, but which have suffered a loss by reason of injury or damage to property in Italy, shall receive compensation in accordance with subparagraph (a) above. This compensation shall be calculated on the basis of the total loss or damage suffered by the corporation or association, and shall bear the same proportion to such loss or damage as the beneficial interests of such nationals in the corporation or association bear to the total capital thereof.[59]

This Treaty provided for similar terms as the 1919 Versailles Treaty, allowing shareholders to bring claims for damages for losses suffered by their company. The calculation of damages is based on the loss suffered and the number of shareholders' shares, which means that a 50% shareholder is entitled to seek damages for 50% of the loss incurred by the company. The shareholder does not have to be a majority shareholder or hold a substantial interest.

It has been argued that this Treaty illustrates 'the existence of what may be called an international rule of equity, supplementing the normal principle of respect for the juridical personality of associations, and allowing of exceptions to it where its application would cause injustice'.[60] If that is the case, the Treaty, perhaps inadvertently, affirms the general principle against a shareholder's right of intervention. The treatment of enemy and allied property was justified by the ICJ in *Barcelona Traction* as:

> an instrument of economic warfare, aimed at denying the enemy the advantages to be derived from the anonymity and separate personality of corporations. Hence the lifting of the veil was regarded as justified ex necessitate and was extended to all entities which were tainted with enemy character, even the nationals of the State enacting the legislation. The provisions of the peace treaties had a very specific function: to protect allied property, and to seize and pool enemy property with a view to covering reparation claims.[61]

The Italian Peace Treaty thus cannot be generalized to support the proposition that shareholders can claim damages suffered by the company under customary international law.

[4]   The Algiers Declaration

The Claims Settlement Declaration ('Algiers Declaration')[62] contains a definition of 'nationals' entitled to bring a claim before the Iran–US Claims Tribunal that includes shareholders. This Declaration is analysed here before considering in detail the earlier ICJ judgment of *Barcelona Traction*, because it is an important example of how

---

59. Treaty of Peace with Italy, Paris, 10 Feb. 1947, United Nations Treaty Series, vol. 49, 126.
60. Jones, 'Claims on Behalf of Nationals Who Are Shareholders in Foreign Companies', 254.
61. *Barcelona Traction*, 39–40, para. 60.
62. Claims Settlement Declaration, Declaration of the Government of the Democratic and Popular Republic of Algeria concerning the settlement of claims by the Government of the United States of America and the Government of the Islamic Republic of Iran, 19 Jan. 1981, *ILM* 20 (1981), 230.

shareholders' rights are recognized at the international level, and is also in line with the treaties discussed above, particularly the Mexican Claims Conventions.

The Algiers Declaration, like the Mexican Claims Conventions, is based on the following principles:

(i) the shareholder must be a controlling shareholder; and
(ii) a claim issued by the shareholder and a claim issued by the company are alternative claims. While the Mexican Claims Conventions provide for an 'allotment', the Algiers Declaration provides that the shareholder has *locus standi* only if the company is not allowed to bring a claim.

Article VII 2 of the Algiers Declaration defines 'Claims of Nationals or Iran or the United States' as:

> claims owned continuously, from the date on which the claim arose to the date on which this agreement enters into force, by nationals of that state, including claims that are owned indirectly by such nationals through ownership of capital stock or other proprietary interests in juridical persons, provided that the ownership interests of such nationals, collectively, were sufficient at the time the claim arose to control the corporation or other entity, and provided, further, that the corporation or other entity is not itself entitled to bring a claim under the terms of this agreement.

The Iran-US Claims Tribunal awards that are relevant in this context concern how damages are awarded to shareholders. This jurisprudence has consistently held that the Claimants are entitled to a proportional share of the corporation's claim.[63] If the Claimant owned 50%, he would receive 50% of the damages. Some shareholders attempted to get a payment of 100% of the claim, even though they were holding a smaller share of the company's capital, because the company was entitled to seek compensation. However, the Tribunal rejected these arguments:

(i) the shareholders' rights were 'an exception to the normal rule of international law that shareholders may not bring the claims of the corporation (as opposed to claims relating to their ownership rights);[64]
(ii) the company may have access to an alternative forum for the redress of its damages; and
(iii) the recovery of 100% could not be justified on the assumption that the shareholder would have given part of the amount awarded to other shareholders not entitled to bring a claim.[65]

---

63. *Blount Bros. Corp. v. Islamic Republic of Iran*, Award No. 215-52-1, 10 Iran-US. Cl. Trib. Rep. 56, at 63; *Harza Scoville and Pabich v. Islamic Republic of Iran*, Award No. 232-97-2, 11 Iran-US. Cl. Trib. Rep. 76 at 85–89; and *Howard Needles Tammen & Bergendoff v. Islamic Republic of Iran*, Award No. 244-68-2, 11 Iran-US. Cl. Trib. Rep. 302 at 312–314. Compare *Foremost-McKesson & others v. Islamic Republic of Iran*, Award No. 220-37/231-1,10 Iran-US Cl. Trib. Rep. 228, at 250, in which the shareholders acted to seek redress in relation to the breach of their rights to dividends and management of the company, which amounted to an indirect expropriation of shares. They did not act in connection with damage suffered by the company.
64. *Harza v. Islamic Republic of Iran*, 87.
65. *See, e.g., Blount Bros. Corp. v. Islamic Republic of Iran*, 64.

The Iran-US Claims Tribunal emphasized that it was rendering an award in favour of a national and not in favour of an ineligible corporation.[66] It also noted that 'in international claims practice, although there have been instances of proportional recovery by shareholders, a conclusive pattern has not been developed especially with regard to treaty language similar to that in issue here'.[67] The issue of creditors' net equity was, regrettably, not addressed. The issue of whether the company could recover its damages in another forum was also omitted because shareholders had *locus standi* only if the company could not bring a claim under the Algiers Declaration. This left open the possibility for the company to recover its damages by other avenues (contractual claims before other tribunals).

Some authors have characterized the Iran – US Claims Tribunal as a 'retrospective BIT':[68] (i) the Algiers Declaration 'tracks the structure of contemporary BITs';[69] and (ii) claims can be brought by nationals of one State against the other State. Despite these similarities, this characterization seems questionable: the right of shareholders to bring a claim in connection with harm suffered by their company is rarely expressly addressed in BITs as it was in the Algiers Declaration, and the interpretation given by certain investment treaty tribunals (as will be addressed later in this chapter) is so broad that it does not resemble the tightly defined shareholders' right in the Algiers Declaration. On the other hand, the amount awarded to shareholders by BIT tribunals resembles the approach taken by the Iran-US Tribunal, as BIT tribunals have often attributed to shareholders a percentage of damages equivalent to their proportion of shares in the company's capital.

§5.03 ICJ JUDGMENTS ON SHAREHOLDERS' RIGHTS

This section considers two well-known ICJ judgments rendered in the context of diplomatic protection (*'Barcelona Traction'* and *'Diallo'*) and another well-known ICJ judgment concerning a Treaty of Friendship, Commerce and Navigation (FCN Treaty) case between Italy and the United States (*ELSI*). These three cases are directly relevant to the analysis of the relationship between international law and municipal law in the context of shareholders' rights.

[A] *Barcelona Traction, Light and Power Company Limited*[70]

Barcelona Traction is the first pronouncement of the ICJ on the right of shareholders in relation to an indirect claim. Partly because it is the first such case, and partly because of the complexity, variety and length of the opinions, *Barcelona Traction* is one of the

---

66. *Id.*, 64.
67. *Id.*, 83.
68. *See* Caron 'The Iran-U.S. Claims Tribunal and Investment Arbitration: Understanding the Claims Settlement Declaration as a Retrospective BIT', in *The Iran-US Claims Tribunal at 25, The Cases Everyone Needs to Know for Investor-State and International Arbitration*, eds. Drahozal and Gibson (Oxford, 2007), 375.
69. *Id.*, 376.
70. *Barcelona Traction*, Judgment of 24 Jul. 1964, in 1964 ICJ, 6, and Judgment of 5 Feb. 1970.

most frequently cited judgments in public international law. Yet, it also suffers from being treated as something of a curiosity, not fully analysed and, because of its position as the first ICJ judgment on the issue, regarded by some scholars as having been left behind by subsequent developments. That assessment is misguided; the principles enunciated in *Barcelona Traction* have been confirmed in the most recent ICJ pronouncement on shareholders' rights, *Diallo*.

Barcelona Traction is a diplomatic protection case. Belgium sought recovery from Spain for damages suffered by Barcelona Traction's shareholders (who were Belgian nationals) as a result of the conduct of various organs of Spain. The company was incorporated in Canada, with the purpose of creating and developing an electric power production and distribution system in Spain. The claim arose from Barcelona Traction's bankruptcy in Spain. Belgium claimed that the majority shareholders were Belgian nationals; Spain challenged this claim.

Barcelona Traction had issued several bonds serviced out through transfers to it by subsidiary companies. In 1936, the Spanish Civil War suspended the servicing of the bonds. After the war, the Spanish exchange control authorities refused to authorize the transfer of foreign currency necessary to service the bonds. In 1948 three bondholders petitioned for Barcelona Traction's bankruptcy in Spain because it had not paid interest on their bonds. The company was declared bankrupt, the management was dismissed, and new shares were issued and bought by Spanish nationals at a public auction. Barcelona Traction's Belgian shareholders initiated several proceedings regarding various irregularities during the bankruptcy proceedings.

The Spanish government raised preliminary objections that were addressed in the first judgment in 1964. These objections included a challenge to the claim's admissibility. Spain argued that Belgium had no *locus standi* because Barcelona Traction was a Canadian company. Spain stated that customary international law –there was no treaty applicable to the dispute – did not contemplate any diplomatic protection of the right of the shareholders other than the State of nationality of the company (Canada). The ICJ found that the question of *locus standi* was inextricably tied to the merits.

The holding in *Barcelona Traction*'s first judgment may be summarized as follows:

(i) International law must recognize institutions of municipal law with regard to the concept of companies' and shareholders' rights since these are not defined by international law.[71] The concept of a limited company is an 'exclusive creation' of municipal law, and international law is 'bound in principle to deal with companies as they are'.[72]

---

71. *Barcelona Traction*, 33 and 34: 'Municipal law determines the legal situation not only of such limited liability companies but also of those persons who hold shares in them.' (para. 41).
72. *Barcelona Traction*, Separate Opinion of Judge Fitzmaurice, at 67, para. 6.

Chapter 5: Shareholders' Rights §5.03[A]

(ii) In municipal law, the concept of the company is distinct from the concept of the company's shareholders. Shareholders do not have rights to the corporate assets as long as the company is in existence. Only the company can seek redress for damages to its assets.[73]

(iii) A wrong done to the company frequently prejudices its shareholders, but this does not mean that they are entitled to a claim for compensation. By the same token, creditors do not have any right to claim compensation in relation to damage suffered by the company-debtor.[74]

(iv) Only the company can challenge an act infringing just the company's rights; while the shareholders can challenge an act infringing their 'direct' rights, such as the right to dividends. These are property rights of the shareholders and not a mere interest.[75]

(v) Diplomatic protection may be exercised by the State of the company's nationality but not by the State of the shareholders' nationality with regard to shareholders' indirect claims. There is a difference between 'injury in respect of a right and injury to a simple interest'.[76]

(vi) There is no rule of international law that expressly confers a right to shareholders in relation with their indirect claims.[77]

(vii) International law may recognize the piercing of the corporate veil.[78]
- Two special situations may arise: (a) the company has ceased to exist; or (b) the protecting State of the company lacks capacity to take action. These two circumstances did not arise in this dispute.[79]

(viii) Under customary international law shareholders have no right to maintain an indirect claim, although such a right could be provided by a treaty.[80]

(ix) The rule of equity was not applicable because it could open the door to an endless number of claims brought by various shareholders with different nationalities, which would create an atmosphere of insecurity in international economic relations.[81]

Barcelona Traction is of overriding importance in characterizing the relationship between international law and municipal law with regard to shareholders' rights. It answers the question of how international law should, on the one hand, recognize the concepts of companies' and shareholders' rights, and on the other hand maintain these two concepts as distinct. International investment law may provide that shareholders can act on behalf of their companies, in which case the wrong done to the company entitles the shareholders to seek damages. However, the content of such shareholders'

---

73. *Id.*, 34–35, paras 41 and 44.
74. *Id.*, 35, para. 44.
75. *Id.*, 36, paras 46 and 47.
76. *Id.*, 36, para. 46.
77. *Ibid.*
78. *Id.*, 39, para. 57.
79. *Id.*, 40–42, paras 64–71.
80. *Id.*, 46–47, para. 90.
81. *Id.*, 48–49, paras 94–96.

rights is remitted to municipal law unless international law provides a specific regulation of these rights under international law.

Barcelona Traction enunciates customary international law with a clarity seldom achieved by earlier or later courts or tribunals. The case may not be 'investor friendly' in certain respects, but it clarifies the distinction between rights and interests, which is often blurred in the jurisprudence of investment treaty tribunals. Dugard's Fourth Report on Diplomatic Protection criticizes *Barcelona Traction* because it was based on company law rather than international law and established an 'unworkable standard'.[82] Yet, the Fourth Report also conceded that *Barcelona Traction* contains a 'true reflection of customary international law'.[83] Moreover, the standard is workable and a *renvoi* to company law does not in any way diminish international law; rather it gives substance to international law.

[B]   *Elettronica Sicula S.p.A.*[84]

ELSI, A 1989 ICJ judgment, concerned a breach of shareholders' rights arising from the 1948 FCN Treaty between Italy and the United States.

ELSI was an Italian company owned by an American company and its subsidiary. It owned a plant that produced electronic components. Although it operated at a profit, the profit was insufficient to offset its accumulated debts. In 1968 the shareholders decided to liquidate the company. Meanwhile, the mayor of Palermo requisitioned the plant. On ELSI's application, the Prefect and the Court of Appeal of Palermo found that the requisition violated Italian administrative law and the Court of Appeal awarded damages for loss of use of the plant. A month after the requisition, ELSI was declared bankrupt.

The United States submitted that the illegal requisition of the plant represented a violation of the FCN Treaty because it denied ELSI's shareholders' the right to liquidate their company in an orderly manner. The ICJ, rejecting Italy's objection to admissibility on the ground of failure to exhaust local remedies, held that Article III of the FCN Treaty – which the United States read as conferring on its shareholders a right to organize and manage ELSI – was not violated because the insolvency was due to ELSI's financial position. That is, ELSI's shareholders were not deprived of their right to conduct an orderly liquidation because it was not established that ELSI could have been liquidated in an orderly manner before the requisition.[85]

ELSI is the second decision where the ICJ addressed a claim brought on behalf of shareholders, even though this decision concerns a claim for a violation of a treaty. The ICJ did not decide whether shareholders were entitled to bring a claim on behalf of their company under customary international law, but considered the shareholders' rights with reference only to the FCN Treaty without taking into account the ruling in

---

82. Fourth report on diplomatic protection by Mr John Dugard, Special Rapporteur, 13 Mar. 2003, UNDoc. A/CN.4/530, para. 16.
83. *Id.*, para. 27.
84. *Elettronica Sicula S.p.A.* ('ELSI') Judgment of 20 Jul. 1989, in ICJ *Reports* (1989), 15.
85. *ELSI*, paras 92, 99 and 101.

Chapter 5: Shareholders' Rights §5.03[B]

Barcelona Traction or any other general statement in this regard. The ICJ also did not consider whether the shareholders' rights in insolvency proceedings were direct rights. In particular, the issue of shareholder protection unfolded on two grounds:

(i) Article III of the FCN Treaty provides expressly for a protection of the right to control and manage. The requisition was unlawful and deprived the shareholders of 'what were at the moment their most crucial rights to control and manage'[86] their company, and it constituted a prima facie violation of their rights. However, because ELSI was insolvent before the requisition, the shareholders' rights of control and management 'would not have existed to be protected by the FCN Treaty'.[87]

(ii) Article V, paragraph 2, of the FCN Treaty provides that its protection 'shall extend to interests held directly or indirectly … by nationals, corporations and associations of either High Contracting Party in property which is taken within the territories of the other High Contracting Party'.[88] The ICJ interpreted this article to protect the shareholders' interests in the company's assets and in their residual value after the liquidation. But because ELSI was insolvent before the requisition, no liquidation could have taken place and consequently there were no assets to be protected from a taking.

ELSI considers specific provisions of an FCN Treaty and applies them to the facts. There was no attempt to broaden the notion of shareholders' rights or to pierce the corporate veil at the international level. As a matter of customary international law (*Barcelona Traction*) and treaty international law (*ELSI*), in decisions some twenty to twenty-five years apart, the ICJ has thus spoken strongly in favour of limiting indirect claims.

Moreover, *ELSI* confirms that even if a treaty confers standing on a shareholder, this does not imply disregard for how municipal law characterizes the shareholder's right. The ICJ analysed the right to manage a company, and whether the company was insolvent under the relevant provisions of Italian law. The existence of 'standing' in the realm of international law and the absence of a definition of the underlying right in international law did not lead the tribunal to create a standing right.

It is also noteworthy that ELSI's shareholders had been involved in several proceedings where ELSI's creditors attempted to pierce the corporate veil at a municipal level and sought declarations that the shareholders were liable for ELSI's debts under Article 2363 of the Italian Civil Code. This article provided that a sole shareholder was liable for all the debts of the company. ELSI had two shareholders, with one being wholly controlled by the other. Some of these proceedings were discontinued and others were rejected by the Italian Court of Cassation.[89] Piercing was thus unsuccessful in all *fora*.

---

86. *Id.*, para. 75.
87. *Id.*, para. 94.
88. *Id.*, para. 118.
89. These proceedings are mentioned at para. 45.

[C] Diallo

After a hiatus of approximately forty years, the ICJ again addressed shareholders' rights under international law in the context of diplomatic protection. Mr Diallo moved to Congo in 1964 and established an import-export company, Africom-Zaire. In 1979 he created another company, Africontainers-Zaire, with the support of two private partners. Towards the end of the 1980s, these two companies began experiencing problems recovering certain debts. In 1995 Zaire issued an order to expel Diallo, and he was deported to Guinea in 1996.

The ICJ considered its jurisdiction on three grounds alleged by Guinea: (i) violation of Diallo's individual rights; (ii) violation of Diallo's direct right as a shareholder in two companies; and (iii) violation of the rights of those companies by 'substitution'. Guinea observed that in *Barcelona Traction* the Court had referred in obiter dictum to an exception to the general rule in the event that the company was incorporated in the State whose responsibility is invoked in the request for diplomatic protection. The ICJ held in *Diallo* that it had jurisdiction over the first two causes of action, but that Guinea was precluded from exercising the companies' right by substitution. The ICJ stated that 'what amounts to the internationally wrongful act, in the case of *associés* or shareholders, is the violation by the respondent State of their direct rights in relation to a legal person, direct rights that are defined by the domestic law of that State, as accepted by both Parties, moreover.'[90]

The ICJ noted the principle set out in *Barcelona Traction* distinguishing between rights of companies and interests of shareholders, and added that:[91]

> The Court, having carefully examined State practice and decisions of international courts and tribunals in respect of diplomatic protection of associés and shareholders, is of the opinion that these do not reveal – at least at the present time – an exception in customary international law allowing for protection by substitution, such as is relied on by Guinea.
>
> The fact invoked by Guinea that various international agreements, such as agreements for the promotion and protection of foreign investments and the Washington Convention, have established special legal régimes governing investment protection, or that provisions in this regard are commonly included in contracts entered into directly between States and foreign investors, is not sufficient to show that there has been a change in the customary rules of diplomatic protection; it could equally show the contrary. The arbitrations relied on by Guinea are also special cases, whether based on specific international agreements between two or more States.[92]

---

90. *Diallo*, para. 64. *See also* the judgment on the merits: *Ahmadou Sadio Diallo (Republic of Guinea v. Democratic Republic of the Congo), Merits, Judgment, I.C.J. Reports 2010*, 639. In a subsequent judgment dated 19 Jun. 2012 *Ahmadou Sadio Diallo (Republic of Guinea v. Democratic Republic of the Congo), Compensation, Judgment, I.C.J. Reports 2012*, 324), the ICJ addressed damages in respect of which compensation was requested in the *Diallo* proceeding. This judgment is not relevant to this Chapter's discussion.
91. 'Not a mere interest affected, but solely a right infringed involves responsibility, so that an act directed against and infringing only the company's rights does not involve responsibility towards the shareholders, even if their interests are affected.' (*Barcelona Traction*, para. 46).
92. *Diallo*, paras 89–90.

The ICJ further explained that protection by substitution:

> seeks indeed to offer protection to the foreign shareholders of a company who could not rely on the benefit of an international treaty and to whom no other remedy is available, the allegedly unlawful acts having been committed against the company by the State of its nationality.[93]

The ICJ listed in its subsequent judgment on the merits, dated 30 November 2010,[94] the rights of Mr Diallo as an individual and his direct rights as an *associé* in Africom-Zaire and Africontainers –Zaire. The ICJ accepted his right to take part and vote in general meetings, the rights relating to the *gérance*; the right to oversee and monitor the management and the right to property of Mr Diallo over his *parts sociales* in Africom-Zaire and Africontainers –Zaire. In doing so, the ICJ applied Congolese law.[95] The ICJ reaffirmed that international law acknowledged the principle of domestic law that the company had a legal personality distinct from its shareholders and that the rights and assets of the company were also distinct from the rights and assets of an *associé*,[96] adding that 'it is legally untenable to consider, as Guinea argues, that the property of the corporation merges with the property of the shareholder.'[97] Thus, this judgment reiterated the principles expressed in *Barcelona Traction*.

From *Diallo*, which was adopted in the context of diplomatic protection, three key principles may be identified:

(i) there is no customary international law allowing for protection by substitution;
(ii) protection by substitution constitutes a last resort – and one that would only be applicable in very limited circumstances; and
(iii) the two special situations, mentioned in *Barcelona Traction* – (a) the company ceased to exist; and (b) the protecting State of the company lacked capacity to take action – do not justify any general exception to the rule of the shareholders' *locus standi*.[98]

It follows from these principles that an investment treaty tribunal should not apply 'substitution' when the investment treaty does not expressly provide for it. In the absence of an express treaty provision, a 'last resort' type of action would permit a tribunal to pierce the corporate veil and to disregard the municipal law rules governing shareholders' rights, and would further introduce uncertainty as to what a shareholder is entitled to do or not do. The fact that it is a 'last resort' action implies that it must be interpreted narrowly and there should be no room to pierce the corporate veil automatically in all disputes concerning the protection of foreign investments, absent

---

93. *Id.*, para. 88.
94. *Ahmadou Sadio Diallo (Republic of Guinea v. Democratic Republic of the Congo), Merits, Judgment, I.C.J. Reports 2010*, 639.
95. *Id.*, paras 103–104.
96. *Id.*, paras 155.
97. *Ibid.*
98. *Barcelona Traction*, para. 64.

of an express treaty provision. Indeed, the ICJ confirmed that the rights of a shareholder must be determined in accordance with the relevant municipal law when it applied the law of Zaire to decide the question of whether Diallo's companies were incorporated in Zaire as a precondition to running their business.

In summary, these three judgments, *Barcelona Traction, ELSI,* and *Diallo,* though often cited in investment treaty disputes, are usually considered by tribunals to *lack* direct applicability on the ground that an investment treaty is a *lex specialis* and is not to be assimilated to diplomatic protection.[99] The inclusion of shares as protected investments in BITs is used to justify the departures from these general principles of international law.[100] However, the principles underlying these judgments are still relevant in the investment context. First, *Barcelona Traction* and *Diallo* held that there are no shareholders' rights in customary international law, but that some treaties do provide these rights. If the treaty in question (whether or not a BIT) does *not* provide for such a right, then shareholders do not have standing under international law. Second, all three judgments indicate how the relationship between international law and municipal law should be characterized: international law can recognize shareholders' rights, but the content is to be remitted to municipal law. *ELSI* considered these rights in the context of a treaty, but because the treaty did not define shareholders' rights, it also referred to the relevant municipal law's definition of these rights.

§5.04 THE ILC'S ARTICLES ON DIPLOMATIC PROTECTION

The ILC's work on Diplomatic Protection indicates that the concept of shareholders' rights remains hotly debated, and that the majority of States do not favour an attempt to adopt a broad view of such rights.

In 2006 the ILC recommended 19 Articles on Diplomatic Protection ('Articles'). Article 11[101] concerns the protection of shareholders in two circumstances:

> (a) the corporation has ceased to exist according to the law of the State of incorporation for a reason unrelated to the injury; or

---

99. *See,* e.g., *CMS Gas Transmission Company v. Argentina,* Decision on Annulment, 25 Sep. 2007, para. 69. *See also* in general Bottini, 'Indirect Shareholders Claims', in *Building International Investment Law, The First 50 Years of ICSID,* eds Kinnear et al. (Kluwer, 2016), 203–218.
100. *See* Bottini, *supra,* 213.
101. Article 11, *Protection of shareholders:*

> A State of nationality of shareholders in a corporation shall not be entitled to exercise diplomatic protection in respect of such shareholders in the case of an injury to the corporation unless:
>
> (a) The corporation has ceased to exist according to the law of the State of incorporation for a reason unrelated to the injury; or
> (b) The corporation had, at the date of injury, the nationality of the State alleged to be responsible for causing the injury, and incorporation in that State was required by it as a precondition for doing business there.

Chapter 5: Shareholders' Rights §5.04

(b) the corporation had, at the date of injury, the nationality of the State alleged to be responsible for causing the injury, and incorporation in that State was required by it as a precondition for doing business there.[102]

As noted above, although Dugard's Fourth Report[103] criticized *Barcelona Traction* and the principles derived from *Barcelona Traction* are not followed in the Articles, the Fourth Report accepted that:

> despite its shortcomings, Barcelona Traction is today, 30 years on, widely viewed not only as an accurate statement of the law on the diplomatic protection of corporations but as a true reflection of customary international law. (...) This was clearly demonstrated by the response of delegates in the Sixth Committee to the question whether the rule in Barcelona Traction should be reconsidered. Of the 15 delegates who spoke on this subject, only one suggested that Barcelona Traction should be reconsidered. Regrettably all but one of the delegates who spoke on this subject represented developed States. However, it is unlikely that developing States would show much enthusiasm for a rule replacing Barcelona Traction that accords more protection to shareholders of foreign companies.[104]

Article 11 takes into account the criticism of *Barcelona Traction*, but recognizes that the case 'enjoys widespread acceptance on the part of States'.[105] Article 11 endorses 'both the primary rule in *Barcelona Traction* – namely that the State of incorporation of a company enjoys the right to exercise diplomatic protection on behalf of the company – and the exceptions to this rule, recognized, to a greater or lesser extent, by the Court'.[106]

Crawford has criticised Article 11's exceptions to the general rule on shareholders' protection:

(i) the two exceptions mentioned in *Barcelona Traction* 'were not actually affirmed' by the ICJ and, accordingly, the 'ILC's formulation in draft Article 11(b) gains little support';[107]
(ii) multiple claims, winding up, and related issues are unresolved;[108]
(iii) in several cases there has been no legal requirement to incorporate a company in a certain State, as Article 11 required;[109] and
(iv) the requirement that the company cease to exist for reasons unrelated to the injury will limit this article's applicability.[110]

---

102. ILC 'Draft Articles on Diplomatic Protection with Commentaries' in *Report of the International Law Commission on the Work of Its Fifty-Eight Session* (1 May 2006 to 9 Jun. 2006; 3 Jul. 2006 to 11 Aug. 2006), Ch. IV, UNDoc A/61/10, 13–10, at 19.
103. Fourth Report on Diplomatic Protection by Mr John Dugard, Special Rapporteur, 13 Mar. 2003, UNDoc. A/CN.4/530.
104. *Id.*, para. 27.
105. *Id.*, para. 47.
106. *Ibid.*
107. Crawford, 'The ILC's Articles on Diplomatic Protection', *SAYIL* 31 (2006), 19, at 39.
108. *Id.*, 40.
109. *Ibid.*
110. *Id.*, 41.

In short, the protection of shareholders' rights envisaged by ILC Article 11 applies not only to a very limited spectrum of cases, but also might not reflect customary international law. ILC Article 11 clearly does not identify a settled principle of shareholders' protection under international law. The views of the delegates of the Sixth Committee show that States are reluctant to confer any protection to shareholders when the alleged misconduct has been directed at the company. Both the ICJ and the Sixth Committee indicate that protection by 'substitution' constitutes a very last resort – and one that would only be applicable in limited circumstances. This may well be relevant in interpreting investment treaties.

§5.05 EUROPEAN COURT OF HUMAN RIGHTS

ECHR precedents further demonstrate a reluctance to adopt a broad interpretation of shareholders' rights under international law. The ECHR's concerns that shareholders' claims may give rise to a double recovery have led it to only permit such claims in a very limited framework.

To date, there have been few ECHR judgments on the issue of shareholders' rights. Moreover, the principles arising from these precedents cannot be invoked *tout court* in the field of investment treaty protection, because the ICJ has held that there is a distinction between diplomatic protection on the one hand and human rights on the other.[111] The ICJ explained that the obligations subject to diplomatic protection are not of the same category as obligations *erga omnes*.[112] Judge Morelli, in his separate opinion appended to *Barcelona Traction*, identified two different sets of international rules: (i) human rights; and (ii) rules on the treatment of foreigners. While the first are considered natural rights, the latter must result from a 'positive legal order'. Municipal law plays a much more important role in defining the content of treatment of foreigners.[113]

Some investment treaty tribunals have also held that they lacked jurisdiction over human rights matters. In *Biloune v. Ghana Investment Centre*, for example, the arbitral tribunal held that:

> This Tribunal's competence is limited to commercial disputes arising under a contract entered into in the context of Ghana's Investment Code. (...) Under the facts of this case it must be concluded that, while the acts alleged to violate the international human rights of Mr Biloune may be relevant in considering the investment dispute under arbitration, this Tribunal lacks jurisdiction to address, as an independent cause of action, a claim of violation of human rights.[114]

---

111. *Barcelona Traction*, paras 33 and 34.
112. *See* Crawford, 'Multilateral Rights and Obligations in International Law', *Recueil des cours* 319 (2006), 329 at 422–425.
113. *Barcelona Traction*, Judge Morelli Separate Opinion, 232–233, paras 2 and 3.
114. *Biloune v. Ghana Investment Centre*, 203.

The Ad Hoc Annulment Committee in *Azurix Corp. v. Argentina*[115] stated that comparisons with differently-worded treaties was of limited utility, especially treaties outside the field of investment protection. The Committee noted that the ECHR held that shareholders in certain circumstances did not have standing to bring a claim for a violation of the company's right's under Article 1 of Protocol No. 1 of the ECHR, but these holdings were not relevant since investment treaty provisions might confer certain rights directly on a shareholder which would be violated by an injury to the company, or answer the question whether the shareholder could have standing to bring a claim in that event.[116]

By contrast, in *Mondev International Ltd v. USA*[117] the tribunal held that although ECHR decisions on Article 6 of the European Convention on Human Rights did not concern investment protection, they provided 'guidance by analogy'[118] on the 'right to a court'. Similar conclusions were reached in *Tulip v. Turkey*.[119]

Despite the differences between human rights and investment protection, the ECHR precedents can still be usefully analysed to consider whether there is a general principle of protection of shareholders' rights with regard to indirect claims. Moreover, investment treaty tribunals and scholars commenting on international investment law have frequently referred to ECHR precedents.[120]

The investment tribunal in *Urbaser v. Argentina*[121] stated that a 'BIT cannot be applied in a vacuum'[122] and therefore although mindful of the purpose of investment treaties to promote investment, cannot exclude taking into account rules of international law. 'The BIT has to be construed in harmony with other rules of international law of which it forms part, including those relating to human rights'.[123] Interpreting investment treaties as part of the system of international law requires then to consider the relevancy of ECHR principles. Accordingly, I briefly review two ECHR judgments.

In the *Agrotexim*[124] case, the applicant companies, joint majority shareholders in a brewery, lodged a complaint against Greece relating to the brewery's development of

---

115. *Azurix Corp. v. The Argentine Republic*, Decision on the Application for Annulment of the Argentine Republic, 1 Sep. 2009, available on Investment Treaty Arbitration website: https://www.italaw.com/sites/default/files/case-documents/ita0065.pdf
116. *Id.*, para. 128.
117. *Mondev International Ltd v. USA*, Award, 11 Oct. 2002, ILR 125 (2004), 110.
118. *Id.*, para. 144.
119. *Tulip Real Estate and Development Netherlands B.V. v. Republic of Turkey*, Decision on Annulment, 30 Dec. 2015, para. 92 (*see also* para. 91), available on Investment Treaty Arbitration website: https://www.italaw.com/sites/default/files/case-documents/italaw7037.pdf.
120. *See*, e.g., Paulsson, *Denial of Justice in International Law* (Cambridge, 2005), 133; and *Mondev International Ltd v. USA*.
121. *Urbaser S.A. and Consorcio de Aguas Bilbao Biskaia, Bilbao Biskaia Ur Partzuergoa v. Argentine Republic*, Award, 8 Dec. 2016, available on Investment Treaty Arbitration website: https://www.italaw.com/sites/default/files/case-documents/italaw8136_1.pdf.
122. *Id.*, para. 1200.
123. *Ibid.*
124. *Agrotexim and others v. Greece*, Judgment of 24 Oct. 1995, available on the ECHR website: http://cmiskp.echr.coe.int/tkp197/view.asp?item=2&portal=hbkm&action=html&highlight=agrotexim&sessionid=6812591&skin=hudoc-en.

a site. The shareholders alleged a violation of their right to the peaceful enjoyment of their property and of ECHR Articles 6 and 13, in that 'it was not possible for them, under Greek law, as Fix Brewery's shareholders to take proceedings in a Court and to secure legal protection of their rights'.[125] The Commission declared the application admissible and opined that there had been a violation of Article 1 of Protocol 1, but not of Article 6 or 13. Greece argued that the applicant companies lacked the status of 'victim' because the shareholders suffered only indirect effects from an injury to their companies.[126]

The ECHR observed that the shareholders had filed an indirect claim: they were claiming damages stemming from the harm suffered by their company and they were victims because they suffered financial losses. The Court made three significant findings. First, whether a shareholder is a victim of measures affecting its company cannot be determined only on the basis of whether he is a majority shareholder.[127] Second, the 'piercing of the "corporate veil", or the disregarding of a company's legal personality, will be justified only in exceptional circumstances, in particular where it is clearly established that it is impossible for the company to apply to the Convention institutions through the organs set up under its articles of incorporation or – in the event of liquidation – through its liquidators'.[128] Third, the application in the particular case should be dismissed on the grounds that the liquidator representing the brewery could have brought the claim before the ECHR.[129]

In *Olczak*,[130] the ECHR reaffirmed the distinction between the shareholders' interest and the rights of a company. The Court stated that piercing the corporate veil and disregarding the company's legal personality can only be justified in exceptional circumstances, and only when the company itself cannot apply to ECHR institutions through its organs, including its liquidators. The ECHR restated the *Barcelona Traction* principle.[131]

---

125. *Id.*, para. 51.
126. *Id.*, para. 59.
127. *Id.*, para. 63. The jurisprudence of the Court indicates that the applicant shareholder(s) must be a majority shareholder or control the company (*see*, e.g., *Yarrow Plc v. United Kingdom*, Decision of 28 Jan. 1983 on admissibility of the application, available on the ECHR website: http://cmiskp.echr.coe.int/tkp197/portal.asp?sessionId = 6822212&skin = hudoc-en&action = request, even though this requirement is insufficient for a successful claim).
128. *Id.*, para. 66.
129. These principles were reiterated in *Khamidov v. Russia*, Judgment of 15 Nov. 2007, available on the ECHR website: http://cmiskp.echr.coe.int/tkp197/view.asp?item = 18&portal = hbkm& action = html&highlight = agrotexim&sessionid = 6822944&skin = hudoc-en, at para. 123. See also *Rahimov v. Azerbaijan*, Decision on Admissibility of 3 Jan. 2008, available at: http://cmiskp.echr.coe.int/tkp197/view.asp?item = 47&portal = hbkm&action = html&highlight = agr otexim&sessionid = 6822944&skin = hudoc-en; and *Teliga and others v. Ukraine*, Judgment of 21 Dec. 2006, available at: http://cmiskp.echr.coe.int/tkp197/view.asp?item = 1&portal = hbk m&action = html&highlight = teliga&sessionid = 6822944&skin = hudoc-en.
130. *Olczak v. Poland*, Decision on Admissibility of 7 Nov. 2002, available at: http://cmiskp.echr. coe.int/tkp197/view.asp?item = 1&portal = hbkm&action = html&highlight = Olczak&sessionid = 6822944&skin = hudoc-en.
131. *Id.*, para. 59.

These ECHR decisions thus set clear boundaries for claims brought by shareholders. Behind the Court's reasoning there is the concern that granting to shareholders an independent right of action would circumvent the rule of exhaustion of local remedies, because the vast majority of municipal laws do not allow shareholders to bring a claim for damages suffered by the company. In addition, the company could always bring an action before the ECHR even if it is a national of the respondent State. Shareholders, the ECHR has repeatedly concluded, should be allowed to bring a claim only in the event that the company itself cannot.

Even if these ECHR principles are not applicable in the investment treat context, they offer guidance regarding to the implications of piercing the corporate veil, the distinction between a company's rights and shareholders' interests, and the potential circumvention of creditors' rights. The ECHR framework is, as noted above, frequently referred to in the investment treaty context.

§5.06 INVESTMENT TREATY DISPUTES

The current trend in investment treaty arbitration is at odds with the ICJ's approach to shareholders' rights, at odds with the conclusions reached by the delegates of the Sixth Committee regarding the ILC Articles on Diplomatic Protection, and at odds with ECHR precedents that circumscribe the standing of shareholders.

Two investment treaty provisions help to clarify the international law position. First, Article 25 of the ICSID Convention shows that parties' consent can overcome the nationality of a company and characterize it as a foreign company if there is foreign control. This provision is designed to address the situation where shareholders bring a claim that should have been brought by the company. Article 25 only concerns jurisdiction, not the merits. From the wording of Article 25, it appears that the consent of the parties can, in this particular instance, disregard the nationality of a company to establish jurisdiction. Second, NAFTA contains a *lex specialis* framework for shareholders' claims and a provision on payment of damages directly to the company to avoid double recovery. A similar framework can be found in the Central America – Dominican Republic – United States Free Trade Agreement (CAFTA – DR);[132] Article 10.16(1) (b) provides that a shareholder can act on behalf of its controlled enterprise and Article 10.26(2) (a) and (b) provides that the award should be paid to the enterprise.

These ICSID and NAFTA provisions are discussed below, with a focus on how they confirm the general rule of separateness between companies and shareholders, and whether international law should refer to municipal law, as far as the contents of companies' and shareholders' rights are concerned.

---

132. Central America – Dominican Republic – United States Free Trade Agreement (CAFTA – DR), 5 Aug. 2004, available on the United States Trade Representative office website: www.ustr.gov/assets/Trade_Agreements/Bilateral/CAFTA/CAFTA-DR_Final_Texts/asset_upload_file328_4718.pdf.

[A] ICSID

Article 25 of the ICSID Convention provides that:

> The jurisdiction of the Centre shall extend to any legal dispute arising directly out of an investment, between a Contracting State (or any constituent subdivision or agency of a Contracting State designated to the Centre by that State) and a national of another Contracting State, which the parties to the dispute consent in writing to submit to the Centre. When the parties have given their consent, no party may withdraw its consent unilaterally.
> (2) 'National of another Contracting State' means:
>   (a) (...); and
>   (b) any juridical person which had the nationality of a Contracting State other than the State party to the dispute on the date on which the parties consented to submit such dispute to conciliation or arbitration and any juridical person which had the nationality of the Contracting State party to the dispute on that date and which, because of foreign control, the parties have agreed should be treated as a national of another Contracting State for the purposes of this Convention.

Article 25 recognizes the possibility of a claim brought on behalf of a company incorporated in the host State if the company is 'controlled' by foreign entities and the parties agree to consider it a national of another State for purposes of the ICSID Convention. Schreuer states that this provision was 'designed to accommodate' the problem of investments carried out through companies organized under the law of the host State.[133] The provision was the result of a long debate; the initial draft had provided that the nationality of companies was defined on the basis of incorporation or foreign control.[134] The emphasis attributed to consent as the basis of the ICSID Convention swayed the debate and therefore it was suggested to leave to the host State the decision on whether to treat a company as a foreign company,[135] and to recognize the concept of foreign control as opposed to a minority share in the company.[136]

The agreement to treat a company as a foreign national must be express, and it is 'essential' to have such an agreement.[137] This provision does not contemplate shareholders' indirect claims, but represents a jurisdictional response to the problem of host State-incorporated companies controlled by foreign nationals and the requirement of an 'investment'. Article 25 indicates that unless there is consent between the Contracting States, an ICSID tribunal has no jurisdiction over disputes arising in relation to investments carried out through locally incorporated companies. The open question is whether shareholders can overcome this exclusion by bringing claims on behalf of locally incorporated companies for which there is no consent to bring ICSID claims.

---

133. Schreuer et al., *The ICSID Convention: A Commentary*, 296.
134. *History of The ICSID Convention* ('Documents Concerning the Origin and Formulation of the Convention on the Settlement of Investment Disputes between States and Nationals of Other States') published by ICSID, vol. I, 122.
135. *Id.*, vol. II (1), 256, 284, 287, 359, 360-361, 450, 539, 580.
136. Schreuer et al., *The ICSID Convention*, 296-297.
137. *Id.*, 299.

[B] NAFTA

NAFTA contains an express provision concerning claims of an investor on behalf of an enterprise.[138] Article 1117 identifies when an investor can bring such a claim, and Article 1135(2) provides that any payment of damages, in the case of a claim under Article 1117, has to be made directly to the *enterprise* that suffered the damage:

> *Article 1117: Claim by an Investor of a Party on Behalf of an Enterprise*
> 1. An investor of a Party, on behalf of an enterprise of another Party that is a juridical person that the investor owns or controls directly or indirectly, may submit to arbitration under this Section a claim that the other Party has breached an obligation under:
> (a) Section A or Article 1503(2) (State Enterprises), or
> (...)
> 2. Where an investor makes a claim under this Article and the investor or a non-controlling investor in the enterprise makes a claim under Article 1116 arising out of the same events that gave rise to the claim under this Article, and two or more of the claims are submitted to arbitration under Article 1120, the claims should be heard together by a Tribunal established under Article 1126, unless the Tribunal finds that the interests of a disputing party would be prejudiced thereby.[139]
>
> *Article 1135: Final Award*
>
> 2. *Subject to paragraph 1, where a claim is made under Article 1117(1):*
>
> (a) an award of restitution of property shall provide that restitution be made to the enterprise;
> (b) an award of monetary damages and any applicable interest shall provide that the sum be paid to the enterprise; and
> (c) the award shall provide that it is made without prejudice to any right that any person may have in the relief under applicable domestic law.[140]

Under Article 1117 the shareholder must control the company and the damage must occur as a result of a breach of Section A of Chapter 11. However, the shareholder is only entitled to bring the claim; he cannot directly benefit from any damages awarded because the amount payable pursuant to the award is due to the company. In short, a domestic company can benefit from the payment of damages for a violation of Section A of Chapter 11 only if its shareholders are foreign and are entitled to bring a claim under NAFTA. Articles 1117 and 1135 thus work around the application of the *Barcelona Traction* principle and recognize a foreign shareholder's right to bring an investment claim. The payment of damages to the vehicle that suffered the loss addresses the problem of circumvention of creditors' rights. NAFTA thereby provides an elegant solution to the problems posed by indirect claims.

---

138. There are several cases on the application of Art. 1117; *see*, e.g., *GAMI v. Mexico*, Final Award of 15 Nov. 2004, with regard to a claim for expropriation of shares, available on Investment Treaty Arbitration website: http://ita.law.uvic.ca/documents/Gami.pdf; *Pope & Talbot Inc. v. Canada*, Award, 11 Oct. 2002; *Waste Management Inc v. United Mexican States*, Award, 30 Apr. 2004; and *Mondev International Ltd v. USA*.
139. *Id.*, 643.
140. *Id.*, 646.

A minority shareholder cannot bring a claim under Article 1117, but may do so under Article 1116.[141] However, the minority or majority shareholder cannot bring a derivative claim under Article 1116.[142] Accordingly, in *Gami*, discussed below, the tribunal should have found the claim to be inadmissible instead of dismissing it on the merits, since derivative claims were vested in the company under Article 1117, and Gami was a minority shareholder that did not qualify for NAFTA protection.[143] Article 1117 addresses the issue of multiple Claimants and contains a provision on consolidation of claims if one claim is brought on behalf of a company under Article 1117 and another claim arising from the same facts is brought under Article 1116. These two articles also avoid the possibility of double recovery[144] by providing that the payment of damages incurred by the company must be made to the company. Additionally, the consolidation of proceedings for damages suffered by the company (claims under Article 1117) and damages suffered by the company's shareholders (claims under Article 1116) concerning the same facts avoids the possibility of conflicting decisions based on the same facts (as in the *CME v. Czech Republic*[145] and *Lauder v. Czech Republic*[146] cases).

[C] Shareholders' Indirect Claims in Investment Treaty Disputes

Investment treaty tribunals have adopted a broad concept of shareholders' rights to bring claims, and have often attributed relevance to shareholders' economic interests in the company injured by allegedly wrongful acts of the State.[147] The expanding

---

141. See *GAMI v. Mexico*, Final Award of 15 Nov. 2004. Art. 1116:

   Claim by an Investor of a Party on Its Own Behalf,
   1. 'An investor of a Party may submit to arbitration under this Section a claim that another Party has breached an obligation under: (a)Section A or Article 1503(2) (State Enterprises), or(b)Article 1502(3)(a) (Monopolies and State Enterprises) where the monopoly has acted in a manner inconsistent with the Party's obligations under Section A,
      (a) Section A or Article 1503(2) (State Enterprises), or
      (b) Article 1502(3)(a) (Monopolies and State Enterprises) where the monopoly has acted in a manner inconsistent with the Party's obligations under Section A,
   2. and that the investor has incurred loss or damage by reason of, or arising out of, that breach.
   3. An investor may not make a claim if more than three years have elapsed from the date on which the investor first acquired, or should have first acquired, knowledge of the alleged breach and knowledge that the investor has incurred loss or damage.

142. See also Douglas, *The International Law of Investment Claims*, 421–425.
143. *Ibid.*
144. Article 1117 was introduced into the NAFTA draft in September 1992 and the first formulation of the article contained a footnote stating that the text should avoid double recovery: See Kinnear, Bjorklund and Hannaford, *Investment Disputes under NAFTA, an Annotated Guide to NAFTA Chapter 11*, Commentary to Art. 1117, 1117-1.
145. *CME v. Czech Republic*, Award, 14 Mar. 2003, available on the Investment Treaty Arbitration website: http://ita.law.uvic.ca/documents/CME-2003-Final_001.pdf.
146. *Lauder v. Czech Republic*, Award, 3 Sep. 2001, available on the Investment Treaty Arbitration website: http://ita.law.uvic.ca/documents/LauderAward.pdf.
147. *See*, on shareholders' right to claim: *Asian Agricultural Products Limited v. Democratic Socialist Republic of Sri Lanka*, Final Award, 27 Jun. 1990, *ILM* 30 (1991), 577; *American Manufacturing*

concept of shareholders' rights has been variously justified on the grounds that: (i) municipal law recognizes 'the real interest involved and not merely observ[es] a corporate formality. The economic choice of maximizing the shareholders' wealth is the underlying rationale for these developments';[148] or (ii) State practice regarding lump sum agreements, the Iran – United States Claims Tribunal, the United Nations Compensation Commission, and the work of the ILC on Diplomatic Protection show

---

& *Trading, Inc. v. Democratic Republic of the Congo*, Final Award, 21 Feb. 1997, *ICSID Reports* 5 (2002), 14; *Antoine Goetz and others v. Republic of Burundi*, Final Award, 10 Feb. 1999, *ICSID Reports* 6 (2004), 5; *Lanco International, Inc. v. Argentine Republic*, Preliminary Decision on Jurisdiction, 8 Dec. 1998, *ICSID Reports*, 5 (2002), 367; *Emilio Agustín Maffezini v. Kingdom of Spain*, Decision on Jurisdiction, 25 Jan. 2000, 212; *Alex Genin, Eastern Credit Limited, Inc. et A.S. Baltoil v. République d'Estonie*, Final Award, 25 Jun. 2001, *ICSID Reports* 6 (2004), 236 paras 319–329; *Azurix Corp. v. Argentine Republic*, Decision on Jurisdiction, 8 Dec. 2003, *ILM* 43 (2004), 262 and Decision on the Application for Annulment of the Argentine Republic, 1 Sep. 2009, available on Investment Treaty Arbitration website: https://www.italaw.com/sites/default/files/case-documents/ita0065.pdf; *LG & E Energy Corp, LG & E Capital Corp. and LG & E International Inc. v. Argentine Republic*, Decision on Objections to Jurisdiction, 30 Apr. 2004, available on the ICSID website: www.worldbank.org/icsid/cases/lge-decision-en.pdf; *LG&E v. Argentina*, Decision on Liability, 3 Oct. 2006, *ICSID Rev. Foreign Inv. L. J.* 21 (2006), 203; *Plama Consortium Limited v. Republic of Bulgaria*, Decision on Jurisdiction, 8 Feb. 2005; *El Paso Energy International company v. Argentina*, Decision on Jurisdiction, 27 Apr. 2006 and Award, 31 Oct. 2011, available on the Investment Treaty Arbitration website: https://www.italaw.com/sites/default/files/case-documents/ita0270.pdf; *Suez, et al. v. Argentine Republic*, Decision on Jurisdiction, 3 Aug. 2006, available on the ICSID website: www.worldbank.org/icsid/cases/pdf/ARB0319_DecisionJurisdiction03-19.pdf; *Pan American Energy LLC, and BP Argentina Exploration Company v. The Argentine Republic, BP America Production Company, Pan American Sur SRL, Pan American Fueguina, SRL and Pan American Continental SRL v. The Argentine Republic*, Decision on Jurisdiction, 27 Jul. 2006, available on the Investment Claims website: www.investmentclaims.com/decisions/PanAmerican_BP-Argentina-Jurisdiction.pdf. *Camuzzi International S.A. v. Argentina*, Decision on Jurisdiction, 11 May 2005, available on the ICSID website: http://icsid.worldbank.org/ICSID/FrontServlet?requestType=CasesRH&actionVal=showDoc&docId=DC510_En&caseId=C10, para. 81; *Enron v. Argentina*, Decision on Jurisdiction, 2 Aug. 2004, available on the ICSID website: http://icsid.worldbank.org/ICSID/FrontServlet?requestType=CasesRH&actionVal=showDoc&docId=DC502_En&caseId=C3 (this decision on the merits, 22 May 2007, was annulled in part, but the *Ad Hoc Committee* confirmed that the minority shareholders had *ius standi* to bring an investment claim – see para. 127 of the Decision on the Application for Annulment of the Argentine Republic, 30 Jul. 2010 available on the Investment Treaty Arbitration website: https://www.italaw.com/sites/default/files/case-documents/ita0299.pdf); *Sempra Energy v. Argentina*, Decision on Jurisdiction, 11 May 2005, available on the ICSID website: http://icsid.worldbank.org/ICSID/FrontServlet?requestType=CasesRH&actionVal=showDoc&docId=DC509_En&caseId=C8, para. 93 (the award on the merits was annulled by the Decision on the Argentina Republic's Application for Annulment of the Award, 29 Jun. 2010, available on the Investment Treaty Arbitration website: https://www.italaw.com/sites/default/files/case-documents/ita0776.pdf. However, the *Ad Hoc Committee* confirmed that Sempra was entitled to bring a claim under the ICSID Convention with regard to its damages arose from its investment represented by a minority shareholdings, *see* para. 103 of the Annulment Decision); *EDF International SA, SAUR International Sa and Leon Participaciones Argentinas v. Argentina*, Decision on Annulment, 5 Feb. 2016, available on the Investment Treaty arbitration website: https://www.italaw.com/sites/default/files/case-documents/italaw7090.pdf; *Postova Banka v. Greece*, Award, 9 Apr. 2015, available on Investment Treaty website: https://www.italaw.com/sites/default/files/case-documents/italaw4238.pdf (Award upheld by the Decision on Partial Annulment).

148. Vicuña, 'The Protection of Shareholders under International Law: Making State Responsibility More Accessible', in *International Responsibility Today, Essay in Memory of Oscar Schachter* (Netherlands, 2005), 161 at 163.

that 'the right being asserted through international claims is no longer that of the State of nationality but that of the affected individual'.[149] It has further been argued that '[i]t does not any longer appear to be a valid proposition to decide this kind of issue by recourse to the domestic law of a given country or even by reference to principles common to various legal systems (...). It is a matter to be decided principally under international law itself, which now has all the necessary legal tools to do so'.[150]

The broad concept and its attempted justification by investment treaty tribunals entails disregarding municipal law and depicting international law as a self-contained set of rules. The central issue is not whether shareholders can claim in their own right and independently from the company, but whether shareholders can claim in relation to damages suffered by their company. Many investment treaties consider shares as a form of investment, and in these cases expropriation of shares or other measures directly affecting shareholders' rights would undoubtedly give standing to shareholders.[151] This is not controversial. But shareholders' entitlement to bring indirect claims[152] is controversial, and two situations need to be examined. The first occurs when shareholders claim for loss of value of their shares in connection with violations of international law obligations *vis-à-vis* the company. The second is when shareholders bring a claim on behalf of the company and have been vested by international law to bring such a claim (e.g., under NAFTA Article 1117).

The starting point, applicable to both instances, is the content of provisions concerning shareholders, if any, in the relevant investment treaty. BITs generally limit their jurisdiction to claims concerning investments and violations of the BIT's provisions (e.g., the requirement of fair and equitable treatment or adequate compensation for expropriation). These treaties often include, within the definition of investments, capital investment made through shares. If this is the case, investment tribunals may entertain jurisdiction over claims brought by shareholders, as investors and shareholders have a right to bring a claim for a violation of the investment treaty in relation to their investment represented by shares in a certain company. The definition of investment may limit investments to majority shareholdings or may include minority shareholdings.

However the concept of investment is formulated, this does not eliminate fundamental differences between shareholders and the companies they invest in. Investments made by the shareholders are separate and distinct from investments made by their companies. The distinction between shareholders and their companies, which is regulated at a municipal level, has to be maintained at an international plane,

---

149. *Id.*, 165.
150. *Id.*, 163.
151. *See Continental Company v. Argentina*, Decision on Jurisdiction, 22 Feb. 2006, available on the Investment Treaty Arbitration website: http://ita.law.uvic.ca/documents/Continental Casualty-Jurisdiction.pdf, Award 5 Sep. 2008 available on the Investment Treaty Arbitration website: http://ita.law.uvic.ca/documents/ContinentalCasualtyAward.pdf. The *Ad Hoc* Committee dismissed the annulment application (Decision on the Application for Partial Annulment of Continental Casualty Company and the Application for Partial Annulment of the Argentine Republic, 16 Sept. 2011, available on the Investment Treaty Arbitration website: https://www.italaw.com/cases/329).
152. Schreuer, 'Shareholder Protection in International Investment Law', 601.

Chapter 5: Shareholders' Rights §5.06[C]

unless the relevant treaty confers on shareholders the right to pursue their indirect claims and consequently to pierce the corporate veil.

Investment treaty tribunals have mainly dealt with issues of loss of value of shares and shareholders' claims on behalf of the company. In the claim for loss of value of the shares suffered as a consequence of a violation of international law *vis-à-vis* the company, a shareholder's claim has been considered by several investment treaty tribunals along the following lines:

(i) jurisdiction is established if there is an investment and if there is a prima facie[153] case of a violation of the relevant investment treaty;
(ii) 'investment' must include shares in its definition;
(iii) the injury must be to the investment, that is, the shares;
(iv) the injury must be caused by an action or an omission in violation of an investment treaty obligation owed by the host State *vis-à-vis* the shareholder; or
(v) the injury must be caused by an action or an omission in violation of an investment treaty obligation owed by the host State *vis-à-vis* the company.

As discussed more fully below, investment treaty tribunals have often failed to consider whether shareholders were acting in connection with a violation of an investment treaty obligation owed by the host State *vis-à-vis* the shareholders or *vis-à-vis* the company. These tribunals have thereby blurred the distinction between the rights pertaining to shareholders and the company's rights in an investment context.

For claims on behalf of the company under an international law provision that allows the shareholder to bring a claim on behalf of his company, the framework has been the following:

(i) the investment tribunal's jurisdiction is established in accordance with an international law provision that grants the shareholder the right to bring an action on behalf of the company;
(ii) the injury must be caused by an action or an omission in violation of an investment treaty obligation owed by the host State *vis-à-vis* the company;
(iii) if the claim is brought under NAFTA Article 1117, a mechanism is in place to pay any damages awarded to the company in order to avoid double recovery damages and depriving creditors of an asset that belongs to the company.

[1] Loss of Value of Shares

If the obligation was owed *vis-à-vis* the company, the claim for loss of value of the shares is a de facto claim on behalf of the company. If there is a breach of an obligation owed *vis-à-vis* the shareholders, the quantification of damages can be carried out on the basis of the loss suffered by the shareholders, which may well include the value of the

---

153. *Continental Company v. Argentina*, Decision on Jurisdiction, para. 60.

shares. But if there is a breach of an obligation owed to the company, it is not clear on which grounds the shareholder is entitled to bring a claim. Some tribunals mention the breach of economic rights of shareholders[154] and have held that the protection contained in an investment treaty 'extends to the standards of protection spelled out in the BIT with regard to the operation of the local company that represents the investment'.[155] Other tribunals have referred to the protection of 'the individual who is the real holder of an economic interest under international law'.[156] These references do not clarify the meaning of economic rights or 'economic interest', and the blurring of a distinction between the terms 'interest' and 'right' is unjustified. What is an economic right (or interest)? Is it a right to a return or to profit from an investment?

Even if the debate on the existence of shareholders' economic rights is put aside, the determination of damages is still at issue: damages may be awarded on a violation of an obligation owed to the shareholder or damages may be awarded in connection with a violation *vis-à-vis* the company. In the event of a claim concerning the violation of an obligation owed to the company, the shareholder is substantially acting on the company's behalf; in order not to deprive the company's creditors of assets, the tribunal must find a remedy that takes into account this reality and does not circumvent any creditors' rights.

Five investment treaty cases are analysed below. In the first, the violation concerns obligations owed to shareholders. In the second, the violation concerns obligations owed to both shareholders and company, but the tribunal did not distinguish between the two and fashioned a remedy that could potentially deprive the company's creditors of their rights. In the third and fourth decisions, the shareholders brought a de facto claim on behalf of the company that was upheld by the tribunal and deprived the bankrupt company's creditors of their assets. In the fifth, the tribunal rejected on jurisdictional grounds a shareholder's claim arising from impairment of assets belonging to the company in which the Claimant/shareholder held shares.

[a]   CMS Gas Transmission Company v. Argentina (CMS v. Argentina)[157]

This case concerned the suspension of 'a tariff adjustment formula for gas transportation applicable to an enterprise in which CMS has an investment'.[158] In 1989, Argentina reorganized its gas industry so that tariffs were calculated in US dollars and expressed in pesos at the exchange rate on the date of the billing. CMS claimed that it invested in the gas transmission system in reliance on the promises made by Argentinian public

---

154. *Id.*, para. 77.
155. *Id.*, para. 79.
156. Vicuña, 'The Protection of Shareholders under International Law: Making State Responsibility More Accessible', 166. *See also* Total SA *v.* Argentina, Decision on Objections to Jurisdiction, 25 Aug. 2006, paras 80 and 81, available on Investment Treaty Arbitration website: https://www.italaw.com/sites/default/files/case-documents/ita0867.pdf.
157. *CMS Gas Transmission Company v. Argentina*, Decision on Jurisdiction, 17 Jul. 2003, *ILM* 42 (2003), 788; Award, 12 May 2005, *ILM* 44 (2005), 1205; and Decision on Annulment, 25 Sep. 2007.
158. *Id.*, Decision on Jurisdiction, para. 1. *See also* Bottini, *supra*, 207–215.

Chapter 5: Shareholders' Rights §5.06[C]

officials that the programme offered a return in dollars. After the financial crisis of 1999, Argentina adopted several measures amending the exchange rate system.

Argentina's objections to CMS's *ius standi* raised two grounds for the tribunal's consideration: (i) whether a shareholder has standing different from that of the company and, if so, whether the shareholders' rights refer only to its status as shareholder or also to substantive rights connected with the legal and economic performance of its investment; and (ii) whether the Claimant satisfied the jurisdictional requirement that the alleged dispute 'arises directly from the investment'.

The tribunal found 'no bar in current international law to the concept of allowing claims by shareholders independently from those of the corporation concerned'.[159] The tribunal also found no such bar under the ICSID Convention.[160] As for the shareholders' right to claim damages suffered by their company, the tribunal held that CMS had a 'direct right of action' as shareholder under the BIT:[161]

> [T]he rights of the Claimant can be asserted independently from the rights of TGN and those relating to the License and because the Claimant has a separate cause of action under the Treaty in connection with the protected investment, the Tribunal concludes that the present dispute arises directly from the investment.[162]

The tribunal concluded that CMS had *jus standi*.

On the merits, the tribunal stated that CMS had the right to a tariff calculated in dollars and converted into pesos on the billing date. By not keeping its obligations, Argentina breached the standard of fair and equitable treatment and the umbrella clause.[163] The tribunal ordered the payment of damages to CMS and upon, payment of such compensation ordered the transfer of the ownership of CMS's shares to Argentina against the payment of a certain sum.

Argentina sought to nullify the award and argued, *inter alia*: (i) lack of jurisdiction, because CMS was seeking compensation for alleged breaches of rights belonging not to it, but to a different company; and (ii) the tribunal was not entitled to exercise jurisdiction over claims by a company's shareholder for income lost by the company.

The Annulment Committee held that jurisdiction was proper.[164] The Committee noted that the definition of investment under the relevant BIT was very broad and included minority shareholders, and that CMS was an investor:

> It asserted causes of action under the BIT in connection with that protected investment. Its claims for violation of its rights under the BIT were accordingly within the jurisdiction of the Tribunal. This is without prejudice to the determination of the extent of those rights, a question to which the Committee will return.[165]

---

159. *Id.*, para. 48.
160. *Id.*, para. 56.
161. *Id.*, para. 65.
162. *Id.*, para. 68.
163. *CMS Gas Transmission Company v. Argentina*, Award, 12 May 2005, paras 138, 252, 281, and 303.
164. *CMS Gas Transmission Company v. Argentina*, Decision on Annulment, 25 Sep. 2007.
165. *Id.*, para. 75.

CMS v. Argentina stands for the following sensible propositions, in view of the terms of the relevant BIT:

(i) a shareholder has standing different from that of its company, and an investment tribunal constituted under the US-Argentina BIT has jurisdiction over shareholders' rights if they relate to an investment;
(ii) shareholders' rights refer to substantive rights connected with the legal and economic performance of their investment;
(iii) the investment was affected by the measures adopted by Argentina after its crisis in 1999; and
(iv) Argentina breached its commitment and obligations *vis-à-vis* the shareholders.

The shareholders' rights were considered much broader than the rights relating to the shareholders' *status*, since the former include economic rights. This accorded with the broad definition of 'investment' in the US – Argentina BIT, a definition that invokes an economic concept rather than a juridical one. Argentina breached its commitment and obligation *vis-à-vis* the shareholders.

[b] Compañia de Aguas del Aconquija SA and Vivendi v. Argentina (Vivendi II)[166]

The arbitration arose out of a concession agreement concerning the privatization of the water and sewage services of the Argentinean Province of Tucumàn. This concession was executed by, *inter alia*, a French company (CGE, subsequently incorporated into Vivendi) and an Argentinian company, Compañia de Aguas del Aconquija SA (CAA). The judgment of interest for present purposes is the award on the merits (the request to annul this award was rejected in 2010), rendered after the first award on the merits was annulled in 2002.

CAA and Vivendi claimed that the French investor was mistreated[167] by the Argentinean authorities, who 'systematically deprived'[168] the Claimants of their rights under the Argentina/France BIT. The actions of the Argentinean authorities allegedly destroyed the concession's economic viability; the Claimants suffered further damages after the concession's termination because they had to provide service before being replaced and were prevented from collecting outstanding bills and enforcing judgments. The Claimants claimed violation of the fair and equitable standard and expropriation of the investment and sought damages to be paid either entirely to CAA or to both CAA and Vivendi in a portion equivalent to their shareholding, 94.4% to Vivendi and 5.6% to CAA.

Argentina challenged CAA's *locus standi* and argued that this case involved only contractual matters falling outside the tribunal's jurisdiction. On the merits, it argued

---

166. *Compañia de Aguas del Aconquija SA and Vivendi v. Argentina*, Award, 20 Aug. 2007, and Decision on the Argentine Republic's Request for Annulment of the Award, 10 Aug. 2010.
167. *Id.*, Award 20 Aug. 2007, 34, para. 3.2.1.
168. *Ibid.*

that the concession doubled the bills without improving the service, that CAA delivered undrinkable water. It further argued that investors should not be protected by the BIT from 'their own mistakes, nor [should the BIT] provide them with an insurance policy against the due exercise of the State's regulatory activity'.[169]

The tribunal determined that CAA was a proper Claimant and that Argentina had violated the fair and equitable treatment standard due to an illegitimate "campaign" against the concession.[170] On the claim of expropriation without compensation, the tribunal concluded that Argentina had expropriated the Claimants' right of use and enjoyment of their investment under the Concession Agreement by enacting measures that 'were not legitimate regulatory responses to CAA's failings, but were sovereign acts designed illegitimately to end the concession or force its renegotiation'[171] and deprived the Claimants of 'the economic use and enjoyment of their investment, the benefits of which (i.e., the right to be paid for services provided) had been effectively neutralized and rendered useless'.[172] The tribunal assessed damages that took into account the concession's market value[173] and arrived at USD 105 million, which included: (1) the initial capital investment of USD 30 million and the additional investment of USD 21 million in CAA; and (2) USD 54 million subsequently invested by way of debt (debt from CAA to Vivendi, as shown from CAA's accounts at the end of 2005).[174]

The tribunal ordered Argentina to pay damages either entirely to CAA or in the proportion of 5.6% to CAA and 94.4% to Vivendi. However, this order involved a potential circumvention of CAA's creditors' rights: CAA no longer had any value and damages awarded in relation to the concession – likely CAA's only remaining asset – could be paid directly to CAA's shareholder, thereby evading the rights of other preferential creditors. The capital investment in CAA and the shareholder's loan could be reimbursed before CAA's other creditors were paid.

Above all, the tribunal failed to distinguish between: (i) damages suffered by the shareholder as one of the signatory parties to the concession agreement that Argentina violated; and (ii) the company that was party to and implemented the concession agreement. The tribunal did not hold that all of Argentina's acts were taken in relation to the foreign controlling shareholder; instead, it held that the Argentinian Province adopted a certain course of action because it opposed the privatization and there was no indication that this course of conduct would have differed if CAA were controlled by an Argentinian company. If this were the case, then it is not clear why damages could be paid to CAA or alternatively to its shareholder.

There was a simple path for the tribunal, represented by one of the Claimant's pleaded remedies: order the damages paid entirely to CAA. This would have avoided a de facto piercing of the corporate veil. However, the tribunal chose to leave in place the

---

169. *Id.*, 37, para. 3.3.3.
170. *Id.*, 209, para. 7.4.19.
171. *Id.*, 231, para. 7.5.22.
172. *Id.*, 237, para. 7.5.34.
173. *Id.*, 245–246, para. 8.2.10: the tribunal affirmed that 'it is appropriate to assess compensation, *at least in part*, based on the fair market value of the concession' (246, para. 8.2.11).
174. *Id.*, 252–254, paras 8.3.17–8.3.20.

alternative payment option, thereby disregarding the difference between the company and its shareholder. This decision was rendered without any explanation in the text of the award, and the Annulment Committee rejected Argentina's annulment application.

[c] Azurix Corp. v. Argentina[175]

Azurix invested in a utility that distributed drinking water and treated sewage in Argentina. The concession had been tendered on the international market; two Azurix group of companies were incorporated in Argentina for the specific purpose of making a bid offer: Azurix AGOSBA S.R.L. ('AAS') and Operadora de Buenos Aires S.R.L. (OBA). AAS and OBA were indirect subsidiaries of Azurix. AAS and OBA won the bid and incorporated Azurix Buenos Aires S.A. (ABA) in Argentina to act as concessionaire. In 1999 the Province of Buenos Aires gave ABA a thirty-year contract.

Azurix alleged that its investment in Argentina was expropriated and that Argentina had, in addition, violated its obligations under the BIT of fair and equitable treatment, non-discrimination, and full protection and security. In 2001, ABA gave notice of termination of the concession and in 2002 filed for bankruptcy. Argentina contended that Azurix had no *jus standi* to 'put forward indirect claims' relating to its investment's contractual rights.[176] The tribunal disagreed on the basis that the BIT's broad definition of investment[177] served to 'protect indirect claims'.[178]

In the merits phase, the tribunal clarified that Argentina and Azurix had no contractual relationship and that the concession agreement was between the Province and ABA.[179] However, the focus of the award was the concession, which was considered the investment subject to the dispute. The tribunal held that: (i) Argentina failed to accord fair and equitable treatment to Azurix's investment; (ii) Argentina failed to accord full protection and security to Azurix's investment; and (iii) Argentina took arbitrary measures that impaired Azurix's use and enjoyment of its investment. The tribunal awarded compensation to Azurix in the amount of the concession's fair market value.

The tribunal decided that the concession entered into by Azurix's Argentinian subsidiary represented Azurix's investment and on that basis awarded damages in the amount of the concession's fair market value (plus additional investments Azurix had made to finance ABA). Meanwhile, the company that entered into the agreement was bankrupt and had no redress at an international level against the Argentinian Province for the breach of the concession. Azurix thus obtained a payment for its investment

---

175. *Azurix Corp. v. Argentina*, Decision on Jurisdiction, 8 Dec. 2003, *ILM* 43 (2004), 259; Award, 14 Jul. 2006, available on ICSID website: http://icsid.worldbank.org/ICSID/FrontServlet?requestType=CasesRH&actionVal=showDoc&docId=DC507_En&caseId=C5; and Decision on the Application for the Annulment of the Argentine Republic, 1 Sep. 2009, available on Investment Treaty Arbitration website: http://ita.law.uvic.ca/documents/Azurix-Annulment.pdf.
176. *Azurix Corp. v. Argentina*, Decision on Jurisdiction, 8 Dec. 2003, para. 43.
177. *Id.*, paras 73 and 74: 'Azurix is the investor that made the investment through indirectly owned and controlled subsidiaries.'
178. *Id.*, para. 73.
179. *Azurix Corp. v. Argentina*, Award, 14 Jul. 2006, para. 52.

before all the creditors of its subsidiary and paid no tax in Argentina on what was a windfall for its Argentinean subsidiary.

The Annulment Committee upheld the decision of the *Azurix* tribunal. The Committee endorsed the approach that a shareholder can bring a claim for a harm done to a company because there has been a diminution of the value of his shares. Any interest the investor had, whether or not it was a right under municipal law, was protected by the BIT. However, the tribunal, and the Committee in upholding the tribunal, failed to understand that although the investor had standing to activate the dispute settlement mechanism under BITs, it did not have *locus standi* to bring a claim related to assets or situations concerning the company it had shares in. The tribunal's reading of the BIT ignored that the term 'investment' included 'any right conferred *by law* or contract, and any licenses and permits pursuant *to law*'.[180] [emphasis added] The BIT does not protect 'whatever interest', but it protects rights conferred by law. In this case the *rights arising from the ABA concession* were *not* granted by any law *to Azurix*. This was the key point.

Azurix appears to be distinguishable from *CMS* in that Azurix and its subsidiary were considered the same entity, although both cases concerned violations of the same BIT. In *CMS* the Claimant alleged a breach of commitments and obligations rendered to itself; in *Azurix*, the concession, even if it was entered into by a different company, was considered an asset belonging to Azurix. *Azurix* is also distinguishable from *Vivendi II*, since in the latter case the concession was granted to CAA and Vivendi, its controlling shareholder.

The fact that Azurix set up the companies for the tender and won the tender justified in the tribunal's collective mind that Azurix should be compensated for any breach of the concession. However, the tribunal disregarded the existence of separate companies, as well as the fact that there were bankruptcy proceedings. No provision was made to avoid Azurix's obtaining money in preference to its subsidiary's creditors. The Committee rejected the application of municipal law because the question of the breach of the BIT had to be determined in accordance with general principles of international law and not in accordance with municipal law.[181] But the application of international law does not exclude per se the application of municipal law, since international law may *renvoi* to municipal law.

Subsequent to the *Azurix* Annulment decision, the *Standard Chartered Bank v. Tanzania*[182] tribunal detailed the requirements that it determined should be placed on shareholder-investors seeking to advance indirect claims under a BIT. The tribunal stated that the investor had to be actively involved in the 'making' of the investment and to 'demonstrate that the investment was made at the Claimant's direction, that the Claimant funded the investment or that the Claimant controlled the investment in an active and direct manner. Passive ownership of shares in a company not controlled by

---

180. Article 1 of the BIT USA – Argentina.
181. *Azurix Corp. v. Argentina*, Decision on the Application for the Annulment of the Argentine Republic, 1 Sep. 2009, para. 146. *See also* para. 151.
182. *Standard Chartered Bank v. Tanzania*, Award, 2 Nov. 2012, available on Investment Treaty Arbitration website: https://www.italaw.com/sites/default/files/case-documents/italaw1184.pdf.

the Claimant where that company in turn owns the investment is not sufficient'.[183] Although the *Standard Chartered* tribunal drew this conclusion from the wording of the particular BIT in the case, its restrictive approach might be adopted by future tribunals in order to narrow the class of indirect investors who may be qualified to bring investment treaty claims for alleged treaty violations against companies in which they own shares.

[d] Enron Corp. and Ponderosa Assets L.P. v. Argentina[184]

Enron participated in the privatization of Transportadora de Gas del Sur ('TGS'), one of the networks for the transportation and distribution of gas produced in Argentina's southern provinces. Enron owned, through two subsidiaries, 50% of the shares of an Argentina-incorporated company that controlled TGS. Enron's claim challenged the issuance of tax assessments by some of the provinces. An auxiliary claim was introduced for disputes concerning tariffs, currency devaluation, and other financial measures adopted by the Argentinian government.

Argentina contended that the tax claim was inadmissible on the grounds that Enron did not have the rights upon which it based its claim. The measures directly affected only TGS, a company incorporated in Argentina. Enron was affected indirectly, as a minority shareholder in TGS. Argentina argued that an investment in shares qualified for protection under the BIT, but in such a case, claims could only be made in respect of 'measures affecting the *qua* shares. (...) Claims by minority shareholders concerning measures that affect the corporation as a separate legal entity cannot be admissible in the context of the Treaty'.[185]

The tribunal held that:

> The question of jus standi thus becomes inseparable from the determination of the Claimant's status as a protected investor. (...) If so, then the inquiry must determine whether these rights refer only to the Claimants' status as shareholders or also to substantive rights connected with the legal and economic performance of the investment made (...) This Tribunal must accordingly conclude that under the provisions of the Bilateral Investment Treaty, broad as they are, claims made by investors that are not in the majority or in the control of the affected corporation when claiming for violations of their rights under such treaty are admissible. Whether the locally incorporated company may further claim for the violation of

---

183. *Id.*, para. 230.
184. *Enron Corp. and Ponderosa Assets L.P. v. Argentina*, Decision on Jurisdiction, 14 Jan. 2004, available on Investment Treaty Arbitration website: http://ita.law.uvic.ca/documents/Enron-Jurisdiction.pdf; and Decision on Ancillary Claims, 2 Aug. 2004, available on the same website: http://ita.law.uvic.ca/documents/Enron-DecisiononJurisdiction-FINAL-English.pdf. Award, 22 May 2007, available on Investment Treaty Arbitration at http://ita.law.uvic.ca/documents/Enron-Award.pdf. This decision on the merits dated 22 May 2007 was annulled in part, but the *Ad Hoc Committee* confirmed that the minority shareholders had *ius standi* to bring an investment claim, *see* para. 127 of the Decision on the Application for Annulment of the Argentine Republic, 30 Jul. 2010 available on the Investment Treaty Arbitration website: https://www.italaw.com/sites/default/files/case-documents/ita0299.pdf.
185. *Enron Corp. and Ponderosa Assets L.P. v. Argentina*, Decision on Jurisdiction, 14 Jan. 2004, para. 35.

its rights under contracts, licences or other instruments, does not affect the direct right of action of foreign shareholders under the Bilateral Investment Treaty for protecting their interests in the qualifying investment.[186]

On the issue of whether the claim was too remotely connected with the investment, the tribunal concluded that:

> The Claimants cannot be considered to be only remotely connected to the legal arrangements governing the privatization, they are beyond any doubt the owners of the investment made and their rights are protected under the Treaty as clearly established treaty-rights and not merely contractual rights related to some intermediary. The fact that the investment was made through CIESA and related companies does not in any way alter this conclusion.[187]

The fact that Enron had been specifically invited to participate in the privatization process and had decision-making power in the subsidiary's management led the tribunal to conclude that the 'cutoff' point for indirect shareholders was not reached and Enron had *jus standi*. Enron was not too remotely connected to the investment, and its claim was admissible.[188] The tribunal also found that it had jurisdiction over other 'ancillary claims' on the same ground that Enron was specifically invited to participate in the privatization process and could not be dissociated from the Argentinian companies it had set up and through which it channelled the investment.

The *Enron* Ad Hoc Annulment Committee confirmed that the Claimants had *ius standi* to bring a BIT claim in respect of any measure of Argentina affecting the investment.[189] The Committee referred to the reasoning adopted in *Azurix* and held that: (i) the proceeding was not an indirect claim brought by the shareholders in respect of their company's rights; (ii) *Barcelona Traction* entailed customary international law and diplomatic protection, and an investment treaty is capable of modifying these rules; and (iii) Claimants invested in Argentina, although they were a minority shareholder in TGS. The Committee rejected the risk of double recovery, endorsing the tribunal's view that such risk had not in fact arisen and there were 'pragmatic ways' of dealing with it.[190]

In reaching these conclusions, the *Enron* tribunal and then the Ad Hoc Committee ignored the existence of different companies and only considered relevant the investment from an economic perspective. The presence of different companies carrying out the investment meant to the tribunal that all the assets and rights of one company became the assets and rights of the other companies involved in the investment. Unfortunately, under this approach legal personality became a meaningless concept, as did the notion of a 'legal dispute arising directly out of an investment', required for the purpose of jurisdiction under Article 25 of the ICSID Convention. The question that this case poses for international lawyers is how a legal dispute can arise out of an

---

186. *Id.*, paras 37 and 49.
187. *Id.*, para. 56.
188. *Id.*, paras 52 and 56.
189. Decision on the Application for Annulment of the Argentine Republic, 30 Jul. 2010, paras 112–127.
190. *Id.*, para. 124.

investment if no consideration is given to the different entities owning the rights and assets in dispute. *Siemens AG v. Argentina*,[191] which held that the definition of investment contained in the Germany–Argentina BIT was very broad, took an approach similar to *Enron*:

> The Treaty does not require that there be no interposed companies between the investment and the ultimate owner of the company. Therefore a literal reading of the Treaty does not support the allegation that the definition of investment excludes indirect investment.[192]

As a matter of international law, both *Enron* and *Siemens* are flawed decisions in that they fail to consider the link between the damage and the investment. These decisions accorded no legal significance to the layers of companies that carried out the investment. The principle of distinct personalities between entities is ignored in favour of the concept of an economic unit. There is no distinction between obligations owed to an entity and conduct carried out by another company. The only relevant factor is that all these companies were in some way involved in the same investment. Legal differences are overruled by alleged economic realities. This devotion to the foreign origins of capital comes at the expense of basic international law principles.[193] The concept of investment implies the existence of a legal entitlement, and therefore the fact that a company invested in another company and expects a return from this investment should not have sufficed to establish the jurisdiction of an investment treaty tribunal.

[e] Poštová Banka As and Istrokapital SE v. The Hellenic Republic[194]

The global financial crisis of 2008 led to Greek public debt being downgraded by rating agencies. In January 2010, Greece submitted to the European Commission a three-year stability programme to reduce its fiscal deficit, which was followed by the adoption of austerity measures.

In 2010, Poštová banka, a Slovak bank, bought EUR 504,000,000.00 of Greek Government Bonds (GGBs). The GGBs acquired by Poštová belonged to five series of GGBs, governed by Greek law, which had been issued by the Hellenic Republic between 2007 and 2010 and matured at various dates between 2012 and 2020. These

---

191. *Siemens AG v. Argentina*, Decision on Jurisdiction, 3 Aug. 2004, *ILM* 44 (2005), 137. In 2009 the parties settled the dispute and discontinued the Annulment proceedings.
192. *Id.*, para. 137.
193. These decisions run contrary to the approach to nationality taken in *Tokios Tokeles v. Ukraine*, where form over substance was the rule. *See* Ch. 3, on nationality.
194. Poštová Banka As and Istrokapital SE *v.* The Hellenic Republic, Award, 9 Apr. 2015, available on Investment Treaty Arbitration website: https://www.italaw.com/sites/default/files/case-documents/italaw4238.pdf. Annulment proceeding ended with the dismissal of Poštová Banka's application for partial annulment of the Award, 9 Apr. 2015 (*see* Decision on Poštová Banka Application for Partial annulment of the Award, 29 Sep. 2016, available on Investment Treaty Arbitration website: https://www.italaw.com/sites/default/files/case-documents/italaw7587.pdf.

Chapter 5: Shareholders' Rights   §5.06[C]

five series of GGBs were among the obligations of the Greek Government that the rating agencies downgraded.

During 2010 and 2011, Greece paid the interest due on its bonds. From July 2011, as Greece's situation continued to deteriorate, the International Monetary Fund, together with Greek and European authorities, determined that 'Private Sector Involvement' was necessary to close a significant funding gap, meaning that private holders of government debt would be required to accept some reduction in the amount due on that debt. In the following months, a second adjustment programme was adopted and Greece initiated a sovereign debt restructuring which was implemented through an exchange of outstanding GGBs for new titles. In 2012 Poštová received new securities in exchange for its GGBs.

Meanwhile the National Bank of Slovakia requested a meeting with Poštová banka to discuss the bank's exposure to GGBs. Istrokapital SE (a European Public Limited Liability Company organized under the laws of Cyprus) held shares in Poštová banka and in 2011 signed a Framework Share Purchase Agreement with J&T Finance for the acquisition by J&T of Istrokapital's shares in Poštová banka. Notwithstanding the sale, the risk associated with GGBs was borne by Istrokapital and the latter assumed an obligation to compensate J&T Finance if the return on the value of the GGBs did not reach the acquisition cost. Several agreements were entered into afterward between Istrokapital and J&T related to the GGBs.

In 2013 Poštová banka and Istrokapital brought an ICSID proceeding on the basis of an alleged impairment of their entitlement in GGBs. Greece objected to jurisdiction on several grounds, including that GGBs were not a protected investment and that Istrokapital had never made a protected investment under the Cyprus-Greece BIT. The tribunal held that it had no jurisdiction over the dispute:

(i) The shareholder had no standing to assert a claim for an impairment of the assets of the company in which it holds shares.
(ii) Shareholders do not have claims arising from rights in the assets of the companies in which they hold shares.[195]

The Poštová tribunal reiterated that the default position in international law is that the company is distinct from its shareholders, and this implies that only the company can protect its own assets. The tribunal reasoned that Istrokapital did not demonstrate that it had any legal or contractual right to the GGBs held by Poštová banka that would allow it to bring a treaty claim against Greece for the impairment of the GGBs. The tribunal clarified that shareholders may well bring a claim in relation to the effects that measures taken against the company have on the value of the Claimants' shares.[196] Assets of companies are not protected investment per se unless the companies are a protected investor and can bring a treaty claim in relation to its assets.[197] The definition of the protected investment in the event of claim brought by a

---
195. *Id.*, paras 229 and 247.
196. *Id.*, para. 232.
197. *Id.*, para. 235. *See* various decisions listed by the tribunal in paras 232–244.

shareholder was limited to the shares, and no claim could be raised by a shareholder in relation to interference with assets belonging to its company.

This well-reasoned decision stands for the proposition that a shareholder of a company incorporated in the host state may assert claims based on measures taken against its company's assets only if the measures impair the value of the shares. Shareholders have no standing to bring claims concerning assets of their company or have any rights over such assets.

[2]   Claims on Behalf of the Company: GAMI v. Mexico

GAMI Investment Inc., a US corporation, brought a NAFTA claim for the value of its minority shareholding in GAM (Grupo Azucarero México SA de CV), a Mexican company controlled by Mexican shareholders. GAMI challenged certain governmental measures, including the expropriation of GAM's sugar mills. There were no contracts between GAM (or GAMI) and Mexico. GAMI alleged, *inter alia*, breach of the fair and equitable treatment standard and wrongful expropriation, arguing that the Mexican measures 'rendered GAMI's investment virtually worthless'.[198]

The tribunal clarified that the issue in dispute was whether the alleged breach 'leads with sufficient directness to loss or damage in respect of a given investment',[199] and in this the distinction between 'de facto expropriation of GAMI's shares in GAM and the de jure expropriation of GAM's five mills is critical'.[200] The tribunal concluded that 'GAMI has not shown that the government's self-assigned duty in the regulatory regime was simple and unequivocal. It is impossible to conclude that the failures in the Sugar Programme were both *directly attributable to the government and directly causative of GAMI's alleged injury*' [emphasis added].[201]

Gami focuses on the difference between damages suffered by the company and damages suffered by the shareholders. To determine whether Mexico had violated the fair and equitable treatment standard, the tribunal required evidence that there was a direct link between the damage to the company and the injury to the shareholders. GAMI could not prove that the value of its shareholding had been destroyed; accordingly, the tribunal declared that it had no jurisdiction over GAMI's claims. The minority shareholder's rights were defined taking into account legal rights, not the economic interests behind the investment. The distinction between the concept of a company and its shareholders was maintained.

As noted above, the NAFTA framework is useful in that it distinguishes shareholders' claims on behalf of the company from shareholders' claims on their own behalf (Articles 1116 and 1117). *GAMI* upheld this distinction.

---

198. *Gami v. Mexico*, para. 28.
199. *Id.*, para. 33.
200. *Id.*, para. 35.
201. *Id.*, para. 110.

§5.07 CONCLUSION

Corporations are entities distinct from their members. This principle applies on the municipal level and on the international plane unless a specific provision of municipal or international law allows for corporate personalities to be disregarded. Flowing from this principle is the rule that a wrong against the corporation does not amount to a wrong against its members, unless, again, there is a specific treaty provision providing such a claim. Based on this principle and rule, only the company is entitled to act to redress an injury directed at itself, in the absence of a specific provision enabling other entities to act on its behalf.

The ICJ expressed this framework in *Barcelona Traction*. Investment arbitrators often state that this case is not relevant, or at least not directly relevant, in the investment treaty context because it arose in the context of diplomatic protection:

> With respect to general international law, the Committee notes that the parties advanced different interpretations of the judgments rendered by the International Court of Justice in the Barcelona Traction case and the ELSI case. Those cases were concerned with diplomatic protection under customary international law and not with the protection of the rights of investors under treaties relating to the protection of investments. As specified by the Tribunal, those judgments are not 'directly relevant to the present dispute.'[202]

However, *Barcelona Traction* and other ICJ judgments *are* relevant to the extent that investment treaties do not expressly regulate shareholders' rights, because these judgments concern and explicate shareholders' rights under customary international law. As the ICJ explained in *Barcelona Traction*:

> Indeed, whether in the form of multilateral or bilateral treaties between States, or in that of agreements between States and companies, there has since the Second World War been considerable development in the protection of foreign investments. The instruments in question contain provisions as to jurisdiction and procedure in case of disputes concerning the treatment of investing companies by the States in which they invest capital. Sometimes companies are themselves vested with a direct right to defend their interests against States through prescribed procedures. No such instrument is in force between the Parties to the present case.[203]

Barcelona Traction and *Diallo* provide, in summary, important guidance for investment treaty tribunals. In particular:

(i) International law must recognize institutions of municipal law with regard to companies' and shareholders' rights since international law does not define these concepts. A limited company is an 'exclusive creation' of municipal law, and international law 'is bound in principle to deal with companies as they are'.[204]

---

202. *CMS Gas Transmission Company v. Argentina*, Decision on Annulment, 25 Sep. 2007, para. 69 (footnotes omitted).
203. *Barcelona Traction*, 47, para. 90.
204. *Id.*, Separate Opinion of Judge Fitzmaurice, 67, para. 6.

(ii) In municipal law, the concept of the company is separate from the concept of the company's shareholders. Shareholders do not have a right to the corporate assets as long as the company is in existence. Only the company can seek redress for wrongs relating to the corporate character.[205]
(iii) A wrong done to the company frequently prejudices its shareholders, but this does not imply that they are entitled to a claim for compensation. By the same token, creditors do not have any right to claim compensation in relation to damages suffered by their company/debtor.[206]
(iv) There is a difference between 'injury in respect of a right and injury to a simple interest'.[207]
(v) No rule of international law expressly confers a right to shareholders in relation to their indirect claim;[208] under customary international law there is no such right of shareholders, even though such a right could be provided by a treaty.[209]
(vi) A shareholder can bring a claim if there has been a complete expropriation of the company's assets. A shareholder can also bring a claim if no remedy is available to the company to obtain redress to its injury or if the company suffered denial of justice.[210]

Applying this customary international law guidance in the investment treaty context requires maintaining a distinction between (i) shareholders' claims brought expressly or de facto on behalf of their company, and (ii) shareholders' claims brought on their own behalf. This difference is clearly enunciated in Articles 1116 and 1117 of NAFTA, while in BITs there is typically no mention of such a difference. However, the absence of provisions similar to Article 1116 or 1117 of NAFTA cannot be treated as a license to disregard the concept of legal personality. In the absence of an express provision in BITs treating shareholders and their company as one entity, there is no basis for mixing shareholders' claims on their own behalf and their claims on behalf of their company.

The most recurrent treaty arbitration scenario is a claim for loss of value of the shares due to a violation of international law *vis-à-vis* the company. The shareholder can, for example, be injured by conduct *vis-à-vis* the company if the host State breaches the fair and equitable treatment standard because the company is owned by foreign shareholders. The appropriate framework for considering such claims is:

(a) the investment tribunals' jurisdiction is established if there is an investment and if there is a prima facie[211] case that the relevant investment treaty was violated;

---

205. *Id.*, 34–35, para. 42.
206. *Id.*, 35, para. 44.
207. *Id.*, para. 46.
208. *Id.*, 37, para. 51.
209. *Id.*, 46–47, paras 89–90.
210. *See* Douglas, *The International Law of Investment Claims*, 427–430.
211. *Continental Company v. Argentina*, Decision on Jurisdiction, para. 60.

(b) 'investment' must include shares in its definition;
(c) the injury must be to the investment, that is, the shares (their use or value); and
(d) the injury must be caused by an action or an omission in violation of an investment treaty obligation owed by the host State *vis-à-vis* the shareholder.

If this framework is adopted, the potential problem of awarding damages suffered by the company to its shareholders, and thereby circumventing creditors' rights and possibly overlooking bankruptcy issues, is resolved.

However, several investment tribunals have inserted in this framework injuries caused by an action or an omission in violation of an investment treaty obligation owed by the host State *vis-à-vis* the company (*see*, e.g., *Azurix*). Shareholders have received damages suffered by their company in preference to other creditors. The failure to consider the difference between shareholders acting in connection with obligations owed *vis-à-vis* the shareholders versus the company is, regrettably, the prevailing trend in investment treaty cases.

The broad definition of investment in several BITs may lead investment tribunals to conclude that economic realities matter more than legal personality. If the breach of the standard of fair and equitable treatment or denial of justice or expropriation of all the assets of the company and of investors' legitimate expectations leads to *locus standi* for any company/individual involved in the investment, legal personality should at least be considered at the damages level. If a company, simply by having participated in a tender process, can seek damages for wrongful conduct carried out *vis-à-vis* another company connected to its group, the award of damages must take the existence of separate entities into account. Shareholders should not be permitted to seek the advantages of a legal personality and, for example, avoid bankruptcy if the company-vehicle of the investment is declared bankrupt, and then be paid for damages suffered by the same vehicle. The arbitral award should put shareholders in the position they would have been in if the injury had not occurred. This does not mean that shareholders are entitled to be in a better position than if the injury had not occurred.

If damages are awarded to the shareholders' vehicle, they are subject to sharing between the vehicle's creditors and to the taxation regime applicable to the vehicle. If damages are awarded to shareholders, however, the vehicle's creditors lose their rights and the taxation regime changes. If the investment treaty does not expressly enable the investment tribunal to disregard creditors' rights and States' taxation rights, a tribunal should not simply ignore them. An award of damages must take into account the existence of the vehicle's creditors, including tax authorities. One solution may be to award compensation on the basis of what would have been the shareholders' dividends after payment of taxes and of the vehicle's creditors, if the State would have paid damages for the injury to the vehicle. Another solution may be to award damages by calculating the value of the shares as if the injury would have never occurred. A third option is that shareholders may seek payment of damages for harm to their vehicle, as was pleaded in *Vivendi*. Finally, the host State can plead that any award of damages is to be paid to the vehicle.

According to one scholar, the emerging trend of investment tribunals is to consider that the 'shareholder's interests in a company includes an interest in the assets of that company, including its licenses, contractual rights, rights under the law, claims to money or economic performance, etc., and in that in finding jurisdiction they based that reasoning on the broad definition of investment in the applicable BITs'.[212] The concept of 'investment' adopted by several tribunals has led them to disregard the existence of a legal dispute in the sense that it was irrelevant to determining which entity had a right versus which entity had an obligation owed to it.

However, this concept of investment does not as a matter of international law permit these tribunals to disregard how municipal law defines certain rights. BITs define the concept of investment by referring to certain rights (e.g., property rights, contracts, shares); these rights are defined by municipal law since no definition exists under international law. Moreover, the definition of investment often refers to shares and identifies direct or indirect shareholdings as a relevant investment. This broad definition of investment cannot justify the claim that assets belonging to the controlled subsidiary are assets belonging to the shareholder.

The Report of the Executive Directors of the International Bank for Reconstruction and Development on the ICSID Convention[213] states that 'consent of the parties is the cornerstone of the jurisdiction of the Centre'.[214] But, the Report added that 'consent alone will not suffice to bring a dispute within its jurisdiction. In keeping with the purpose of the Convention, the jurisdiction of the Centre is further limited by reference to the nature of the dispute and the parties thereto'.[215] The expression 'legal dispute' in Article 25(i) 'has been used to make clear that while conflicts of rights are within the jurisdiction of the Centre, mere conflicts of interests are not. The dispute must concern the existence or scope of a legal right or obligation, or the nature or extent of the reparation to be made for breach of a legal obligation'.[216]

It has been argued that the recent trend of investment awards 'performs a true measure of justice in the international community (...). A major historical distortion based on the exclusion of corporate claims or their modalities stands now to be corrected'.[217] This perspective ignores that this 'true measure of justice' in a number of cases would violate the rights of the injured company's creditors and would expose the host State to a multitude of potential parallel claims as well as double recoveries. Moreover, the recent trend circumvents the requirement concerning the nationality of the parties, namely, that a company incorporated in the host State cannot bring an ICSID claim against its State unless there is an agreement and there is foreign control.

---

212. Schreuer, 'Shareholder Protection in International Investment Law', 618, quoting Alexandrov, 'The Baby Boom of Treaty-Based Arbitrations and the Jurisdiction of ICSID Tribunals: Shareholders as "Investors" and Jurisdiction *Ratione Temporis*', *The Law and Practice of International Courts and Tribunals* 4 (2005), 19, at 27.
213. Section V on the jurisdiction of the Centre, available on the ICSID website: http://icsid.worldbank.org/ICSID/StaticFiles/basicdoc/partB.htm.
214. *Id.*, para. 23.
215. *Id.*, para. 25.
216. *Id.*, para. 26.
217. Vicuña, 'The Protection of Shareholders Under International Law: Making State Responsibility More Accessible', 170.

Barcelona Traction may be ignored or rejected by an increasing number of international investment tribunals, but that does not mean that it should be ignored or rejected: *Barcelona Traction* speaks directly to crucial and difficult issues in investment treaty arbitration.

CHAPTER 6
Treaty Versus Contract Claims, and Umbrella Clauses: When a Contract Breach May Become a Treaty Breach

§6.01 INTRODUCTION

As a matter of customary international law, a State's breach of a contract between an alien and the State does not automatically entail State responsibility.[1] Brownlie explained that the 'position is regulated by the general principles governing the treatment of aliens. Thus the act of the contracting government will entail state responsibility if, by itself or in combination with other circumstances, it constitutes a denial of justice or an expropriation contrary to international law'.[2]

An exception to this general principle occurs when the contract is governed by international law or when a breach of contract constitutes a violation of a treaty. States are at liberty to enter into any type of agreement governed by any law or set of rules. As Crawford states 'there is no a priori limitation on the scope or content of treaty obligations, even those concerning what would otherwise be internal affairs'.[3] The PCIJ's holding in *The Wimbledon* expresses this principle: 'if states could not enter into binding international obligations, they would lack an attribute of statehood'.[4]

---

1. *See, e.g.*, Brownlie, *Principles of Public International Law, supra*, 627–629; Jennings & Watts, *Oppenheim's International Law: Peace*, vol. 1, Parts 2 to 4 (London, 927); Mann, 'State Contract and State Responsibility', *Am. J. Int'l. L.* 54 (1960), 572; Mann, 'The Consequences of an International Wrong in International and National Law', *BYIL* 49 (1978), 1; and Amerasinghe, 'State Breaches of Contract with Aliens and International Law', *AJIL* 58 (1964), 881.
2. Brownlie, *Principles of Public International Law*, 627.
3. Crawford, 'Treaty and Contract in Investment Arbitration', Arb Int'l 24 (2008) 351, at 354.
4. *Id.*, 4; *see also* ILC Art. 12 on State Responsibility, in Crawford, *The International Law Commission's Articles on State Responsibility ('The ILC's Articles on State Responsibility'), supra*, 128.

A treaty can also expressly exclude treaty jurisdiction for breach of contract. For example, in the NAFTA framework, a breach of contract is not relevant since Article 1116 provides that an investor may submit to arbitration under Chapter 11 'a claim that another Party has breached an obligation' under the specific provisions of the Chapter. Therefore, an arbitral tribunal constituted under Chapter 11 would (or at least should) *not* entertain jurisdiction over contract claims,[5] whereas an arbitral tribunal constituted under a BIT might well entertain jurisdiction over an alleged breach of contract arising out of an investment (depending on the terms of the BIT).

A contract between a State and an individual or a private entity is not regulated *only* by the governing law elected by the parties or identified through the relevant conflict of law rules.[6] However, absent an international law principle and factual circumstances that would render municipal law regulation internationally wrongful, municipal law should stand as the prevailing law.

Sandline International Inc v. Papua New Guinea[7] demonstrates that while tribunals have rightly understood that, as a matter of international law, the governing law provision is not necessarily the only relevant law, they have been in certain situations, too quick to jettison municipal law. The case concerned a contract under which Sandline would have provided military services to overcome rebels in an area of Papua New Guinea. This mercenary agreement was executed in part and then repudiated by Papua New Guinea, which claimed that this agreement was unenforceable because it was illegal under its Constitution and other statutes, and that its performance was accordingly unlawful in the only place where performance was possible.

The *Sandline* tribunal held that a contract between a private party and a State is an international contract, notwithstanding that the contract contains a choice of law provision designating particular State's law as governing. Accordingly, Papua New Guinea could not rely 'upon its own internal laws as the basis for a plea that a contract concluded by it is illegal'.[8] The tribunal ruled that Papua New Guinea was therefore liable to Sandline for the repudiation of the contract.

In *Sandline*, the defence based on the illegality of the contract was dismissed because a State cannot simply rely on its law. However, the full reasoning behind the holding is unclear. The State's attempt to rely on its municipal law related to the legality of the contract, which should in fact be assessed pursuant to municipal law, as discussed in Chapter 4. International law principles should not necessarily have enabled the tribunal to disregard the proper law of the contract.

In the investment disputes arena, the issue of the relevance of a breach of contract remains controversial. Contract breaches, if related to an investment, are often

---

5. Crawford, qualifies this comment, stating: 'Indeed in some cases it has been clear that there were breaches of the investment contract by State organs: that might conceivably be taken into account in applying the minimum standard of treatment in Article 1105(1) on the NAFTA but it would only be relevant incidentally.' (Crawford, 'Treaty and Contract in Investment Arbitration', 362)
6. Mann, *State Contract and State Responsibility*, 581.
7. This award is reported in part in the unsuccessful appeal procedure before the Australian Supreme Court of Queensland, Judgment of 30 Mar. 1999, in *ILR* 117 (2000), 565.
8. *Id.*, in particular, 571.

Chapter 6: Treaty Versus Contract Claims, and Umbrella Clauses §6.01

included in bilateral investment treaties as being within an investment tribunal's jurisdiction. However, this does not mean that *any* breach of contract constitutes a breach of an investment treaty at the merits stage: there must be a violation of the treaty to find liability. The particular investment treaty's wording of course carries primary importance, and a breach of contract must be characterized as a violation of the relevant treaty.

Perhaps the leading case on this issue is the Annulment Committee's decision in *Vivendi*,[9] which distinguished treaty from contract claims and proposed a framework for assessing the distinction. Although this decision has been followed by some tribunals, it has been substantially ignored by others, which have instead relied on the distinction between *acta iure imperii* and *acta iure gestionis*. In the latter category, the tribunals have considered any breach of contract pursuant to governmental action or purpose to be a violation of an investment treaty, even if the relevant treaty does not mention such an action or purpose, and the contract is governed by a municipal law. Some of these tribunals have considered any breach of contract to be a violation of the fair and equitable treatment standard, and have thereby opened the door to the automatic equation of contract and treaty breaches.

This Chapter first analyses the history of the distinction between treaty and contract claims. It then considers the principles of international law that govern this issue, and examines how international investment tribunals have addressed these principles – properly or improperly. The second part of the Chapter focuses on umbrella clauses, commonly understood as provisions that seek to ensure that each Party to the treaty will respect specific undertakings towards nationals of the other Party.[10] These clauses can also include general undertakings granted by the State to a class of investors, often regulated by municipal law, which become relevant under international law because of a provision contained in the investment treaty.

Umbrella clauses have a chequered history with arbitral tribunals and commentators expressing a variety of views. The range of views largely reflects the differing

---

9. *Vivendi, supra*, Decision on Annulment, para. 95.
10. Dolzer & Stevens, *Bilateral Investment Treaties*, 166. *See, generally*, Alexandrov, 'Breach of Treaty Claims and Breach of Contract Claims: Is It Still Unknown Territory' in *Arbitration Under Investment Agreement*, ed. Yannaca-Small (Oxford, 2010), 323–350; Schreuer, 'Investment Treaty Arbitration and Jurisdiction over Contract Claims – The *Vivendi I* case Considered', available online: http://www.univie.ac.at/intlaw/pdf/cschapter_76.pdf ; and Gaillard, 'Investment Treaty Arbitration and Jurisdiction over Contract Claims – the *SGS Cases* Considered' available online: http://www.shearman.com/ ~ /media/Files/NewsInsights/Publications/2005/01/Investment-Treaty-Arbitration-and-Jurisdiction-o__/Files/IA_Investment-Treaty-Arbitration_040308_10/FileAttachment/IA_Investment-Treaty-Arbitration_040308_10.pdf ; Yannaca-Small '*Interpretation of the Umbrella Clause in Investment Agreements*', OECD Working Papers on International Investment, Number 2006/3, October 2006; Alexandrov, 'Breaches of Contract and Breaches of Treaty – The Jurisdiction of Treaty-Based Arbitration Tribunals to Decide Breach of Contract Claims in *SGS v. Pakistan* and *SGS v. Philippines*' in *TDM 5 (2006), in Case Comments & Awards*; McLachlan, Shore & Weiniger, *International Investment Arbitration Substantive Principles, supra*, 109–120; Crawford, 'Treaty and Contract in Investment Arbitration', *supra*, 366–370; Dolzer & Schreuer, *Principles of International Investment Law, supra*, 166–178.

attitudes of arbitrators to the role of municipal versus international law in investment treaty arbitration. For example, if it is established that, under an umbrella clause, a breach of a 'domestic' commitment is to be considered a breach of an international obligation, how should an international investment tribunal determine the substantive law that applies pursuant to the umbrella clause? That is, if an investor contends that the host State has breached a contractual commitment regarding its investment, what law determines whether the host State has breached the investment treaty: (a) is it the proper law of the contract (usually the law of the host State)? Or (b) does the umbrella clause render the proper law of the contract a secondary consideration to other legal principles?

§6.02 HISTORY OF THE DISTINCTION BETWEEN TREATY AND CONTRACT CLAIMS

The debate on whether a breach of a State contract automatically becomes a violation of international law has occupied the international arena for several decades. This section summarizes key aspects of this debate in order to identify the principles of international law relevant to the analysis of breach of contract versus breach of treaty. The section first considers draft conventions that have addressed the issue of breach of contract and state responsibility,[11] and then analyses several arbitral awards that have repeatedly been cited in this regard.

[A] Draft Conventions or Codifications

Jurists attempted to formulate a rule on breach of contract in the international arena. However, no consensus was reached on whether or in what circumstances a breach of contract would be relevant from an international perspective. What emerges from a review of draft conventions or codifications is that breaches of contract per se lack international standing (excluding the case when the contract is subject to international law or a treaty provision attributes international relevance to breach of contract).[12] The law applicable to the contract therefore still governs the contract.

[1] Garcìa Amador Reports on State Responsibility

The ILC's Garcìa Amador Reports on State Responsibility contain a provision on non-performance of contractual obligations (Article 10) that was distinct from 'public

---

11. Draft conventions on the taking of property, which include contractual rights in the definition of property, are discussed in Ch. 4.
12. Brownlie, *Principles of Public International Law, supra*, 629: '[i]n the proceedings arising from the Iranian cancellation of the 1933 Concession Agreement between the Iranian government and the Anglo-Iranian Oil Company, the UK contended that violation of an explicit undertaking in a concession by the government party not to annul was unlawful *per se*. This view almost certainly does not represent the law but it is not without merit'.

debt'. The last of these six Reports declare that the State was responsible for the non-performance of obligations in certain circumstances.[13]

Although Article 10 states that contractual non-performance triggers State responsibility, it contains two important exclusions: (i) public interest, and (ii) economic necessity of the State. Thus, a State could always justify its non-performance by invocation of the public interest. A State's non-payment of its contractual debts to invest further funds in medical research, to give one example, would be excluded under Article 10. Moreover, pursuant to this Draft Report, the possibility of a waiver to avoid the applicability of State responsibility would simply result in a standard waiver in any State contract.

[2] Harvard Draft Convention on International Responsibility of States for Injuries to Aliens (1961) ('The Harvard Draft')

The Harvard Draft sought to protect against, *inter alia*, breaches of contracts and concessions. Article 12 provides that the 'violation through an arbitrary action of the State of a contract or concession to which the central government of that State and an alien are parties is wrongful'.[14]

The central point of interest here is that despite the drafters' acknowledgment that neither international nor municipal law can exclusively govern breach of contracts or concessions, the solution they offer limits State responsibility to a denial of justice or to any breach characterized as 'arbitrary' or 'tortious'. The drafters conceded that 'arbitrary' or 'tortious' breach is vague and imprecise,[15] and there is still the need to establish a *quid pluris* to a simple breach of contract. This further element may be 'a clear and discriminatory departure from the proper law of the contract or concession as that law existed at the time of the alleged violation' (as indicated in Article 12, subparagraph 1(a)). However, the Harvard Draft accepts that a mere breach does not mean that international law would apply in lieu of the governing law.

[3] Foreign Relations Law of the United States (Restatement 3rd of Foreign Relations Law)

State practice in the United States regarding diplomatic protection and breach of State contracts has been that the United States would assist its citizens only in the case of an

---

13. *Article 10. – Non-performance of contractual obligations in general*, '1. The State is responsible for the non-performance of obligations stipulated in a contract entered into with an alien or in a concession granted to him, if the non-performance is not justified on grounds of public interest or of the economic necessity of the State, or if there is imputable to the State a "denial of justice" within the meaning of Art. 3 of this draft. 2. The foregoing provision shall not apply if the contract or concession contains a clause of the nature described in Art. 19, para. 2. 3. If the contract or concession is governed by international law, or by legal principles of an international character, the State is responsible by reason of the mere fact of the non-performance of the obligations stipulated in the said contract or concession': ILC *Yearbook*, 1961, vol. II, 47.
14. Harvard Draft Convention, 567. This article sets out a 'non-exhaustive' (*see* the commentary, 570) list of 'arbitrary' acts of State.
15. *Ibid.*

'arbitrary wrong, lack of good faith or abuse',[16] where the foreign government acted in a tortious manner in addition to having breached the contract. This approach was broadened in Section 712 of *Restatement 3rd of Foreign Relations Law* (adopted in 1986), to include breaches 'motivated by other non-commercial considerations'. Section 712 states in pertinent part:

> A State is responsible under international law for injury resulting from:
> (...)
> (2) a repudiation or breach by the State of a contract with a national of another State where the repudiation or breach is: (i) discriminatory; or (ii) motivated by non-commercial considerations and compensatory damages are not paid; or where the foreign national is not given an adequate forum to determine his claim of repudiation or breach or is not compensated for any breach determined to have occurred.

The commentary to Section 712 notes that a State 'is responsible under international law for ... breach only if it is discriminatory ... or it is akin to an expropriation in that the contract is repudiated or breached for governmental rather than commercial reasons and the State is not prepared to pay damages'.[17]

This US approach posits the relevance under international law of a State seeking to avoid its obligations towards an alien 'by altering the content of the governing law or by otherwise evading the terms of its commitments'.[18] However, the Restatement does not contain any justification for attributing relevance to breach of contracts for governmental ('non-commercial') rather than commercial reasons. It cites jurisprudence or customary international law rule to support this proposition.

In the field of State responsibility, the ILC has stated that the difference between *acta iure imperii* and *acta iure gestionis* is irrelevant for the purpose of attributing the act of a State organ.[19] As noted in Chapter 1, the ILC sought the views of governments on whether 'all conduct of an organ of a State is attributable to that State under Article 5 (attribution to the State of the conduct of its organs), irrespective of the *iure gestionis* or *iure imperii* nature of the conduct?'[20] The irrelevance of such a distinction was 'affirmed by all those members of the Sixth Committee who responded'.[21]

If the difference between *acta iure imperii* and *acta iure gestionis* is irrelevant for the purpose of attribution of the conduct of a State organ, this difference must also be irrelevant for the conduct of the State. To suggest otherwise would mean that State responsibility would vary according to the classification of the act performed, whether it is *iure imperii* or *iure gestionis*, while this difference would be irrelevant for State

---

16. Mann, 'State Contract and State Responsibility', 578; see on the general view that a breach of contract does not create state responsibility on the international plane, Brownlie, *Principles of Public International Law*, 627.
17. Schwebel, *Justice in International Law*, (Cambridge, 1994), 426 at 428–429.
18. *Ibid.*
19. *See* Crawford, *The International Law Commission's Articles on State Responsibility*, 96, and 'Treaty and Contract in Investment Arbitration', 357. *See also* Bishop, Crawford & Reisman, *Foreign Investment Disputes*, 581–582 and Ch. 7.
20. Report of the International Law Commission on the work of its fiftieth session, 20 Apr. 1988 to 12 Jun. 1988 and 27 Jul. 1988 to 14 Aug. 1998, A/53/10, 17, para. 35.
21. *See* Crawford, *The International Law Commission's Articles on State Responsibility*, 96.

organs. Moreover, the commentaries on the ILC's Articles on State Responsibility make it clear that a breach by a State of a contract 'does not as such entail a breach of international law';[22] an additional element is required to trigger a State's responsibility.

Article 12 of the ILC's Articles on State Responsibility further provides that '[t]here is a breach of an international obligation by a State when an act of that State is not in conformity with what is required of it by that obligation, regardless of its origin or character'.[23] The existence of a breach of an international obligation does not take into account how the breach is characterized, such as being for a governmental purpose or arising from any particular motive of the State.[24] There is no reason to depart from the governing law of the State contract in the event that a breach of contract is discriminatory or if the contract is repudiated or breached for governmental reasons.

[B] Awards and Judgments

The analysis of the awards and judgments below focuses on the issue of whether a mere breach of contract is a violation of international law. Tribunals and courts (outside of the modern investment treaty context) have consistently rejected this simple equation, unless a treaty provides for it.

[1] Affaire Martini[25]

Perhaps 'leading case'[26] on breach of contract and its relevance on the international plane, *Affaire Martini* concerned a concession between Venezuela and the Martini Company for the exploitation of a mine. In 1904–1905, Venezuela sued Martini; as a result of these proceedings the Venezuelan Court of Cassation annulled the concession and ordered Martini to pay damages. Martini claimed that the Court's decision was manifestly unjust and amounted to a denial of justice. A *compromis* between Italy and Venezuela was signed, the dispute was referred to arbitration, and the arbitral tribunal found that four out of the five grounds on which the Venezuelan Court's judgment was based were groundless and unjust. However, one ground, annulment of the concession pursuant to Martini's failure to pay rent, was deemed to be neither a denial of justice nor a flagrant injustice.

The majority of the arbitral tribunal held that Venezuelan law justified the Venezuelan Court's decision to annul the contract on the basis of non-payment of rent.

---

22. *Ibid.*
23. *Id.*, 125.
24. Crawford, 'Treaty and Contract in Investment Arbitration', 356: '[t]here are only two questions: what is the State obliged to do or refrain from doing, and has it complied with that obligation? Unless the primary rule which is the source of the obligation requires it, there is no third question, how to characterize the breach. Still less is there any requirement to prove any particular motive, whether financial or "governmental"'.
25. *Affaire Martini (Italy v. Venezuela)*, 3 May 1930, RIAA, vol. II, 975 (French), and in AJIL 25 (1931), 554 (English).
26. Amerasinghe, 'State Breaches of Contract with Aliens and International Law', 891.

The damages sought by Martini, on the other hand, were based on the absence of legal grounds for such annulment. The tribunal rejected Martini's request for relief on the grounds that the annulment for non-payment of the rent was not illegal.

In the *Affaire Martini*, the analysis of the breach of contract was carried out pursuant to municipal law; terminating the concession for non-payment of the rent did not constitute an international wrong, even though the Venezuelan Court's judgment had been 'unjust'. Two rulings from the same pre-World War II time frame as the *Affaire Martini*, by an arbitral body established under a US-Mexico treaty, shed further light on early approaches to the breach of contract / breach of treaty issue: *Illinois Central Railroad* and *International Fisheries Company*.

[2]   Illinois Central Railroad Company (USA) v. United Mexican States[27]

This case arose from the sale of locomotive engines to Mexico, and Mexico's non-payment of certain amounts for the engines. Mexico challenged the claim on the bases that: (a) non-performance of contractual obligation was outside the jurisdiction of the International Commission, the body established by the relevant US-Mexico treaty; and (b) there was no dispute between the parties, because Mexico did not deny the obligation to pay the outstanding amount for the sale of engines (a position that could be said to reiterate Mexico's primary argument that the Commission lacked jurisdiction).

The Commission rejected Mexico's jurisdictional challenge, holding that it could decide contractual claims because the relevant treaty granted it the power to decide 'all claims against one Government by nationals of the other for losses or damages suffered by such nationals or by their property'.[28] The Commission noted that there was no consistent international law approach to contract claims; based on the treaty provision that claims had to be decided in accordance with international law principles, the Commission inferred that cases in which there was an international law *renvoi* to municipal law were still claims under the treaty.[29] The treaty's wording was broad enough to include contractual claims arising out of State contracts.

In this particular case, there was no contractual jurisdictional clause that would have led to a different conclusion. In an earlier arbitration, the *Woodruff* case,[30] it was held that, given the existence of a jurisdictional clause in the disputed contract, all

---

27. *Illinois Central Railroad Company (USA) v. United Mexican States*, 31 Mar. 1926, RIAA, vol. IV, 21. The subsequent decision, *Illinois Central Railroad Company (USA) v. United Mexican States*, 6 Dec. 1926, RIAA, vol. IV, 134, is irrelevant for present purposes since it concerns the payment of interest.
28. *Id.*, 22.
29. *Id.*, 23–24: '[c]laims as between a citizen of one country and the government of another country acting in its civil capacity. These claims too are international in their character, and they too must be decided in accordance with the principles of international law, even in cases where international law should merely declare the municipal law of one of the countries involved to be applicable'.
30. *Woodruff* case, 1903–1903, RIAA, vol. IX, 213.

disputes arising out of the contract had to be referred to the Court identified in the jurisdictional clause. This clause would not, however, encompass all claims under international law, such as denial of justice or undue delay in the administration of justice.

The *Illinois Central Railroad* Commission's holding that it had jurisdiction over the contract claims did not imply that a breach of contract is necessarily relevant on the international plane. As will be seen in the discussion below of *Vivendi*, an international investment tribunal can have jurisdiction over an investment, which may include the right arising out of a contract, but this does not mean that any breach of such contract should be considered a violation of the relevant treaty from a substantive perspective. The investor must still prove a violation of the treaty to obtain relief.

[3] International Fisheries Company (USA) v. United Mexican States[31]

International Fisheries was a shareholder of a Mexican company and claimed damages for the termination of a concession. The concession contained a Calvo clause, whereby the Mexican company was obliged to submit all disputes to the Mexican courts and waive diplomatic protection. Mexico challenged the Commission's jurisdiction on the basis of the Calvo clause. The Commission majority agreed with Mexico, and held that this clause was effective vis-à-vis International Fisheries; therefore the Commission lacked jurisdiction. In particular, the Commission ruled that Mexico's termination of the concession did not entail any act of 'international delinquency'[32] or an arbitrary act 'which in itself might be considered as a violation of some rule or principle of international law'.[33] Again, then, the potential relevance of a mere breach of contract on the international plane was rejected.

[4] The PCIJ and the ICJ

Two cases often cited in the debate on the international relevance of breach of contract are *Losinger & Co.* case and the *Ambatielos* case, the former a PCIJ proceeding and the latter an ICJ decision.[34]

Losinger & Co. concerned a concession, which contained an arbitration clause, between a Swiss company and the Government of Yugoslavia. Losinger, also a Swiss company, became party to a certain part of the concession. Subsequently, a dispute arose, Losinger initiated arbitration proceedings, and in 1934 an award was rendered. In the meantime, the Yugoslav government terminated the concession and, also in 1934, enacted a law providing that any proceedings against the State had to be brought before a judicial court. Losinger then commenced another arbitration, in which

---

31. *International Fisheries Company (USA) v. United Mexican States*, July 1931, RIAA, vol. 4, 691.
32. *Id.*, 701.
33. *Id.*, 699.
34. *Losinger & Co.* case, Order of 27 Jun. 1936, PCIJ, Series A/B, 27, 15; and *Ambatielos* case, Preliminary Objections, 1 Jul. 1952, ICJ *Reports* (1952), 28, and Judgment (Merits), 19 May 1953, ICJ *Reports* (1953), 10.

Yugoslavia pleaded lack of jurisdiction pursuant to this 1934 law and invited Losinger to file its suit before a Yugoslav Court. The sole arbitrator ruled that he was not permitted to rule on a plea as to the validity of the arbitration clause, and suspended the arbitral proceedings 'until the law had been ascertained'.[35] Switzerland sought a declaration in the PCIJ that Yugoslavia could not be released from the terms of the arbitration clause by enacting such subsequent legislation.

The PCIJ never ruled on the merits of this case or on jurisdiction; it joined the jurisdictional objections Yugoslavia raised to the merits stage, and the proceedings were discontinued when the parties reached a settlement. However, both Switzerland and Yugoslavia had set out their jurisdictional positions, with Yugoslavia insisting on an alleged 'exhaustion of remedies' requirement under Yugoslavian law, and Switzerland arguing that the exhaustion objection was not available where a State had breached a contractual obligation and thereby prevented the counter-party from going before a competent tribunal. The Yugoslav government, however, observed that an arbitration agreement is like any other contract, and the applicable law of this agreement was Yugoslav law, under which the parties had to be referred to the Yugoslav courts.

Seventeen years later, in *Ambatielos*, the ICJ did rule on Greece's contention, similar to that of Switzerland in *Losinger & Co.*, that an arbitration agreement in a treaty had to be enforced in preference to municipal court jurisdiction. Greece commenced proceedings against the United Kingdom before the ICJ, claiming that one of its nationals suffered a substantial loss from a contract entered into with the United Kingdom as a result of certain UK Court decisions, as well as denial of justice in the course of the UK proceedings. Greece claimed that the arbitration procedure provided by the Treaties of 1886 and 1926 between Greece and the United Kingdom had to be implemented, and sought a declaration on whether the dispute should be referred to the ICJ or to another tribunal of competent jurisdiction.

The ICJ found that: (a) it had jurisdiction to determine whether the UK was obliged to submit to arbitration, insofar as the Ambatielos claim was based on the Treaty of 1886; but (b) it did not have jurisdiction to decide the underlying contractual claim, because while the ICJ had jurisdiction to interpret the Treaty, any dispute as to the claim's validity had to be referred to arbitration.[36] In its subsequent judgment on the 'merits', the ICJ held that the dispute should be submitted to arbitration.[37] The ICJ reiterated that it had to refrain from pronouncing judgment on the underlying contractual claim, since the scope of its jurisdiction was to determine whether the Treaty of 1886 bound the United Kingdom to refer the dispute to arbitration.[38] The ICJ thus carefully limited its jurisdiction to the determination of the State's obligation to submit to arbitration, and did not address any issue of fact or law that would have been

---

35. *Losinger & Co.* case, 21.
36. *Ambatielos* (Preliminary Objection), 44.
37. *Ambatielos* (Merits), 23.
38. *Id.*, 16.

under the jurisdiction of the Commission of Arbitration pursuant to the Treaty of 1886.[39]

It would be incorrect to conclude from the *Ambatielos* case that the PCIJ would have ruled against Yugoslavia. If the PCIJ had agreed that Yugoslav law governed the arbitration agreement, the issue would have been whether Yugoslavia was right to insist that its courts first had to determine whether the State's interpretation of the agreement was correct, and, concomitantly, whether an exhaustion requirement should be upheld. Thus, the question of breach of the arbitration agreement in the treaty would have been a matter of municipal law, which the PCIJ might well have determined was a matter for the municipal courts, not an international tribunal, to decide.

A possible determination in favour of the municipal courts in *Losinger & Co.* is suggested by the ICJ's judgment in the *Norwegian Loans* case.[40] Similar to its ruling in *Ambatielos*, the ICJ did not address the issue of breach of contract. France claimed that Norway could not issue several bonds containing a gold clause and later promulgate a law abrogating that clause. France argued that Norway was internationally responsible for breach of contract. Norway responded that the dispute's subject matter was 'within the domain of municipal law and not international law, whereas the compulsory jurisdiction of the Court in relation to the Parties involved is restricted, by their Declarations of ..., to disputes concerning international law'.[41] The ICJ held that it did not have jurisdiction to hear the claim. Specifically, the ICJ endorsed Norway's argument that the condition of reciprocity entitled it to invoke the reservation relating to national jurisdiction contained in the French Declaration: '[t]his Declaration does not apply to differences relating to matters which are essentially within the national jurisdiction as understood by the Government of the French Republic'.[42]

The ICJ did not address the issue of whether the contracts were governed by municipal law or international law. However, Judge Lauterpacht stated in his separate opinion that even if these contracts were governed by a municipal law, they were not outside the realm of international law.[43] He posited the question of a State's treatment of property rights owned by aliens, and stated that to this extent municipal law could not be the exclusive source of obligations. Lauterpacht emphasized that municipal law's applicability would not exclude the application of international law if there were an internationally wrongful act. However, he did not advocate the theory that a mere breach of contract would automatically have relevance on the international plane.

These ICJ and PCIJ cases also do not support an attempt to equate breaches of a State contract with breaches of an international obligation.

---

39. *Ambatielos* (Preliminary Objections), 44.
40. *See* Mann, *State Contract and State Responsibility*, 578.
41. *Case of Norwegian Loans*, Judgment, 6 Jul. 1957, ICJ *Reports* (1957), 9, at 13.
42. *Id.*, 21.
43. *Id.*, 37.

[C] Principles to Be Drawn from Draft Conventions/Codifications and Awards/Judgments

The above review indicates that breach of a State contract is not per se a breach of international law.[44] For a breach of contract to be relevant on the international plane, it must be accompanied by an internationally wrongful act. Thus, a departure from the contract's governing law should not be permitted if there is no internationally wrongful act in addition to the breach of contract.

Mann proposed the following framework[45] for deciding when a breach of contract is relevant under international law: (i) the contract must be governed by the law of the State that is party to the contract and has committed the wrong; (ii) the breach of contract must be 'so grave and so specific a breach as to constitute an international wrong';[46] and (iii) the issue before the tribunal must be contractual rather than proprietary. However, his view does not take into account the circumstance that, if the contract is governed by a law different from the law of the State committing the international wrong, the contract would not be insulated from any international wrong. Moreover, whether the disputed issue is contractual or proprietary seems to be irrelevant if, in addition to the breach of contract, it is necessary to determine the existence of an international wrong.[47]

Jennings has instead argued that international law may attribute relevance to breaches of contract based mainly on the doctrines of acquired rights and *pacta sunt servanda*.[48] He also emphasized that, in the context of nationality, rights are created under a municipal law but should be assessed pursuant to international law standards. His conclusions are: (i) the structure of international law, and the relationship between international law and municipal law, does not prevent a choice of international law as the law governing the contract;[49] (ii) municipal law must conform to international law, which means that international law is relevant even if the contract is subject to a municipal law; (iii) a termination of a contract by a change in the governing law may violate international law even if does not violate the relevant municipal law; (iv) international law cannot be considered irrelevant because by subjecting the contract to municipal law, there is an expectation that such law can be changed; (v) the determination of whether the State is entitled to change the law must be resolved in accordance with international law; and (vi) the 'delictual form of action will be necessary', but *de lege ferenda* the law may develop and confer relevance to contractual breaches.

---

44. Amerasinghe, 'State Breaches of Contract with Aliens and International Law', 897.
45. Mann, 'The Consequences of an International Wrong in International and National Law', 188–191.
46. *Id.*, 189.
47. The Commentary on ILC Art. 12 on State Responsibility, in Crawford, *The International Law Commission's Articles on State Responsibility*, 127, para. (5) states that: '[a]s far as the origin of the obligation breached is concerned there is a single general regime of State responsibility'.
48. Jennings, 'State Contracts in International Law', BYIL 37 (1961), 156, at 173–179; Hyde, 'Economic Development Agreements', *Recueil des cours* 105 (1962), I, 271 at 315–318.
49. Jennings, 'State Contracts in International Law', BYIL 37 (1961), 156, at 181.

The Jennings approach may be superficially attractive to practitioners with a strongly internationalist bent. However, as a matter of international law, the approach has no substance; it does not demonstrate or establish that contractual breaches are (or should be) per se relevant under international law. Indeed, it would be difficult for the Jennings approach to do so, given that more than one hundred years of authority has reached the opposite conclusion. In short, by seeking to render municipal law irrelevant, the Jennings approach imagines an international law construct that does not exist.

Another school of thought, significantly less extreme than the Jennings approach, regards the breach of a State contract by the State as an act entailing State responsibility. Switzerland's submissions before the PCIJ in the *Losinger Case*,[50] and Greece's submissions in the *Ambatielos*[51] case, discussed above, have been cited as prominent expressions of this school. A number of scholars, however, have dismissed this approach on the ground that there is 'little evidence that the 'internationalized contract' idea corresponds to the existing law'.[52] In fact, if one considers the jurisprudential positions of leading capital-exporting States (e.g., the United States and the United Kingdom), it is apparent that a breach of contract requires additional elements to create international responsibility.[53]

Moreover, the ICJ in *Ambatielos* did not hold that breach of State contracts would automatically constitute a breach of international law (and there is no basis for an assessment that the PCIJ in *Losinger & Co.* would have reached such a conclusion has it decided the case). In *Ambatielos*, the ICJ held that it had to refrain from considering the underlying contractual claim since the scope of its jurisdiction was limited to determining whether a treaty bound the United Kingdom to submit to the dispute to arbitration.[54] In another case concerning a concession contract, *Anglo-Iranian Oil Co.*, the ICJ emphasized that a State contract did *not* constitute a treaty.[55]

As for other decisions that have been cited in support of the position that a breach of a State contract not governed by international law nonetheless amounts to a breach of international law, it has rightly been observed that they are not on point, 'either because the tribunal was not applying international law or because the decision rested on some element apart from the breach of contract'.[56] There also is no evidence that principles of acquired rights or *pacta sunt servanda* have the consequences claimed by the practitioners who propound the 'breach of State contact equal breach of international obligation' approach.[57]

Some scholars, in particular Schwebel, have purportedly taken a 'middle' position between the prevalent schools of thought. This 'middle' position asserts that:

---

50. *See* Schwebel, *Justice in International Law, supra*, 427.
51. *Ibid.*
52. Brownlie, *Principles of Public International Law*, 628.
53. *Id.*, 627–629 and Mann, 'State Contract and State Responsibility', 578–579.
54. *Ambatielos* case (Merits), 16.
55. The *Anglo-Iranian Oil Co* case, Judgment 22 Jul. 1952, ICJ *Reports* (1952), 93.
56. Brownlie, *Principles of Public International Law*, 628.
57. *Ibid.*

while a mere breach by a State of a contract with an alien (whose proper law is not international law) is not a violation of international law, a 'non-commercial' act of a State contrary to such contract may be. That is to say, the breach of such a contract by a State in ordinary commercial intercourse is not, in the predominant view, a violation of international law, but the use of sovereign authority of a State, contrary to the expectations of the parties, to abrogate or violate a contract with an alien, is a violation of international law.[58]

The American Law Institute endorses this 'middle' position. As noted above, Section 712 of the *Restatement 3rd of Foreign Relations Law* opines that a 'State is responsible under international law for injury resulting from ... a repudiation or breach by the State of a contract with a national of another State where the repudiation or breach is: (i) discriminatory; or (ii) motivated by other non-commercial considerations and compensatory damages are not paid'.

However, the 'middle' position fails to come to terms with the irrelevance of the difference between *acta iure imperii and acta iure gestionis* in the context of State responsibility and attribution of the conduct of a State organ. Moreover, the middle position gives relevance to motives, since 'even if the underlying relationship and the breach are clearly commercial, the motives of a government for a certain act may still be governmental'.[59] There is the additional problem that the search for a government's motives would render State responsibility even more unpredictable, and would give arbitral tribunals a wide margin of discretion (not subject to appeal), in assessing whether there was in fact a plausible governmental reason for the action taken. The significance of such motives should instead be expressed in a treaty, and cannot plausibly be inferred from the general principles of international law. An international breach of contract should not depend upon the state of mind of a government. Accordingly, the American Law Institute's (and Schwebel's) 'middle' position should not be regarded as a correct interpretation of international law.

Placing the breach of a State contract in the context of the principle of State responsibility provides a sounder analysis of the relationship between international and municipal law in international investment claims. The analytical starting point is an examination of the elements of an internationally wrongful act of a State, as set out in Article 2 of the ILC's Articles on State Responsibility:[60] (i) whether the alleged wrongful act is attributable to the State under international law; and (ii) whether the alleged wrongful act constitutes a breach of an international obligation of the State. These two main questions must be addressed in order to determine whether there is an investment treaty breach. International law regulates both questions. However, as discussed below, municipal law may be relevant to the formulation of the applicable international law standard if the subject matter of the standard is a contract governed by municipal law. There is no basis for the position that a breach of contract by a State actor – without something more – points to international State responsibility.[61]

---

58. *See* Schwebel, *Justice in International Law, supra* 431–432.
59. Dolzer & Schreuer, *Principles of International Investment Law*, 154.
60. Crawford, *The International Law Commission's Articles on State Responsibility*, 81.
61. Brownlie, *Principles of Public International Law*, 627.

The threshold issue for an investment treaty arbitral tribunal should be whether the Claimant-investor alleges a breach of a provision of the treaty, unless the investment treaty itself provides that the State parties have consented to refer contractual claims to arbitration.[62] Apart from whether any such consent is given, the treaty terms themselves constitute a fundamental part of the law applicable to the dispute. Although in certain circumstances a claim could comprise a breach of contract and a breach of treaty, a breach of the investment treaty must be alleged and shown.[63]

Several arbitral tribunals have had to address the question of the boundary between treaty and contract when an investor has claimed that the breach of the contract between the State and the investor was a breach of international law. The asserted overlaps between the treaty and contractual claims and the interplay between international law and municipal law in this context have raised difficult questions, which are considered below.

§6.03 DISTINCTION BETWEEN TREATY AND CONTRACT CLAIMS IN INTERNATIONAL INVESTMENT DISPUTES

The distinction between treaty and contract claims in investment treaty cases was addressed at length in the *Vivendi* annulment proceedings. However, the interpretation of *Vivendi* by subsequent arbitral tribunals has fostered an uncertain legacy: some tribunals have blurred the distinction between treaty and contractual claims (*Noble Ventures v. Romania*) and/or attributed relevance to the difference between contractual and governmental acts of State in seeking to distinguish contractual and treaty claims (e.g., *Eureko v. Poland, Biwater Gauff (Tanzania) v. Tanzania,* and *Tulip Real Estate and Development Netherlands B.V. v. Turkey*), while others have maintained a rigid distinction (*Waste Management Inc v. Mexico*). A brief review of these varying decisions and awards will help explicate whether and how a breach of contract is relevant in the international investment arena.[64]

---

62. Article 25 of the ICSID Convention provides that the jurisdiction of a tribunal constituted under the auspices of ICSID extends 'to any legal dispute arising out of an investment, between a Contracting States (...) and a national of another Contracting State, which the parties to the dispute consent in writing to submit to the Centre'. The unambiguous wording 'any legal dispute' indicates that the parties can consent to submit treaty and contractual disputes to ICSID.
63. *See also* the discussion below with regard to umbrella clauses.
64. Dolzer & Schreuer, *Principles of International Investment Law*, 140–142; Crawford, 'Treaty and Contract in Investment Arbitration', 351; McLachlan, Shore & Weiniger, *International Investment Arbitration: Substantive Principles*, 117–120; Alexandrov, 'Breaches of Contract and Breaches of Treaty – The Jurisdiction of Treaty-Based Arbitration Tribunals to Decide Breach of Contract Claims in *SGS v. Pakistan* and *SGS v. Philippines*', TDM 3 (2006), 555; Schreuer, 'Investment Treaty Arbitration and Jurisdiction over Contract Claims – The *Vivendi I* case Considered', and Gaillard, 'Investment Treaty Arbitration and Jurisdiction over Contract Claims – the *SGS Cases* Considered', in *International Investment Law and Arbitration: Leading Cases from the ICSID, NAFTA, Bilateral Treaties and Customary International* Law, respectively 281 and 325; Siwy, 'Contract Claims and Treaty Claims' in *ICSID Convention after 50 Years, Unsettled Issues* (Kluwer, 2017), 209–225.

[A] *Aguas del Aconquija – Vivendi* and the Separation Between Treaty and Contact Claims

As discussed previously, the underlying dispute in the *Aguas del Aconquija – Vivendi* ('*Vivendi*') annulment proceedings arose out of the termination of a concession contract between Vivendi and the Argentinean province of Tucumán. Vivendi claimed a breach of the BIT between France and Argentina. The tribunal rejected Argentina's jurisdictional objections, but also rejected Vivendi's claims concerning the acts of the Province of Tucumán on the ground that it was impossible to separate 'potential breaches of contract claims from BIT violations without interpreting and applying the Concession contract, a task that the contract assigned expressly to the local courts'.[65]

The *Ad Hoc* Annulment Committee ruled that the tribunal had correctly concluded that it had jurisdiction over the claims. The BIT conferred jurisdiction in relation to any dispute concerning investments: '[r]ead literally, the requirements for arbitral jurisdiction in Article 8 do not necessitate that the Claimant allege a breach of the BIT itself: it is sufficient that the dispute relate to an investment made under the BIT'.[66] However, the Annulment Committee annulled the tribunal's decision to decline to decide the merits of the claims concerning the Province's actions under the BIT.

The Annulment Committee explained that:

(i) a particular dispute may at the same time involve issues of interpretation of contract and issues relating to the relevant BIT;[67]
(ii) the fact that the Concession contract referred some disputes to the administrative courts did not impinge on the jurisdiction of the arbitral tribunal in connection with a claim based on the BIT;[68]
(iii) a State could breach a treaty without breaching a contract and could breach a contract without breaching a treaty;[69] In particular:

Articles 3 and 5 of the BIT do not relate directly to breach of a municipal contract. Rather they set an independent standard. A State may breach a treaty without breaching a contract and vice versa, and this is certainly true of these provisions of the BIT. The point is made clear in Article 3 of the ILC Articles, which is entitled 'Characterisation of an act of a State as internationally wrongful';[70]

(iv) therefore each type of claim – breach of contract and breach of treaty – would be 'determined by reference to its own proper or applicable law – in the case of the BIT, by international law; in the case of the Concession Contract, by the proper law of the contract, in other words, the law of Tucumán';[71] and

---

65. *Vivendi*, Decision on Annulment, para. 41.
66. *Id.*, para. 55.
67. *Id.*, para. 60.
68. *Id.*, para. 76.
69. *Id.*, para. 95.
70. *Ibid.*
71. *Id.*, para. 96.

(v) In cases where there is a contractual claim, 'the tribunal will give effect to any valid choice of forum clause in the contract'.[72] On the other hand, a jurisdiction clause does not limit claims concerning the violation of international law.[73]

The *Vivendi* Annulment Committee emphasized the distinction between the roles of international and municipal law, and quoted the ICJ's judgment in *ELSI*:

> Compliance with municipal law and compliance with the provisions of a treaty are different questions. What is a breach of treaty may be lawful in the municipal law and what is unlawful in the municipal law may be wholly innocent of violation of a treaty provision.[74]

Thus, where a claim's foundation is a treaty containing an independent standard for assessing the parties' conduct, an exclusive jurisdiction clause in a contract 'cannot operate as a bar to the application of the treaty standard'.[75] Although the arbitral tribunal correctly declined to exercise contractual jurisdiction because breaches of the contract did not amount to violations of the BIT, the tribunal could still 'take into account the terms of a contract in determining whether there has been a breach of a distinct standard of international law'.[76] The *Ad Hoc* Committee explained that a tribunal having jurisdiction under a BIT is required to undertake an inquiry 'governed by the ICSID Convention, by the BIT and by applicable international law. Such an inquiry is neither in principle determined, nor precluded, by any issue of municipal law including municipal law agreement of the parties'.[77] However, municipal law would be relevant to determining whether there had been a breach of the treaty when, for example, the rule of international law makes municipal law relevant by 'incorporating the standard of compliance' with municipal law 'as the applicable international standard or as an aspect of it'.[78] In concluding that a treaty cause of action differs from a contractual cause of action because 'it requires a clear showing of conduct which is in the circumstances contrary to the relevant treaty standard',[79] the Annulment Committee by no means dismissed municipal law's potential relevance to the determination of the applicable treaty standard.

The significance of *Vivendi* is that the Annulment Committee shifted the relevant analysis from a mechanical characterization of the investor's claims ('contract versus treaty') to the legal standards applicable to claims brought under an investment treaty. It explained that an investment treaty case turns on whether the alleged breach constitutes a treaty violation under international law – which would *not* necessarily

---

72. *Id.*, para. 98. The Committee cited a decision of the American-Venezuelan Mixed Commission of 1903, the *Woodruff* case, cited above in this Chapter.
73. *Id.*, para. 99.
74. *ELSI*, para. 73.
75. *Vivendi*, para. 101.
76. *Id.*, para. 105.
77. *Id.*, para. 102.
78. *Id.*, para. 97 (quoting paras 4 and 7 of the Commentaries to Art. 3 of Crawford, *The International Law Commission's Articles on State Responsibility*, 88–89).
79. *Id.*, para. 113.

ignore municipal law – and not on whether the conduct portrayed in the claims weighed more in 'treaty' than in 'contract'.

From a substantive law perspective, a contract claim entails applying the law governing the contract, usually a municipal law. From a procedural perspective, if there is a jurisdiction clause, it must be given effect and the dispute must be referred to the tribunal identified in that clause. If the contract is governed by international law, or the investment treaty is applicable to State contracts and the contract contains a jurisdiction clause, then this clause may be applicable on the grounds of *generalia specialibus non derogant* or on the grounds that the parties' clear intention is to exclude the jurisdiction provided by the investment treaty.[80]

The Annulment Committee's decision is clearly expressed and well founded. The next question is the extent to which subsequent arbitral tribunals have followed the Annulment Committee's approach, with particular regard to how these tribunals have dealt with, or should have dealt with, the relationship between international and municipal law.

[B] *Noble Ventures v. Romania* and the Violation of the FET Standard

Some arbitral tribunals have blurred the distinction between treaty and contractual claims to the point where a breach of contract claim is assessed under a treaty standard that completely disregards the law applicable to the contract. The *Noble Ventures* case arose out of a privatization agreement between the Romanian State Ownership Fund (SOF) and Noble Ventures, a US company. Noble Ventures claimed, *inter alia*, that Romania violated the standard of fair and equitable treatment, adopted arbitrary and discriminatory measures, and failed to provide full protection and security.

After stating that it is difficult to define the standard of fair and equitable treatment and the obligation not to adopt arbitrary or discriminatory measures, the arbitral tribunal held that:

> one can consider this to be a more general standard which finds its specific application in inter alia the duty to provide full protection and security, the prohibition of arbitrary and discriminatory measures and the obligation to observe contractual obligations towards the investor.[81]

The tribunal concluded that Romania had not breached this standard. However, the assertion that the standard of fair and equitable treatment is violated by a breach of contractual obligations renders any breach of contract relevant in the international investment arena. This award has been cited to support the theory that '[c]ontractual agreements are the classical instrument in most, if not all, legal systems for the creation of legal stability and predictability. Therefore, *pacta sunt servanda* would seem to be an obvious application of the stability requirement that is so prominent in the FET

---

80. *Vivendi*, para. 76.
81. *Noble Ventures v. Romania*, *supra*, para. 182.

standard'.[82] Unfortunately, this theory transforms any breach of contract into a breach of an investment treaty, and disregards the application of the governing law to the contract even when the treaty does not expressly equate breach of contract and breach of treaty.

The *Parkerings v. Lithuania* tribunal, on the other hand, correctly stated that 'not every hope amounts to an expectation under international law. The expectation a party to an agreement may have of the regular fulfilment of the obligation by the other party is not necessarily an expectation protected by international law'.[83] In other words, contracts entail expectations from each party that are not necessarily transformed into obligations relevant under international law. Along the same lines, *WNC Factoring LTD v. Czech Republic*[84] explained that the 'scope of the obligation to observe an undertaking is separate and distinct from other obligations under international law'.[85] Thus, even if an entity might have 'legitimate expectations in relation to an undertaking, that does not convert it into the beneficiary of the undertaking'.[86]

In short, a breach of contract cannot be automatically equated to a violation of the fair and equitable treatment standard, unless the treaty expressly includes breach of contract as a basis for such a violation. A number of scholars and arbitrators are unhappy with the general principle of international law that mere contract breaches are not relevant on the international plane unless they are accompanied by an internationally wrongful act, but they have no sound basis for failing to apply it.

[C] The Relevance of Contractual versus Governmental Acts

Other tribunals have attributed relevance to the difference between contractual and governmental acts of States in seeking to distinguish contractual and treaty claims. But this approach also lacks a sound legal foundation. *Eureko v. Poland* turned a breach of contract into a breach of treaty, contrary to the prevailing view in international law. The *Eureko* majority attempted to support this holding on the ground that the State's conduct was based on 'arbitrary reasons linked to the interplay of Polish politics and nationalistic reasons of a discriminatory character',[87] and such conduct – i.e., its apparent *motive* or *purpose* for breaching the contract – violated the fair and equitable treatment standard. However, the *Eureko* majority did not supply any reasons that

---

82. Dolzer & Schreuer, *Principles of International Investment Law*, 152. The two authors did recognize, however, that '[p]ractice demonstrates that the view that a simple breach of contract is insufficient to amount to a breach of the FET standard is clearly prevalent' (154).
83. *Parkerings v. Lithuania*, Award, 11 Sep. 2007, para. 344, available on Investment Treaty Arbitration website: http://www.italaw.com/sites/default/files/case-documents/ita0619.pdf. See also Crawford, 'Treaty and Contract in Investment Arbitration', *supra*, 374: 'the doctrine of legitimate expectation should not be used as a substitute for the actual arrangement agreed between the parties, or a supervening or overriding source of applicable law'.
84. *WNC Factoring LTD v. Czech Republic*, Award, 22 Feb. 2017, available on Investment Treaty Arbitration website: http://www.italaw.com/sites/default/files/case-documents/italaw8533.pdf.
85. *Id.*, para. 324.
86. *Ibid.*
87. *Eureko*, para. 233.

would support the conclusion that the investor was treated 'in such an unjust or arbitrary manner that the treatment rises to the level that is unacceptable from the international perspective'.[88] The *Eureko* award clearly attributes relevance under international law to a breach of contract together with the finding that Poland committed the breach for *governmental* reasons. However, the purpose behind a State's breach of contract is irrelevant under international law, and, accordingly, whether the State breached for governmental as opposed to commercial reasons is irrelevant.

The same flawed conclusion regarding the relevance of '*puissance publique*' is present in several other cases. The *Biwater Gauff (Tanzania) v. Tanzania*[89] tribunal, having stated that a breach of contract does not per se constitute a breach of international law for the purpose of expropriation,[90] nonetheless held that 'the critical distinction is between situations in which a State acts merely as a contractual partner and cases in which it acts *iure imperii*, exercising elements of its governmental authority'.[91] The tribunal majority characterized Tanzania's action as a contractual matter since it was carried out pursuant to a lease contract; on this basis, the majority ruled that there was no expropriation. But as the Dissenting Opinion correctly observed, this type of assessment, by focusing on governmental versus commercial actions, led the tribunal majority to consider Tanzania's *taking* of a performance bond – a hallmark of expropriatory action – to be a contractual matter, and not an expropriation.

In *Tulip Real Estate and Development Netherlands B.V. v. Turkey*,[92] the tribunal majority accepted that it did not have jurisdiction over purely contractual disputes,[93] and then proceeded to ascertain whether the contractual obligations relevant to the dispute would be construed as treaty obligation by virtue of the umbrella clause in the BIT.[94] The majority reached the conclusion that '[i]n order to amount to a treaty claim, the conduct said to amount to a BIT violation must be capable of characterisation as sovereign conduct, involving the invocation of *puissance publique*'.[95] The majority considered the issue intertwined with the issue of attribution, and, since it held that the

---

88. *S.D. Myers Inc. v. Canada*, Partial Award, 13 Nov. 2000, para. 263: www.dfait-maeci.gc.ca/tna-nac/documents/myersvcanadapartialaward_final_13-11-00.pdf
89. *Biwater Gauff (Tanzania) Ltd v. Tanzania*, Award, 24 Jul. 2008, available on Investment Treaty Arbitration website: http://ita.law.uvic.ca/documents/Biwateraward.pdf
90. *Id*, para. 457.
91. *Id.*, para. 458.
92. *Tulip Real Estate and Development Netherlands B.V. v. Turkey*, Award, 10 Mar. 2014, available on Investment Treaty Arbitration website: http://www.italaw.com/sites/default/files/case-documents/italaw3126.pdf The Decision on Annulment, 30 Dec. 2015, dismissed Tulip's application for annulment in its entirety (available on Investment Treaty Arbitration website: http://www.italaw.com/sites/default/files/case-documents/italaw7037.pdf).
93. *Id.*, para. 348.
94. *Id.*, para. 352.
95. *Id.*, para. 352. *See* i) *Impregilo S.p.A. v. Islamic Republic of Pakistan*, Decision on Jurisdiction (22 Apr. 2005), para. 260: 'Only the State in the exercise of its sovereign authority ("*puissance publique*"), and not as a contracting party, may breach the obligations assumed under the BIT. In other words, the investment protection treaty only provides a remedy to the investor where the investor proves that the alleged damages were a consequence of the behaviour of the Host State acting in breach of the obligations it had assumed under the treaty': available on

conduct of the para-statal entity party to the contract was not attributable to the State, the majority concluded that there was no evidence of sovereign interference in the contractual relationship. That is, since the para-statal entity acted as a commercial party in pursuit of its commercial interests, this conduct could not be characterized as treaty claim.[96] Again, the approach taken is that a breach of contract is a breach of international law if the State's motive for breaching may be characterized as 'governmental'.

This approach echoes Section 712 of the *Restatement 3rd of Foreign Relations Law of the United States*: a State is responsible under international law for breaches 'motivated by other non-commercial considerations'. Stated differently, these scholars and arbitrators consider that a contract breached for 'governmental' rather than commercial reasons may trigger international law responsibility. However, as discussed above, the characterization of the State's motives for such violation are irrelevant under international law. What is relevant is whether the standard set out by the investment treaty has been violated, *Vivendi* clearly explained. The search for State motives is, in this respect, a diversion from sound international law analysis and should not be undertaken.

[D] *Waste Management Inc v. Mexico*

Other arbitral tribunals have insisted on maintaining the distinction between treaty and contract claims. *Waste Management Inc. II v. Mexico* is a case in point.

As previously described, this dispute arose in connection with a concession for providing waste disposal services in Acapulco. The tribunal was constituted under NAFTA Chapter 11, which, as the tribunal observed, does not give jurisdiction over the breach of an investment contract. Therefore, the tribunal affirmed that 'showing a breach of contract is not enough'.[97]

The tribunal determined that persistent non-payment of debts assumed by a State in breach of a contract cannot be equated with a violation of an investment treaty provision, including expropriation, if it does 'not amount to an outright and unjustified repudiation of the transaction and provided that some remedy is open to the creditor to address the problem'.[98] The tribunal examined Waste Management's claim that its contractual rights were an asset that was expropriated and whether Mexico's conduct 'had an effect equivalent to the taking of the enterprise in whole or substantial part'.[99] The tribunal concluded that 'an enterprise is not expropriated just because its debts are

---

Investment Treaty Arbitration website http://www.italaw.com/sites/default/files/case-documents/ita0422.pdf ; and ii) *Bayindir İnşaat Turizm Ticaret ve Sanayi A.Ş v. Islamic Republic of Pakistan*, Award, dated 27 Aug. 2009, para. 180 ('because a treaty breach is different from a contract violation, the Tribunal considers that the Claimant must establish a breach different in nature from a simple contract violation, in other words one which the State commits in the exercise of its sovereign power') available on Investment Treaty Arbitration website: http://www.italaw.com/sites/default/files/case-documents/ita0075.pdf

96. *Tulip Real Estate and Development Netherlands B.V. v. Turkey*, paras 357–361.
97. *Waste Management Inc v. United Mexican States*, para. 73.
98. *Id.*, para. 115.
99. *Id.*, para. 155.

not paid or other contractual obligations towards it are breached. (...) It is not the function of Article 1110 to compensate for failed business venture, absent arbitrary intervention by the State amounting to a virtual taking or sterilizing of the enterprise'.[100] The *Waste Management* tribunal further emphasized that '*some* distinction must be made: if certain cases of contractual non-performance may amount to expropriation, it must be possible to say, in principle, which ones, otherwise the distinction between contractual and treaty claims disappears'.[101] Waste Management 'did not lose its contractual rights, which it was free to pursue before the contractually chosen forum'.[102]

The *Waste Management* tribunal thus kept the contractual and treaty claims separate, and applied different standards to determine whether there had been a violation of international law. Further, this award emphasized that a contract claim had to be assessed in the parties' selected contractual forum and not before the international tribunal constituted to determine whether there was a breach of the investment treaty. Whatever questions that scholars may otherwise raise about the *Waste Management* award, the tribunal members persuasively analysed this contract/treaty issue.

§6.04 THE HISTORICAL BACKGROUND OF UMBRELLA CLAUSES

Brownlie characterized umbrella clauses as a 'shortcut to enforce contractual obligations'.[103] Breach of treaty and breach of contract discussions in investment treaty disputes almost invariably concern umbrella clauses.

An initial and important point is that the term 'umbrella clause' covers a range of provisions, differently worded, and each with its own negotiating history. The first step in interpreting any umbrella clause claim must be to examine the ordinary meaning of the words of the clause, pursuant to the Vienna Convention on the Law of Treaties.

In *Salini v. Jordan*,[104] an ICSID tribunal emphasized the importance of the language of an umbrella clause. The clause in that case provided that each State party to a BIT was obliged 'to create and maintain a legal framework apt to guarantee investors the continuity of legal treatment including the compliance in good faith of all undertakings assumed with regard to each specific investor'. The tribunal held that this clause did not by its terms commit each Contracting Party to observe any obligation or commitment with respect to the investment of the investors of the other Contracting Party – as distinct from maintaining a domestic legal framework that assured sanctity of contract. Under this clause, the Contracting Parties were bound to their contractual obligations, but no contractual undertaking was reiterated or guaranteed in the BIT.[105]

---

100. *Id.*, para. 160.
101. *Id.*, para. 171.
102. *Id.*, para. 175.
103. Brownlie, *Principles of Public International Law*, 631.
104. *Salini v. Jordan*, Decision on Jurisdiction, 29 Nov. 2004, *ILM* 44 (2005), 569.
105. *Id.*, para. 127.

Chapter 6: Treaty Versus Contract Claims, and Umbrella Clauses §6.04

Any dispute arising from the contract therefore had to be resolved before domestic courts, pursuant to the dispute mechanism contained in the contract.[106]

The *Salini* tribunal did not purport to link its holding to any interpretive approach beyond its reading of the plain meaning of the clause's language of the clause. On the basis of that language, the provision that the Claimant contended was an 'umbrella clause' did not actually constitute such a clause; it merely required that the State 'create and maintain a legal framework', rather than undertake to perform an obligation.

Even in the context of 'properly' designated umbrella clauses, the precise language still matters: a universally agreed model 'umbrella clause' does not exist. The core element is a commitment by the State to comply with its undertakings. An umbrella clause of some type is contained in a significant percentage of BITs,[107] as well as in the ECT,[108] the UK Model BIT,[109] and the 2004 US Model BIT.[110]

A recurring question is whether an umbrella clause protects investors' rights against *any* breach of a State commitment or undertaking, which may be represented by a contract, administrative acts or, in certain cases, legislative acts (i.e., *ad hoc* legislation adopted in relation to an investor or an investment), such that a breach of this type would also constitute a breach of an international obligation protected by the treaty. The history of umbrella clauses, discussed below, supports giving these clauses a broad scope, though in the end the question is one of interpretation of particular words. History cannot overcome a narrowly drafted clause in a particular investment treaty.

Sinclair has opined that the 'origin of the notion that a treaty can be used to elevate a contract between an investor and a host state to the level of an inter-state obligation between the host state and the national state of the investor can be traced to advice provided by Elihu Lauterpacht in late 1953 and early 1954 to the Anglo-Iranian Oil Company in connection with the settlement of the Iranian oil nationalization dispute'.[111] Lauterpacht's advice was that a clause could be designed to give to the

---

106. *Id.*, paras 126–129.
107. It has been estimated that 40% of the BITs currently in existence contain an umbrella clause. *See* Yannaca-Small, 'What About This Umbrella Clause', *supra*, 5 (citing Gill, Gearing & Birt, 'Contractual Claims and Bilateral Investment Treaties: A Comparative Review of the SGS Cases', *J. Int'l. Arb.* 21(5) (2004), 397 at fn. 31).
108. Article 10(1) of the Energy Charter Treaty provides that 'Each Contracting Party shall observe any obligations it has entered into with an Investor or an Investment of an Investor of any other Contracting Party', Annex IA allows the Contracting Parties to opt out of this provision; as of this date Australia, Canada, Hungary, and Norway have opted out.
109. Article 2(2), UK Model BIT, states that 'Each Contracting Party shall observe any obligation it may have entered into with regard to investments of nationals or companies of the other Contracting Party', available on http://investmentpolicyhub.unctad.org/Download/TreatyFile/2847.
110. Article 24(1), 2004 US Model BIT, states that 'In the event that a disputing party considers that an investment dispute cannot be settled by consultation or negotiation: a) the claimant, on its own behalf, may submit to arbitration under this Section a claim (i) that the Respondent has breached ... (B) an investment authorization or (C) an investment agreement ...', in Bishop, Crawford & Reisman, *Foreign Investment Disputes*, 66.
111. Sinclair, 'The Origins of the Umbrella Clause in the International Law of Investment Protection', *Arb. Int.* 20(4) (2004), 411. *See, generally,* Yannaca-Small, 'What About This Umbrella Clause', in *Arbitration Under Investment Agreement*, ed. Yannaca Small (Oxford, 2010), 479–503; Sinclair, 'Umbrella Clause', in *International Investment Law*, eds Bungenberg et al.

terms of the contract between the State and the investor a 'stability guaranteed by treaty between the States most directly concerned'.[112] The investor would receive an added and alternative protection to the dispute settlement mechanism contained in its contract with the State, with the alternative providing recourse to the avenue of diplomatic protection. This meant, in the situation Lauterpacht was addressing, that the parties to the dispute would be the UK and Iranian governments, with the compulsory jurisdiction of the ICJ ultimately being triggered.[113]

In the background of Lauterpacht's advice was the ICJ judgment in the *Anglo-Iranian Oil Co.* case (Preliminary Objection) of 22 July 1952, which held that the contract between the Iranian government and the Anglo-Persian Oil Company could not be considered a treaty and, accordingly, did not regulate relations between two governments.[114] The ICJ explained that the United Kingdom was not a party to the contract (between the company and Iran), which therefore did not regulate the relations between the two States. The ICJ stated that under the contract, Iran could not claim from the United Kingdom any rights that it might claim from the Anglo-Iranian Oil Company, nor could it be called upon to perform for the United Kingdom any obligations that it was bound to perform for the Company.

[A] Premise: Abs-Shawcross Draft Convention 1959, First Modern BIT, OECD Draft Convention, and 1998 Draft MAI

The earliest general umbrella clauses appeared in the 1956–1959 Abs Draft International Convention for the Mutual Protection of Private and Property Rights and in the 1959 Abs-Shawcross Draft Convention on Foreign Investments (hereafter Abs-Shawcross Draft).[115] The wording of the clause in Abs-Shawcross Draft is of particular note:

> Each Party shall at all times ensure the observance of any undertakings which it may have given in relation to investments made by nationals of any other Party.[116]

This provision was intended to cover contractual undertakings between States and private investors as well as unilateral undertakings made by States.[117] Its purpose was to clarify that 'unilateral violation of a concession contract is an international

---

(Hart-Nomos, 2015), 887–958; Rigo Sureda, 'The Umbrella Clause', in *The First 50 Years of ICSID*, eds Kinnear et al. (Kluwer, 2016), 375–387; Pereira & Fleury, 'Umbrella Clauses: A Trend Toward Elimination', *Arb. In.* 31(4) (2015); Antony, 'Umbrella Clauses since *SGS v. Pakistan* and *SGS v. Philippines*—A Developing Consensus', *Arb. In.* 29(4) (2013).

112. *Id.*, 416, quoting Lauterpacht, 'Anglo-Iranian Oil Company Ltd Persian Settlement – Note', 12 Mar. 1954, 18.
113. *Id.*, 417.
114. Case of *Anglo-Iranian Oil Co.*, Judgment, 22 Jul. 1952, ICJ *Reports* (1952), 93, at 112–114.
115. *See* Sinclair, 'The Origins of the Umbrella Clause in the International Law of Investment Protection', 418 and Yannaca-Small, '*Interpretation of the Umbrella Clause in Investment Agreements*', 4.
116. Abs-Shawcross Draft Convention, Art. 2.
117. Schwarzenberger, *Foreign Investments and International Law*, 116.

wrong'.[118] However, at this early stage it was not contemplated that private investors would have *locus standi* against the State, and therefore the question of whether such a clause might potentially trigger a multitude of international law claims was not considered.[119]

The first modern BIT, between Germany and Pakistan (1959), contained an umbrella clause.[120] This is apparent from the Article 7 phrase, 'obligation ... entered into'. Here, the intention seems to have been protection of contractual obligations rather than the broader concept of 'undertaking'. However, there is no contemporaneous commentary that interprets this particular umbrella clause.

The 1967 OECD Draft Convention contains an umbrella clause and is accompanied by a commentary. The umbrella clause reads as follows: 'Each Party shall at all times ensure the observance of undertakings given by it in relation to property of nationals of any other Party' (Article 2). The OECD Commentaries described this provision as 'an application of the general principle of *pacta sunt servanda*' (Article 2). The Commentaries explained that 'property' is to be interpreted in the 'widest sense' and is not limited to investments, though 'undertakings' must '*relate* to the property concerned: it is not sufficient if the link is incidental' (emphasis in the original). The OECD Commentaries also clarified that the link between the property and the undertaking is *not* incidental when the undertaking is granted in specific terms that serve to identify either the property or the undertaking's recipient. Alternatively, an undertaking rendered in general terms may nonetheless carry treaty protection if it can be 'proved or presumed' that the investor 'acted in reliance' on the undertaking.[121]

More recently – though still prior to the leading cases – the 1998 Draft Multilateral Agreement on Investment (MAI) sought to provide two alternative umbrella clause ('respect clause') formulations:

(i) each Contracting Party 'shall observe any obligation it has entered into with regard to a specific investment of an investor of another Contracting Party'; or
(ii) each Contracting Party shall observe any obligation 'in writing', though 'disputes arising from such obligations shall only be settled under the terms of the contracts underlying the obligations'.[122]

The second formulation may be regarded as a gloss on the history of umbrella clauses, seeking to draw a line between the respective tasks of international tribunals and domestic courts, and imposing an exhaustion of contractual remedies requirement

---

118. Seidl-Hohenveldern, 'The Abs-Shawcross Draft Convention to Protect Private Foreign Investment: Comments on the Round-Table', 104. Lauterpacht, 'Drafting of Treaties for the Protection of Investment', in *The Encouragement and Protection of Investment in Developing Countries*, ICLQ, Suppl. 3, 1962, 18.
119. Sinclair, 'The Origins of the Umbrella Clause in the International Law of Investment Protection', 417, quoting Lauterpacht, who 'believed it to be unlikely "that the Government of the United Kingdom and Iran would be directly involved in every minor dispute, which may arise in connection with the Settlement"'.
120. Article 7.
121. *See* Sinclair, 429 (quoting para. 3, Notes and Comments to Art. 2).
122. 1998 Draft Multilateral Agreement on Investment, 115–116.

on the investor if the contract's terms include a dispute resolution provision. Under this approach, if States are to be held to their agreements, so should investors. The MAI thus attempted to break with the past by circumscribing the scope of umbrella clauses. This is also the path taken by the United States in the 2004 US Model BIT (and confirmed in the 2012 US Model BIT), which modified the provision contained in the 1983, 1984, and 1987 US Model BITs concerning a general undertaking to observe any obligation entered into with regard to an investment.[123] The 2004 and the 2012 US Model BITs contain a more narrowly drafted clause, which suggests a concern that the past clauses and the history of umbrella clauses have created extensive obligations on States and were not confined to certain types of contracts or to contracts entered into in the exercise of State sovereignty.

[B] Outcome: Umbrella Clauses and Draft Conventions

One scholar has proposed that the purpose behind the draft conventions (with the exception of the MAI, which he did not consider) and the 1959 Germany–Pakistan BIT was to protect investors that entered into concession contracts.[124] However, this purpose is not reflected in the wording of those draft conventions or in any Model BIT or in the Germany–Pakistan BIT, which simply refer to 'undertakings' or 'obligations'.

It has also been suggested that the 'framers of the original *pacta sunt servanda* clause assumed as evident that the State conduct targeted by the clause had to be qualified as "governmental". The idea that the clause would be applied to any commercial contract concluded by the State entities in their "fisc", that is, private law, role did not occur to them – and therefore was not debated'.[125] According to this view, there is no evidence that the clause's original drafters ever intended to create a 'treaty-based forum for adjudicating all the contractual disputes between State entities and foreigners'. On the basis of this lack of evidence, some commentators and arbitrators seek to limit the applicability of umbrella clauses to governmental contracts. But the difficulty they face is that the language of many of these clauses is broad and unrestricted.

---

123. www.ustr.gov/assets/Trade_Sectors/Investment/Model_BIT/asset_upload_file847_6897.pdf. *See* Kantor, 'The New Draft Model U.S. BIT: Noteworthy Developments', *J. Int. Arb.* (2004), 383. The author mentions the disappearance of the general undertaking provision without suggesting any reason behind such deletion (p. 385). It appears that there has not been any published commentary on the 2004 US Model BIT (Congressional, State Department, or otherwise) that mentions this umbrella clause development. *See also* Alvarez, 'The Evolving BIT' in TDM, June 2009, 2–19, stating that the 2004 Model BIT limits the extent to which an investor can bring a claim for breach of contract since it eliminated the umbrella clause: 'a breach of a written investment contract no longer suffices to prompt an investor-State treaty claim', 9. Alvarez stated also that under the US 2004 Model Bit an investor can bring a claim for a breach of a written investment agreement only if the host State violated other provisions such the fair and equitable treatment or violation of the national treatment standards. On the 1983 US Model BIT, Art. II(4), *see* Vandevelde, *United States Investment Treaties: Policy and Practice* (The Netherlands, 1992), Appendix A-2.
124. Wälde, 'The "Umbrella" Clause in Investment Arbitration: A Comment on Original Intentions and Recent Cases', *J. World Inv. and Trade* 6 (2005), 183, at 204–205.
125. *Id.*, 205.

The history of umbrella clauses does not disclose a clear purpose or common interpretive direction, apart from the very general point that these clauses were intended to broaden the scope of investor protection and therefore should, if the wording permits (and depending on one's view of their purpose), be construed broadly. Some understandings can nonetheless be said to emerge from a study of the historical origins. Chief among these are:

(i) Umbrella clauses protect an investor against 'any interference with his contractual rights, whether it results from a mere breach of contract or a legislative or administrative act, and independently of the question whether or no such interference amounts to expropriation'.[126]

(ii) An umbrella clause may cover, depending on its wording, the observance of any obligation/undertaking. This terminology was adopted by early drafters in its 'widest' sense. The terms 'undertaking' and (perhaps) 'obligation' have a broader scope than the term 'contract', although it is still necessary that the undertaking must relate to the property concerned.[127]

The historical background has informed the approaches adopted by arbitral tribunals in resolving recent umbrella clause claims. However, the background does not assist on the question whether the presence of an umbrella clause transforms the substantive law applicable to the underlying undertaking.

§6.05 FOUR SCHOOLS OF THOUGHT CONCERNING UMBRELLA CLAUSES

Given the different accounts of the history of umbrella clauses, it is not surprising that international investment tribunals have adopted significantly different approaches in deciding umbrella clause claims. The cases examined below focus on the scope of umbrella clauses, and fall into four categories. Following a description of these categories and a discussion of attribution, this Chapter assesses the relative merits of the four schools of thought.

[A] The 'Negative' Interpretation: *Société Générale du Surveillance SA v. Pakistan*[128]

In 1994, SGS, a Swiss company, entered into a pre-shipment inspection agreement with Pakistan. This agreement contained an arbitration clause providing for *ad hoc* arbitration in Islamabad under Pakistani law. Pakistan terminated the agreement in 1996, and SGS first initiated proceedings for unlawful termination in the Swiss Courts; this claim

---

126. Mann, 'British Treaties for the Promotion and Protection of Investments', *BYIL* 52 (1981), 241, at 246.
127. 'Draft Convention on the Protection of Foreign Property and Resolution of the Council of OECD on the Draft Convention', Notes and Comments to Art. 2, 32.
128. *Société Générale du Surveillance SA v. Pakistan (SGS v. Pakistan)*, Decision on Objections to Jurisdiction of 6 Aug. 2003, *ICSID Reports*, vol. 8, 383.

eventually failed on the ground of sovereign immunity. In the meantime, in 2000, Pakistan applied to the Court in Islamabad for an order that the dispute be referred to an arbitral tribunal in Islamabad.

In 2001, SGS initiated proceedings under the 1995 Swiss-Pakistan BIT seeking compensation for Pakistan's termination of the inspection agreement. In the course of the BIT arbitral proceedings, SGS applied to the Court in Islamabad for a stay of the Pakistani arbitration proceedings and argued before the BIT tribunal that it had jurisdiction over the contractual claims pursuant to the umbrella clause, Article 11 of the BIT.[129] SGS submitted that the umbrella clause elevated all contractual claims to the level of claims for a breach of the BIT, and therefore its contractual claims constituted claims under international law.

The BIT tribunal disagreed with SGS; it read Article 11 of the BIT very narrowly. The tribunal held that for SGS's claim to succeed, Article 11 should have been worded in a manner that would sustain a broad interpretation; the treaty wording instead enhanced 'mutuality' and the balance of benefits 'in the inter-relation of different agreements located in differing legal orders'.[130]

The *SGS v. Pakistan* tribunal's reasoning may be summarized as follows:

(i) The term 'commitment' is very broad and appears 'susceptible of almost indefinite expansion', since it would imply incorporating by reference 'an unlimited number of State contracts'.[131] However, the text of Article 11 'does not purport to state that breaches of contract alleged by an investor in relation to a contract it has concluded with a State (widely considered to be matter of municipal rather than international law) are automatically "elevated" to the level of breaches of international treaty law'.[132]

(ii) Taking into account, on the one hand, that breaches of a contract entered into with the State do not by themselves constitute a breach of international law, and on the other the far-reaching and burdensome consequences for the State Contracting Party to the BIT, it was necessary to show '[c]lear and convincing evidence' that the shared intent of Switzerland and Pakistan was that any alleged breach of a contract with the State was a breach of the BIT.[133]

(iii) SGS's reading of the umbrella clause 'tends to make Articles 3 to 7 of the BIT substantially superfluous'.[134] Furthermore, an investor could render inoperative any dispute resolution mechanism freely inserted in a contract with a State by making an umbrella clause claim.

---

129. Article 11 provides that '[e]ither Contracting Party shall constantly guarantees the observance of the commitments it has entered into with respect to the investments of the investors of the other Contracting Party', para. 53.
130. *SGS v. Pakistan*, para. 168.
131. *Id.*, paras 166, 168.
132. *Id.*, para. 166.
133. *Id.*, para. 167. On 1 Oct. 2003, the Swiss government sent a letter to ICSID about its intentions when concluding the BIT (19 Mealey's International Arbitration Reports (2004), issue 2, 3.
134. *SGS v. Pakistan*, para. 168.

(iv) Since the umbrella clause was not placed together with the Contracting Parties' substantive obligations, the umbrella clause is not a substantive obligation.[135]

(v) The interpretative approach expressed in the principle *in dubio mitius* (when in doubt, the milder course should be followed) is to be preferred.[136]

[B] The 'Automatic' Interpretation: *Fedax N.V. v. Venezuela; CMS Gas Transmission Company v. Argentina; LG&E Energy Corp., LG&E Capital Corp., and LG&E International Inc. v. Argentina*

A second school of thought, taking the opposite position from *SGS v. Pakistan*, submits that an umbrella clause automatically transforms an obligation in a contract between a State and an investor into an international obligation.

Fedax v. Venezuela includes an interpretation of an umbrella clause, though it does not provide an in-depth analysis of the clause. The underlying claim by the investor was that Venezuela had failed to honour certain of its promissory notes. The tribunal held that under the Netherlands-Venezuela BIT's umbrella clause (Article 3[137]), 'the Republic of Venezuela is under the obligation to honour precisely the terms and conditions governing such investments, laid down mainly in Article 3 of the [BIT] as well as to honour the specific payments established in the promissory notes issued'.[138] The tribunal's view was that a breach of contract was a breach of treaty, without explaining in any detail the reasoning behind this holding.

The 'automatic' school of thought received further expression in *LG&E v. Argentina*. The tribunal held that Argentina, by enacting a Gas Law and other regulations and then advertising these guarantees in an Offering Memorandum, induced the 'entry of foreign capital to fund the privatization programme in its public sector. These laws and regulations became obligations within the meaning of [the umbrella clause], by virtue of targeting foreign investors and applying specifically to their investments, that gave rise to liability under the umbrella clause'.[139]

A similar conclusion had previously been reached in *CMS Gas Transmission Company v. Argentina*. The *CMS* tribunal held that the obligations under the umbrella clause (i.e., the obligations not to freeze the tariff regime or subject it to price controls and not to alter the rules governing the license without consent) were breached 'to the extent that legal and contractual obligations pertinent to the investment have been breached and have resulted in the violation of the standards of protection under the

---

135. *Id.*, para. 170.
136. *Id.*, para. 171.
137. Article 3: 'Each Contracting Party shall observe any obligation it may have entered into with regard to the treatment of investments of national of the other Contacting Party.'
138. *Fedax v. Venezuela*, Award 9 Mar. 1998, para. 29.
139. *LG&E Energy Corp. LG&E Capital Corp. and LG&E International INC v. Argentina*, Decision on Liability, 3 Oct. 2006, para. 175.

Treaty'.[140] However, the *Ad Hoc* Committee annulled this ruling on the grounds of manifest excess of powers, since it was not clear from the award how the tribunal reached the conclusion that CMS could enforce the umbrella clause. (The tribunal's finding on liability was not affected because the 'award on damages was made on the basis of independent findings' of violations of the BIT).[141]

In relation to the umbrella clause, the *Ad Hoc* Committee drew back from affirming the automatic interpretation and clarified that the term 'obligations' in the clause meant legal obligations and not legitimate expectations.[142] The Committee listed the primary difficulties arising from a broad interpretation of the umbrella clause and commented that:

> The effect of the umbrella clause is not to transform the obligation which is relied on into something else; the content of the obligation is unaffected, as is its proper law. If this is so, it would appear that the parties to the obligation (i.e., the persons bound by it and entitled to rely on it) are likewise not changed by reason of the umbrella clause.[143]

[C] The 'Iure Imperii' Interpretation: *Pan American Energy LLC and Bp Argentina Exploration Company v. Argentina*;[144] *El Paso Energy International Company v. Argentina*[145]

A third school of thought advances the view that a tribunal constituted under a BIT containing an umbrella clause only has jurisdiction over treaty claims, including claims based on the violation of an investment agreement entered into by the foreign investor and the State *as a sovereign*, but not claims where the State acted other than as a sovereign.

The tribunals in *Pan American Energy* and *El Paso Energy*, ruling on jurisdiction in two very similar cases and applying the umbrella clause in the same BIT, reached identical conclusions. The two tribunals emphasized that a balanced interpretation of a BIT is necessary, taking into account both the State's interests and the necessity to

---

140. *CMS Gas Transmission Company v. Argentina*, para. 86. See also *LESI DI PENTA v. Algeria (Consorzio Groupment LESI – DIPENTA v. People's Democratic Republic of Algeria*, Award, 10 Jan. 2005, *ICSID Rev.* 19 – *FILJ* 426 (2004)), where the absence of an umbrella clause in the relevant BIT 'confirmed' that the tribunal's jurisdiction was limited to violations of BIT and not to breaches of contracts (para. 25 (ii)).
141. *CMS Gas Transmission Company v. Argentina*, Decision of the *Ad Hoc* Committee, para. 100.
142. *Id.*, para. 89.
143. *Id.*, para. 95.
144. *Pan American Energy LLC and BP Argentina Exploration Company v. Argentina*, Decision on Preliminary Objections dated 27 Jul. 2006, available on Investment Claims website: www.investmentclaims.com/decisions/PanAmerican_BP-Argentina-Jurisdiction.pdf
145. *El Paso Energy International Company v. Argentina*, Decision on Jurisdiction dated 27 Apr. 2006, available on the ICSID website: www.worldbank.org/icsid/cases/ARB0315-DOJ-E.pdf The application for annulment of this award was dismissed on 22 Sep. 2014, the Decision of the *Ad Hoc* Committee is available on the Investment treaty arbitration website http://www.italaw.com/sites/default/files/case-documents/italaw4007_0.pdf

Chapter 6: Treaty Versus Contract Claims, and Umbrella Clauses   §6.05[D]

protect foreign investment and its continuing flow.[146] Such an interpretation meant rejecting the approach of construing the umbrella clause simply to mean the transformation of a contract claim into a treaty claim.[147]

The *Pan American/El Paso* tribunals read the umbrella clause in conjunction with the BIT provision concerning investment disputes. They held that the umbrella clause 'will not extend the Treaty protection to breaches of an ordinary commercial contract entered into by the State or a State-owned entity, but will cover additional investment protections contractually agreed by the State as a sovereign inserted in an investment agreement'.[148] Pursuant to this approach, a State's violation of an investment agreement that it entered into in its capacity as a sovereign could give rise to a treaty claim.[149]

[D] The 'Enforcement' Approach: *Société Générale Du Surveillance SA v. Philippines*[150]

In another case where SGS was the Claimant, subsequent to the decision in *SGS v. Pakistan*, the arbitral tribunal in *SGS v. Philippines* addressed the question of umbrella clauses in greater depth. Although SGS again failed to achieve its objective of remitting the dispute to the immediate jurisdiction of the arbitral tribunal under the umbrella clause, the tribunal's reasoning differed substantially from *SGS v. Pakistan*.

In 1991, SGS entered into a contract with the Philippines, and in 1997 the Switzerland–Philippines BIT entered in force. In 2002, SGS issued proceedings under this BIT, claiming amounts allegedly unpaid under the 1991 contract. SGS argued, *inter alia*, that the umbrella clause, Article X(2) of the BIT, gave the tribunal jurisdiction over contractual disputes.

The tribunal, having in mind *SGS v. Pakistan*, first clarified that there is no doctrine of precedent in international. The *SGS v. Philippines* tribunal then determined that:

(i) The umbrella clause provision used the 'mandatory term "shall"'.[151]
(ii) The 'object and purpose of the BIT supports an effective interpretation of Article X(2)'. Therefore, '[i]t is legitimate to resolve uncertainties in its interpretation so as to favour the protection of the covered investments'.[152]
(iii) In the event that commitments made by the State in relation to a specific investments 'involve binding obligations or commitments under the applicable law, it seems entirely consistent with the object and purpose of the BIT

---

146. *Pan American and BP v. Argentina*, para. 99.
147. *Id.*, para. 110.
148. *Id.*, para. 109.
149. *Id.*, para. 113.
150. *Société Générale du Surveillance SA v. Philippines*, Decision on Objections to Jurisdiction of 29 Jan. 2004, *ICSID Reports*, vol. 8, 515.
151. *SGS v. Philippines*, para. 115.
152. *Id.*, para. 116.

to hold that they are incorporated and brought within the framework of the BIT'.[153]

(iv) *SGS v. Pakistan* failed to give a 'clear meaning' to the umbrella clause.[154] Moreover, the clause in the Switzerland--Pakistan BIT was 'less clear and categorical' than the equivalent provision in the Switzerland – Philippines BIT.[155] Further, the tribunal disagreed with the application of a 'presumption against the broad interpretation of [an umbrella clause]'.[156] It did not accept *SGS v. Pakistan's* conclusion that the contractual dispute mechanism clause would be overridden by the umbrella clause if the latter provision were interpreted broadly,[157] and it declined to attribute any decisive importance to the location of the umbrella clause within the BIT.[158]

(v) The tribunal rejected the theory that an umbrella clause would 'convert questions of contract law into questions of treaty law'. The umbrella clause did not 'change the proper law of (the Agreement between SGS and the Philippines) from the law of the Philippines to international law'.[159] In particular, the umbrella clause addressed 'the performance' and not the 'scope' of the commitments assumed by the State in connection with a specific investment.

The *SGS v. Philippines* tribunal, by a majority, therefore stayed the investment arbitration pending a decision on the unpaid amount under the 1991 contract, to be determined in accordance with the dispute settlement mechanism provided in the contract.

Crivellaro dissented on the decision to stay the proceedings. He opined that the BIT 'created a completely new law and has conferred on SGS new or additional rights of forum selection. They include, in particular, the right to select the forum *after that the dispute has arisen*'.[160] Crivellaro stated that the BIT was *posterior* to the contract and granted more favourable treatment to the investor than the contract. The dissent's overriding concern was that the Tribunal was restricting 'in practice, its jurisdiction to BIT claims only, after affirming, in theory, that Articles VIII and X(2) of the BIT confer on the Tribunal jurisdiction over also purely contractual claims'.[161]

Thus, Crivellaro seemed to adhere to the 'automatic' interpretation, described above, while the tribunal majority, though it criticized the *SGS v. Pakistan* 'negative' interpretation, nonetheless fashioned a framework that sets very high bar for investors seeking to avoid a contractual dispute resolution mechanism.

---

153. *Id.*, para. 117.
154. *Id.*, para. 125.
155. *Id.*, para. 119.
156. *Id.*, para. 122.
157. *Id.*, para. 123.
158. *Id.*, para. 124.
159. *Id.*, para. 126.
160. *Id.*, para. 2 of Crivellaro's Declaration (emphasis in the original).
161. *Id.*, para. 12 of Prof. Crivellaro's Declaration.

Chapter 6: Treaty Versus Contract Claims, and Umbrella Clauses §6.05[D]

The majority's approach in *SGS v. Philippines* was endorsed in two cases, *Bivac v. Paraguay*[162] and *Toto Costruzioni Generali Spa v. Lebanon*,[163] although the conclusions reached were slightly different. *Bivac* postponed to the merits stage the decision on whether to dismiss the claim or to stay it until proceedings in the city of Asunción courts would be commenced and completed. In *Toto Costruzioni Generali*, instead, the tribunal held that it lacked jurisdiction because of the contract's dispute resolution clause.

The *Bivac* tribunal interpreted the clause before it as establishing an international obligation to observe any contractual obligations with respect to investors. The tribunal concluded that '[t]he words "any obligation" are all encompassing. They are not limited to international obligations, or non-contractual obligations, so that they appear without apparent limitation with respect to commitments that impose legal obligations. On a plain meaning they are undoubtedly capable of being read to include a contractual arrangement' between the Claimant and the Respondent.[164] Since the umbrella clause imported all the obligations under the contract into the BIT, this included the obligation to ensure that the tribunals of the city of Asunción would resolve any dispute arising under the contract: the 'effect of an umbrella clause is one issue; a different issue is whether such a clause may be invoked in circumstances where the parties have clearly agreed on an exclusive jurisdiction for the resolution of contractual disputes that may fall within the terms of the umbrella clause'.[165] The tribunal concluded that in order to respect the autonomy and will of the parties, parties cannot 'pick and choose'[166] the parts of the contract to incorporate into an umbrella clause and to ignore other provisions of the contract.[167]

---

162. *Bureau Veritas, Inspection, Valuation, Assessment and Control, BIVAC B.V v. Paraguay*, Decision of the Tribunal on Objections to Jurisdiction, 29 May 2009, available on investment treaty arbitration website: http://www.italaw.com/sites/default/files/case-documents/ita0103.pdf and Further Decision on Objections to Jurisdiction, 9 Oct. 2012, available on investment treaty arbitration website: http://www.italaw.com/sites/default/files/case-documents/italaw1109.pdf
163. *Toto Costruzioni Generali Spa v. Lebanon*, Decision on Jurisdiction, 11 Sep. 2009, available on investment treaty arbitration website: http://www.italaw.com/sites/default/files/case-documents/ita0869.pdf. There was also an award on the merits and proceedings were discontinued in 2013.
164. *Bureau Veritas, Inspection, Valuation, Assessment and Control, BIVAC B.V v. Paraguay*, para. 141.
165. *Id.*, para. 142.
166. *Id.*, para. 148.
167. *Id.*, para. 161: 'we have heard no argument from the Respondent seeking to dissuade us from adopting the approach taken by the Tribunal in *SGS v. Philippines*, which decided to stay proceedings. In the absence of argument by either party, and having found that the claim under Article 3(4) is inadmissible, we consider that the most prudent approach is to join to the merits the limited issue of whether the Tribunal should *either* dismiss the claim under Article 3(4) of the BIT *or* stay the exercise of jurisdiction indefinitely or for some other period of time or until some other circumstances pertain.' In its Further Decision on Objections to Jurisdiction, the tribunal stayed the proceeding for a period of three months, within which period the Claimant could file a claim for breach of the Contract before the tribunals of the City of Asunción. In the event that such a claim was not filed, the Tribunal would render its award and terminate the arbitration. The ICSID proceeding was in fact discontinued in 2014.

In *Toto Costruzioni Generali*, the tribunal stated that umbrella clauses might form the basis for treaty claims without transforming contractual claims into treaty claims.[168] The tribunal characterized the umbrella clause as 'a mechanism for the enforcement of claims, it does not elevate pure contractual claims into treaty claims. The contractual claims remain based upon the contract; they are governed by the law of the contract and may be affected by the other provisions of the contract. In the case at hand that implies that they remain subject to the contractual jurisdiction clause and have to be submitted exclusively to the Lebanese courts for settlement'.[169] The tribunal held that it lacked jurisdiction to hear the contract claim before it, and indeed referred to *SGS v. Pakistan* to support this decision.

On the other hand, Crivellaro's dissenting opinion in *SGS v. Philippines* was endorsed in *SGS v. Paraguay*.[170] There the tribunal concluded that an umbrella clause 'establishes an international obligation for the parties to the BIT to observe contractual obligation[s] with respect to investors'.[171] Having established its jurisdiction over a claim stemming from a violation of the umbrella clause, the tribunal had to determine whether to hear the claim or remand it to the forum selected in the relevant contract. The tribunal decided to hear the claim because: (i) the Claimant's claims were not only contractual, since there were other alleged commitments relied by SGS and therefore not all the umbrella clause claims would fall into the contract forum selection clause;[172] (ii) the enforcement of the forum selection clause would result in limiting BIT tribunals' jurisdictions to 'empty shell and depriving the BIT dispute resolution process of any meaning';[173] and (iii) a decision that an umbrella claim is inadmissible can be read as an implied waiver of BIT rights. The tribunal quoted Crivellaro to support the proposition that the BIT settlement provision and the contractual forum selection should survive and coexist with the contractual forum not being the exclusive forum. To exclude all the contractual claims would render *inutile* the BIT's umbrella provision.

---

168. *Toto Costruzioni Generali Spa v. Lebanon*, para. 200.
169. *Id.*, para. 202.
170. *Société Générale du Surveillance SA v. Paraguay*, Decision on Jurisdiction, 12 Feb. 2010, available on investment treaty arbitration website: http://www.italaw.com/sites/default/files/case-documents/italaw1526.pdf and the Award, 10 Feb. 2012, available on investment treaty arbitration website: http://www.italaw.com/sites/default/files/case-documents/italaw1525.pdf Annulment proceedings were dismissed with the Decision on Annulment dated 19 May 2014, available on investment treaty arbitration website: http://www.italaw.com/sites/default/files/case-documents/italaw3236.pdf. In particular the *Ad Hoc* Committee held that: 'This Committee cannot act as an appeals tribunal and review whether the interpretation of the umbrella clause and the forum-selection clause by the Tribunal were correct. The Committee could only annul the award upon verification of the existence of a manifest excess of powers on the part of the Tribunal, which can be easily perceived and does not require extensive interpretation of the Award to be perceived. This is not the case in the Tribunal's Award' (para. 130).
171. *Ibid.*
172. *Id.*, para. 173.
173. *Id.*, para. 176.

§6.06 UMBRELLA CLAUSES: ATTRIBUTION AND PARTIES TO THE UNDERTAKING

A final issue concerns (i) the applicability of an umbrella clause provision to contracts entered into by a State entity with a separate personality from the State, and (ii) whether the umbrella clause transforms the substantive law applicable to the undertaking as far as the parties to the agreement are concerned.[174]

If the umbrella clause refers only to the undertakings granted by each Contracting Party, the question to resolve is whether an undertaking granted by a municipality or any other State instrumentality with a separate personality can be attributed to the State.

The rules on attribution of State responsibility in relation to State instrumentalities cannot be invoked, because such rules apply only to the exercise of governmental acts, and the entering into a contract cannot be characterized as a governmental act.[175] Moreover, a breach of an undertaking given by a State instrumentality, without clear wording in the investment treaty, cannot be considered an internationally wrongful act: in the absence of a violation of a primary rule (i.e., the violation of an international law obligation) the rules on State responsibility, which are secondary rules, cannot be invoked.[176] In other words, the offer to arbitrate contained in investment treaties concerns States' undertakings and not State-owned entities' undertakings. The view that umbrella clauses would encompass contracts 'made with the State itself – and the term may fairly be said to comprise its instrumentalities, even if they are separate legal entities, as well as companies of which it is the sole shareholder'[177] – does not explain why the mere presence of an umbrella clause would permit the piercing of the corporate veil and treating a contract entered into by an entity which is not a State organ as a State contract.

The question whether an umbrella clause claim may be maintained with regard to breach of contracts entered into by parties different from those to the arbitral proceedings has arisen in several cases. In *Azurix Corp. v. Argentina, Siemens AG v. Argentina, CMS Gas Transmission Company v. Argentina,* and *LG&E Energy Corp. LG&E v. Argentina*, the contract for which umbrella clause protection was sought was entered into by the Claimant's subsidiary.

In *Azurix Corp. v. Argentina*, Argentina argued that neither it nor its province undertook any contractual obligation with the Claimant. Azurix contended that the umbrella clause referred to any obligation, including obligations arising under international law as well as municipal law. The tribunal held that 'none of the contractual claims as such refer to a contract between the parties to these proceedings: neither the

---

174. *Noble Ventures Inc. v. Romania*. See Dolzer & Schreuer, 175–177. *See* Gallus, 'An Umbrella Just for Two? BIT Obligations Observance Clauses and the Parties to a Contract', *Arb. Int.* 24(1) (2008), 157; and Mann, 'British Treaties for the Promotion and Protection of Investments', 246.
175. Crawford, 'International Law and Foreign Sovereigns: Distinguishing Immune Transactions', BYIL 54 (1983), 75 at 101, citing the State Immunity Act 1978, which confirms that commercial acts of instrumentalities cannot be attributed to the State in the context of State immunity.
176. Crawford, *The International Law Commission's Articles on State Responsibility*, 75.
177. Mann, 'British Treaties for the Promotion and Protection of Investments', 246.

Province nor ABA are parties to them. While Azurix may submit a claim under the BIT for breaches by Argentina, there is no undertaking to be honoured by Argentina to Azurix other than the obligations under the BIT'.[178] The *Siemens* tribunal took the same approach.[179]

However, a different conclusion was reached, at least implicitly, by the *CMS v. Argentina* tribunal. As noted above, this tribunal ruled that an umbrella clause elevates contractual obligations into treaty obligations. It did not address the point (which had been raised by Argentina) that CMS was not party to the contract in connection with which the breach of contract, that is, the breach of treaty, was submitted. This ruling was annulled; the *Ad Hoc* Committee held that 'the *parties* to the obligation (i.e., the persons bound by it and entitled to rely on it) are likewise not changed by reason of the umbrella clause'.[180]

Burlington v. Ecuador[181] discusses the concept of privity in umbrella clauses. The ordinary meaning of 'obligation' entails a party bound by it and another one benefitting from it. Furthermore, 'an obligation does not exist in a vacuum. It is subject to a governing law. Although the notion of obligation is used in an international treaty, the court or tribunal interpreting the treaty may have to look to municipal law to give it content'.[182] In this case, the tribunal concluded, it was not alleged that under Ecuadorian law, the non-signatory parent of a contracting party might directly enforce its subsidiary's rights.[183] The tribunal stated that the link between the obligation and the investment did not replace but qualified the notion of obligation. There had to be an obligation in the first place, and this obligation must have a link with an investment.[184]

Finally, in *WNC Factoring v. Czech Republic*[185] the tribunal noted that the term umbrella clause does not expand the scope of the obligation to observe an undertaking. The obligation to observe an undertaking is owed by the State that has given the undertaking and it is owed to the party to which the undertaking has been given, '[i]t is not a freely transferrable obligation, without the consent of the State that has given the undertaking (although such consent can be identified in different ways, including by way of a treaty or a contract governed by municipal law)'.[186] The requisite elements

---

178. *Azurix Corp. v. Argentina*, Award, para. 384. The tribunal rejected Azurix's claim concerning the breach of the umbrella clause and the Annulment Committee dismissed the application in its entirety.
179. *Siemens AG v. Argentina*, Award, 6 Feb. 2007, para. 204 (annulment proceeding was discontinued).
180. *CMS Gas Transmission Company v. Argentina*, Award 12 May 2005, paras 303 and 378 and Annulment Decision, paras 93–100.
181. *Burlington Resources Inc. v. Ecuador*, Decision on Liability, 14 Dec. 2012, available on investment treaty arbitration website: http://www.italaw.com/sites/default/files/case-documents/italaw1094_0.pdf.
182. *Id.*, para. 214.
183. *Id.*, para. 215.
184. *Id.*, paras 216–217.
185. *WNC Factoring Ltd v. Czech Republic*, Award, 22 Feb. 2017, available on investment treaty arbitration website: http://www.italaw.com/sites/default/files/case-documents/italaw8533.pdf.
186. *Id.*, paras 321–323.

of an undertaking to be observed under international law are a specific, clear, and direct commitment from a State to an identified beneficiary. Thus, under international law if a State owes an obligation to observe an undertaking to a company, it does not mean that the State owes the same obligation to the company's shareholders.[187]

§6.07 ASSESSMENT OF THE FOUR SCHOOLS OF THOUGHT

The four interpretations of umbrella clauses, discussed above, lead to different understandings of the relationship between municipal law and international law – on the international plane – when tribunals have to decide these claims.

The 'negative' approach adopts an extremely narrow reading of an umbrella clause, effectively rendering its presence in a treaty irrelevant. Although this school's argument that the investor's ability to render the dispute resolution clause in the underlying contract a nullity supports a tribunal's proper reluctance to treat contract claims as treaty claims, the remainder of the reasoning was clearly designed to reach a conclusion that arbitrators believed they should reach, but that could not be firmly grounded in international law.

For example, the *SGS v. Pakistan* tribunal divests the umbrella clause provision of its meaning by requiring supplemental evidence as to the clause's interpretation and disregarding the provision's plain language. This approach is inconsistent with Articles 31 and 32 of the Vienna Convention on the Law of the Treaties. Moreover, the umbrella clause does not render the rest of the BIT meaningless, contrary to the position of the *SGS v. Pakistan* tribunal. Provisions concerning expropriation and fair and equitable treatment would still be applicable. The umbrella clause would therefore protect the investor from undertakings given in circumstances different from those giving rise to a claim for expropriation or denial of fair and equitable treatment.

Still, the *SGS v. Pakistan* tribunal was not unreasonable in its concern over upholding a clause that incorporates by reference an unlimited number of State contracts as well as other municipal law instruments setting out State commitments, including unilateral commitments to an investor of the other Contracting Party. As the tribunal put it, '[a]ny alleged violation of those contracts and other instruments would be treated as a breach of the BIT'.[188] *SGS v. Pakistan*'s unwillingness to accept the elimination of all differences between a breach of contract and a breach of treaty is an unsurprising position for an international investment tribunal to take. But the fear of misapplying the umbrella clause cannot justify an interpretation that does not take the clause's wording into account. The 'negative' school of thought is not a viable international law approach and does not provide proper guidance for future investment treaty tribunals.

The 'automatic' approach is also deeply flawed, though for the opposite reason: it eliminates any distinction between contractual and treaty claims. This approach has been supported by some commentators who consider that the mere presence of an

---

187. *Id.*, para. 323.
188. *SGS v. Pakistan*, para. 168.

umbrella clause would 'transform' the contractual obligation between the State and the investor into an international obligation between the two Contracting States in order to protect the contract by sanctioning any breach of the treaty.[189] Under a similar view, the relationship between the State and the investors is simply 'doubled' by the undertakings between the State hosting the investment and the State to which the investor belongs. In effect, there are two distinct and parallel relationships: one between the parties to the contract, which is subject to the *lex contractus*; and one between the States, which is regulated by *jus gentium*. The fact that the breach of contractual obligations would constitute at the same time a breach of international law does not modify the nature of the breach.[190]

According to this reasoning, the mere presence of an umbrella clause attributes relevance under international law to any breach of State contracts. It is irrelevant if such contracts contain a jurisdictional clause, since the investor can refer any breach to the investment tribunal. The investor can 'cherry pick' among the contractual provisions, while the State is bound to the contract in its entirety. This can hardly be consistent with the object and purpose of an investment protection treaty.

The 'automatic' school's justification for eliminating of any distinction between municipal and international law is the fact that the State entered into a BIT or a multilateral investment convention containing an umbrella clause. But this justification is flawed. The 'automatic' school fails to adhere to the direction under Article 31 of the Vienna Convention to interpret a treaty's terms in their context *and in the light of its object and purpose.*

The *iure imperii* approach seems to be consistent with the 'sovereignty' perspective on the historical origins of the umbrella clause. However, the limitation of 'exercise of sovereignty' to, e.g., concession contracts or a breach constituting an act of sovereignty is not supported by any contemporaneous evidence. There is no reference in the 1967 OECD Draft or Commentaries to the umbrella clause being limited to concession contracts or to contracts entered into by the State in the exercise of its sovereignty. The reference to the term 'undertakings' in the 1967 OECD Draft and Commentaries (as well as in the 1959 Abs-Shawcross Draft) suggests coverage that is broader than concession/sovereign commitments alone.[191]

The *iure imperii* school narrows the scope of the umbrella clause *ratione materiae* and applies it only to contracts entered into or breaches committed by the State in the

---

189. Weil, 'Problèmes relatifs aux contrats passés entre un état et un particulier', *Recueil des cours* 128 (1969), III, 37, at 130. *See also* Shihata, *The World Bank in a Changing World: Selected Essays and Lectures*, vol. II (Netherlands, 1995), 601; and Schreuer, 'Travelling the BIT Route: Of Waiting Periods, Umbrella Clauses and Forks in the Roads', *J. World Inv and Trade* 5 (2004), 231. UNCTAD Series, *Bilateral Investment Treaties in the Mid-1990s* (United Nations, 1998) at 56 states that an umbrella clause 'might possibly alter the legal regime and make the agreement subject to the rules of international law'. *See* Gaillard, 'L'arbitrage sur le fondement des traits de protection des investissements', *Revue de l'Arbitrage* (2003), 868, in which umbrella clauses are defined as 'clauses with a mirror effect': i.e., clauses which reflect the contractual breach at the international level.
190. Mayer, 'La neutralisation du pouvoir normatif de l'Etat en matière de contracts d'Etat', *JDI* 1 (1986), 1, at 36–37.
191. *See* Lauterpacht, 'Drafting Conventions for the Protection of Investment', at 29.

exercise of its sovereignty.¹⁹² A tribunal following this approach could consider a commercial contract, but could only apply the umbrella clause to the use (and abuse) of governmental powers against contracts.¹⁹³ Accordingly, the tribunal would have to imply a 'balanced' reading requirement into BITs. International law does not justify this implication. Moreover, the ILC has rejected the view (as a general matter) that breaches of treaties have to involve *acta jure imperii*. There is no basis for applying the distinction to determine whether there has been a breach of treaty when the relevance of the distinction was expressly rejected in the context of attribution.

Even if one seeks to apply the criterion *acta iure imperii* versus *acta iure gestionis*, there would be many difficulties in doing so, including the characterization of the government's conduct and motives in committing the (alleged) breach (i.e., how to determine whether the intention to terminate a contract is governmental or commercial). The classification of a State's function as governmental or non-governmental is determined according to municipal law and varies according to different perspectives on what is governmental.¹⁹⁴ A State's act does not become commercial merely because it has been performed with respect to a commercial transaction, particularly one between other parties.¹⁹⁵

Pursuant to the *iure imperii* school, unless and until the breach is committed, there is no possibility of determining whether a certain breach is relevant as a breach of the umbrella clause and consequently of the investment treaty. This uncertainty as to whether measures adopted in connection with a contract are relevant under international law would leave the investors in limbo during the contract's performance or after its breach, if the circumstances surrounding the breach are unclear. Thus, there cannot be any a priori rule to interpreting umbrella clauses on the basis of the distinction between *acta iure imperii* and *acta iure gestionis*, notwithstanding the umbrella clause's wording. The PCIJ noted that in the presence of a clear text, a 'restrictive interpretation would be contrary to the plain terms of the article and would destroy what has been clearly granted'.¹⁹⁶ Finally, the *iure imperii* school disregards Article 12 of the ILC's Articles on State Responsibility, which does not accord any relevance to the characterization of the wrongful act as either governmental or commercial.¹⁹⁷

In a variation of the *iure imperii* approach, one scholar has submitted that the umbrella clause would operate as an enforcement device in the case of an ordinary contract claim: if the State had interfered in the contract, for example by subsequent

---

192. Brower, 'The Future of Foreign Investment – Recent Developments in the International Law of Expropriation and Compensation', in *Private Investors Abroad – Problems and Solutions* (Dallas, 1975), 93, at 94–97.
193. Wälde, 'The "Umbrella" Clause in Investment Arbitration: A Comment on Original Intentions and Recent Cases', *J. World Inv. and Trade* 6 (2005), 183, at 233–236.
194. *See*, with regard to the difficulties concerning the distinction between *acta iure imperii* and *acta iure gestionis* in the context of State Immunity, Crawford, 'International Law and Foreign Sovereigns: Distinguishing Immune Transactions', 75.
195. *Id.*, 101.
196. Case of *SS Wimbledon*, Judgment, 17 Aug. 1923 PCIJ, Series A, No. 1, 15 at 25.
197. Crawford, *The International Law Commission's Articles on State Responsibility*, 125; and Crawford, 'Treaty and Contract in Investment Arbitration', 356.

changes in the law that defeated a specific undertaking, the umbrella clause would provide 'an independent treaty standard pursuant to which the investor could require the host State to honour its original bargain irrespective of subsequent changes in its law'.[198] In this scenario, the umbrella clause would operate 'in that bulwark role, if and to the extent that, the alternative contractual forum could not (as a matter of applicable law) or did not, uphold the undertaking of the State regardless of any such exercises of sovereign authority'.[199] This approach considers the umbrella clause to be a stabilization clause in the event that the State exercises its sovereign authority. However, umbrella clauses and stabilization clauses are different, just as laws are different from obligations entered into by the State: 'in the absence of express stabilization, investors take the risk that the obligations of the host State under its own law may change, and the umbrella clause makes no difference to this basic proposition'.[200] Thus, neither the *iure imperii* school nor this variation offers satisfying international law formulations.

The 'enforcement' approach expressed by the *SGS v. Philippines* tribunal addressed the *SGS v. Pakistan* concern that the contractual dispute resolution mechanism would be overridden if the umbrella clause were applied. The *SGS v. Philippines* interpretation of the umbrella clause preserved the contractual dispute provision *and* maintained the distinction between contract claims and international law claims. If the State had been found liable under the contract (perhaps unlikely, given the dispute resolution method in the contract) and had repudiated its obligation to pay, the tribunal would likely have decided that the Philippines had violated the umbrella clause provision.

The Crivellaro dissent advanced the valid criticism that the tribunal majority restricted its jurisdiction to BIT claims after affirming that, in theory, the umbrella clause comprised contract claims. But the Crivellaro dissent had no persuasive response to the majority's 'performance/scope' distinction; the dissent's position meant that the umbrella clause would override contractual dispute resolution provisions, although there was no evidence that the BIT intended to override such provisions.

SGS v. Philippines explains that the umbrella clause does not transform the law applicable to the contract into international law, and that the contractual provisions remain applicable and binding between the parties to the contract (the State and the investor). The performance, not the scope, of the contract is relevant under international law: '[t]he umbrella clause is an extra mechanism for the enforcement of claims, but the basis of the transaction remains the same'.[201] Under the *SGS v. Philippines* 'enforcement' school of thought, international law and municipal law are distinct, but municipal law still plays a role that an international arbitral tribunal must recognize and take into account.

---

198. McLachlan, Shore & Weiniger, *International Investment Arbitration: Substantive Principles*, 116.
199. *Id.*, 117.
200. Crawford, 'Treaty and Contract in Investment Arbitration', 370.
201. *Ibid.*

Chapter 6: Treaty Versus Contract Claims, and Umbrella Clauses §6.08

The 'enforcement' school is consistent with the approach adopted by the second MAI formulation, discussed above: each Contracting Party shall observe any obligation 'in writing', although any 'dispute arising from such obligations shall only be settled under the terms of the contract underlying the obligation'. In particular, the MAI's 'carve out' provision, by which the dispute resolution clause of the underlying contract is adhered to by an international arbitral tribunal, supports the 'enforcement' approach. For all the above reasons, this Chapter submits that the *SGS v. Philippines* 'enforcement approach', although not entirely satisfactory, provides the most appropriate guidance for future international tribunals. Unfortunately, an entirely satisfactory approach is unlikely to emerge, given that umbrella clauses, by their terms, place international law and municipal into a relationship that does not permit either its full expression.

§6.08 CONCLUSION

Investment treaties (with the notable exception of NAFTA) often confer jurisdiction over breaches of contract if they arise from an investment.[202] This does not mean that a breach of contract automatically constitutes a violation of the investment treaty, because such a violation entails analysing whether the breach of contract is a violation of international law under the treaty's or the contract's wording, which may be governed by international law. A State may breach a treaty without breaching a State contract and may breach a State contract without breaching a treaty.

Each type of claim – breach of contract and breach of treaty – has to be determined under its own applicable law. Although it would be improper for an international investment tribunal to exercise contractual jurisdiction, unless consented to by the parties, it may be necessary for a tribunal to take into account a contract's terms in determining whether there has been a breach of a distinct standard of international law.

Municipal law usually governs a contract claim. International law determines a treaty claim. However, international law does not in principle preclude a point of municipal law, including a municipal law agreement of the parties, from being considered in determining a breach of the treaty. In the event that municipal law is deemed relevant to a treaty claim, international tribunals should examine how it has been applied by municipal courts.[203]

The 'hybrid' nature of investment treaty arbitration is often remarked upon, with the hybrid usually depicted as being the co-existence of contract and treaty claims and the difficulties in keeping the two types of claims separate. However, this depiction does not fully express another aspect of the hybrid nature: the need, in certain cases, for international investment tribunals to take municipal law into account in determining the international law content of the treaty standard.

---

202. *Id.*, 361.
203. *Case concerning the Payment in Gold of the Brazilian Federal Loans Issued in France*, 12 Jul. 1929, PCIJ, Series A, No. 15, 93 at 123–125.

§6.08

The ILC's Articles on State Responsibility place important boundaries on the application of municipal law: (a) 'the characterization of an act as internationally wrongful is governed by international law'; (b) '[s]uch characterization is not affected by the characterization of the same act as lawful by internal law';[204] and (c) the 'responsible State may not rely on the provisions of its internal law as justification for failure to comply with its obligations under this Part'.[205] These Articles are relevant in the investment treaty context, because, for the purpose of State responsibility, the relevant conduct must be attributable to the State.

To interpret umbrella clauses, it is necessary to refer to the Vienna Convention on the Law of Treaties. Article 31 of the Vienna Convention provides that a 'treaty shall be interpreted in good faith in accordance with the ordinary meaning to be given to the terms of the treaty in their context and in the light of its object and purpose'. Article 32 further provides that 'recourse may be had to supplementary means of interpretation, including the preparatory work of the treaty and the circumstances of its conclusion, in order to confirm the meaning resulting' from Article 31. The use of the term 'obligation' in an umbrella clause arguably invokes the concept of a contract rather than a legislative or administrative act as a source of commitment. On the other hand, the use of the terms 'commitments' or 'undertakings' suggest broader coverage than 'contract', and arguably comprises any administrative or legislative act as a source of undertakings.

Some commentators and arbitral tribunals have proposed that umbrella clauses were originally intended to protect investors solely in relation to contracts entered into by a State in the exercise of its sovereign powers or where a State was engaging in governmental abuse. This theory lacks evidentiary support. Reliance on the Abs-Shawcross and OECD Draft Conventions does not take into account: (a) the absence of a reference to any such limitation in those drafts; and (b) the conclusions reached by the ILC regarding the irrelevance of the distinction between *acta iure imperii* and *acta iure gestionis* in relation to breach of treaties. The historical background of umbrella clauses indicates, instead, a clear preference for broader coverage.

However, in a contract between an investor and a State, the investor must observe the contract in its entirety; the investor cannot 'cherry pick' the commitments that he believes have been breached. The contract's dispute resolution terms must be adhered to. It would be an overreach of jurisdiction for a BIT tribunal to fail to observe the underlying contract's dispute resolution terms,[206] and no historical analysis of umbrella clauses or interpretation of the object of a BIT demonstrates otherwise.

On this basis, the majority decision in *SGS v. Philippines* provides the soundest international law approach to the analysis of umbrella clauses, though such an approach inevitably curtails the jurisdictional scope of investment treaty tribunals. At least this approach, unlike others, neither disregards the wording of umbrella clauses nor eliminates the divide between treaty and contract claims.

---

204. *See* Art. 3, ILC's Articles on State Responsibility.
205. *See* Art. 32, ILC's Articles on State Responsibility.
206. The 2004 US model BIT is revealing in this regard. According to this Model BIT, the umbrella clause only covers an investment agreement *strictu sensu*.

Umbrella clauses provide for a standard of protection under international law that cannot operate without the content of municipal law, if municipal law governs the undertakings given by the State. International law must, in such cases, refer to municipal law in order to fill in the standard of protection. In the event that the undertaking is constituted by a contract with an exclusive jurisdiction clause, the investor, as well as the State, is bound by the contract in its entirety. International tribunals should, as a matter of international law, require the application of municipal law – not by the BIT tribunal itself, but by the forum indicated in the underlying contract or undertaking.

Conclusion: The Unsettled Relationship Between International and Municipal Law

In *Barcelona Traction*, the ICJ stated that 'international law is called upon to recognize institutions of municipal law that have an important and extensive role in the international field'.[1] The ICJ cautioned that this 'does not necessarily imply drawing any analogy'[2] between its own institutions and those of municipal law, 'nor does it amount to making rules of international law dependent upon categories of municipal law'.[3] Rather, it meant that, in the case of shareholders' rights, international law had to recognize 'the corporate entity as an institution created by States in a domain essentially within their domestic jurisdiction'.[4] Where international law has not established its own rules concerning the treatment and rights of companies and shareholders, 'it has to refer to the relevant rules of municipal law'.[5]

The jurisprudence on Article 6 of the ECHR provides a useful example of this *renvoi*. Article 6 guarantees the right of access to a court in relation to rights that the European Convention does not regulate. Because the Convention does not provide any particular content for such rights, the European Court cannot itself create a right to access to a court in relation to rights that have no legal basis in the Contracting States.[6] In *Masson and Van Zon v. the Netherlands*,[7] the Court held that: (i) if the Convention does not grant a right, the question whether a right exists must be answered with reference to municipal law;[8] and (ii) in deciding whether a right exists under a municipal law, the Court must consider the wording of the provisions of the relevant

---

1. *Barcelona Traction*, 33–34, para. 38.
2. *Ibid.*
3. *Ibid.*
4. *Ibid.*
5. *Ibid.*
6. *Roche v. United Kingdom*, Judgment, 19 Oct. 2005, available on the ECHR website: http://cmiskp.echr.coe.int/tkp197/view.asp?item = 1&portal = hbkm&action = html&highlight = roche%20%7C%20united%20%7C%20kingdom&sessionid = 17314843&skin = hudoc-en, para. 117.
7. *Masson and Van Zon v. Netherlands*, Judgment, 28 Sep. 1995, available on the ECHR website: http://cmiskp.echr.coe.int/tkp197/view.asp?item = 1&portal = hbkm&action = html&highlight = masson%20%7C%20van%20%7C%20zon&sessionid = 17314843&skin = hudoc-en.
8. *Id.*, para. 49, 12.

municipal law and how the national courts have interpreted them.[9] Although the provisions of the relevant municipal law are the 'starting point': the Court may nonetheless find the existence of a right recognized by municipal law that is contrary to the view held by national courts. However, it would need 'strong reasons to differ from the conclusion'[10] reached by national courts.

Under the ECHR's Article 6 approach, municipal law is relied upon to determine whether a substantive right exists, but the application of international law cannot be subordinated to the sovereign will of a State. In the investment treaty context, the same approach applies: international law regulates the standard of protection granted by a treaty, and the application of municipal law to govern the treaty's subject matter cannot affect this standard of protection. Thus, an investment tribunal will want to consider the substance of the provisions of municipal law in applying the standard of protection (the *renvoi*), but the tribunal may need to depart from the municipal law if it circumvents the international law standard (i.e., the *renvoi* is not necessarily dispositive).

International law has no code of company law, no substantive regulation of contracts or property. However, these rights may well be relevant on the international plane. What rules govern contracts, property rights, shares and shareholders' rights when they are relevant on the international plane? There are two basic alternatives: either an 'international law of contracts' (or of property rights or of shareholders' rights) must be created, as asserted by Arbitrator R.-J. Dupuy in the *Texaco* case,[11] or there must be a reference to the regime of such rights as contained in some municipal law.

The preceding chapters strongly disagree with Dupuy's approach, pursuant to which international investment tribunals have to play a quasi-legislative role, since there are no rules of international law on the substance of contracts or other private law rights. That approach would entail disregard of the fundamental difference between rights and interests: any investment arbitral tribunal would have the discretion to convert an interest, for example an economic interest, into a right. International tribunals would then have broad discretion, detached from rules of law, in deciding a dispute.

Would such discretion be too broad? Hersch Lauterpacht argued that it was absurd to conceive a change from interests to rights by a unilateral *ipse dixit*.[12] There must be a set of rules that provides the contents of these rights, and, if one follows Lauterpacht's reasoning, these rules cannot be the *ad hoc* creation of variously constituted arbitral tribunals. Lauterpacht also argued that the distinction between legal and political disputes (i.e., disputes with claims based on political, economic, or moral grounds) was endorsed in several international conventions concerning settlement of disputes,[13] which defined arbitration as the means to resolve *legal* disputes

---

9. *Ibid.*
10. *Roche v. United Kingdom*, para. 120.
11. *Texaco Overseas Petroleum Company v. Libyan Arab Republic*, 447–448.
12. Hersch Lauterpacht, *The Function of Law in the International Community* (Oxford, 1933), 357.
13. *Id.*, 353.

Conclusion: Relationship Between International and Municipal Law

while mediation was restricted to the resolution of conflicts of interests. He concluded that '[t]he judicial character of international arbitration is a matter of historical fact and of positive international law'.[14] Unless the treaty states otherwise, when the resolution of a dispute is submitted to an international arbitral tribunal, the dispute concerns a right rather than an interest.

A definition of rights under investment treaties that disregards the content of municipal law would be an *ad hoc* definition, adopted for the purpose of resolving a single dispute. In such circumstances, there will be no certainty as to the content of the subject matters of treaties.

As discussed in previous Chapters, if municipal law is to be applied, a question remains: is the reference intended to be to some generic concept of municipal law, as the ICJ majority stated in *Barcelona Traction*, or to a specific municipal law, as proposed by Judge Morelli in his separate opinion? This book has argued that approach of the *Barcelona Traction* majority does not adequately address the issue of identifying a set of rules governing the rights that are the subject matter of treaties. A universal set of rules can be as generic as the various attempts by arbitral tribunals to 'internationalize' rights of foreign investors,[15] which transforms the rights of foreign investors into vague concepts, remitted to the broad discretion of international tribunals.

Morelli's 'specific municipal law' approach is the better answer. Indeed, in *Diallo*, the ICJ looked to Congolese law, rather than a generalized system, to determine the shareholders' rights.[16] To be sure, Morelli's approach is flawed to the extent it suggests the possibility that municipal law can remit the application of international law to the sovereign will of a State, which could improperly contravene international law. Accordingly, the approach proposed in this book is to consider municipal law as the starting point of the analysis. The characterization of an act as internationally wrongful pertains to the realm of international law. If the application of municipal law affects the international characterization of the disputed act, the municipal law of the host State should be disregarded and reliance should instead be placed on the 'municipal legal system' identified by the ICJ majority in *Barcelona Traction*. Thus, the *renvoi* should not necessarily terminate with the application of the host State's municipal law, though it should not commence by looking to municipal legal systems.

I THE NECESSITY OF *RENVOI* IN THE INVESTMENT TREATY CONTEXT

Since international law instruments do not define many of the key terms and concepts in the international investment field, arbitral tribunals need to search for definitions in the relevant municipal law and, if necessary, to import rules of municipal law into an international context. The absence of a definition in international law of terms such as

---

14. *Id.*, 381.
15. *See*, e.g., *Antoine Goetz, and others v. Republic of Burundi*, Award, 10 Feb. 1999, Y.B. Com. Arb. 26 (2001): 24, 31; 'the national law of the host state is totally irrelevant or inapplicable in favour of the exclusive role played by international law'.
16. *Diallo*, Preliminary Objections, Judgment of May 24 May 2007, paras 62 and 94.

contract, property rights and shareholders' rights does not permit investment tribunals to create *ad hoc* definitions.

Similarly, the broad description of 'investment' in BITs, which has led many arbitral tribunals to adopt a broad interpretation of this concept, does not, as a matter of international law, permit these tribunals to disregard how rights are defined under municipal law. A broad treaty description of investment cannot justify a claim concerning an economic interest, such as a shareholder's claim that assets belonging to a controlled subsidiary are assets belonging to the shareholder. To ignore the concept of rights may also lead to several competing claims – by shareholders, the company, and its creditors – in connection with the same facts.

The necessity for a *renvoi* in these circumstances is clear. This book has sought to demonstrate how the framework adopted in *Barcelona Traction* on the interplay of international and municipal law should be applied in the investment treaty context. The adoption of a *renvoi* in the absence of an express definition in the investment treaty is the only approach consistent with the application of the principle of sovereignty as expressed by the PCIJ in the *Wimbledon* case. Entering into international treaties is an 'attribute of State sovereignty',[17] and in doing so a State has agreed to limit the exercise of some of its sovereign rights. However, this limitation must result from the treaty itself. If the treaty makes no reference to international law as the law governing the investment, and the parties, including the host State, previously elected a municipal law as the governing law of the investment, the subsequent invocation of an investment treaty does not transform the applicable law?

Investment treaties are intended to protect foreign investors from host State's improper behaviour, but these treaties do not stand as a substitute for the legal systems of host States. Host States have the right to regulate admission of foreign investments, and, once admitted, foreign investors must in principle comply with the host State's legislation. Investments, then, are not insulated from municipal law. This principle is reiterated in the World Bank Guidelines on the Treatment of Foreign Direct Investment,[18] which refer to 'existing and new investments established and operating at all times as bona fide private foreign investments, in full conformity with the laws and regulations of the host State',[19] and which further explain that host States have 'the right to make regulations to govern the admission of private foreign investments'.[20]

In *Barcelona Traction*, the ICJ emphasized that when a State admits foreign investors into its territory, 'it is bound to extend to them the protection of the law and assumes obligations concerning the treatment to be afforded them'.[21] The law of the host State regulates the investment. The existence of an investment treaty does not change how the host State regulates the investment, but simply provides for an overlay

---

17. Case of *SS Wimbledon*, 25.
18. A copy of these Guidelines is set out in McLachlan, Shore & Weiniger, *International Investment Arbitration: Substantive Principles*, *supra*, Appendix 13, 587–591.
19. *Id.*, S. I.2, 587.
20. *Id.*, S. II.3, 588.
21. *Barcelona Traction*, para. 32, 33.

of protection in the event of State conduct contrary to international law.[22] Investment treaties do not 'rewrite' the terms on which investments are made.[23] When a State admits foreign investments into its territory, it is bound to protect the investments under municipal law and international law. However, the host State does not become an insurer of the foreign investment.[24] Every investment of this kind carries certain risks, and these risks are relevant in the realm of international law only to the extent they are protected by investment treaties.[25] The question is whether a right has been violated, which right could only be regulated either directly by international law, if it is so defined in the investment treaty, or by international law through a *renvoi* to municipal law, with the limitations set out above.

An individual investment tribunal cannot be empowered to regulate subject matters of an investment treaty absent an express provision in the treaty. To allow an arbitral tribunal to do so without such a provision would imply that a State waived its sovereign authority to regulate foreign investment in favour of arbitral tribunals constituted on an *ad hoc* basis, with almost unbounded discretionary authority. This approach has no foundation in international law.

The principle of *renvoi* does not affect the supremacy of international law. It permits the application of concepts developed for many years at a municipal level when such application does not conflict with international law and does not affect the characterization of an act as internationally wrongful. Conflicts between international and municipal law are seldom encountered because international law does not contain substantive definitions of the subject matters of investment treaties. An example of such a conflict would be as follows: arbitrary conduct against a company may constitute an internationally wrongful act against the company's shareholders under an investment treaty if it constitutes a breach of the fair and equitable treatment standard *vis-à-vis* the shareholders. In this instance, even if the shareholders are a different entity from the company and would not have a right under municipal law, they can avail themselves of the investment treaty's protection, because one of the treaty's standards has been violated.

Some scholars have emphasized the need to consider whether an investment effectively belongs to a particular economy. They have attributed importance to the economic links between the foreign national and the investment.[26] Mere economic links, however, cannot alone suffice to trigger the protection granted by investment treaties. Although these treaties require the existence of an investment, they also require the existence of a right. The economic links are necessary, because in their absence the protection of investment treaties will not be triggered. But economic links are not sufficient; investors are entitled to treaty protection only if they have a right.

---

22. Crawford, 'Treaty and Contract in Investment Arbitration', *supra*, 374.
23. *Ibid.*
24. *Barcelona Traction*, para. 87, 47.
25. Crawford, 'Treaty and Contract in Investment Arbitration', 374.
26. *Barcelona Traction*, Gros' separate opinion, paras 9–13, 272–275.

II *RENVOI* IN THIS BOOK'S SIX CHAPTERS

To briefly summarize what I have presented in this book's chapters:

Chapter 1 discussed *renvoi* and the rules on attribution. International law remits to municipal law the classification of State organs and entities acting on behalf of the State. The framework I have proposed for the definition of State organs first requires the determination of the relevant rules to define the term 'organ' in the investment treaty. If the treaty does not provide a definition, the rules are encapsulated by the ILC Article 4 on State Responsibility, which is a codification of customary international law rules (as held by the ICJ in the *Genocide* case). 'State organ' pursuant to ILC Article 4 is a broader category under international law than municipal law, but municipal law *must* be referred to in order to determine the content of the international law category. This book relies on the definition of the roles of municipal law and international law as set out in ILC Article 4: (a) international law refers to municipal law for the definition of organ; (b) if an individual or an entity is an organ under municipal law, it is automatically an organ on the international plane; (c) if the entity or the individual or the entity is not a de jure organ, this entity or individual may still qualify as an organ on the international plane if it is shown that the entity or individual is controlled by and dependent on the State. To determine whether in such instances the entity or the individual is an organ under international law, the starting point is to consider whether the entity or individual is treated an organ under the municipal law of other States.

In relation to State entities, the text of the investment treaty must, again, first be analysed to determine if it contains any relevant rule on attribution. In the absence of a relevant rule on attribution in the text of the investment treaty, ILC Article 5 on State Responsibility sets out the exceptions to the rule of separateness between the State and State-owned entities. Under Article 5, internationally wrongful acts of a separate entity that exercises 'elements of governmental authority' are attributable to the State. The relationship between municipal law and international law is captured in the definition of 'governmental' activity: municipal law plays a role in the sense that it must authorize the entity's conduct as 'involving the exercise of public authority'. The first step, again, is to review the relevant municipal law and determine whether the activity carried out by the purported organ is a public function. The second step, in the event that the analysis of the relevant municipal law leads to a formalistic definition of public function, is to give weight to the State's history and practices in order to determine whether the activity in dispute is a de facto governmental activity.

Chapter 2 focused on the law applicable to the merits of a dispute of an ICSID treaty arbitration, i.e., the substantive law as opposed to the procedural law. In the event that the investment treaty does *not* include a provision on applicable law, the second sentence of Article 42(1) becomes relevant. It is this part of Article 42 that has been the subject of vigorous debate on the question of the centrality of municipal law and the limits, if any, to the application of international law in treaty arbitration. Aron Broches's guidance is the appropriate framework for interpreting and applying Article 42(1), when investor-state arbitral tribunals must make the crucial decision of identifying the law applicable to the merits of the dispute:

Conclusion: Relationship Between International and Municipal Law

The tribunal 'may' apply international law when:

(i) national law calls for its application;
(ii) where international law directly regulates the subject matter;
(iii) where national law or action taken under such law violates international law.

Absent the circumstances set out in points (i) through (iii) above, and absent an agreement by the Contracting Parties to apply international law, ICSID tribunals should apply municipal law to the merits of the dispute. The Broches approach may seem uncomfortably non-international to arbitrators appointed to ICSID tribunals, but it is what the ICSID Convention requires that they implement.

Chapter 3 concerned the determination of an investor's nationality. If the investor is an entity, municipal law may be relevant in assessing the threshold issue of whether the entity has a legal personality different from its participants before reaching the question of nationality. For an individual, there is no similar threshold issue; nationality is the only matter to be determined. The application of municipal law to establish the investor's nationality may raise difficulties when, for example, the links with the State of origin are tenuous. Moreover, the applicability of municipal law does not imply that international law is divested of any role; customary international law may limit a State's determination of its nationals. International conventions may also place limitations on States, although BITs and MITs usually do not elaborate upon the concept of nationality and simply identify the laws of the Contracting Parties as the applicable law in establishing the investor's nationality. International investment tribunals have the power to apply municipal law in determining the issue of nationality, and may need to determine whether consular or other municipally issued certificates were obtained through fraud or error. Tribunals are not bound by a municipal authority's determination of nationality.

Chapter 4 analysed 'investment' and protection of a property right. Investment treaties identify the category 'investment', which requires municipal law to determine whether there is an underlying right deriving from, for example, a contract or if a share or a bond has been issued. Several arbitral decisions have attempted to identify the features of an 'objective' notion of investment, independent from the existence of an underlying right. Such features are vague and difficult to apply in an analytically sound manner. Some tribunals have allegedly determined these features on the basis of municipal rules, and others have done so on the grounds of some undefined international law principles. Neither approach assists in differentiating between 'investment' and 'ordinary commercial transaction'. The framework proposed in Chapter 4 for the concept of investment is, in the absence of a detailed definition of the underlying rights in the investment treaty, a *renvoi* to municipal law in order to determine whether a valid right exists. However, international law may limit a State's determination of a valid right. For example, if a municipal law denies rights to foreign investors simply on the grounds of their nationality, arbitral tribunals must disregard the municipal law.

Although customary international law lacks of a general definition of property, States are free to define the content of property rights for the purpose of a particular treaty. International law may elect to protect certain interests that municipal law does not characterize as property rights. However, unless stated otherwise by international law, the content of these interests must be considered in accordance with municipal law. Chapter 4 also considered investment treaty tribunal decisions concerning intangibles. The approach often adopted by investment tribunals, which Chapter 4 criticizes, is to conflate an economic interest or 'legitimate expectation' and a right, in the absence of an international treaty expressly providing for such economic interests or legitimate expectation to be considered a right. A right cannot be determined in the absence of a *renvoi* to municipal law, unless international law contains a substantive definition of the right in dispute.

Chapter 5 addressed shareholders' claims and developed an argument from the principle that corporations are distinct entities from their members. This principle, accepted in many municipal legal systems as well as in customary international law, does not allow for corporate personality to be disregarded. Flowing from this is the principle that a wrong against the corporation does not constitute a wrong against its members, unless there is a treaty provision stating otherwise. However, in the investment treaty context, in addition to an express provision in the investment treaty, the corporate vehicle may be disregarded if arbitrary conduct towards a corporation is considered a breach of the fair and equitable treatment standard *vis-à-vis* the company's shareholders.

Three shareholders' rights situations were analysed. In the first, where shareholders may bring a claim in relation to their 'direct rights', the shareholder can claim that the State is using his foreign nationality to deny him his right to dividends or his right to participate in the company's management. Here, the breach of shareholders' rights may amount to an expropriation of their shares, where foreign shareholders are deprived of their use and enjoyment of their shares. In this scenario, the separation between companies and shareholders provided by municipal law and recognized by international law is maintained.

The second situation occurs when shareholders claim for loss of value of their shares in connection with violations of international law obligations towards the company. For example, the shareholder can be injured where there is a breach by the host State of the fair and equitable treatment standard *vis-à-vis* the shareholders. Such a breach renders the State's conduct internationally wrongful, even if this conduct is taken against the company. In this case, the principle of separation between shareholders and their company adopted at a municipal level must be disregarded. The framework that tribunals should follow in deciding these claims is as follows:

(a) the tribunal's jurisdiction is established if there is an investment and a *prima facie* violation of the relevant treaty;
(b) 'investment' must include shares in its definition;
(c) the injury must be to the investment, that is, the shares or the company; and
(d) the injury must be caused by an action or omission that violates an investment treaty obligation owed by the host State *vis-à-vis* the shareholder.

If this framework is adopted, the potential problem of awarding to shareholders the damages suffered by the company, and thereby circumventing creditors' rights and possibly overlooking bankruptcy issues, is resolved. Shareholders would only recover if the injury were *vis-à-vis* themselves.

There is a third situation, where shareholders claim for loss of value of their shares in connection with violations of international law obligations *vis-à-vis* the company. Shareholders may bring a claim on behalf of the company only if international law expressly allows such a claim (*see, e.g.*, NAFTA Article 1117). This type of claim constitutes a *lex specialis* scenario.

Chapter 6 considered 'treaty versus contract claims' and umbrella clauses. A State may breach a treaty without breaching a State contract, and may breach a State contract without breaching a treaty. Breach of an investment treaty must be assessed according to independent international standards. In this respect, each type of claim – breach of contract and breach of treaty – has to be determined under its own proper law. The *renvoi* would be conclusive if international law does not regulate the contract. Municipal law may also be relevant in supplying facts for applying the international standard or by incorporating the standard of compliance with municipal law into the applicable international standard.

Umbrella clauses do not provide for a 'transformation' of the law applicable to the undertakings given by the State. Umbrella clauses attribute relevance on the international plane to a breach of the State's performance of undertakings, but they do not affect the scope of such undertakings. Where a contract contains an exclusive jurisdiction clause, the investor, as well as the State, is bound by the contract in its entirety. The investor cannot 'cherry pick' the commitments that he believes have been breached. Accordingly, the contract's dispute resolution terms must be followed, and contractual disputes are to be decided pursuant to their own applicable law. Tribunals must, as a matter of international law, require the application of municipal law, with this to be performed by the forum indicated in the contract.

III THE NEED FOR TREATY ARBITRATORS TO APPLY MUNICIPAL LAW

The relationship between municipal law and international law is often tangled, but a systematic approach can nonetheless be followed. This approach must avoid the adoption of allegedly objective criteria, resting solely on international law, for deciding the content of rights relevant in the investment treaty domain. Investment treaties concern rights, the determination of which involves application of international law and municipal law. If international law does not provide a substantive definition of a right, then international law must make a *renvoi* to municipal law and its provisions concerning the existence and validity of such a right. However, such a *renvoi* cannot overrule the principle of characterization of an act as internationally wrongful and its possible determination as such under international law. This approach preserves international law's supremacy.

Many arbitral tribunals tend to ignore municipal law's role as well as the principle that an investor is entitled to protection under investment treaties only if she has a right, which must – if not defined under international law – be defined under an existing set of rules and not by rules created for the purpose of a particular dispute. The creation of rules on an ad hoc ad hoc basis does not contribute to the development of international law; it increases uncertainty and unpredictability and replaces the concept of rights with vague and undefined interests.

The history of the ICSID Convention confirms that the *renvoi* approach is the preferable solution. ICSID left host States free to establish their relationships with investors on whatever basis they deemed proper.[27] The existence of an investment agreement implied a limitation of national sovereignty, but *not* the abdication of the regulation of foreign investments. Investment treaties do not regulate the admission criteria for foreign investments or the regulation of investors' legal rights.

Investment treaties protect investors from host States' improper behaviour. The main purpose of these treaties is to 'insulate disputes from the realm of politics and diplomacy',[28] not to transform economic interests into legal obligations. The existence of an investment attracts treaty protection, but investors still must show that they have certain rights and that the host State has violated their rights under these treaties. The *renvoi* approach addresses the criticism that investment treaties are uneven, with obligations only on one side, that of the host State.[29] This approach ensures that investors are protected only and to the extent of their having carried out a *bona fide* investment that conforms to the host State's legislation.

This book has proposed a framework for applicable law in investment treaty disputes, taking into account the absence of substantive *international* law to govern these rights. A *renvoi* to municipal law is essential to give content to subject matters of investment treaties. The ILC Articles on State Responsibility remain applicable, with their significant constraints on the relevance of municipal law, pursuant to Article 3. The *renvoi* is nonetheless called for; investment treaties do not provide for a transformation of the law applicable to the subject matter of investment treaties.

---

27. History of the ICSID Convention, vol. II (1), 242.
28. *Id.*, 303.
29. Muchlinski, 'Policy Issues', *The Oxford Handbook on International Investment Law*, 3.

Appendices

Appendices

APPENDIX I
Hermann Abs and Lord Shawcross, *Draft Convention on Investments Abroad* (1959)

Hermann Abs and Lord Shawcross, *Draft Convention on Investments Abroad* (1959)[1]

Draft Convention on Investment Abroad (Abs-Shawcross Draft Convention)

The High Contracting Parties:

>believing that peace, security, and progress in the world can only be attained and ensured by fruitful co-operation between all peoples on a basis of international law and mutual confidence;
>
>appreciating also the importance of encouraging commercial relations and promoting the flow of capital for economic activity and development; and considering the contribution which may be made towards these-ends by a restatement of principles of conduct relating to foreign investments; have resolved for this purpose to conclude the present Convention.

Article I:

Each Party shall at all times ensure fair and equitable treatment to the property of the nationals of the other Parties. Such property shall be accorded the most constant protection and security within the territories shall not in any way be impaired by unreasonable or discriminatory measures.

---

1. Reproduced with the kind permission of the Emory University School of Law. Previously published as Hermann Abs & Lord Shawcross, *Draft Convention on Investment Abroad*, 9 J.Pub.L. 116 (1960).

Appendix I

Article II:

Each Party shall at all times ensure the observance of any undertakings, which it may have given in relation to investments made by nationals of any other Party.

Article III:

No Party shall take any measures against nationals of another Party to deprive them directly or indirectly of their property except under due process of law and provided that such measures are not discriminatory or contrary to undertakings given by that Party and are accompanied by the payment of just and effective compensation. Adequate provision shall have been made at or prior to the time of deprivation for the prompt determination and payment of such compensation, which shall represent the genuine value of the property affected, be made in transferable form, and be paid without undue delay.

Article IV:

Any breach of this Convention shall entail the obligation to make full reparation. The Parties shall not recognise or enforce within their territories any measures conflicting with the principles of this Convention and affecting the property of nationals of any of the Parties until reparation is made or secured.

Article V:

No Party may take measures derogating from the present Convention unless it is involved in war, hostilities, or other public emergency, which threatens its life; and such measures shall be limited in extent and duration to those strictly required by the exigencies of the situation. Nothing in this Article shall be construed as superseding the generally accepted laws of war.

Article VI:

The provisions of this Convention shall not prejudice the application of any present or future treaty or municipal law under which more favourable treatment is accorded to nationals of any of the Parties.

Article VII:

1. Any dispute as to the interpretation or application of the present Convention may, with the consent of the interested Parties, be submitted to an Arbitral Tribunal set up in accordance with the provisions of the Annex to this Convention. Such consent may take the form of specific agreements or of unilateral declarations. In the absence of such consent or of agreement for settlement by other specific means, the dispute may be submitted by either Party to the International Court of Justice.

Appendix I

2. A national of one of the Parties claiming that he has been injured by measures in breach of this Convention may institute proceedings against the Party responsible for such measures before the Arbitral Tribunal referred to in paragraph 1 of this Article, provided that the Party against which the claim is made has declared that it accepts the jurisdiction of the said Arbitral Tribunal in respect of claims by nationals of one or more Parties, including the Party concerned.

Article VIII:

If a Party against which a judgement or award is given fails to comply with the terms thereof, the other Parties shall be entitled, individually or collectively, to take such measures as are strictly required to give effect to that judgement or award.

Article IX:

For the purposes of this Convention,

a. 'nationals' in relation to a Party includes (i) companies which under the municipal law of that Party are considered national companies of that Party and (ii) companies in which nationals of that Party have directly or indirectly a controlling interest. 'Companies' includes both juridical persons recognised as such by the law of a Party and associations even if they do not possess legal personality.
b. 'property' includes all property, rights, and interests, whether held directly or indirectly. A member of a company shall be deemed to have an interest in the property of the company.

Article X:

Final clauses relating to ratification, entry into force, accession, deposit, etc.

ANNEX RELATING TO THE ARBITRAL TRIBUNAL

1. The Arbitral Tribunal referred to in Article VII of the Convention shall consist of three persons appointed as follows: one arbitrator shall be appointed by each of the parties to the arbitration proceedings; a third arbitrator (hereinafter sometimes called 'the Umpire') shall be appointed by agreement of the parties or, if they shall not agree, by the President of the International Court of Justice, or failing appointment by him, by the Secretary-General of the United Nations. If either of the parties shall fail to appoint an arbitrator, such arbitrator shall be appointed by the Umpire. In case any arbitrator appointed in accordance with this Article shall resign, die, or become unable to act, a, successor arbitrator shall be appointed in the same manner as herein prescribed for the appointment of the original arbitrator and such successor shall have all the powers and duties of such original arbitrator.

Appendix I

2. Arbitration proceedings may be instituted upon notice by the party instituting such proceedings (whether a Party to the Convention or a national of a Party to the Convention, as the case may be) to the other-party. Such notice shall contain a statement setting forth the nature of the relief sought, and the name of the arbitrator appointed by the party instituting such proceedings. Within 30 days after the giving of such notice, the adverse party shall notify the party instituting proceedings of the name of the arbitrator appointed by such adverse party.

3. If, within 60 days after the giving of such notice instituting the arbitration proceedings, the parties shall not have agreed upon an Umpire, either party may request the appointment of an Umpire as provided in, Article 1 of this Annex.

4. The Arbitral Tribunal shall convene at such time and place as shall be fixed by the Umpire. Thereafter, the Arbitral Tribunal shall determine where and when it shall sit.

5. Subject to the provisions of this Annex and except as the parties shall otherwise agree, the Arbitral Tribunal, shall decide all questions relating to its competence and, shall determine its procedure and all questions relating to costs. All decisions of the Arbitral Tribunal shall be by majority vote.

6. The Arbitral Tribunal shall afford to all parties a fair hearing and shall render its award in writing. Such award may be rendered by default. An award signed by the majority of the Arbitral Tribunal shall constitute the award of such Tribunal. A signed counterpart of the award shall be transmitted to each party. Any such award rendered in accordance with the provisions of this Annex shall be final and binding upon the parties and shall be published. Each party shall abide by and comply with any such award rendered by the Arbitral Tribunal.

APPENDIX II
Treaty Between the Federal Republic of Germany and Pakistan for the Promotion and Protection of Investments (1959)

Treaty between the Federal Republic of Germany and Pakistan for the Promotion and Protection of Investments (1959)[1]

No. 6575. TREATY[2] BETWEEN THE FEDERAL REPUBLIC OF GERMANY AND PAKISTAN FOR THE PROMOTION AND PROTECTION OF INVESTMENTS. SIGNED AT BONN, ON 25 NOVEMBER 1959

The Federal Republic of Germany and Pakistan,

Desiring to intensify economic co-operation between the two States,

Intending to create favourable conditions for investments by nationals and companies of either State in the territory of the other State, and

Recognizing that an understanding reached between the two States is likely to promote investment, encourage private industrial and financial enterprise and to increase the prosperity of both the States,

Have agreed as follows:

Article 1:

1. Each contracting State hereafter called in this Treaty a Party will endeavour to admit in its territory, in accordance with its legislation and rules and regulations framed thereunder the investing of capital by nationals or companies of the other Party and to promote such investments and will give sympathetic consideration to requests for the

---

1. Reproduced with the kind permission of the United Nations Conference on Trade and Development (UNCTAD). For the original document see < www.unctad.org/sections/dite/iia/docs/bits/germany_pakistan.pdf >.
2. Came into force on 28 April 1962, one month after the date of exchange of the instruments of ratification which took place on 28 March 1962, in accordance with article 14.

grant of necessary permissions. In the case of Pakistan such permissions shall be given with due regard also to their published plans and policies.

2. Capital investments by nationals or companies of either Party in the territory of the other Party shall not be subjected to any discriminatory treatment on the ground that ownership of or influence upon it is vested in nationals or companies of the former Party, unless legislation and rules and regulations framed thereunder existing at the time of coming into force of this Treaty provide otherwise.

Article 2:

Neither Party shall subject to discriminatory treatment any activities carried on in connection with investments including the effective management, use or enjoyment of such investments by the nationals or companies of either Party in the territory of the other Party unless specific stipulations are made in the documents of admission of an investment.

Article 3:

1. Investments by nationals or companies of either Party shall enjoy protection and security in the territory of the other Party.

2. Nationals or companies of either Party shall not be subjected to expropriation of their investments in the territory of the other Party except for public benefit against compensation, which shall represent the equivalent of the investments affected. Such compensation shall be actually realizable and freely transferable in the currency of the other Party without undue delay. Adequate provision shall be made at or prior to the time of expropriation for the determination and the grant of such compensation. The legality of any such expropriation and the amount of compensation shall be subject to review by due process of law.

3. Nationals or companies of either Party who owing to war or other armed conflict, revolution or revolt in the territory of the other Party suffer the loss of investments situate there, shall be accorded treatment no less favourable by such other Party than the treatment that Party accords to persons residing within its territory and to nationals or companies of a third party, as regards restitution, indemnification, compensation or other considerations. With respect to the transfer of such payments each Party shall accord to the requests of nationals or companies of the other Party treatment no less favourable than is accorded to comparable requests made by nationals or companies of a third party.

Article 4:

Either Party shall in respect of all investments guarantee to nationals or companies of the other Party the transfer of the invested capital, of the returns therefrom and in the event of liquidation, the proceeds of such liquidation.

Article 5:

If a claim arising out of a guarantee given for an investment is brought against a Party, the latter shall without prejudice to its rights under Article 11, be authorised, on the conditions stipulated by its predecessor in title, to exercise the rights having devolved on such Party by law or having been assigned to it by the predecessor in title (devolved interest). As regards the transfer of payments to be made by virtue of the devolved interest to the Party concerned, paragraphs (2) and (3) of Article 3 as well as Article 4 shall apply *mutatis mutandis*.

Article 6:

1. Transfers under paragraphs (2) or (3) of Article 3, under Article 4 or Article 5 shall be made without undue delay and at rates of exchange applicable to current transactions on the date the transfer is made.

2. The rate applicable to current transactions shall be based on the par value agreed with the International Monetary Fund taking into account the provisions of Section 3 of Article 4 of the Articles of Agreement establishing the International Monetary Fund.[3]

3. In case no rate of exchange within the meaning of paragraph (2) above exists at the time of transfer the appropriate authorities of the Party in the territory of which the investment is situated shall admit a rate of exchange which is just and reasonable.

Article 7:

If the legislation of either Party or international obligations existing at present or established hereafter between the Parties in addition to the present Treaty, result in a position entitling investments by nationals or companies of the other Party to treatment more favourable than is provided for by the present Treaty, such position shall not be affected by the present Treaty. Either Party shall observe any other obligation it may have entered into with regard to investments by nationals or companies of the other Party.

Article 8:

1. *(a)* The term 'investment' shall comprise capital brought into the territory of the other Party for investment in various forms in the shape of assets such as foreign exchange, goods, property rights, patents and technical knowledge. The term 'investment' shall also include the returns derived from and ploughed back into such 'investment'.

---

3. United Nations, *Treaty Series*, Vol. 2, p. 40; Vol. 19, p. 280; Vol. 141, p. 355; Vol. 199, p. 308; Vol. 260, p. 432; Vol. 287, p. 260; Vol. 303, p. 284; Vol. 316, p. 269; Vol. 406, p. 282, and Vol. 426, p. 334.

Appendix II

(b) Any partnerships, companies or assets of similar kind, created by the utilisation of the above mentioned assets shall be regarded as 'investment'.

2. The term 'return' shall mean the amounts derived from investments as profits or interest for a specified period.

3. The term 'nationals' shall mean

   aa) in respect of the Federal Republic of Germany, Germans within the meaning of the Basic Law for the Federal Republic of Germany;
   ba) in respect of Pakistan, a person who is a citizen of Pakistan according to its laws.

4. The term 'companies' shall comprise

   aa) in respect of the Federal Republic of Germany, any juridical person, any commercial company or any other company or association, with or without legal personality, having its seat in the territory of the Federal Republic of Germany and lawfully existing in accordance with its legislation, irrespective of whether the liability of its partners, associates or members is limited or unlimited and whether or not its activities are directed to pecuniary gain;
   ba) in respect to Pakistan, any juridical person or any company or association, incorporated in the territory of Pakistan and lawfully existing in accordance with its legislation.

Article 9:

The present Treaty shall also apply to approved investments made prior to its entry into force but not earlier than 1st September, 1954, by nationals or companies of either Party in the territory of the other Party unless in any case it is specifically provided otherwise. This provision shall not affect the Agreement of 27th February 1953, on German External Debts.[4]

Article 10:

Each Party shall co-operate with the other in furthering the interchange and use of scientific and technical knowledge and development of training facilities particularly in the interest of increasing productivity and improving standards of living in their territories.

---

4. United Nations, *Treaty Series*, Vol. 333, p. 3 and Vol. 437, p. 367.

Appendix II

Article 11:

1. In the event of disputes as to the interpretation or application of the present Treaty, the Parties shall enter into consultation for the purpose of finding a solution in a spirit of friendship.

2. If no such solution is forthcoming, the dispute shall be submitted

   aa) to the International Court of Justice if both Parties so agree or
   ba) if they do not so agree to an arbitration tribunal upon the request of either Party.

3. *(a)* The tribunal referred to in paragraph (2) *(b)* above shall be formed in respect of each specific case and it shall consist of three arbitrators. Each Party shall appoint one arbitrator and the two members so appointed shall appoint a chairman who shall be a national of a third country.

   (b) Each Party shall appoint its arbitrator within two months after a request to this effect has been made by either Party. If either Party fails to comply with this obligation the arbitrator shall be appointed upon the request of the other Party by the President of the International Court of Justice.

   (c) If within one month from the date of their appointment the arbitrators are unable to agree on the chairman of the arbitration tribunal such chairman shall upon the request of either Party be appointed by the President of the International Court of Justice.

   (d) If the President of the International Court of Justice is prevented from acting upon a request under sub-paragraph *(b)* or sub-paragraph *(c)* of the present paragraph or if the President is a national of either Party the Vice-President shall make the appointment. If the Vice-President is prevented or if he is a national of either Party the appointment shall be made by the seniormost member of the International Court of Justice who is not a national of either Party.

   (e) Unless the Parties otherwise decide, the arbitration tribunal shall determine its own rules of procedure.

   (f) The arbitration tribunal shall take its decisions by a majority of votes. Such decisions shall be binding upon the Parties and shall be carried out by them.

Article 12:

The provisions of the present Treaty shall remain in force also in the event of a conflict arising between the Parties without prejudice to the right of taking such temporary measures as are permitted under international law and are indispensable for assuring a supervision of investments. Measures of this kind shall be repealed not later than the

Appendix II

date of termination of the conflict, irrespective of whether or not diplomatic relations have been re-established.

Article 13:

The present Treaty shall also apply to *Land* Berlin, provided that the Government of the Federal Republic of Germany has not made a contrary declaration to the Government of Pakistan within three months from the entry into force of the present Treaty.

Article 14:

1. The present Treaty shall be ratified and the instruments of ratification shall be exchanged as soon as possible.

2. The present Treaty shall enter into force one month after the date of exchange of the instruments of ratification. It shall remain in force for a period of ten years and shall continue in force thereafter for an unlimited period unless notice of termination is given in writing by either Party one year before its expiry. After the expiry of the period of ten years, the present Treaty may be terminated at any time by either Party giving one year's notice.

3. In respect of investments made prior to the date of expiry of the present Treaty, the provisions of Articles 1 to 13 shall continue to be effective for a further period of ten years from the date of expiry of the present Treaty.

Done at Bonn on the twenty fifth day of November in the year nineteen hundred and fifty nine in duplicate, in the German and English languages, both texts being equally authentic.

For the Federal Republic of Germany:
von Brentano
For Pakistan:
S. A. Hasnie

PROTOCOL

On signing the Treaty for the Promotion and Protection of Investments concluded between the Federal Republic of Germany and Pakistan,[5] the undersigned plenipotentiaries have, in addition, agreed to the following provisions which should be regarded as an integral part of the said Treaty:

> 1. The Parties shall within one year after signing this Treaty enter into negotiations to conclude an establishment treaty which shall, *inter alia*, make provision for the following:

---

5. See p. 24 of this volume.

Immigration and emigration, temporary and permanent residence, protection from expulsion, taking up and carrying on business and professional activities on a basis of employment or self-employment, particularly in respect of managerial and technical staff, foundation of and participation in enterprises, protection and security of persons and property, free access to courts, freedom to contract, acquisition of real estate and other property and admission as arbitrator.

2. The following shall in particular be deemed discrimination referred to in Article 2:

    Restricting the purchase of raw or auxiliary materials, of power or fuel, or of means of production or operation of any kind, impeding the marketing of products within or outside the country, as well as any other measures not applied to the same extent either to persons residing within the country and to nationals of third states or to investments of such persons.

    Measures taken for reasons of public security and order, public health or morality shall not be deemed as discrimination within the meaning of Article 2.

3. The term "expropriation" within the meaning of paragraph (2) of Article 3 shall also pertain to acts of sovereign power which are tantamount to expropriation, as well as measures of nationalization.

4. With a view to ensuring an equitable share of cargo to their respective shipping either Party shall abstain from any discriminatory measures which, contrary to the principles of free competition are designed to eliminate or impair the participation of ships of the other Party in transporting the following goods:

    aa) goods which represent an investment and are transported by sea-going vessels,

    ba) goods which for the purpose of operating an enterprise in the territory of one Party are purchased by means of capital invested in the territory of that Party by nationals or companies of the other Party.

5. Without prejudice to any other method of determining nationality, any person shall be deemed to be a national of a Party who is in possession of a national passport issued by the appropriate authority of the Party concerned or of a valid identity document of one of the following types:

    aa) In respect of the Federal Republic of Germany, a valid identity card (*Personaiaus-weis*) of the Federal Republic of Germany or a valid identity card (*Personalausweis*) of Land Berlin or a seaman book (*Seefahrtbuch*) issued by an appropriate authority of the Federal Republic of Germany provided that the bearer of the seaman book is entered therein as a German;

    ba) In respect of Pakistan, the documents for determining the nationality of Pakistanis in Germany at a particular time may in addition to the national passports be (1) Crew Member Certificates in respect of airmen, and (2) Continuous Discharge Certificates or Nullies in respect of seamen.

Appendix II

Done at Bonn on the twenty fifth day of November in the year nineteen hundred and fifty nine in duplicate, in the German and English languages, both texts being equally authentic.
For the Federal Republic of Germany:
von Brentano
For Pakistan:
S. A. Hasnie

EXCHANGE OF NOTES

I

Bonn, 25 November 1959
MINISTRY OF FINANCE GOVERNMENT OF PAKISTAN
Excellency,
It is our understanding that the term 'investment' wherever it is used in this Treaty[6] or in the letters annexed refers in respect of Pakistan to investments approved by the Government agencies authorizing such investments. If at any time later free investment is allowed in Pakistan the term 'investment' will cover all investments made in the territory of Pakistan.
The same term refers in respect of the Federal Republic of Germany to all investments made in accordance with its legislation.
It is also our understanding that for the purpose of admission of capital investments the value of the assets mentioned in paragraph (1) of Article 8 may be determined by the appropriate agencies of the Party concerned.
I shall be grateful if you would kindly confirm the above understanding. Accept, Excellency, the assurance of my highest consideration.
S. A. Hasnie
Secretary
His Excellency Dr. Heinrich von Brentano
Federal Minister for Foreign Affairs
Bonn

II

[German text – Texte Allemand]
der bundesminister des auswärtigen
Bonn, den 25. November 1959
Herr Staatssekretär,
Ich beehre mich, den Empfang Ihres Schreibens vom 25. November 1959 zu bestätigen, das folgenden Wortlaut hat:

---

6. See p. 24 of this volume.

Appendix II

"Zwischen uns besteht Einverständnis darüber, daß der Ausdruck 'Kapitalanlagen' in diesem Vertrag und den ihm beigefügten Schreiben sich hinsichtlich Pakistans auf Kapitalanlagen bezieht, die von den dafür zuständigen Regierungsstellen genehmigt worden sind. Falls zu einem späteren Zeitpunkt die freie Anlage von Kapital in Pakistan gestattet wird, umfaßt dann der genannte Ausdruck alle im Hoheitsgebiet Pakistans vorgenommenen Kapitalanlagen.
Der genannte Ausdruck bezieht sich hinsichtlich der Bundesrepublik Deutschland auf alle Kapitalanlagen, die im Rahmen ihrer Rechtsvorschriften vorgenommen werden.
Wir sind uns ferner darüber einig, daß für den Zweck der Zulassung der Kapitalanlage der Wert der in Artikel 8 Absatz (1) erwähnten Vermögenswerte von den zuständigen Stellen der betreffenden Partei festgesetzt werden kann.
Ich wäre Ihnen dankbar, wenn Sie dieses Einverständnis bestätigen würden."
Ich bestätige, daß dies unserem Einverständnis in dieser Angelegenheit entspricht.
Genehmigen Sie, Herr Staatssekretär, die Versicherung meiner ausgezeichnetsten Hochachtung.
von Brentano
An den Staatssekretär im Finanzministerium
der Regierung von Pakistan
Herrn S. A. Hasnie
z. Z. Bonn
[Translation – Traduction]
federal minister for foreign affairs
Bonn, 25 November 1959
Sir,
I have the honour to acknowledge receipt of your note of 25 November 1959 reading as follows:
[See note I]
I confirm that this agrees with our understanding in this matter.
I have the honour to be, etc.
von Brentano
Mr. S. A. Hasnie
Secretary, Ministry of Finance
Government of Pakistan
Bonn

III

Bonn, 25 November 1959
ministry of finance
government of pakistan
Excellency,
During our discussion on the type and nature of treatment to be accorded by either Party to the nationals and companies of the other Party we realised that it would be neither desirable nor practicable to comprehend in this Treaty the extent and scope of

Appendix II

favours and immunities which may be granted by either Party to the investments of nationals or companies of the other Party in specific cases. It was therefore agreed that without prejudice to the provisions of this Treaty any concessions that are granted by either Party to the nationals or companies of the other Party shall be governed by the documents of admission, namely the Memoranda or the Articles of Association established for the creation and operation of a particular enterprise or such other instruments as either Party may choose keeping in view the requirements of each case. In admittng investments by nationals or companies of the other Party each Party may in the documents of admission mentioned above impose conditions regarding the administration, use or enjoyment of an investment or regarding the operation of an enterprise based on such investment or regarding the training and employment of nationals of the Party concerned.

The favours and immunities mentioned in the first paragraph above and the conditions mentioned in the second paragraph above may fall outside the scope of national or most-favoured-nation treatment.

I shall be grateful if you would kindly confirm the above understanding.

Accept, Excellency, the assurance of my highest consideration.

S. A. Hasnie
Secretary
His Excellency Dr. Heinrich von Brentano
Federal Minister for Foreign Affairs
Bonn

[Translation – Traduction]

federal minister for foreign affairs
Bonn, 25 November 1959

Sir,

I have the honour to acknowledge receipt of your note of 25 November 1959 reading as follows:

[See note III]

I confirm that this agrees with our understanding in this matter.

I have the honour to be, etc.

von Brentano
Mr. S. A. Hasnie
Secretary, Ministry of Finance
Government of Pakistan
Bonn

V

Bonn, 25 November 1959
ministry of finance
government of pakistan

Excellency,

It is our understanding that, intending to facilitate and promote investments by German nationals or companies in Pakistan, the Government of Pakistan will, prior to the entry into force of an establishment treaty the negotiation of which has been provided for, grant necessary permits to German nationals who desire to enter, stay and carry on activities in Pakistan in connection with investments by German nationals or companies except in so far as reasons of public security and order, public health or morality may warrant otherwise.

The appropriate Government agencies of the Federal Republic of Germany will endeavour to persuade German nationals or companies to provide progressive employment and training facilities for Pakistan nationals.

I shall be grateful if you would kindly confirm the above understanding.

Accept, Excellency, the assurance of my highest consideration.

S. A. Hasnie
Secretary
His Excellency Dr. Heinrich von Brentano
Federal Minister for Foreign Affairs
Bonn

VI

[German text – Texte allemand]
der bundesminister des auswärtigen
Bonn, den 25. November 1959
Herr Staatssekretar,
Ich beehre mich, den Empfang Ihres Schreibens vom 25. November 1959 zu bestätigen, das folgenden Wortlaut hat:
"Zwischen uns besteht Einverständnis darüber, daß die Regierung von Pakistan in der Absicht, Kapitalanlagen deutscher Staatsangehöriger oder Gesellschaften in Pakistan zu erleichtern und zu fördern, bereits vor dem Inkraft-treten eines Niederlassungsvertrags, über dessen Abschluß Verhandlungen vor-gesehen sind, deutschen Staatsangehörigen, die im Zusammenhang mit Kapitalanlagen deutscher Staatsangehöriger oder Gesellschaften nach Pakistan einreisen, sich dort aufhalten und dort tätig werden wollen, die erforderlichen Erlaubnisse erteilt, soweit nicht Gründe der öffentlichen Sicherheit und Ordnung, der Volksgesundheit oder Sittlichkeit entgegenstehen.

Die zuständigen Regierungsstellen der Bundesrepublik Deutschland werden sich bemühen, deutschen Staatsangehörigen und Gesellschaften nahezulegen, für pakistanische Staatsangehörige in fortschreitendem Maße Arbeitsplätze und Ausbildungsmöglichkeiten zu schaffen.

Ich wäre Ihnen dankbar, wenn Sie dieses Einverständnis bestatigen würden." Ich bestätige, daß dies unserem Einverständnis in dieser Angelegenheit entspricht.

Genehmigen Sie, Herr Staatssekretär, die Versicherung meiner ausgezeichnetsten Hochachtung.

von Brentano
An den Staatssekretär im Finanzministerium

Appendix II

der Regierung von Pakistan
Herrn S.A. Hasnie
z. Z. Bonn
[Translation – Traduction]
federal minister for foreign affairs
Bonn, 25 November 1959
Sir,
I have the honour to acknowledge receipt of your note of 25 November 1959 reading as follows:
[See note V]
I confirm that this agrees with our understanding in this matter.
I have the honour to be, etc.
von Brentano
Mr. S. A. Hasnie
Secretary, Ministry of Finance
Government of Pakistan
Bonn

APPENDIX III

Harvard Draft Convention on the International Responsibility of States for Injuries to Aliens (1961)

Harvard Draft Convention on the International Responsibility of States for Injuries to Aliens (1961)[1]
Draft Convention on the International Responsibility of States for Injuries to Aliens

SECTION A GENERAL PRINCIPLES AND SCOPE

Article 1: (Basic Principles of State Responsibility)

1. A State is internationally responsible for an act or omission which, under international law, is wrongful, is attributable to that State, and causes an injury to an alien. A State which is responsible for such an act or omission has a duty to make reparation therefor to the injured alien or an alien claiming through him, or to the State entitled to present a claim on behalf of the individual claimant.

2. (a) An alien is entitled to present an international claim under this Convention only after he has exhausted the local remedies provided by the State against which the claim is made.

    (b) A State is entitled to present a claim under this Convention only on behalf of a person who is its national, and only if the local remedies and any special

---

1. Reproduced with the kind permission of the *American Journal of International Law*. Previously published as 'Draft Convention on International Responsibility of States for Injuries to Aliens', in Louis B. Sohn & R.R. Baxter, 'Responsibility of States for Injuries to the Economic Interests of Aliens', *American Journal of International Law* 55 (1961): 545–551.

Appendix III

international remedies provided by the State against which the claim is made have been exhausted.

Article 2: (Primacy of International Law)

1. The responsibility of a State under Article 1 is to be determined according to this Convention and international law, by application of the sources and subsidiary means set forth in paragraph 1 of Article 38 of the Statute of the International Court of Justice.

2. A State cannot avoid international responsibility by invoking its municipal law.

3. Nothing in this Convention shall adversely affect any right which an alien enjoys under the municipal law of the State against which the claim is made if that law is more favorable to him than this Convention.

SECTION B WRONGFUL ACTS AND OMISSIONS

Article 3: (Categories of Wrongful Acts and Omissions)

1. An act or omission which is attributable to a State and causes an injury to an alien is 'wrongful,' as the term is used in this Convention:

   (a) if, without sufficient justification, it is intended to cause, or to facilitate the causing of, injury;
   (b) if, without sufficient justification, it creates an unreasonable risk of injury through a failure to exercise due care;
   (c) if it is an act or omission defined in Articles 5 to 12; or
   (d) if it violates a treaty.

2. The wrongfulness of such an act or omission may be the result of the fact that the law of the State does not conform to international standards or of the fact that the law, although conforming to international standards, has been misapplied.

Article 4: (Sufficiency of Justification)

1. The imposition of punishment for the commission of a crime for which such punishment has been provided by law is a 'sufficient justification' within the meaning of sub-paragraph 1(a) of Article 3, except when the decision imposing the punishment is wrongful under Article 8.

2. The actual necessity of maintaining public order, health, or morality in accordance with laws enacted for that purpose is a 'sufficient justification' within the meaning of sub-paragraphs 1(a) and 1(b) of Article 3, except when the measures taken against the injured alien clearly depart from the law of the respondent State or unreasonably depart

from the principles of justice or the principles governing the action of the authorities of the State in the maintenance of public order, health, or morality recognized by the principal legal systems of the world.

3. The valid exercise of belligerent or neutral rights or duties under international law is a 'sufficient justification' within the meaning of sub-paragraphs 1(a) and 1(b) of Article 3.

4. The contributory fault of the injured alien, or his voluntary participation in activities involving an unreasonable risk of injury, to the extent that such fault or voluntary participation bars the claim of a person under both the law of the respondent State and the principles recognized by the principal legal systems of the world, is a 'sufficient justification' within the meaning of sub-paragraph 1(b) of Article 3.

5. In circumstances other than those enumerated in paragraphs 1 to 4 of this Article, 'sufficient justification' within the meaning of sub-paragraphs 1(a) and 1(b) of Article 3 exists only when the particular circumstances are recognized by the principal legal systems of the world as constituting such justification.

Article 5: (Arrest and Detention)

1. The arrest or detention of an alien is wrongful:

   (a) if it is a clear and discriminatory violation of the law of the arresting or detaining State;
   (b) if the cause or manner of the arrest or detention unreasonably departs from the principles recognized by the principal legal systems of the world;
   (c) if the State does not have jurisdiction over the alien; or
   (d) if the arrest or detention otherwise involves a violation by the State of a treaty.

2. The detention of an alien becomes wrongful after the State has failed:

   (a) to inform him promptly of the cause of his arrest or detention, or to inform him within a reasonable time after his arrest or detention of the specific charges against him;
   (b) to grant him prompt access to a tribunal empowered both to determine whether his arrest or detention is lawful and to order his release if the arrest or detention is determined to be unlawful;
   (c) to grant him a prompt trial; or
   (d) to ensure that his trial and any appellate proceedings are not unduly prolonged.

3. The mistreatment of an alien during his detention is wrongful.

Article 6: (Denial of Access to a Tribunal or an Administrative Authority)

The denial to an alien of the right to initiate, or to participate in, proceedings in a tribunal or an administrative authority to determine his civil rights or obligations is wrongful:

(a) if it is a clear and discriminatory violation of the law of the State denying such access;
(b) if it unreasonably departs from those rules of access to tribunals or administrative authorities which are recognized by the principal legal systems of the world; or
(c) if it otherwise involves a violation by the State of a treaty.

Article 7: (Denial of a Fair Hearing)

The denial to an alien by a tribunal or an administrative authority of a fair hearing in a proceeding involving the determination of his civil rights or obligations or of any criminal charges against him is wrongful if a decision or judgment is rendered against him or he is accorded an inadequate recovery. In determining the fairness of any hearing, it is relevant to consider whether it was held before an independent tribunal and whether the alien was denied:

(a) specific information in advance of the hearing of any claim or charge against him;
(b) adequate time to prepare his case;
(c) full opportunity to know the substance and source of any evidence against him and to contest its validity;
(d) full opportunity to have compulsory process for obtaining witnesses and evidence;
(e) full opportunity to have legal representation of his own choice;
(f) free or assisted legal representation on the same basis as nationals of the State concerned or on the basis recognized by the principal legal systems of the world, whichever standard is higher;
(g) the services of a competent interpreter during the proceedings if he cannot fully understand or speak the language used in the tribunal;
(h) full opportunity to communicate with a representative of the government of the State entitled to extend its diplomatic protection to him;
(i) full opportunity to have such a representative present at any judicial or administrative proceeding in accordance with the rules of procedure of the tribunal or administrative agency;
(j) disposition of his case with reasonable dispatch at all stages of the proceedings; or
(k) any other procedural right conferred by a treaty or recognized by the principal legal systems of the world.

Article 8: (Adverse Decisions and Judgments)

A decision or judgment of a tribunal or an administrative authority rendered in a proceeding involving the determination of the civil rights or obligations of an alien or of any criminal charges against him, and either denying him recovery in whole or in part or granting recovery against him or imposing a penalty, whether civil or criminal, upon him is wrongful:

   (a) if it is a clear and discriminatory violation of the law of the State concerned;
   (b) if it unreasonably departs from the principles of justice recognized by the principal legal systems of the world; or
   (c) if it otherwise involves a violation by the State of a treaty.

Article 9: (Destruction of and Damage to Property)

1. Deliberate destruction of or damage to the properly of an alien is wrongful, unless it was required by circumstances of urgent necessity not reasonably admitting of any other course of action.

2. A destruction of the property of an alien resulting from the judgment of a competent tribunal or from the action of the competent authorities of the State in the maintenance of public order, health, or morality shall not be considered wrongful, provided there has not been:

   (a) a clear and discriminatory violation of the law of the State concerned;
   (b) a violation of any provision of Articles 6 to 8 of this Convention;
   (c) an unreasonable departure from the principles of justice recognized by the principal legal systems of the world; or
   (d) an abuse of the powers specified in this paragraph for the purpose of depriving an alien of his property.

APPENDIX IV

Organisation for Economic Co-operation and Development Draft Convention on the Protection of Foreign Property (1967)

Organisation for Economic Co-operation and Development Draft Convention on the Protection of Foreign Property (1967)[1]
On 12th October, 1967, the Council of the Organisation for Economic Co-operation and Development adopted a Resolution on the Draft Convention on the Protection of Foreign Property, which was drawn up by one of the Committees of the Organisation.
The text of that Resolution is reproduced hereafter.
RESOLUTION OF THE COUNCIL
ON THE DRAFT CONVENTION ON THE PROTECTION OF FOREIGN PROPERTY
(Adopted by the Council at its 150th meeting, on 12th October, 1967)[2]
The Council
HAVING REGARD to the provisions of the Convention on the Organisation for Economic Co-operation and Development concerning economic expansion and assistance to developing countries;
HAVING REGARD to the Reports by the Committee for Invisible Transactions and the Comments by the Payments Committee on the Draft Convention on the Protection of Foreign Property;
HAVING REGARD to the text of the Draft Convention on the Protection of Foreign Property and to the Notes and Comments constituting its interpretation (hereinafter called the 'Draft Convention');
OBSERVING that the Draft Convention embodies recognised principles relating to the protection of foreign property, combined with rules to render more effective the application of these principles;

---

1. Reproduced with the kind permission of the Organisation for Economic Co-operation and Development (OECD). For the original document see 7 ILM 117 (1968).
2. The Delegates for Spain and Turkey abstained.

CONSIDERING that a clear statement of these principles will be a valuable contribution towards the strengthening of international economic co-operation on the basis of international law and mutual confidence;

CONSIDERING that a wider application of these principles in domestic legislation and in international agreements would encourage foreign investments;

BELIEVING that the Draft Convention will be a useful document in the preparation of agreements on the protection of foreign property;

NOTING the conclusion of a Convention on the Settlement of Investment Disputes between States and Nationals of Other States;

> I. REAFFIRMS the adherence of Member States to the principles of international law embodied in the Draft Convention;
> II. COMMENDS the Draft Convention as a basis for further extending and rendering more effective the application of these principles;
> III. APPROVES the publication of the Draft Convention as well as this Resolution.

DRAFT CONVENTION *ON THE* PROTECTION OF FOREIGN PROPERTY
Text with Notes and Comments
PREAMBLE
DESIROUS of strengthening international economic cooperation on a basis of international law and mutual confidence;

RECOGNISING the importance of promoting the flow of capital for economic activity and development;

CONSIDERING the contribution which will be made towards this end by a clear statement of recognised principles relating to the protection of foreign property, combined with rules designed to render more effective the application of these principles within the territories of the Parties to this Convention; and

DESIROUS that other States will join them in this endeavour by acceding to this Convention;

The STATES signatory to this Convention HAVE AGREED as follows:

Article 1: Treatment of Foreign Property

> (a) Each Party shall at all times ensure fair and equitable treatment to the property of the nationals of the other Parties. It shall accord within its territory the most constant protection and security to such property and shall not in any way impair the management, maintenance, use, enjoyment or disposal thereof by unreasonable or discriminatory measures. The fact that certain nationals of any State are accorded treatment more favourable than that provided for in this Convention shall not be regarded as discriminatory against nationals of a Party by reason only of the fact that such treatment is not accorded to the latter.
> (b) The provisions of this Convention shall not affect the right of any Party to allow or prohibit the acquisition of property or the investment of capital within its territory by nationals of another Party.

Appendix IV

NOTES AND COMMENTS TO ARTICLE 1

Paragraph (a) General Standard of Treatment of Foreign Property

1. The Obligations

It is a well-established general principle of international law that a State is bound to respect and protect the property of nationals of other States. From this basic principle flow the three rules contained in paragraph (a) of Article 1 – that is to say, that, as towards the other Parties to the Convention, each Party must assure to the property of its nationals which comes within its jurisdiction (A) fair and equitable treatment; (B) most constant protection and security; and (C) that each Party must ensure that the exercise of rights relating to such property and mentioned in paragraph (a) shall not be impaired by unreasonable or discriminatory measures. Each of these rules is discussed in turn in Notes 4 to 8. That, however, Article 1 (or, for that matter, the other provisions of the Convention) does not provide a right for a national of one Party to acquire property in the territories of other Parties, nor for their duty to admit his property or investments, is expressly stated in paragraph (b) of Article 1 (see Note 9 below).

2. Object of Protection: Property

   (a) In international law the rules contained in the Convention – and therefore in Article 1 – apply to property in the widest sense of the term which includes, but is not limited to, investments. For a definition of 'property' see Article 9 (c) of the Convention and the Notes thereto.
   (b) Within the jurisdiction of a Party, the provisions of the Convention apply to all property of nationals of the other Parties irrespective of whether it was acquired before or after the date on which the Convention has come into force as regards the Party concerned. However, legislative or administrative measures taken by that Party before that date and relating to such property are not covered by the Convention as such [see Article 12 (c)]. Generally, to come within the provisions of the Convention, the property must be lawfully acquired or invested by the foreign national or his predecessor in title.

3. Nationals

The duty of a State to respect the property of alien nationals is owed, in the first instance, not to the alien concerned, but to his State; it is only on behalf of its own nationals that the State may claim from other States compliance with that duty. This right is necessarily so limited because – in the words of the Permanent Court of International Justice[3] – 'it is the bond of nationality between the State and the individual which alone confers upon the State the right to diplomatic protection' [see

---

3. The Panevezys-Saldutiskis Railway Case, quoted in Edvard Hambro, The Case Law of the International Court, Vol. I, (hereinafter referred to as 'Hambro I') No. 348, p. 289.

Appendix IV

also on the concept of nationality in relation to diplomatic protection Article 9(a) and Note 1 to that Article]. And, again, as that Court said in another case[4] : 'By taking up the case of one of its subjects and by resorting to diplomatic action or international judicial proceedings on its behalf, a State is in reality asserting its own rights – its right to ensure, in the person of its subjects, respect for the rules of international law'. The bond of nationality becomes apparent not only in the person of the national who is abroad, but also in his property within the jurisdiction of another State while he himself may remain within his own country.

First Rule Fair and Equitable Treatment

4. (a) The phrase 'fair and equitable treatment', customary in relevant bilateral agreements, indicates the standard set by international law for the treatment due by each State with regard to the property of foreign nationals. The standard requires that – subject to essential security interests [see Article 6 (i)] – protection afforded under the Convention shall be that generally accorded by the Party concerned to its own nationals, but, being set by international law, the standard may be more exacting where rules of national law or national administrative practices fall short of the requirements of international law. The standard required conforms in effect to the 'minimum standard' which forms part of customary international law.

> (b) Each Party must not only grant, but 'ensure', fair and equitable treatment of the property of nationals of the other Parties. It will, of course, incur responsibility for any acts or omissions which may be properly attributed to it under customary international law (see Article 5).

Second Rule Most Constant Protection and Security

5. 'Most constant protection and security' must be accorded in the territory of each Party to the property of nationals of the other Parties. Couched in language traditionally used in the United States Bilateral Treaties,[5] the rule indicates the obligation of each Party to exercise due diligence as regards actions by public authorities as well as others in relation to such property.

Third rule Exclusion of Unreasonable and Discriminatory Measures

6. General

> (a) In addition to the obligations examined in Notes 4 and 5, Article 1 provides that 'management, maintenance, use, enjoyment or disposal' of property of

---

4. Mavrommatis Case, quoted in Hambro I, No. 347, p. 239.
5. See, for instance, United States-German Treaty, Article V (1); United States-Nicaraguan Treaty, Article VI (1); and also United Kingdom-Iranian Treaty, Article 8 (1).

nationals of other Parties shall not 'in any way' be impaired by unreasonable or discriminatory measures.[6] 'Maintenance' is probably implicit in the concept of 'management' and, moreover, as a precondition, in 'use' and 'enjoyment'. The term is added for the sake of clarity. It is more doubtful whether 'disposal' is implicit in these notions. Yet knowledge alone of measures taken that prevent or limit the 'disposal' of the property reduces its value and interferes with its 'enjoyment'. The term indicates therefore with greater precision the limits to which, under the Convention, the exercise of rights arising out of property is protected. It cannot, on the other hand, be assumed that the right to 'enjoyment' of property implies for the Party concerned the obligation to permit automatically transfers in connection with that property.

(b) Exercise of the rights quoted in the preceding paragraph shall not in any way be 'impaired' by unreasonable or discriminatory measures. This means that a breach of the obligation is established if it can be shown that a certain measure:

　(i) is 'unreasonable' or 'discriminatory' – for an analysis of these terms see Notes 7 and 8 below;
　(ii) may be attributed to the Party against whom complaint is made – see Article 5; and that it
　(iii) impairs the exercise of any of the rights quoted. Thus it is insufficient to prove – as in the case of 'fair and equitable treatment' (see Note 4) – that the measure complained of is contrary to a standard set by international law; it must also be established that, as its consequence, actual possibilities for the exercise of the right in question are reduced.

7. Unreasonable Measures

(a) A breach of obligations by a Party is established if it can be shown that the exercise of any right referred to in Article 1 is impaired by an 'unreasonable' measure that may be attributed to that Party (see Article 5).

(b) The measure in issue may have been taken by or on behalf of the Party concerned in the exercise of its sovereign powers. The fact that it has thus been taken will undoubtedly carry weight in the determination of the question whether it is lawful. However, though the power by virtue of which the measure is taken may not be contested, the latter may be unlawful in view of the manner or circumstances in which the power has been exercised. In many cases such a measure will also violate the standard of 'fair and equitable treatment' (see Note 4).

---

6. Recent bilateral treaties frequently provide for the exclusion of unreasonable and discriminatory measures. See United States-Netherlands Treaty, Article VI (3): also United States-Japanese Treaty, Article V (1); United Kingdom-Iranian Treaty, Article 8 (2), etc.

(c) Thus, in interpreting Article 4 of the United Nations Charter, concerned with the admission to the United Nations, Judge Azvedo (quoting Brazilian, Soviet and Swiss law) in his Individual Opinion declared that under any legal system a right must be exercised in accordance with standards of what is normal, having in view the social purpose of the law and that there are, moreover, restrictions on an arbitrary decision taken in the exercise of the right in question.[7] Again, it has been repeatedly held by the Permanent Court of International Justice that the abuse or misuse of a right would endow an act otherwise lawful with the character of a breach of treaty.[8]

(d) That a measure is unreasonable cannot be presumed; it must be proved.

8. Discriminatory Measures

(a) A breach of obligations by a Party is established if it can be shown that the exercise of any right relating to property referred to in Article 1 is impaired by a 'discriminatory' measure that can be attributed to that Party (see Note 1 to Article 5).

(b) This, again, is a restatement of the law. For the very fact that the history of international relations abounds in examples of representations by Governments against measures of economic discrimination resulting in injury, implies the recognition of the principle that measures, otherwise lawful, may be deprived of the protection of the law on the grounds of discrimination. Prohibition of discrimination is in accordance with the principles laid down by the Permanent Court of International Justice in the Case of Certain German Interests in Polish Upper Silesia and the Case of Treatment of Polish Nationals in Danzig.[9]

(c) It is immaterial whether the measure complained of is expressly or exclusively directed against the property of the national for whom redress is sought or is couched in general terms which bring such property within its scope. In other words, 'de facto discrimination' is unlawful.

(d) The essence of discrimination, from the point of view of Article 1, is differentiation introduced in the treatment of property as a result of the measures in question, which is not justified by legitimate considerations. That differentiation consisting in the more favourable treatment of certain persons – whatever their nationality – does not constitute in itself discrimination against other nationals, is reaffirmed in the last sentence of paragraph (a).

---

7. Advisory Opinion on Conditions of Admission to the United Nations, ICJ Report 1947-48, p. 57 to p. 80: see also p. 83.
8. Polish Upper Silesia Case and Free Zones of Upper Savoy Case, quoted in Hambro I, Nos.100-101, p. 73.
9. See Hambro I, Nos 246 and 315, at pp. 201 and 261.

(e) Such discrimination may take four forms, viz. represent differentiation as regards the treatment of property of: (i) nationals of the same (foreign) Party to the Convention; (ii) nationals of different Parties; (iii) nationals of a Party and of those of a third State; and (iv) nationals of another Party and of its own nationals.

Paragraph (b) The Convention and the Acquisition of Property

9. (a) While respect is owed by each State to property of aliens which is in its jurisdiction (see Note 1), no State is bound – unless it agrees otherwise – to admit aliens into, or permit the acquisition of property by aliens in, its territory. Consequently, paragraph (b) of Article 1 confirms that the provisions of the Convention do not affect the right of each Party to control the acquisition of property and investment of capital by nationals of other Parties within its territory. The Convention is designed to safeguard property after its acquisition or investments after they have been made.

(b) Nothing in the Convention should be construed as prohibiting a Party from requiring divestiture of property obtained by inheritance by foreign nationals, provided that where such requirements are imposed, such nationals are allowed reasonable time and conditions in which to dispose of the property so obtained.

Article 2: Observance of Undertakings

Each Party shall at all times ensure the observance of undertakings given by it in relation to property of nationals of any other Party.

NOTES AND COMMENTS TO ARTICLE 2

1. Purpose of the Article

(a) Article 2 represents an application of the general principle of pacta sunt servanda – the maintenance of the pledged word. This principle is undoubtedly the basic norm of any system of law relating to agreements. It also applies to agreements between States and foreign nationals.

(b) If a Party should fail to observe an undertaking given in relation to property on the ground that that undertaking was contrary to its constitutional laws, it will be obliged to provide just compensation where required under this Convention. In giving an undertaking to a national of another Party relating to his investment or concession, a Party acts in the exercise of its sovereignty. At the same time, it is free to provide that, after a period, the terms of its undertaking might be altered or that the undertaking might altogether lapse; the undertaking itself might be governed by its own national law. However, any right originating under such an undertaking gives rise to an international right that the Party of the national concerned or of his successor in title is entitled to protect.[10] The validity of this principle has not been challenged. Thus, the basis of the decisions of the Permanent Court of International Justice in the cases of the Serbian and Brazilian Loans was that States were not entitled unilaterally to modify or abrogate such agreements.[11]

2. Object of Protection: Property

The provisions of Article 2 apply to 'property' in the widest sense of the term which includes, but is not limited to, investments (see Note 2 to Article 1; for a definition of 'property', see Article 9 (c) of the Convention and the Notes thereto). On the other hand, it goes without saying that the special protection enjoyed by property under Article 2 owing to an undertaking given in relation thereto by a Party which must carry it out, does not take the place of the general protection provided in Article 1 but is additional to the latter.

3. Nature of the Undertakings

   (a) An undertaking may be embodied in a contract or in a concession – it is not possible on legal grounds to draw a distinction between the two, and such an undertaking may represent a consensual or a unilateral engagement on the part of the Party concerned. However, it must relate to the property concerned; it is not sufficient if the link is incidental. Such a link may be established either:
      (i) owing to the form or specific terms in which the undertaking was couched which as such identify either the property or the recipient of the undertaking; or
      (ii) owing to the fact that though the undertaking was originally couched in general terms (e.g. a general exchange licence), the national concerned – as can be proved or presumed – acted in reliance on it. In such cases, in accordance with the principles of international law, a situation must be protected in which a Party by its conduct had given rise to a legitimate expectation of the continuance of a particular state of affairs.
   (b) The provisions of Article 2 do not apply, on the other hand, in respect of undertakings incidentally affecting the property of a foreign national. Thus the Article would apply to undertakings given e.g. in respect of transfers of earnings from an investment or taxation thereof (e.g. a tax holiday) or to a promise that there will be no expropriation for, for instance, ten years; but a

---

10. See The Right Honourable Lord Shawcross, Q.C.: The Problems of Foreign Investment in International Law, in Hague Recueil, 1961.
11. (1929) Series A, Nos. 20/21. In his lecture (ibidem) Lord Shawcross quotes other authorities in support of this principle.

promise of political rights for the national concerned would not be within its scope.
(c) Unless the undertaking expressly excludes it, it operates in favour of a lawful successor to the title to the property to which it relates.
(d) Undertakings given in relation to property of nationals of any other Party are not prejudiced by the provisions of Article 1 (b).

Article 3: Taking of Property

No Party shall take any measures depriving, directly or indirectly, of his property a national of another Party unless the following conditions are complied with:

(i) The measures are taken in the public interest and under due process of law;
(ii) The measures are not discriminatory; and
(iii) The measures are accompanied by provision for the payment of just compensation. Such compensation shall represent the genuine value of the property affected, shall be paid without undue delay, and shall be transferable to the extent necessary to make it effective for the national entitled thereto.

NOTES AND COMMENTS TO ARTICLE 3

A Requirements for a Lawful Taking of Property

1. Nature of Obligation and its Scope

(a) Article 3 acknowledges, by implication, the sovereign right of a State, under international law, to deprive owners, including aliens, of property which is within its territory in the pursuit of its political, social or economic ends. To deny such a right would be to attempt to interfere with its powers to regulate – by virtue of its independence and autonomy, equally recognised by international law – its political and social existence.[12] The right is reconciled with the obligation of the State to respect and protect the property of aliens (see Note 1 to Article 1) by the existing requirements for its exercise – before all, the requirement to pay the alien compensation if his property is taken.

(b) Thus, the Article restates[13] the five conditions which must be complied with in this connection according to recognised rules of international law: the measures in question must be taken (i) in the public interest; (ii) under due process of law; (iii) not be discriminatory; and, furthermore, (iv) just and

---

12. Sir Hersch Lauterpacht, Règles générales du Droit de la Paix. In Hague Recueil, 1937 (iv), pp. 95 et seq., and p. 346.
13. See e.g. United States-German Treaty, Article V (4): United States-Italian Treaty, Article V (2), Not all United States Bilateral Treaties refer, however, to 'due process of law' as a requirement: see e.g. United States-Greek Treaty, Article 7 (3).

effective compensation must be paid. Paragraph (iii) sets out the basic elements of the notion of 'just compensation'.

2. Relation to Article 2

Nothing in Article 3 relieves a Party which has given an undertaking in relation to property from the obligation imposed by Article 2.

3. Object of Protection: Property

Article 3 refers to property in general. This term is used in the Convention in the widest sense and includes contractual rights [see Note 2 to Article 1 and Article 9 (c)].

4. Taking of Property

(a) In the case of direct deprivation ('expropriation' or 'nationalisation') the loss of the property rights concerned is the avowed object of the measure. By using the phrase 'to deprive ... directly or indirectly ...' in the text of the Article it is, however, intended to bring within its compass any measures taken with the intent of wrongfully depriving the national concerned of the substance of his rights and resulting in such loss (e.g. prohibiting the national to sell his property or forcing him to do so at a fraction of the fair market price).

(b) Article 3 deals with deprivation of property. Protection against wrongful interference with its use by unreasonable or discriminatory measures is, in principle, provided in Article 1. Yet such interference might amount to indirect deprivation. Whether it does, will depend on its extent and duration. Though it may purport to be temporary, there comes a stage at which there is no immediate prospect that the owner will be able to resume the enjoyment of his property. Thus, in particular, Article 3 is meant to cover 'creeping nationalisation', recently practised by certain States. Under it, measures otherwise lawful are applied in such a way as to deprive ultimately the alien of the enjoyment or value of his property, without any specific act being identifiable as outright deprivation. As instances, may be quoted excessive or arbitrary taxation; prohibition of dividend distribution coupled with compulsory loans; imposition of administrators; prohibition of dismissal of staff; refusal of access to raw materials or of essential export or import licences.

(c) The taking of property, within the meaning of the Article, must result in a loss of title or substance – otherwise a claim will not lie.[14]

5. Public Interest

In order to be in conformity with the rules of international law, the taking of property must be justified by public interest, i.e. the measures must be adopted in the interest of

---

14. See B.A. Wortley, Expropriation in Public International Law, Cambridge, 1959, p. 139.

the State or any political subdivision thereof. Thus seizure undertaken ostensibly for public purposes but, in fact, to be used by persons connected therewith solely for private gain is unlawful and gives rise to a claim for damages.[15] On the other hand, provided the taking is in the public interest, it is immaterial whether the title in the property passes to the State or, as part of the design, to one of its nationals, the undertaking thus remaining in the 'private sector'.

6. The Notion of Due Process of Law

(a) In essence, the contents of the notion of due process of law make it akin to the requirements of the 'Rule of Law', an Anglo-Saxon notion, or of the 'Rechtsstaat', as understood in continental law. Used in an international agreement, the content of this notion is not exhausted by a reference to the national law of the Parties concerned.[16] The 'due process of law' of each of them must correspond to the principles of international law.

(b) In view of the variety of national rules that give expression to the notion, its precise definition in terms of international law is difficult. On analysis, this term – which is used in some United States Bilateral Treaties[17] – implies that whenever a State seizes property, the measures taken must be free from arbitrariness. Safeguards existing in its Constitution or other laws or established by judicial precedent must be fully observed; administrative or judicial machinery used or available must correspond at least to the minimum standard required by international law. Thus, the term contains both substantive and procedural elements.

(c) One safeguard, specifically recognised in some bilateral agreements,[18] deserves special mention in view of its importance; the legality of the measures taken by the expropriating State and – wherever the constitutional rules of the State concerned permit it – the amount of compensation fixed should be subject to judicial review. This principle does not, of course, prejudice the form the judicial review should take, i.e. whether it should be carried out by ordinary or administrative Courts, as long as the independence of the Judge and the fundamentals of fair hearing are ensured – i.e. the rights to be heard, if possible, in public; to have advance knowledge of the rules governing the hearing; to adequate representations; etc.

(d) This analysis shows that, used in the context of an international agreement, the notion of 'due process of law' means that the national of a Party may be deprived of his property by measures taken by another Party only subject to the safeguards and conditions provided for by national law and by the principles of international law.

---

15. Arbitral Award in the United States-Cuban claim, W. Fletcher Smith, (1929) Reports of International Arbitral Awards, Vol. II, pp. 915–918.
16. See R.R. Wilson, United States Commercial Treaties and International Law, New Orleans, La., 1960, p. 115.
17. See footnote 11 p. 242.
18. See, for instance, German-Pakistan Treaty, Art. III (2) and German-Togoland Treaty, Art. 3 (2).

Appendix IV

7. 'Discriminatory'

Under Article 1 (a) of the Convention 'the management maintenance, use, enjoyment and disposal' of property shall not be impaired by discriminatory measures. The prohibition extends under Article 3 to the deprivation of property, this being the most incisive measure against an investment. Thus, measures of deprivation of this type are prohibited absolutely. If they are taken, there is – as in the case of a breach of any other condition set out in Article 3 – a duty of the Party to make 'full reparation' under Article 5.

B The Elements of just and Effective Compensation

8. Just and Effective Compensation

Paragraph (iii) of Article 3 sets out the elements of 'just compensation'. The phrase appears in some United States Bilateral Treaties.[19] Other treaties of that group speak of 'just and effective compensation'.[20] They provide that 'just compensation' shall represent the equivalent of the property taken and shall be made in an effectively realisable form and without unnecessary delay. Adequate provision shall have been made, at the latest, by the time of the taking for the determination and the giving of the compensation.[21] The United Kingdom-Iranian Treaty provides for 'prompt, adequate and effective compensation' for any measure of deprivation (Article 15). The German-Pakistan Treaty speaks of 'compensation which shall represent the equivalent of the investments affected'; the German-Togoland Treaty, of compensation that must 'correspond to the value of the expropriated investment'; in the case of each of these two Treaties compensation must be 'actually realisable', 'freely transferable' and paid without undue delay (Article 3).

9. 'Just' Compensation

    (a) The standard of 'just' compensation, equivalent to 'fair compensation' or 'just price', has been accepted in a number of important decisions of international tribunals. It implies that compensation should represent – as Article 3 (iii) provides – the 'genuine value of the property affected' at the moment of deprivation. As a rule, this will correspond to the fair market value of the property without reduction in that value due to the method by which the payment is calculated: to the manner in which it is made; or to any special tax or charges levied on it. Furthermore, the value must remain unaffected by artificial factors such as deterioration due to the prospect of the very seizure which ultimately occurs, similar seizures by the Party concerned or the

---

19. United States-Japanese Treaty, Article VI (3); United States-German Treaty, Article V (4); United States-Netherlands Treaty, Article VI (4).
20. United States-Ethiopian Treaty, Article VIII (2).
21. See footnote 9, page 240.

general conduct of that Party towards property of aliens which makes such seizures likely.

(b) The determination of the 'genuine value' must initially be referred to the national body to which is entrusted the task of assessing compensation unless the value of the property or the method of ascertaining it is stipulated in an undertaking within the meaning of Article 2. To the amount assessed should be added interest from the day of the taking to the day on which compensation is paid. In appropriate cases profitability is an elment in the computation of the value of the property.

10. Absence of Delay

Compensation must be paid 'without undue delay'. This does not affect the legality of procedures under which compensation is payable after the measures of deprivation have been taken. Yet Article 3 (iii) requires that measures constituting the taking of the property must be 'accompanied' by provision for the payment of compensation – thereby emphasizing the close link, as regards time, between the deprivation, the assessment of compensation, and its receipt.

11. Effectiveness and Transferability

Compensation must be paid in a form which is of real practical use to the person entitled thereto, having regard to his particular situation (for example his occupation, residence, etc.) – that is to say, it must be 'effective' for him. In some cases, compensation in non-transferable form may be effective in this sense – for example, in the case of a person permanently resident in the expropriating State at the time of expropriation who voluntarily continues to reside there thereafter, provided always that it is possible for him to re-invest the funds reveived by way of compensation in the country of his residence. In other cases, where the economic system with which the person concerned is primarily connected is that of a State other than the expropriating State, it may be necessary to pay compensation in a form transferable into the currency of that other State in order to make it effective for him. Article 3 (iii) accordingly provides that compensation shall be 'transferable to the extent necessary to make it effective' for the person concerned. A transfer through the market, for instance in security sterling, would represent a proper discharge of the obligations contained in the Article provided it did not entail an undue reduction in the genuine value.

12. The Recipient of Compensation

(a) The recipient of the compensation, 'the national entitled thereto', may be (i) the national [see Article 9 (a)] of a Party other than that from which it is due, who has been deprived of his property; or (ii) a national of such other Party who lawfully derives (e.g. by succession) his title to compensation from the national who lost his property. Voluntary assignments of claims need not be recognised if they are not so recognised under domestic law.

(b) From the point of view of the entitlement as such, the residence of the recipient is immaterial: he may reside in the territory of the Party which owes him compensation; in the territory of any other Party; or elsewhere – he is entitled to compensation.

Article 4: Recommendation on Transfers

Each Party recognises, with respect to property in its territory owned by a national of another Party, the principle of the freedom of transfer of the current income from, and proceeds upon liquidation of, such property, to such national of a Party as is entitled to them. While this Recommendation does not contain any obligation in this respect, each Party will endeavour to grant the necessary authorisations for such transfers to the country of the residence of that national and in the currency thereof.

NOTES AND COMMENTS TO ARTICLE 4

Recognising the principle that transfer of the current income from, and the proceeds of the liquidation of, foreign property should be free but without accepting any obligation in this respect, the Parties, in Article 4, declare that they will endeavour to give effect to this principle by authorising appropriate transfer operations. Thus the text has, as it expressly indicates, the nature of a recommendation. It follows that it contains no obligation suitable for implementation by an international tribunal. The text of the Recommendation cannot prejudice the application of any obligation assumed by a Party by virtue of this Convention or any other international agreement.

Article 5: Breaches of the Convention

Any breach of this Convention shall entail the obligation of the Party responsible therefor to make full reparation.

NOTES AND COMMENTS TO ARTICLE 5

1. Responsibility and Attribution

(a) To establish responsibility of a Party under Article 5 it must be shown that, in accordance with the general rules of international law, the breach is attributable to the Party against whom the complaint is made.
(b) Questions concerning recognition by a Party of measures contrary to the provisions of the Convention shall be determined in accordance with such principles of international law as may apply.

2. 'Full Reparation'

- (a) Article 5 reaffirms the principle, contained in the very notion of an illegal act, that its chief consequence must be full reparation of the wrong done. 'Reparation', stated the Permanent Court of International Justice, 'must, as far as possible, wipe out all the consequences of the illegal act and re-establish the situation which would, in all probability, have existed if that act had not been committed'.[22] In practice, such reparation will generally take the form of damages.
- (b) In cases in which full reparation takes the form of, or includes, the payment of damages, the payment must cover all loss (damnum emergens and lucrum cessans) flowing from the wrongful act and, where required, must be transferable.

Article 6: Derogations

A Party may take measures in derogation of this Convention only if:

- (i) involved in war, hostilities or other grave national emergency due to force majeure or provoked by unforeseen circumstances or threatening its essential security interests; or
- (ii) taken pursuant to decisions of the Security Council of the United Nations or to recommendations of the Security Council or General Assembly of the United Nations relating to the maintenance or restoration of international peace and security.

Any such measures shall be limited in extent and duration to those strictly required by the exigencies of the situation.

NOTES AND COMMENTS TO ARTICLE 6

1. The Legal Nature of the Derogations

- (a) Article 6 provides for two groups of cases in which a Party may be justified in derogating from the Convention. These derogation clauses are declaratory of existing rules of international law. The Article, however, deals only with 'derogations' in the strict sense of the word, that is to say measures which in its absence would not otherwise be justifiable. No attempt is made here to provide for those cases of State action which, without being of a discriminatory character, limit freedom of ownership or disposition of property but which are accepted as part of the normal governmental process. The imposition of taxation of a general and non-confiscatory character; the forfeiture of goods smuggled through the customs; the confiscation of obscene literature or

---

22. Chorzow Factory Case, (1928) Series A, No. 17, p. 47.

dangerous drugs; the payment of fines upon conviction for crime; the enforcement of court judgments – these are all examples of measures which Parties are entitled to take and the legality of which, in relation to the Convention, is not dependent upon the invocation of a derogation clause.

(b) Contingencies in which measures taken in derogation of the Convention are justified are transient in character. Therefore, in conformity with existing international law, Article 6 requires the measures to be limited in extent and duration to those strictly required by the exigencies of the situation. Thus, the measures must be taken while a war or other hostilities last and cannot be continued after the cessation of hostilities (even though a peace treaty might not yet have been concluded). The Convention as such remains binding. Compliance with its terms must be resumed as soon as the emergency is over. 'La force majeure disparue', says Rousseau, 'l'obligation d'exécution reparaîtra – ce qui prouve bien que le traité subsiste'.[23]

(c) Finally, the measures must be legitimate, i.e. in conformity with the existing rules of international law which Article 6 is not designed to supersede.

2. The Notion of 'Public Emergency'

(a) In the event of war, multilateral treaties are suspended as regards their effect on relations between opposing belligerents. Even in relation to an ally, as between a belligerent and a neutral, or as between neutrals, legitimate measures of self-defence are justified. This principle applies, more widely, in the event of other public emergencies.[24]

(b) The nature and degree of the emergency in which derogations are admissible are, however, qualified by the provisions of Article 6. Thus, the emergency must (A) be not only 'grave' in itself but have 'national' repercussions; and (B)(i) be due to force majeure; or (ii) be provoked by unforeseen circumstances; or (iii) threaten the essential security interests of the Party concerned. Civil war, riots or other widespread civil disturbances may clearly come within the first two of these three categories. So also may major emergencies arising from natural causes – such as storm damage, earthquakes, volcanic eruptions, etc. – with effects on a national scale.

(c) As regards the third category, the measures taken will normally relate to defence or aspects connected with the external relations of the Party concerned. On the other hand, they need not presuppose circumstances that are

---

23. Charles Rousseau, Principes Généraux du Droit International Public. Tome I, p. 573.
24. '... Necessity may excuse the non-observance of international obligations ... the plea of necessity ... by definition implies the impossibility of proceeding by any other method than the one contrary to law', declared Judge Anzilotti in the Oscar China Case (P.C.I.J. Series A/B No. 63, p. 114).

unforeseen or amount to force majeure. The derogation provided for corresponds to analogous provisions in the United States Bilateral Treaties.[25]

3. Maintenance of Peace

Article 103 of the United Nations Charter lays down that in the event of a conflict between the obligations of the Members of the United Nations under the Charter and their obligations under any other international agreement, their obligations under the Charter shall prevail. A similar principle underlies the provisions of Article 6 (ii) of the Convention. As compared with Article 103, they apply, of course, as between all the Parties to the Convention – whether they are Members of the United Nations or not. They are, however, limited to derogations designed to serve the maintenance of international peace and security – which Article 103 is not. Within this limitation, they apply equally to measures taken pursuant to decisions or to recommendations of the competent organs of the United Nations.

Article 7: Disputes

(a) Any dispute between Parties as to the interpretation or application of this Convention may be submitted by agreement between them either to an Arbitral Tribunal established in accordance with the provisions of the Annex to this Convention, which shall form an integral part thereof, or to any other international tribunal. If no agreement is reached for this purpose between the Parties within a period of sixty days from the date on which written notice of intention to institute proceedings is given, it is hereby agreed that an Arbitral Tribunal established in accordance with that Annex shall have jurisdiction.

(b) A national of a Party claiming that he has been injured by measures in breach of this Convention may, without prejudice to any right or obligation he may have to resort to another tribunal, national or international, institute proceedings against any other Party responsible for such measures before the Arbitral Tribunal referred to in paragraph (a), provided that:
 (i) the Party against which the claim is made has accepted the jurisdiction of that Arbitral Tribunal by a declaration which covers that claim; and
 (ii) the Party of which he is a national has indicated that it will not institute proceedings under paragraph (a) or, within six months of receiving a written request from its national for the institution of such proceedings, has not instituted them.

(c) The declaration referred to in paragraph (b)(i), whether general or particular, may be made or revoked at any time. In respect of claims arising out of or in connection with rights acquired during the period of the validity of such

---

25. See, for example, United States-Italian Treaty, Article XXIV; United States-Greece Treaty, Article XXIII; United States-Federal Germany Treaty, Article XXIV; United States-Nicaraguan Treaty, Article XXI; and also Norwegian-Japanese Treaty, Article XVI.

declaration, it shall continue to apply for a period of five years after its revocation.

(d) At any time after the expiry of the period of six months referred to in paragraph (b)(ii), the Party concerned may institute proceedings in accordance with paragraph (a). In this case proceedings instituted in accordance with paragraph (b) shall be suspended until the proceedings instituted in accordance with paragraph (a) are terminated.

NOTES AND COMMENTS TO ARTICLE 7

1. Purpose of the Article

In the event of a dispute that arises under the Convention, the Parties thereto may, in accordance with existing practice, attempt to settle it by diplomatic means. However, in the case of an instrument dedicated to the creation of an atmosphere of confidence there is a vital need to make also provision for the effective adjudication of such disputes. This is particularly true in view of the nature of the provisions of the Convention, the generality of the terms employed therein, and the complexity of the facts that might have to be elucidated. Article 7 serves this purpose.

2. Machinery Provided

Article 7 provides that in the event of a dispute relating to the interpretation or application of the Convention:

(A) a Party may under paragraph (a):
  (i) in agreement with the other Party, submit the dispute to an Arbitral Tribunal established ad hoc in accordance with the Annex to the Convention (the 'A.T.') or to any other international tribunal; or
  (ii) if no agreement is reached within sixty days, submit the dispute to the A.T.; and that
(B) under paragraph (b), a national of any Party, injured by measures in breach of the Convention, may submit the dispute to the A.T., provided that:
  (i) the Party against which his claim is made has accepted its jurisdiction by a declaration which covers his claim; and that
  (ii) the Party of which he himself is a national has not itself instituted proceedings within six months from being requested to do so.

Paragraph (a) Disputes between the Parties

3. Agreement on Jurisdiction

(a) Faced with the issue whether, in the absence of agreement between the Parties on the tribunal, there should be compulsory jurisdiction of the International Court of Justice (the 'I.C.J.') or of the A.T., the jurisdiction of the

A.T. was ultimately preferred on the grounds, among others, that (i) the A.T. was a forum more appropriate for disputes, many of which were of a technical nature; (ii) the A.T. was easy to convene and a country in the process of economic development might feel reassured by the possibility of choosing one of its members; (iii) its decision was given in a shorter time and the procedure entailed less cost; and that (iv) countries in the process of economic development might prefer the A.T. because disputes could be determined there without much publicity. In the event of a dispute of major political importance, on the other hand, the Parties could, as is open to them with regard to any dispute, agree to submit it to the I.C.J. or any other international tribunal.

(b) Thus, the effect of the provisions of paragraph (a) is that:

    A. no question of jurisdiction arises where the Parties agree to submit their dispute to the A.T., the I.C.J. or some other international tribunal, as provided for in that paragraph; and that

    B. if there is no agreement reached, the Party alleging the breach of the Convention can initiate proceedings before the A.T. whose jurisdiction then becomes binding on the other Party.

4. Form of Agreement

Agreement between the Parties to the dispute concerning jurisdiction of the A.T. or another international tribunal may take the form of a special agreement relating to that dispute ('compromis'), to all disputes or to certain disputes arising under the Convention, or of unilateral declarations to that effect. Such agreement may also be inferred from certain acts of the Parties concerned. It would be for the tribunal to determine whether the Party had in fact agreed on its jurisdiction [see Paragraph 6 (a) of the Annex to the Convention].

The rules relating to the establishment of the A.T. and some basic rules of its procedure are contained in the Annex to the Convention (pp. 59 and 60).

5. Compulsory Jurisdiction of the Arbitral Tribunal

In order to institute proceedings before the A.T. by virtue of its compulsory jurisdiction, the Party concerned must be able to show that:

(i) it has given written notice of its intention to institute proceedings to the Party which it alleges is responsible for a breach of the Convention (as distinct from the notice instituting proceedings before the A.T. – see Paragraph 2 of the Annex to the Convention); and that

(ii) sixty days have elapsed since such notice was given without agreement on the tribunal for the dispute having been reached between the Parties.

Appendix IV

Paragraph (b) Claims by Nationals

6. The Rule and its Limitations

   (a) The notion that an individual may enjoy access directly to an international tribunal is not new. Not only was procedural capacity enjoyed by individuals in relation to the Central American Court of Justice and certain Mixed Arbitral Tribunals, but it is enjoyed today with regard to the Court of the European Communities, the European Commission of Human Rights and Administrative Tribunals of intergovernmental organisations.

   (b) Under paragraph (b) of Article 7, nationals of the Parties may submit disputes under the Convention to the A.T. [as to the definition of a 'national', see Article 9 (a)] without prejudice, however, to a right that a national may have to resort to the tribunal of his State or to another international tribunal and without prejudice to obligations which may exist for him to exhaust local or other remedies. As regards such obligations, paragraph (b) implies that all appropriate legal remedies short of the process provided for in the Convention must be exhausted – local remedies or others (such as remedies under an agreement between a Party and a national of another Party which contains a provision for the submission of all disputes to arbitration).

   (c) Otherwise, the right of a national to institute proceedings under paragraph (b) of Article 7 is subject only to the conditions set out in sub-paragraphs (i) and (ii) of that paragraph (see Note 7). After the institution of proceedings his claim may be espoused by his own State (see Note 8). Furthermore, the A.T. has powers to order security for costs or to dismiss the claim if the institution of proceedings appears frivolous or vexatious. [Paragraph 6(c) of the Annex to the Convention].

7. Acceptance of Jurisdiction

   (a) Under paragraph (b), jurisdiction of the A.T. as regards claims by nationals of the Parties exists only if it has been accepted by the respondent Party. Acceptance is effected by a unilateral declaration.

   (b) The use of the words 'whether general or particular' in paragraph (c) indicates that the Parties are free to limit the scope of their declaration (i) in time; (ii) in substantive scope; and (iii) in the range of nationals who may benefit under it. Thus, a Party may limit its declaration to one specific claim. It may also, if it wishes, make it a pre-condition of a claim that the individual concerned should have first exhausted other possibilities of redress that may be open to him.

   (c) The declaration may be revoked by the Party concerned at any time – unless the declaration itself states the contrary. The effect of the revocation is, however, not absolute. According to paragraph (c) of Article 7, jurisdiction of the A.T. continues to exist for five years in respect of claims arising out of, or in connection with, rights acquired while the declaration was valid.

8. The Right of Espousel

(a) The right of the national to submit a claim to the A.T. is, under paragraphs (b) and (d) of Article 7, subject to the general principle of international law that, as regards international process, the State of the national concerned has the right of espousel, i.e. the right to present his claim directly to the respondent Party or to bring it before an international tribunal in accordance with the provisions of paragraph (a).
(b) This principle limits the right of the national concerned in two respects:
   (i) He must, in the first place, request in writing the appropriate authorities of his own State to institute proceedings against the respondent Party and can only institute proceedings himself provided that his State, within a period of six months from the receipt of his request, has not instituted such proceedings or otherwise indicated that it will not institute them [paragraph (b)(ii)];
   (ii) If, after the expiry of this period, his State, at any time, institutes proceedings in conformity with paragraph (a), the proceedings instituted by him must be suspended by the A.T. until the former proceedings are terminated [paragraph (d)].
(c) Under these rules the State of the national concerned may espouse his claim at any time and submit it, in accordance with paragraph (a), to the A.T. or – in agreement with the respondent Party – to the I.C.J. or any other international tribunal. But it cannot, after the expiry of the six months' period, prevent the national concerned from exercising his rights under paragraph (b), by advising him or the A.T. that it is dealing with the claim on the diplomatic level.

GENERAL POINTS

9. Parallel Remedies

The Convention contains no specific provisions dealing with the possibility that more than one international remedy may be available in relation to any given factual situation. Any attempt to deal with this problem would involve a degree of detailed regulations disproportionate to the likelihood of its occurence. The difficulties which might arise out of overlapping claims by States and individuals can to a large extent be controlled by the terms of the declarations which States make under paragraph (b) (i) of Article 7 [see Note 7 (b) above]. In addition, the A.T. is given in Paragraph 6 (b)(iii) of the Annex the power to stay proceedings – a power which it would be free to exercise if proceedings involving substantially the same facts, parties and issues were pending before another international tribunal or commission.

Appendix IV

Article 8: Other International Agreements

Where a matter is covered both by the provisions of this Convention and any other international agreement nothing in this Convention shall prevent a national of one Party who holds property in the territory of another Party from benefiting by the provisions that are most favourable to him.

Article 9: Definitions

For the purposes of this Convention:

(a) 'National' includes both natural persons and companies. It does not, however, include nationals of a Party who belong to any territory to which this Convention may be extended pursuant to Article 11 but has not been so extended.

(b) 'Company' means any entity which, under the law of a Party, either is recognized as a legal person or, as an entity or through its members, has the capacity to dispose of property or to institute legal proceedings.

(c) 'Property' means all property, rights and interests, whether held directly or indirectly, including the interest which a member of a company is deemed to have in the property of the company. However, no claim shall be made under this Convention in respect of the interest of a member of a company:

(i) if the company is a national of a Party other than the Party which has taken the measures affecting the property of the company; or

(ii) in the case of a company which is a national of a Party by whose measures its property is affected, if the interest of the member of the company does not arise out of and, at the time of such measures, does not represent either an investment of foreign funds made by him or his predecessor in title or an investment of compensation or damages paid in accordance with the provisions of this Convention.

NOTES AND COMMENTS TO ARTICLE 9

1. 'National': Physical Persons

(a) Paragraph (a) of Article 9 includes a reference both to physical persons and to 'companies'. According to the rules of international law the nationality of physical persons is, in general, determined by the national law of the State concerned.[26] A Party to the Convention cannot, however, claim the protection of its national if he 'belongs' to a territory for whose international relations it

---

26. See The Permanent Court of International Justice in the Tunis and Morocco Nationality Decrees Case: 'In the present state of international law, questions of nationality are ... in principle ... solely within the jurisdiction of a State' (P.C.I.J., Series B, No. 4, p. 24): also Sir Hersch

is responsible where, though it could have done so in accordance with Article 11, it did not, by notification to the depositary of the Convention, extend the application thereof to that territory. Thus, although under Section 4 of the British Nationality Act, 1948, every person born within the United Kingdom and Colonies after 1st January, 1949, shall be, as a rule, a citizen of the United Kingdom and Colonies (as well as a 'British subject' and a 'Commonwealth citizen'), a person born in a colony of the United Kingdom and residing there will not enjoy protection under the Convention unless the British Government extends its application to that colony.

(b) It is nationality that confers the right to diplomatic protection (see Note 3 to Article 1). Thus, as a rule it will be for the Party that intervenes on behalf of the claimant, or for the claimant himself, to show that he is its national in conformity with its law. Conflicts may, however, arise in cases of dual nationality. The respondent Party may, for instance, contend that the claimant is, or has been, its own national as well and invoke the rule that a State is ordinarily not entitled to the protection of its nationals who are also nationals of another State as against the latter.[27] Where recent naturalisation by the Party which seeks to protect its national is involved, the conflict will be resolved by the rule that the person concerned must be not only its national when diplomatic protection is exercised, but also at the time of the injury.[28] In the case of other conflicts preference will have to be given – in accordance with the principle recognized by the International Court of Justice[29] – 'to the real and effective nationality, that which accorded with the facts, that based on stronger factual ties between the person concerned and one of the States whose nationality is involved'. One may speak generally of 'the antipathy of international law to plural nationality'.[30]

2. 'National': Companies

(a) The definition of 'national' in paragraph (a) also includes 'companies', a term which – in accordance with paragraph (b) – comprises all entities which, under the law of a Party, have legal personality or at least the capacity to dispose of property or to institute legal proceedings. It is immaterial in this respect whether such capacity arises because the law in question attributes it

---

Lauterpacht: 'It is not for international law but for municipal law to determine who is, and who is not, to be considered a subject' (Oppenheim-Lauterpacht, International Law, Vol.I, 8th Ed., p. 643).

27. See Strupp – Schlochauer, Wörterbuch des Völkerrechts, Vol. I, p. 381; see also The Hague Convention of 1930 on Certain Questions relating to the Conflict of Nationality Laws, Article 14.
28. Sir Hersch Lauterpacht, The Development of International Law by the International Court, London, 1958, p. 183; for exceptions to this rule, see ibidem, p. 352 and Andrew Martin, Private Property Rights, and Interests in the Paris Peace Treaties, in (1947) B.Y.I.L., Vol. 24, p. 288.
29. Nottebohm Case (2nd phase), quoted in Hambro II, No. 138, pp. 193–195; see also The Hague Convention of 1930, Article 5.
30. Clive Parry, Nationality and Citizenship Laws of the Commonwealth, London, 1957, p. 26.

to the entity as such or because such capacity is attributed by the law to its members. The object of the provision is to bring within the protection of the Convention not only joint stock companies but various kinds of consortia, partnerships and other entities recognized by the national laws of the Parties and active in the field of foreign investment. In particular, it is intended to cover partnerships under English law and the Offene Handelsgesellschaft, the Gesellschaft des Buergerlichen Gesetzbuches, and the Gesamthandsgemeinschaften under German law.

(b) In ascribing nationality to companies the Convention does not define the connecting factors that entitle a Party to take up, or a company to claim, protection under it. Such factors will have to be determined in accordance with international judicial and treaty practice.[31]

3. 'Property'

(a) The definition of this term in paragraph (c), which is in conformity with international judicial practice, shows that it is meant to be used in its widest sense which includes, but is not limited to, investments. To come within the provisions of the Convention, property must be lawfully acquired [see Note 2 (b) to Article 1].

(b) The definition includes – subject to the two exceptions set out under (i) and (ii) in paragraph (c) – the interest which a member of a company is deemed to have in its property. The term 'member' is used in preference to 'shareholder', as in some legal systems the latter applies only in relation to joint stock companies, but not to other commercial entities (e.g. a 'société à responsabilité limitée') which should also come within the definition. It should be noted that a 'company' within the meaning of paragraphs (a) and (b) may be a 'member' in another company.

(c) Sub-paragraph (ii) of Article 9 (c) is included for the purpose of limiting the right of protection of foreign shareholders to those cases where the interest of the foreign shareholder arises out of an investment of foreign capital in the economy of the State. If, for any reason, the original investment of foreign funds is liquidated and the proceeds of the sale of the shares are remitted abroad, then the shares lose the protection of the sub-paragraph until such time as they may once again be acquired by the investment of foreign funds.

Article 10: Ratification

This Convention shall be subject to ratification by the signatory States. Instruments of ratification shall be deposited with the [depositary Organisation/depositary

---

31. See R.L. Bindschedler, La protection de la propriété privée en droit international public, in Hague Recueil, 1956 (ii), p. 179, as to the tests applied in the post-war compensation treaties, see I. Foighel, Nationalisation, London, 1957, pp. 110–111.

Government], which shall notify the (other) signatory States and all acceding States of each deposit.

Article 11: Territorial Application

Any State may at the time of signature, ratification or accession to this Convention or at any time thereafter declare by notification given to the [depositary Organisation/depositary Government] that the Convention shall extend to any of the territories for whose international relations it is responsible, and the Convention shall, from the date of the receipt of the notification or the date on which the Convention takes effect for the notifying State – whichever is the later – extend to the territories named therein.

Article 12: Coming into Force

(a) This Convention shall come into force on the date of the deposit of the Xth instrument of ratification or accession.
(b) The Convention shall thereafter take effect for each ratifying or acceding State on the date of the deposit of its instrument of ratification or accession.
(c) Any measure taken by a Party before the date of the coming into force of this Convention for it shall not be affected by the Convention as such. The provisions of this Convention shall apply to measures taken after such date, whether in pursuance of legislative or administrative authority existing before such date or otherwise.

Notes and Comments to Article 12

The provisions of the Convention apply to property irrespective of whether it was acquired before or after the date on which the Convention comes into force as regards the Party concerned (see Note 2 to Article 1). In this respect paragraph (c) of Article 12 is designed to clarify two questions. In the first place, paragraph (c) renders it clear that the provisions of the Convention do not apply to measures relating to such property taken by a Party before the Convention comes into force with regard to it, though, of course, existing rules of customary international law and other relevant treaties will continue to apply to such measures. Secondly, paragraph (c) deals with the question of application of the Convention to measures taken after the date on which the Convention has come into force. Such measures will be covered by the Convention, even where the legislative or administative authority on which they are based originated before the date on which the Convention comes into force.

Article 13: Termination

Any Party may terminate the application of this Convention to itself or to any territory to which it has extended the Convention by notification pursuant to Article 11 by giving notice to this effect to the [depositary Organisation/depositary Government] which shall notify the (other) Parties thereof. The termination shall take effect one year after such notice has been received by the [depositary Organisation/depositary Government]. In respect of property acquired or investments made before the date on which the termination takes effect, the provisions of Articles 1 to 12 of this Convention shall continue to apply for a further period of 15 years from that date.

Article 14: Signature and Accession

(pro memoria)
FINAL CLAUSE
(pro memoria)

ANNEX RELATING TO THE STATUTE OF THE ARBITRAL TRIBUNAL

1. The Arbitral Tribunal referred to in Article 7 of the Convention shall consist of three persons appointed as follows: one arbitrator shall be appointed by each party to the arbitration proceedings and a third arbitrator, who shall also act as Chairman of the Tribunal (hereinafter sometimes called the 'Chairman of the Tribunal'), shall be appointed by agreement of the parties.

2. Arbitration proceedings shall be instituted upon notice by the party instituting such proceedings (whether a Party to the Convention or a national of a Party to the Convention, as the case may be) to the other party. Such notice shall contain a statement setting forth in summary form the grounds of the claim, the nature of the relief sought, and the name of the arbitrator appointed by the party instituting such proceedings. Within 30 days after the giving of such notice, the respondent party shall notify the party instituting proceedings of the name of the arbitrator appointed by the respondent party.

3. If, within 60 days after the giving of notice instituting the arbitration proceedings, the parties shall not have agreed upon a Chairman of the Tribunal, either party may request the President of the International Court of Justice, or if he is unable to act, the Vice-President of the International Court of Justice, to make the appointment. If either of the parties shall fail to appoint an arbitrator, such arbitrator shall be appointed by the Chairman of the Tribunal.

4. In case any arbitrator appointed as provided in this Annex shall resign, die, or otherwise become unable to act, a successor arbitrator shall be appointed in the same manner as herein prescribed for the appointment of the original arbitrator and his successor shall have all the powers and duties of the original arbitrator.

5. The Arbitral Tribunal shall convene at such times and places as shall be fixed by the Chairman of the Tribunal. Thereafter, the Tribunal shall determine where and when it shall sit.

6. (a) The Arbitral Tribunal shall decide all questions relating to its competence and shall, taking into consideration any agreement of the parties, determine its procedure and all questions relating to costs.

(b) In particular, the Arbitral Tribunal may:
   (i) permit intervention by a Party which considers that it has an interest of a legal nature which may be affected by the decision in the case;
   (ii) consolidate pending proceedings with the agreement, where necessary, of any other Arbitral Tribunal established in accordance with this Annex; and
   (iii) provided that no objection is made by any Party to such proceedings, stay proceedings if other proceedings arising out of the same facts and raising substantially the same issues are pending before any other international Tribunal or Commission.
(c) The Arbitral Tribunal may also, in the case of proceedings instituted by a national of a Party to the Convention and upon preliminary application by the respondent:
   (i) order that national to give security for costs; or
   (ii) dismiss the claim if, from the statements made by that national to the Tribunal, the institution of the proceedings appears frivolous or vexatious.
(d) Decisions of the Arbitral Tribunal may be made by a majority vote.

7. The Arbitral Tribunal shall afford to all parties a fair hearing. It may render an award on the default of a party. Any award shall be rendered in writing, signed by the majority of the Arbitral Tribunal, and delivered publicly. A signed counterpart of the award shall be transmitted to each party. Any such award shall be final. Each party to the proceedings shall comply with any such award rendered by the Arbitral Tribunal.

INTERNATIONAL ARBITRATION LAW LIBRARY

1. Moshe Hirsch, *The Arbitration Mechanism of the International Center for the Settlement of Investment Disputes*, 1993 (ISBN 07-923-1993-1).
2. Aida B. Avanessian, *Iran-United States Claims Tribunal in Action*, 1993 (ISBN 18-533-3902-4).
3. Isaak I. Dore, *The UNCITRAL Framework for Arbitration in Contemporary Perspective*, 1993 (ISBN 18-533-3573-8).
4. Vesna Lazić, *Insolvency Proceedings and Commercial Arbitration*, 1998 (ISBN 90-411-1115-8).
5. Joachim Frick, *Arbitration in Complex International Contracts*, 2001 (ISBN 90-411-1662-1).
6. Katherine Lynch, *The Forces of Economic Globalization: Challenges to the Regime of International Commercial Arbitration*, 2003 (ISBN 90-411-1994-9).
7. Christoph Liebscher, *The Healthy Award: Challenge in International Commercial Arbitration*, 2003 (ISBN 90-411-2011-4).
8. Hamid G. Gharavi, *The International Effectiveness of the Annulment of an Arbitral Award*, 2003 (ISBN 90-411-1717-2).
9. Abdulhay Sayed, *Corruption in International Trade and Commercial Arbitration*, 2004 (ISBN 90-411-2236-2).
10. Gabrielle Kaufmann-Kohler & Thomas Schultz, *Online Dispute Resolution: Challenges for Contemporary Justice*, 2004 (ISBN 90-411-2318-0).
11. Christopher R. Drahozal & Richard W. Naimark (eds), *Towards a Science of International Arbitration: Collected Empirical Research*, 2005 (ISBN 90-411-2322-9).
12. Ali Yeşilirmak, *Provisional Measures in International Commercial Arbitration*, 2005 (ISBN 90-411-2353-9).
13. Christian Bühring-Uhle, *Arbitration and Mediation in International Business*, second revised edition, 2006 (ISBN 978-9-041-12256-8).
14. Bernard Hanotiau, *Complex Arbitrations: Multiparty, Multicontract, Multiissue and Class Actions*, 2006 (ISBN 978-9-041-12442-5).
15. Loukas A. Mistelis & Julian D.M. Lew (eds), *Pervasive Problems in International Arbitration*, 2006 (ISBN 978-9-041-12450-0).
16. Julian D.M. Lew & Loukas A. Mistelis (eds), *Arbitration Insights – Twenty Years of the Annual Lecture of the School of International Arbitration, Sponsored by Freshfields Bruckhaus Deringer*, 2006 (ISBN 978-9-041-12606-1).
17. Mark Kantor, *Valuation for Arbitration: Compensation Standards, Valuation Methods and Expert Evidence*, 2008 (ISBN 978-9-041-12735-8).
18. Christoph Brunner, *Force Majeure and Hardship under General Contract Principles: Exemption for Non-Performance in International Arbitration*, 2009 (ISBN 978-90-411-2792-1).

19. Loukas A. Mistelis & Stavros L. Brekoulakis (eds), *Arbitrability: International & Comparative Perspectives*, 2009 (ISBN 978-90-411-2730-3).
20. Sam Luttrell, *Bias Challenges in International Commercial Arbitration: The Need for a 'Real Danger' Test*, 2009 (ISBN 978-90-411-3191-1).
21. Monique Sasson, *Substantive Law in Investment Treaty Arbitration: The Unsettled Relationship Between International Law and Municipal Law*, Second Edition, 2017 (ISBN 978-90-411-6103-1).
22. Ileana M. Smeureanu, *Confidentiality in International Commercial Arbitration*, 2011 (ISBN 978-90-411-3226-0).
23. Won Kidane, *China-Africa Dispute Settlement: The Law, Economics and Culture of Arbitration*, 2011 (ISBN 978-90-411-3674-9).
24. Karel Daele, *Challenge and Disqualification of Arbitrators in International Arbitration*, 2012 (ISBN 978-90-411-3799-9).
25. Crina Baltag, *The Energy Charter Treaty: The Notion of Investor*, 2012 (ISBN 978-90-411-3428-8).
26. Alexandra Diehl, *The Core Standard of International Investment Protection: Fair and Equitable Treatment*, 2012 (ISBN 978-90-411-3869-9).
27. Manuel Indlekofer, *International Arbitration and the Permanent Court of Arbitration*, 2013 (ISBN 978-90-411-4766-0).
28. Günther J. Horvath & Stephan Wilske (eds), *Guerrilla Tactics in International Arbitration*, 2013 (ISBN 978-90-411-4002-9).
29. Albert Badia, *Piercing the Veil of State Enterprises in International Arbitration*, 2014 (ISBN 978-90-411-5162-9).
30. Nadja Erk, *Parallel Proceedings in International Arbitration: A Comparative European Perspective*, 2014 (ISBN 978-90-411-5264-0).
31. Simon Vorburger, *International Arbitration and Cross-Border Insolvency: Comparative Perspectives*, 2014 (ISBN 978-90-411-5419-4).
32. Ahmad Ali Ghouri, *Interaction and Conflict of Treaties in Investment Arbitration*, 2015 (ISBN 978-90-411-5417-0).
33. Reto Marghitola, *Document Production in International Arbitration*, 2015 (ISBN 978-90-411-5159-9).
34. Alfonso Gómez-Acebo, *Party-Appointed Arbitrators in International Commercial Arbitration*, 2016 (ISBN 978-90-411-6671-5).
35. Jonas von Goeler, *Third-Party Funding in International Arbitration and Its Impact on Procedure*, 2016 (ISBN 978-90-411-5015-8).
36. Dean Lewis, *The Interpretation and Uniformity of the UNCITRAL Model Law on International Commercial Arbitration: Focusing on Australia, Hong Kong and Singapore*, 2016 (ISBN 978-90-411-6700-2).
37. Stavros Brekoulakis, Julian D.M. Lew & Loukas Mistelis (eds), *The Evolution and Future of International Arbitration*, 2016 (ISBN 978-90-411-7004-0).
38. Rémy Gerbay, *The Functions of Arbitral Institutions*, 2016 (ISBN 978-90-411-6217-5).

39. Maximilian Clasmeier, *Arbitral Awards as Investments: Treaty Interpretation and the Dynamics of International Investment Law*, 2017 (ISBN 978-90-411-8357-6).
40. Tony Cole (ed.), *The Roles of Psychology in International Arbitration*, 2017 (ISBN 978-90-411-5921-2).
41. Pietro Ferrario, *The Adaptation of Long-Term Gas Sale Agreements by Arbitrators*, 2017 (ISBN 978-90-411-8232-6).
42. Jacob B. van de Velden, *Finality in Litigation: The Law and Practice of Preclusion – Res Judicata (Merger and Estoppel), Abuse of Process and Recognition of Foreign Judgments*, 2017 (ISBN 978-90-411-8342-2).
43. Dolores Bentolila, *Arbitrators as Lawmakers*, 2017 (ISBN 978-90-411-8354-5).
44. Giacomo Marchisio, *The Notion of Award in International Commercial Arbitration: A Comparative Analysis of French Law, English Law, and the UNCITRAL Model Law*, 2017 (ISBN 978-90-411-8391-0).